THE
SUBLIME
QURAN

TRANSLATED BY
LALEH BAKHTIAR

BASED ON THE
HANAFI, MALIKI AND SHAFII SCHOOLS OF LAW

islamicworld.com

Library of Congress Cataloging-in-Publication Data

Koran. English. The Sublime Quran translation by Laleh Bakhtiar.

Includes bibliographical references and index.
I. Bakhtiar, Laleh. II. Title.

BP109 2006
297.1'22521-dc22   2004041455
ISBN: 1-56744-750-3

In the Name of God
I dedicate this translation
with the hope that this
humble effort will
in some measure
—through a fresh view of Quranic discernment—
improve understanding
between Muslim men and women

Published by
islamicworld.com
Distributed by
Kazi Publications
3023 West Belmont Avenue
Chicago IL 60618
(T) 773-267-7001; (F) 773-267-7002
email: info@kazi.org   www.kazi.org
www.sublimequran.org

Contents

CHAPTER 3: THE FAMILY OF IMRAN (*Āl-i ᶜImrān*) • 55
Number of Signs in Chapter: 200 Signs
Number of Words: 3542 words
Number of Letters: 15,336 letters

• Contents •

CHAPTER 4: THE WOMEN (al-Nisā᾽) • 87

Number of Signs in Chapter: 176 Signs
Number of Words: 3045 words
Number of Letters: 16,030 letters

• Contents •

CHAPTER 6: THE FLOCKS (*al-An^c am*) • **144**
Number of Signs in Chapter: 165 Signs
Number of Words: 3100 words
Number of Letters: 12,935 letters

CHAPTER 8: THE SPOILS OF WAR (*al-Anfāl*) • 201
Number of Signs in Chapter: 75 Signs
Number of Words: 1075 words
Number of Letters: 5080 letters

Part 10 (8:41-9:92) • 206

CHAPTER 9: REPENTANCE (*al-Tawbah*) • 212
Number of Signs in Chapter: 129 Signs
Number of Words: 4078 words
Number of Letters: 10,488 letters

CHAPTER 11: HUD (*Hūd*) • 251
Number of Signs in Chapter: 123 Signs
Number of Words: 1600 words
Number of Letters: 9567 letters

Part 12 (11:6-12:52) • 252

CHAPTER 12: JOSEPH (*Yūsuf*) • 268
Number of Signs in Chapter: 111 Signs
Number of Words: 1600 words
Number of Letters: 7166 letters

CHAPTER 13: THUNDER (*al-Raᶜd*) • 284
Number of Signs in Chapter: 43 Signs
Number of Words: 855 words
Number of Letters: 3506 letters

CHAPTER 14: ABRAHAM (*Ibrāhīm*) • 292
Number of Signs in Chapter: 52 Signs
Number of Words: 868 words
Number of Letters: 3433 letters

CHAPTER 17: THE JOURNEY BY NIGHT (*al-Isrāʾ*) • 322
Number of Signs in Chapter: 111 Signs
Number of Words: 533 words
Number of Letters: 3460 letters

Stage 4 (Chapter 17 through Chapter 25) • 322
Part 15: (17:1-18:74) • 322

• Contents •

• Contents •

CHAPTER 25: THE CRITERION (*al-Furqān*) • 414
Number of Signs in Chapter: 77 Signs
Number of Words: 892 words
Number of Letters: 3703 letters

Part 19 (25:21-27:59) • 416

Stage 5 (Chapter 26 through Chapter 36) •423

CHAPTER 26: THE POETS (*al-Shuᶜarāʾ*) • 423
Number of Signs in Chapter: 227 Signs
Number of Words: 1279 words
Number of Letters: 5540 letters

Sec. 1: *Ṭā Sīn Mīm; these* are *the Signs of the clear Book*

CHAPTER 27: THE ANT (*al-Naml*) • 435
Number of Signs in Chapter: 93 Signs
Number of Words: 1317 words
Number of Letters: 4799 letters

Part 20 (27:60-29:45) • 441

CHAPTER 28: THE STORY (*al-Qaṣaṣ*) • 445
Number of Signs in Chapter: 88 Signs
Number of Words: 431 words
Number of Letters: 5800 letters

CHAPTER 29: THE SPIDER (*al-ᶜAnkabūt*) • 458
Number of Signs in Chapter: 69 Signs
Number of Words: 980 words
Number of Letters: 4165 letters

Part 21 (29:46-33:30) • 464

CHAPTER 30: THE ROMANS (*al-Rūm*) • 467
Number of Signs in Chapter: 60 Signs
Number of Words: 819 words
Number of Letters: 3534 letters

• Contents •

Number of Letters: 2191 letters

Part 26 (46:01-51:30) • 582

CHAPTER 46: THE CURVING SANDHILLS (*al-Aḥqāf*) • 582
Number of Signs in Chapter: 35 Signs
Number of Words: 644 words
Number of Letters: 2598 letters

CHAPTER 47: MUHAMMAD (*Muḥammad*) • 588
Number of Signs in Chapter: 38 Signs
Number of Words: 539 words
Number of Letters: 2349 letters

CHAPTER 48: THE VICTORY (*al-Fatḥ*) • 593
Number of Signs in Chapter: 29 Signs
Number of Words: 560 words
Number of Letters: 2408 letters

• Contents •

Number of Words: 540 Arabic words
Number of Letters: 2476 Arabic letters

CHAPTER 58: SHE WHO DISPUTES (al-Mujādilah) • 631
Number of Signs in Chapter: 22 Signs
Number of Words: 473 Arabic words
Number of Letters: 1792 Arabic letters

CHAPTER 59: THE BANISHMENT (al-Ḥashr) • 636
Number of Signs in Chapter: 24 Signs
Number of Words: 445 Arabic words
Number of Letters: 1913 Arabic letters

CHAPTER 60: SHE WHO IS PUT TO A TEST (al-Mumtaḥinah) • 640
Number of Signs in Chapter: 13 Signs
Number of Words: 348 Arabic words
Number of Letters: 1500 Arabic letters

CHAPTER 61: THE RANKS (al-Ṣaff) • 643
Number of Signs in Chapter: 14 Signs
Number of Words: 221 Arabic words

• Contents •

Number of Letters: 900 Arabic letters

• Contents •

• Contents •

Number of Letters: 1054 Arabic letters

• Contents •

• Contents •

• Contents •

In the Name of God, the Merciful, the Compassionate

Preface

After having spent many years studying the various English translations of the Quran and realizing the sincere efforts of the translators in this great, divinely blessed task, it became clear to me that English translations lack internal consistency and reliability.

Clearly no translation of the Quran can compare in beauty and style with the original Arabic, which has been described as: "by turns, striking, soaring, vivid, terrible, tender and breathtaking."[1] However, I found, when the context is the same, if the same English word is not used for the same Arabic word throughout the translation, it becomes difficult for someone who wants to learn to correlate the English and the Arabic to be able to do so. In other words, the twenty or so English translations put emphasis on interpreting a Quranic verse without precisely representing the original Arabic word. For example, in one translation, the English verb "to turn" is used for over forty-three different Arabic words and the noun "sin," twenty-three.

For the Muslim, the Quran is the Word (Logos) of God much as Jesus is the Word of God for Christians. Just as a Christian believer wants to learn as much as possible about the life of Jesus, so the Muslim wants to know more about each word that God chose for His revelation through the Quran. This realization, in turn, prompted this present translation, an attempt to give the sense of unity within the revelation to a non-Arabic speaking reader.

The method used by English translators of the Quran to date is to start at the beginning of the sacred text and work through translating until the end. I used the same method in translating over thirty books before I earned a Ph. D. in educational psychology much later in life. Armed with this science, I began this translation as a scientific study to see if it was possible to apply these principles to a translation by finding a different English equivalent for each Arabic verb or noun in order to achieve a translation of a sacred text that has internal consistency and reliability.

As I am unlettered, so to speak, in modern Arabic, I relied upon my many years of tutoring in classical Quranic Arabic grammar. It was at that time that I had become familiar with the *al-Muʿjim al-mufahris: al-lafāḍ al-qurʾān al-karīm*. The *Muʿjim* lists every

Arabic root and its derivative(s) found in the Quran as verbs, nouns and some particles (adverbs, prepositions, conjunctions or interjections). Each time a specific word appears, the relevant part of the verse containing that word is quoted with reference to Chapter and Sign (verse). They are listed under their three-letter or four-letter roots. I transliterated the words according to the system of transliteration developed by the American Library Association/ Library of Congress 1997 Romanization Tables in preparing an accompanying Concordance.[2] I then found a viable English equivalent that I would not repeat for another Arabic word. I found that there are 3600+ different Arabic verbs and nouns, excluding most prepositions, that appear at least one time in the Quran. Only in some 50+ cases was it necessary to use the same English word twice for two different Arabic words. For example, there are two different Arabic words for parents, or the number "three," or the word "year," and three for the word "time."

For every Arabic verb's perfect (past tense), imperfect (present and future tense), and imperative form, the same basic English equivalent is used adjusted according to whether it is past, present or a command. A different English equivalent is used for a verbal noun, an active or passive participle, and a noun, again, adjusted according to its usage. The English equivalents for these verbs and nouns are then studied in context and, where necessary for correct meaning, an alternative equivalent that has not been previously used elsewhere in the text is used. This resulted in 5800+ unique English equivalents. I then added the some 50,000+ particles (adverbs, prepositions, conjunctions or interjections not listed in the *al-Mu^cjim*) to the 40,000 I had to complete the data base.

Beginning this process seven years ago with the words instead of the first sentence, I later learned that this was much the method, called formal equivalence, used in the translation of the King James Version of the Bible first published in 1611 CE. This translation, then, is one of formal equivalence in order to be as close to the original as possible. This is the most objective type of translation, as compared to a translation using dynamic equivalence, where the translator attempts to translate the ideas or thoughts of a text, rather than the words, which results in a much more subjective translation.

Another distinction between this translation and other present English translations arises from the fact that this is the first English translation of the Quran by an American woman. Just as I found a lack of internal consistency in previous English translations, I also found that little attention had been given to the woman's point of view.

While the absence of a woman's point of view for over 1440 years since the revelation began, clearly needs to change, it must be acknowledged that there are many men who have been supportive of the view of women as complements to themselves, as the completion of their human unity. To them, I and other Muslim women are eternally grateful. They relate to women as the Quran and Hadith intended. The criticism women have is towards those men who are not open to this understanding, who are exclusive in opposition to the Quran and Sunnah's inclusiveness.

Clearly the intention of the Quran is to see man and woman as complements of one another, not as superior-inferior. Consequently, in the introduction and translation, I address a main criticism of Islam made in regard to the inferiority of women, namely, that a husband can beat his wife (4:34) after two stages of trying to discipline her.

In addition, when words in a verse refer directly to a woman or women or wife or wives and the corresponding pronouns such as (they, them, those), I have placed an (f) after the word to indicate the word refers to the feminine gender specifically.[3] Otherwise, in the Arabic language (as in Spanish), the masculine pronoun may be used generically to include both male and female human beings.

In regard to 25:62, all English translations checked by the translator agreed with the translation given by Yusuf Ali except the translation by Arberry. There is a significant difference between the translations which has to be brought to the reader's attention. Yusuf Ali translates: *"And it is He Who made the night and the day to follow each other: For such as have the will to celebrate His praises, or to show their gratitude"* (25:62). This example says that the individual can will to praise God or show their gratitude to God or can will not to. This contradicts many verses of the Quran that point out: *"But they will not remember unless God will,"* (74:54; see also 76:30; 81:29 among others). Arberry translates 25:62 in the following way: *"And it is He who made the night and day a succession for whom He desires to remember or He desires to be thankful."* This present translation follows what Arberry has understood.

When an English speaker reads the translation of the Quran, it is not clear which are the Qualities and Attributes of God that he or she may be reciting. This present translation recognizes them by presenting the definite article (the) with a capital letter. In this way, one can make the connection between one of the Attributes of God they are reciting and a Quranic verse in which it appears.

Words not appearing in the Arabic, but necessary for English, have been put in italics along with interpretative words or phrases to clarify the context. An example is that often the Quran refers to someone's being struck blind, deaf and dumb. The meaning refers to someone who is "*unwilling* to see, hear or speak," not someone who is physically disabled. Therefore, I have added in italics the word "*unwilling*."

Another unique aspect of this translation in comparison to other English translations is to present a translation of the Quran that is universal, for all times, related to the Quran's eternality and not to it as a text frozen in the time period of its revelation. To this end, there are no parenthetical phrases further interpreting and elaborating a verse, thus allowing the translation to be free of any transient political, denominational or doctrinal bias.

In addition to the translation being unbounded by time, in several sensitive cases, the word chosen to translate an Arabic word is also of a universal rather than a particular nature. This then broadens the perspective and scope of the Quran so that it becomes inclusive rather than exclusive to one particular group of people. In other words, in this way a larger audience can relate to its message. Examples of this would be the translation of the derivatives of kfr, literally meaning: To hide or cover over something. Most English translations use the verb "to disbelieve" making the active participle "one who disbelieves" or "one who is an infidel." In the present translation the more inclusive viable terminology is used, namely, "to be ungrateful," the active participle being "one who is ungrateful."

The Quran itself declares its timelessness and universality. Therefore, its understanding or interpretation must also be eternal and for all time, inclusive of all of humanity rather than exclusive to one group of people. Applying the above criterion to the word *asla - ma*, "he who submits," in the eight times that it appears in the form of *islam*, it is translated according to its universal meaning as "submission,"and the forty-two times that its form as *muslim*, it is translated according to its universal meaning, "one who submits." Or *zakat* usually translated as alms does not give the universal meaning of the Arabic. *Zakat* has been translated in the present translation as "purifying alms" because the important aspect of paying the religious tax is that it purifies the rest of one's wealth.

At this point I should say that there will be those who see me as a person having a particular Muslim point of view. Let me assure the reader that I am most certainly a Muslim woman. I have been schooled in Sufism which includes both the Jafari (Shia) and Hanafi, Hanbali, Maliki and Shafii (Sunni) points of view. As an adult, I lived nine years in a Jafari community in Iran and have been living in a Hanafi community in Chicago for the past fifteen years with Maliki and Shafii friends. While I understand the positions of each group, I do not represent any specific one as I find living in America makes it difficult enough to be a Muslim, much less to choose to follow one sect or another. However in this translation I have not added any indication of differences in interpretation between the sects so that it does represent the majority view. At the same time, I have chosen to continuously engage in the greater struggle of self-improvement. This is the beginning stage of the Sufi path and I cannot even claim that I have moved beyond that. God knows best.

I grew up in the United States with a single parent, a Christian, American mother. My father, an Iranian, lived in Iran. I was an adult before I came to know him. He was not religious, but spiritual, devoting his life as a physician to help to heal the suffering of people.

My mother was not a Catholic, but she sent me to a Catholic school. At the age of eight I wanted to become a Catholic, to which she had no objection. When I was twenty-four, I went to Iran for the first time as an adult, not speaking a word of Persian, with my former husband and our children. I began taking classes taught in English at Tehran University. The classes on Islamic culture and civilization were being taught by Seyyed Hossein Nasr. One day he asked me what religion I followed, and I said that I had been brought up as a Christian. He said: Well, now that you are in Iran and your father is Muslim, everyone will expect you to be Muslim. I said: I don't know anything about Islam. He said: Well, learn! And that was the beginning of my journey culminating in this translation.

The English speaking reader will find another difference from previous translations, and that is the translation of the active participle when used nominally and not as an adjective. Active participles indicate the person or thing undertaking the action of the verb. Instead of creating English words that would not readily resonate with the reader, the translator has used "one who" for the animate and "that which" for the inanimate. The caution to the reader, however, is that this translation should be read with a "fresh eye" and rather than expecting an English equivalent as used in previous translations.

In terms of presentation, most English translations of the Quran presently available translate and present the translation Sign by Sign (or verse by verse), much like a translation of the Old or New Testament.[4] As the Quran was revealed in the oral tradition and is still recited in Arabic as it was revealed, this English translation is arranged to match the Arabic oral recitation.[5]

The number and name of each **Chapter** (*sūrah*) appears on the side of each page of the translation along with the **Stage** (*manzil*, division of the Quran into seven parts so it can be read in its entirety in a week), **Part** (*juz³* or *para*, division of the Quran into thirty parts so that the entire Quran can be read during the month of Ramadan), **Section** (*rukū^c*, an indication to bow the head), and the **Signs** (*āyāt*) on that page. Putting this information on the side instead of at the top of the page furthers the sense of the oral tradition of the Quran and the importance of its recitation.

There are various marks used in the science of recitation that are marked in the English translation as well so that one can read the English translation as one listens to the recitation. This will be even more useful in the bi-lingual edition to follow. There, also, the English translation will be more exact for those who wish to learn Quranic Arabic. That translation will distinguish between 2nd person singular (i.e., thee, thou, thine, thy) and 2nd person plural (you, your) which the present translation does not do. This is by special request from English speaking readers who find it difficult to relate to the usage of thee, thou and thine and the relevant verb forms. As a compromise to them, when the reader finds the word you in bold (**you**) or the word your in bold (**your**), that indicates that the original was thou, thee or thine, thy in the Arabic.

The sign ^ before and after a phrase, as worked out by early commentators of the Quran, indicate that the phrase can either be recited as part of the previous phrase or as the beginning of the next one.

A warning not to stop (as a stop would change the meaning) is designated by (*lā*) in the Arabic followed by the symbol: • in English. This is placed in the column to the left of the English translation. The Arabic letter (*m*) indicates a necessary stop. This is marked at the end of a line of English translation with a period (.) followed by the symbol: •. The Arabic letter (*j*) indicates a non-obligatory, but preferred stop. This is marked at the end of a line of English translation with a period (.) followed by the symbol: °. The Arabic letters (*ṣl*) indicate that a pause is preferred and permissible. This is marked at the end of a line of English translation with a semi-colon (;) followed by the symbol: °. The Arabic letters (*ql*) mark a permissible stop, but continuing is better. This is marked at the end of a line of English translation with a comma (,) followed by the symbol: °. The Arabic letter (*ᶜayn*) appears inside a circle in an Arabic text denoting the end of a Sign and indicating a stop unless it is superceded by a contrary symbol written above it to continue. The reader will find a period (.) at the end of a line of English translation unless the discussion continues to the next Sign. When the English sentence requires a ? or an ! and it is followed by °, the Arabic text may be indicating a (*j*) or (*ql*) or (*ṣl*). A period (.), question mark (?) or exclamation point (!) not followed by ° has been used by the translator as normal English punctuation. Each section (*rukū*) of each Chapter has been indicated in the margin and numbered consecutively. The fourteen Signs where a prostration is obligatory are indicated at the end of the English line of translation with the symbol: ‡.

The numbering of Signs used in this translation is based on the Kufi numbering system.[6] The number of words and letters found in the Table of Contents are based on *Kashf al-asrār wa ᶜuddat al-abrar* by Khawjah ᶜAbdullāh Anṣārī. The translation is based on Ḥafs version of the reading of Asim which is the most popular reading throughout the Islamic world.[7]

Therefore, this translation differs from previous English translations in that there has been a conscious attempt to present a translation of the sacred text that has internal consistency and reliability. It is the first English translation by an American woman who includes the view of women in the Signs (verses) wherever relevant. The translation is consciously a universal, inclusive one widening the relevance of the sacred text to a larger community. The translation is presented line by line in a larger font size so that it can be read and understood more easily while listening to the Arabic recitation.

Let is also be said that this translation was undertaken by a woman to bring both men and women to equity so that the message of fairness and justice between the sexes can be accepted in Truth by both genders. God knows best.

*****

While I have personally been blessed by my contacts with the most understanding and compassionate of men in my lifetime, and I have never found myself in a situation of being physically threatened or beaten, reading about and hearing first hand stories of women who have, I felt the deep sense that I am essentially and spiritually one with them by my very existence. The question I kept asking myself during the years of working on the translation: How could God, the Merciful, the Compassionate, sanction husbands beating their wives?

The feeling, however, did not rise to the surface until the day I first publicly presented the results of this translation of the *Sublime Quran* at the WISE (Women's Islamic Initiative in Spirituality and Equity) Conference (November, 2006) where 150 Muslim women from all over the world had gathered to discuss the possibility of forming a Women's Islamic Council. I gave the logic as to why the word "to beat" in 4:34 has been a misinterpretation. At the end of the session, two Muslim women approached me. They said that they work in shelters for battered women and that they and the women in the shelters have been waiting for over 1400 years for someone to pay attention to this issue through a translation of the Quran. The heavy weight of responsibility suddenly fell upon my shoulders. I had to publish my findings as soon as possible to initiate a dialogue with the exclusivists. Hopefully the initiating of a dialogue will further open the minds and awaken to consciousness and conscience those men who place their hand on the Word of God giving themselves permission to beat their wife.

I ask for the forgiveness of the One God for any errors in this translation, at the same time that I ask for His blessings.

Laleh Bakhtiar, Chicago, March 2007

Notes to the Preface

1 Mohammad Khalifa in notes to the translator.

2 American Library Association/Library of Congress, 1997. ALC/LC Romanization Tables: Transliteration Schemes for Non-Roman Script.

3 See the excellent work by Margot Badran on "Feminism and the Quran,""Gender in the Quran," and "Sisters," as well as "Gender Journeys in/to Arabic."

4. The same method is used by A. J. Arberry in the *Koran Interpreted* and Sayyid Ali Quli Qarai, *The Qur'an with English Paraphrase*.

5 There are seven famous historic reciters of the Quran. Imām ibn Kaṣīr who died in Mecca in 120 A.H; Imām ᶜĀsim of Kufa who it is recorded as having learned this way of reciting the Quran from ᶜAbd al-Raḥmān al-Salāmī who had been taught by the rightly-guided caliphs ᶜUthmān and ᶜAlī ibn Abī Ṭālīb; Imām Abū ᶜUmr, born in Mecca and died in Kufa in 154 A.H.; Imām Ḥamzah of Kufa, born in 80 A.H. and died in 156 A.H.; Imām al-Kisāʾī who died in Tus in 182 A.H; Imām Nāfiʾ of Madina who died in 169 A.H.; and Imām Ibn ᶜĀmir from Syria whose dates are uncertain. See Hughes, *Dictionary of Islam*, p. 478.

6 The Quran has been reprinted millions of times in Arabic throughout the Muslim world without the slightest change of a sentence, a word, or even a letter. The order of the verses has not changed, nor the 114 chapters. There are only a few discrepancies of diacritics which effect some vowels that may emphasize a different shade of meaning of specific words and a different numbering of the verses: 6239 (Kufa), 6204 (Basra), 6225 (Damascus), 6219 (Mecca) and 6211 (Medina) but they all contain the same number of words and the same number of letters.

7 See Hughes, Dictionary of Islam, p 492.

Introduction

The Quran is the Word of God for those who submit to the Will of God (*muslim*). Prophet Muhammad (ﷺ) did not believe that he was bringing a new religion. Rather, as the Last and Final Prophet, he was teaching "submission," something that the First Prophet (ﷺ) had initiated. Therefore, for those who follow "submission" as their way of life, Prophet Muhammad (ﷺ) completed the message of a way of life that has existed continuously from ancient times. Submission is an open system with no beginning and no finite end. It has existed in the past but begins again in the present and goes on for an eternity making it an example of an open history—no beginning and no end—eternal. The message for the present, as it was for Prophets such as Abraham (ﷺ), Moses (ﷺ) and Jesus (ﷺ), is: "There is no god but God," Who alone is to be worshiped. This is the central message of *tawhid* or the Oneness of God. The concept of "submission" connected itself little by little through transition from one Prophet to another, culminating in this message of the Quran. Here the universal rules are preserved.

The Quran was revealed to the Prophet in the Arabic language and it is the Arabic of the Quran which is considered to be the Word of God. Any and every translation is considered to be, to a greater or lesser extent, an interpretation of the Quran and not the Quran itself.

For the Muslim, the Quran, meaning "Recitation," is the eternal Word of God revealed to the Prophet Muhammad (ﷺ) over a period of twenty-two years and five months. This is considered to be the greatest miracle of Prophet Muhammad (ﷺ). He was unlettered, yet he was chosen to receive the Arabic Recitation (Quran), which is considered to be unique in style, possessing a sense of unity in language and level of discourse.

During the moments of revelation and afterwards, his Companions were encouraged to memorize the verses under the supervision of the Prophet. Abdullah bin Masud narrated: God's Prophet said to me, "Recite for me." I said: "Shall I recite it to you although it has been revealed to you?" He said: "I like to hear it from others."[1] One of the greatest acts of worship for a Muslim, then, is to memorize the Arabic Recitation. One who does so is

1

called a *ḥāfiẓ*.

During his lifetime, Prophet Muhammad (ﷺ) divided the Recitation (Quran) into 114 Chapters or "Enclosures." These 114 Chapters each begin with the words: *In the Name of God, The Merciful, The Compassionate,* except for the ninth Chapter where the same words appear in the text. The 114 Chapters (or Enclosures) are divided into more than six thousand Signs or verses (*āyah*)² and 558 sections (*rukūᵓ*, literally "bowing of the head)." The text is organized more or less by length of chapter and is not in chronological order. For one who wants to begin to savor the Quran, it is best to read it randomly and not from beginning to end.

The Quran began as an oral recitation, and oral transmission remained important even after it was transcribed into the written form we now have. The Quran is the first book-length example of Arabic literature.³ It is the bridge between the pre-Islamic oral tradition that focused on narrative or poetic traditions and the written language that rapidly produced great works of prose and poetry. It was compiled into the form of a book by scribes who had written down the verses as they were revealed to the Prophet, verses written on pieces of parchment, leather, stone tablets, animal shoulder blades, palm leaf stems and pieces of cloth. This was done within twenty-one years of the death of the Prophet.

The particular details and practices to be followed are found in the *Sunnah*—the exemplary practice of the Prophet that was recorded in the *Ḥadīth* or Traditions. A person considers himself or herself a good example of submission if he or she follows the example or *Sunnah* of the Prophet—acting and saying as he acted and said. The *Sunnah* consists of the sayings and actions of the Prophet and is considered to be a legally accepted way of interpreting the Signs of the Quran. The *Sunnah* has been compiled in six canonical works, that which the Hanafi, Hanbali, Maliki and Shafii schools of law follow; the Jafari school has a different but similar in content set of canonical works.

The Quran refers to the Recitation by different names, one of which is *The Sublime Quran* (*al-quran al-ᶜaẓīm*, 15:87), the name chosen for this present translation. Being sublime refers to the Quran's spiritual value. In its sublimity it guides and inspires beyond the material world that it transcends. This can only happen when one begins with some standard that establishes a system based in justice and fairness in order to be able to enter the world of the spiritual and intuition. One has to begin with some criterion.

Another of the names the Quran gives itself is *al-furqān*[4] or The Criterion: The discernment between moral and immoral, right and wrong, good and evil, lawful and unlawful, truth and falsehood. The Quran, as The Criterion, is the standard by which to determine the correctness of a judgment or conclusion. It is the measure, the reference point against which other things may be evaluated.

For the Muslim, the Prophet (ﷺ) is the living Quran, the living Criterion. If there was a command to good: fasting, daily formal prayers, pilgrimage, alms, charity, he performed these commands. If it was to prevent a wrong like drinking alcohol, gambling or eating pork, he refrained from these things. As the living Quran, the life, sayings and behavior of the Prophet serve as a model for all Muslims.

In all of the canonical works there is no reference to Prophet Muhammad (ﷺ) having ever beaten women himself. On several occasions when the issue arose, he said, as recorded in the written *Sunnah* or *Hadith*, that he opposed any such practice.[5]

While this translation differs in multiple ways from previous English translations (see Preface), it is the interpretation of the word "to beat" in 4:34 that this translation challenges. We begin with two premises: Islam encourages marriage and divorce, while allowed, is discouraged. The Prophet said: Marriage is half of faith. He also said: Divorce is deplorable.

The relevant part of 4:34 is translated by Muhammad Asad, as an example, in the following way: "*And as for those women whose ill-will you have reason to fear, admonish them [first]; then leave them alone in bed; then **beat** them; and if thereupon they pay you heed, do not seek to harm them. Behold, God is indeed most high, great!*" (4:34)[6]

In recent translations, the last part of the verse reads as follows: "*As for those of whom you fear perversity, admonish them; then leave them alone in bed; then **spank** them,*" (4:34) while another: "*If you fear high-handedness from your wives, remind them [of the teachings of God], then ignore them when you go to bed, then **hit** them.*" The words "beat," "spank," and "hit" are English translations of the Arabic imperative form of the verb, *ḍaraba*, namely, "***iḍrib***" yet the Prophet never carried out this imperative.[7]

This is the first argument for why the interpretation of the word "*iḍrib*" must revert to its interpretation as understood by the Prophet. Since he chose not to beat, "not beating" is the *Sunnah*.

Perhaps he did not "beat" because he understood the word *ḍaraba* to have a different meaning. This second argument, then, for why there needs to be a revert interpretation: The verb form of *ḍaraba* and subsequently its imperative form of *iḍrib* has many meanings in Form I, as found in Arabic lexicons like *Tāj al-ʿArūs*. A legal jurist would say: "We have to choose the one that suits most the general Quranic principles and rules, not a meaning that contradicts them."[8] why chose to interpret the word as "to beat" when it also can mean "to go away." This is what the Prophet did when he faced difficulties with his wives. This is the *Sunnah*. This is an argument accepted by inclusivists while it should be convincing to exclusivists.

That is, husbands in submission to God, the way of life emphasized in both the Quran and the *Sunnah*, have admonished their wives and left their bed, and yet their wives are still resistant. Husbands at that point should submit to God, let God handle it—go away from them and let God work His Will instead of a human being inflicting pain and suffering on another human being in the Name of God.

The third argument comes from the Quran itself. When speaking about divorce, the Quran says to husbands: "*And when you divorce wives and they (f) are about to reach their (f) term, then hold them (f) back honorably or set them (f) free honorably; and hold them (f) not back by injuring them (ḍirar: hurting, using force, harming) so that you commit aggression; whoever commits that, then, indeed, he does wrong to himself; and take not to yourselves the Signs of God in mockery; and remember the divine blessing of God on you and what He sent forth to you of the Book and wisdom; He admonishes you with it; and be Godfearing of God and know that God is Knowing of everything*" (2:231).

God **admonishes** husbands not to injure, use force, hurt or harm their wives; not to commit aggression; not to take His Signs (verses) in mockery. Looking at the commentaries on the Quran by Maulana Maududi, Ibn Kathir, Ayatullah Tabatabie and Sayyid Qutb in regard to 2:231, only Sayyid Qutb has relevant commentary beyond the translation. He says: "Married life must be built on a spirit of mutual kindness, fairness and compassion, and this spirit must be evident even if the relationship has to be severed. Malice and ill-will (i.e., *ḍirar*, injuring, using force, hurting or harming) must not be allowed to cloud this relationship. But, this can only be attained if the parties concerned are guided by faith in God and are conscious of their accountability to Him in the hereafter. . . . Keeping a wife against her will, or mistreating her, would be akin to harming one-self, because she is a fellow human being, with dignity and feelings. A man would be doing himself injustice, too, by allowing himself to act in defiance of God's guidance and teachings. . . . Men who abuse . . . . in order to malign or ill-treat (i.e., *ḍirar*, injuring, using force, hurting or harming) their estranged wives, are violating God's will and subverting His instructions. Regrettably, such blatant abuse is quite widespread in many Muslim communities today, where men tend to do all they can to evade the proper conduct taught by Islam."[9]

What this tells us is that if a wife wants a divorce, a husband is **forbidden** from **harming, hurting, injuring or using force** against her while if a wife wants to stay married, it is **permissible** for her husband to **beat** her!!! Recall our premise: Islam encourages marriage. If women were aware of this contradiction, what woman would chose to stay married and be beaten rather than be divorced and unharmed?

The Arabic Word of God was, is and remains the Word of God. There is no change in the Arabic. The change is in our perception, our interpretation. The understanding of saying "go away" is a revert interpretation to how the blessed Prophet understood it. Whoever believes in and follows the *Sunnah* should logically agree with reverting the interpretation to the way he understood it because interpreting the Arabic word *iḍrib* as "beat" contradicts 2:231 and fosters divorce rather than marriage, commands to immorality and prohibits morality which is one of the definitions of a hypocrite in the Quran (see 9:67).

The *Sublime Quran* calls out *"not to take its Signs (verses) in mock - ery"* yet through exclusivity of gender, jurists and scholars have done just that in interpreting one Sign (verse) in contradiction to another. May God forgive them their error and awaken their con-sciousness and conscience. If they admit that 2:231 prohibits hus-bands from "injuring, using force, harming or hurting" their wives when they want a divorce, then they must logically and rationally— not allowing emotion or irrational feelings to influence their judgment—accept *idrib* in 4:34 to mean "to go away" in order to foster marriage and the *Sunnah* of the Prophet. "Beat them" should be reverted to the meaning as the Prophet understood it—"go away."

In the present translation, based on the fact that the Prophet never beat his wives clearly having understood the word in another sense, and noting that practices in Islam are based on what Prophet Muhammad (ﷺ) did, 4:34 should be: *Men are supporters of wives because God has given some of them an advantage over others and because they spend of their wealth. So the ones (f) who are in accord with morality are the ones (f) who are morally obligated, the ones (f) who guard the unseen of what God has kept safe. But those (f) whose resistance you fear, then admonish them (f) and abandon them (f) in their sleeping place; then go away from them (f); and if they (f) obey you, surely look not for any way against them (f); truly God is Lofty, Great.*

Hopefully all future translations of the Quran in whatever language will revert the interpretation back to the *Sunnah* of the blessed Prophet. Peace.

Notes to the Introduction

1 *Ṣaḥīḥ al-Bukhārī*, Vol. VI, No.106.

2 See Table of Contents.

3 *Encyclopedia of the Quran*, Vol. 1, p. 316; Hanna Kassis, *The Concordance of the Quran*, p. xxvi.

4 *Furqān* is the name of Chapter 25 of the Quran and is mentioned in other Signs as well. The Signs are 2:53, 2:181, 2:185, 3:2, 3:4, 8:29, 8:41, and 21:48. It is also a name given to the Torah revealed to Moses. The Signs referring to the Torah as The Criterion are 2:50 and 21:49.

5 The Prophet said: "Do not beat the women servants of God." He asked: "Do you beat your wife like you beat your camel, for you will be flogging her early in the day and taking her to bed at night." (Seyyed Qutb, *In the Shade of the Quran*, Vol. 3, p 138.) Also, "the best among you are those who are best to their family and I am the best of you to my family," (al-Tirmidhi and al-Tabarani p 138, Seyyed Qutb v. 3.) and "if you act with kindness and are Godfearing, surely God is aware of all that you do" (El-Ḥareere, *Mukāmāt*, pp 465 and 553.).

6 See Amina Wadud, *Quran and Woman*, pp 66-78 for an excellent discussion of many of the significant words in 4:34.

7 There are twelve uses of the imperative form of this verb in the Quran. Four instances relate to Moses "striking" his staff before Pharaoh; four relate to propounding or striking parables; ones relates to the after life; one relates to war; and one relates to the story of Prophet Job. The last historically relates to striking women but hopefully through dialogue this understanding will revert the interpretation to its original meaning as understood and practiced by the Prophet. The traditional Stories of the Prophets have expanded the story of Job. In order to keep his oath that he would strike his wife, Job is told to take a bundle of grass and strike with it in order not to break his oath. Being submissive, he does so. See *From Judges to Monarchy*, pp 13-14. See website www.sublimequran.org for examples of many presently available English translations.

8 Havva Guney-Ruebenacker, presently an S.J.D. candidate at Harvard Law School. She also quite rightly points out that "the meaning of 'beating' also contradicts the verse that follows, namely 4:35 which suggests a way of conflict resolution among spouses, namely arbitration. There is no point in recommending a peaceful method of conflict resolution among spouses after allegedly permitting a physical violence in the preceding verse." (email March 11, 2007)

9 Seyyed Qutb, *In the Shade of the Quran*, Vol. 1, pp 364-365.

Acknowledgements

The translator wishes to thank God for His blessings, guidance and for the presence of the mercy to humanity, Prophet Muhammad, peace and the mercy of God be upon him, and the following teachers, friends and family in my life:

Seyyed Hossein Nasr for his spiritual presence in the life of this translator;

Liaquat Ali and Kazi Publications for believing that this project could, if God will, reach fruition;

Muhammad Nur (Jay R. Crook), Ph. D., for his invaluable advice and editing. It would not have reached its present form without his help.

Shireen Blair, Muhammad Munir Chaudry, Ph. D., Usama Hussein and Abdullah Clark whose careful reading, comments and questions improved the translation;

Sheila Musaji who mentioned to Daisy Khan that she thought I should say a few words about my work; and to Daisy Khan for hosting the WISE Conference and accepting.

Khalilah Karim-Rushdan, MSW, LCSW, Chaplain to the Muslim Community, Smith College, who has been relentless in her encouragement, support and help since we met at the WISE Conference;

Havva Guney-Ruebenacker, S.J.D. candidate, Harvard Law School, for her advice on issues of Islamic jurisprudence;

Margot Badran, Ph. D., for sharing her work on gender equity.

The two Muslim women I met who work in the shelters for battered women and who handed me the mandate;

Hujjat al-Islam Mojtaba Musavi Lari who agrees that the interpretation of "beat them" must change;

Harold Voglaar, Ph. D., who suggested a more accurate translation for Chapter 112;

Nasif Mahmoud, Attorney-at-Law, who has encouraged me from the beginning;

Bill Beeman, Ph. D., who has put me in touch with others in the publishing industry;

Abdul Majid (Frank Vriale) for producing the first English audio recitation of the Quran by a woman;

Mani Farhadi and Rodd Farhadi, for their creative energies, comments and suggestions regarding the cover design;

Iran Davar Ardalan, for her creative insights, knowledge of the media and constant awakenings to reality;

Saied Ghaffari, for his creative imagination, insightful comments and suggestions and

Karim Ardalan for his creative abilities, advice and magnificent website design, www.sublimequran.org

Stage 1

Part 1

CHAPTER 1
THE OPENING (*al-Fātiḥah*)

1:1
·

In the Name of God,
The Merciful, The Compassionate.

1:2

The Praise *belongs* to God
Lord of the worlds,

1:3

The Merciful, The Compassionate,

1:4

One Who is Sovereign of the Day of Judgment.

1:5

You alone we worship,
and to **You** alone we pray for help.

1:6

Guide us to the straight path,

1:7
·

the path of those to whom
You have been gracious,
not ones against whom **You** are angry,
nor the ones who go astray.

*

CHAPTER 2
THE COW (*al-Baqarah*)

In the Name of God,

Sec. 1

The Merciful, The Compassionate

2:1

Alif Lām Mīm;°

2:2

that *is* the Book—there *is* no doubt in it,
a guidance for the ones who *are* Godfearing:

2:3

Those who believe in the unseen
and perform the formal prayer
and they spend from what We have provided them

2:4

and those who believe
in what was sent forth to **you**
and what was sent forth before **you**
and they are certain of the world to come.

2:5

Those *are* on a guidance from their Lord;°
and those, they *are* the ones who prosper.

2:6

Truly those who are ungrateful,
it *is* all the same to them
whether **you** have warned them
or **you** have warned them not;
they believe not.

God has set a seal on their hearts
and on their *inner* hearing
and a blindfold on their *inner* sight;°
and *there is* a tremendous punishment for them.

*

Among humanity *are* those who say:
We have believed in God and in the Last Day;
and yet they *are* not among the ones who believe.
They seek to trick God,
and those who have believed
while they deceive none but themselves,
except they are not aware.
There is a sickness in their hearts.
Then God has increased them in sickness;°
and *there is* a painful punishment for them
because they were liars.
When it was said to them:
Make not corruption in and on the earth,
they said: We *are* not but
ones who make things right.
Truly they *are* the ones who make corruption,
except they are not aware.
When it is said to them:
Believe as humanity believes,
they would say: Shall we believe
as the fools have believed?°
They truly they *are* the fools,
but they know not.
When they met those who have believed,
they said: We have believed,
but when they go privately to their satans,
they said: Truly we *are* with you,
truly we *were* nothing but ones who ridicule.
God ridicules them,
and causes them to increase in their defiance.
They wander *unwilling* to see.
They, those bought misjudgment
for guidance,
so their trade *was* not to be bettered

nor were they ones who were truly guided.

Their parable *is* like a parable
of him who lit a fire,
then when it illuminated what *was* around him,
God took away their light
and left them in shadows
where they perceive not.

Unwilling to hear, speak, or see,
then they shall not return.

Or like a cloudburst from heaven
in which *there are* shadows,
and thunder and lightning.
They lay their fingertips in their ears
against the thunderbolts, fearful of death;°
and God is One Who Encloses
the ones who are ungrateful.

The lightning almost snatches their sight;°
whenever it illuminates for them,
they walk in it;
and when it grows dark against them,
they stand still;°
and had God willed, He would have taken away
their having the ability to hear and their sight.°
Truly God *is* Powerful over everything.

*

Sec. 3

O humanity! Worship your Lord
Who created you
and those *that were* before you
so that perhaps you would be Godfearing.

It is He Who assigned the earth for you
as a place of restfulness
and heaven as a canopy;
and He sent forth water from heaven
and drove out fruit of trees by it
as provision for you;°
so assign not rivals to God
while you know.

If you are in doubt
about what We have sent down to Our servant,

then approach with a chapter of the Quran
—the like of it—
and call to your witnesses, other than God,
if you are the ones who are truthful.
But if you accomplish *it* not, 2:24
and you shall never accomplish it,
then be Godfearing of the fire
whose fuel *is* humanity and rocks,°
that is prepared for the ones who are ungrateful.
Give **you** good tidings to those who have believed, 2:25
and have acted in accord with morality,
that for them *shall be* Gardens
beneath which rivers run.°
Whenever they are provided from there
of its fruit as provision,
they would say:
This *is* what we were provided before;°
and they were given
ones that were alike from there;°
and for them in it
shall be purified spouses;°
and they, ones who shall dwell in them forever!
Truly God is not ashamed 2:26
to propound a parable
even of a gnat or something above it;°
as for those who have believed,
then they know that it *is* the truth
from their Lord;°
but then as for those who are ungrateful, they say:
What would God mean by this parable?•
He causes many to go astray by it,
and He guides many by it;°
but He causes none to go astray by it
except the ones who disobey—
those who break the compact of God 2:27
after a solemn promise,
and sever what God has commanded
that it be joined,
and make corruption in and on the earth.°

Those, they *shall be* the ones who are losers!

How is *it* you are ungrateful to God
as you were lifeless
and then He gave you life;°
then He shall cause you to die,
and He shall give you life
and you shall be returned to Him?

2:29
It is He Who created for you
all that *is* in and on the earth;
then He turned His attention to heaven,
and He shaped them into seven heavens;°
and He *is* Knowing of everything.

Sec. 4
*

2:30
When **your** Lord said to the angels:
Truly I *am* assigning on the earth
a viceregent;°
they said:
Shall **You** be one who makes on it *him*
who shall make corruption in and on it
and shall shed blood,
while we glorify **Your** praise
and sanctify **You**?°
He said: Truly I know what you know not!

2:31
He taught Adam the names, all of them;
then He presented them to the angels and said:
Communicate to Me the names of these
if you be ones who are sincere.

2:32
They said: Glory be to **You**!
We *have* no knowledge
except what **You** have taught us;°
truly **You, You** alone *are*
The Knowing, The Wise.

2:33
He said: O Adam!
Communicate to them their names;°
and when he had communicated to them
their names,
He said: Have I not said to you:
Truly I know the unseen
in the heavens and the earth

5

and that I know what you show,
and what you keep back?
When We said to the angels: 2:34
Prostrate before Adam!
They then prostrated except Iblis.
He refused and grew arrogant;
he was among the ones who have been ungrateful.
We said: O Adam!   2:35
Inhabit the Garden, **you** and **your** spouse,
and both of you eat freely from it
wherever you both have willed,
but come not near this tree
so that **you** both not be among ones who are unjust.
Then Satan caused both of them to slide back   2:36
from there and drove both of them out
from that in which they were;
and We said: Get down,
some of you an enemy to one another;°
and for you on the earth,
an appointed time and sustenance for awhile.
Adam then had received words from his Lord   2:37
and He turned to him in forgiveness;°
truly He, He *is* The Compassioned
Accepter of Repentance.
We said: Get down altogether from here;°   2:38
yet whenever guidance arrives from Me for you,
whoever heeds My guidance,
there is neither fear in them
nor *shall* they feel remorse.
But those who are ungrateful and deny Our Signs,   2:39
those *shall be* the Companions of the Fire;°
they *are* ones who shall dwell in it forever!
*   Sec. 5

O Children of Israel!   2:40
Remember My divine blessing
with which I was gracious to you,
and live up to the compact *with* Me;
I shall live up to the compact *with* you;
then have reverence for Me.

2:41	Believe in what I have sent forth,
	establishing as true what *is* with you;
	be not the first one who is ungrateful for it;°
	exchange not My Signs for a little price;
	and be Godfearing of Me alone.
2:42	Confuse not The Truth with falsehood
	nor keep back The Truth while you know.
2:43	Perform the formal prayer;
	give the purifying alms;
	and bow down with the ones who bow down.
2:44	Would you command humanity
	to virtuous conduct,
	while you yourselves forget
	as you recount the Book?°
	Shall you not be reasonable?
2:45	Pray for help with patience
	and formal prayer;°
	and truly it is not easy
	except for the ones who are humble,
2:46	who bear in mind that
	they *shall be* the ones who encounter their Lord
	and that they truly
	shall be ones who return to Him.

Sec. 6

*

2:47	O Children of Israel!
	Remember My divine blessing
	with which I was gracious to you,
	and that I gave advantage to you over the worlds.
2:48	Be Godfearing of the day
	when no soul shall give recompense
	for another soul at all,
	nor shall intercession be accepted from it,
	nor an equivalent be taken from it,
	nor shall they be helped.
2:49	*Recall* when We delivered you
	from the people of Pharaoh
	who caused an affliction to befall on you
	of a terrible punishment,
	slaughtering your sons

and saving alive your women;°
and in that there *was*
a tremendous trial from your Lord.
Recall when We separated the sea for you;   2:50
We rescued you,
and We drowned the people of Pharaoh
while you looked on:
Recall when We appointed for Moses   2:51
forty nights,
then you took the calf to yourselves
after him,
and you were ones who were unjust.
Recall then after that We pardoned you,   2:52
so that perhaps you would give thanks.
Recall when We gave Moses the Book   2:53
and the Criterion between right and wrong
so that perhaps you would be truly guided.
Recall when Moses said to his folk: 2:54
O my folk!
Truly you have done wrong against yourselves
by your taking the calf to yourselves,
so repent to the One Who is your Fashioner,
and kill your souls;
that *would be* better for you
with the One Who is your Fashioner;
then He shall turn to you in forgiveness;°
truly He *is* The Compassioned
Accepter of Repentance.
Recall when you said: 2:55
O Moses! We shall never believe **you**
until we see God publicly;
so the thunderbolt took you
while you looked on.
Then We raised you up after your death   2:56
so that perhaps you would give thanks.
We shaded you with   2:57
cloud shadows
and sent forth to you the manna and the quails:°
Eat of what is good

that We have provided for you;°
and they did not wrong Us,
but they did wrong themselves.

2:58　　*Recall* when We said: Enter this town,
and eat freely from it whatever you willed,
and enter the doors as one who prostrates,
and say: Unburden *us of sin*!
We shall forgive your transgressions.°
Soon We shall increase
the ones who are doers of good.

2:59　　But those did wrong, who substituted a saying
—other than what had been said to them—
so We sent forth on those who did wrong
wrath from heaven
because they were disobedient.

Sec. 7
*

2:60　　*Recall* when Moses asked for water for his folk,
We said: Strike the rock with **your** scepter!°
So twelve springs ran out from it;°
every clan knew its drinking place:°
Eat and drink of the provisions of God,
and do no mischief in and on the earth
as ones who make corruption.

2:61　　*Recall* when you said: O Moses!
We shall not endure patiently with one *kind of* food,
so call to **your** Lord for us to drive out for us
of what the earth brings forth of its green herbs,
and its cucumbers and its garlic,
and its lentils and its onions;°
he said: Would you *have* in exchange
what *is* lesser for what *is* higher?°
Get down to a settled country,
and so truly for you *is* what
you have asked;°
and they were stamped
with abasement and wretchedness.
They drew the burden of anger from God;°
that *was* because they were ungrateful
for the Signs of God,

9

and killed the Prophets without right;°
that because they rebelled
and committed aggression.

*

Truly those who have believed,   2:62
and those who have become Jews,
and the Christians and the Sabaeans,
whoever has believed in God and the Last Day,
and *is* one who has acted in accord with morality,
then for them,
their compensation *is* with their Lord;
there is neither fear in them
nor *shall* they feel remorse.
When We took your solemn promise,   2:63
and We exalted the mount above you:°
Take what We have given you firmly
and remember what *is* in it,
so that perhaps you would be Godfearing.
Then after that you turned away;°   2:64
and were it not for the grace of God on you
and His mercy,
indeed you would have been
among the ones who are losers.
Indeed you knew those among you   2:65
who committed aggression against the Sabbath.
Then We said to them:
Be you loathed apes.
We made this an exemplary punishment   2:66
for the former
and for succeeding generations
and an admonishment
for the ones who are Godfearing.
Recall when Moses said to his folk: 2:67
Truly God commands that you sacrifice a cow;°
they said: Have **you** taken us to **yourself**
in mockery?°
He said: I take refuge in God
that I not be among the ones who are ignorant!
They said: Call to **your** Lord for us   2:68

to make manifest to us what she *is* like!°
He said: Truly He says: She should be a cow
neither old nor immature;
middle-aged between that;°
so accomplish what you are commanded.

2:69　　　They said: Call to **your** Lord for us
to make manifest to us what its hue *is*.°
He said: Truly He says:
She *is* a saffron-colored cow,
one that is bright in hue
that makes the ones who look *upon her* happy.

2:70　　　They said: Call to **your** Lord for us
to make manifest to us what she *is*.
Truly cows are alike to us
and truly had God willed,
we shall be ones who are truly guided.

2:71　　　He said: Truly He says she *is* a cow,
neither broken to plow the earth
nor to draw water for cultivation,
that *is* to be handed over
without blemish on her.°
They said: Now **you** have brought about
The Truth.°
So they sacrificed her
while they almost accomplished it not.

Sec. 9　　　　　　　*

2:72　　　*Recall* when you killed a soul,
then you put up an argument over it;°
but God was One Who Drove Out
what you were keeping back.

2:73　　　So We said: Strike him with some of it!°
Thus God gives life to the dead,
and He causes you to see His Signs
so that perhaps you would be reasonable.

2:74　　　Then after that your hearts became hard,
so that they *were* as rocks or more hardened.°
For truly *there are* some rocks
from which rivers gush forth;°
and truly *there are* some of them

11

that split open
so water goes forth from them;°
and truly there *are* some of them
that crash down, dreading God;°
and God *is* not One Heedless
of what you do.
Are you desirous   2:75
that they should believe in you,
while indeed a group of people among them
would hear the assertion of God,
then while they knew
they would tamper with it
after they had discerned it?
When they met those who have believed,   2:76
they said: We have believed;°
but when they go privately
—some of them with some others—
they said: Shall you divulge to them
what God has opened to you
so that they may argue with you about it
before your Lord?°
Shall you not be reasonable?
Know they not that God knows   2:77
what they keep secret
and what they speak openly.
Among them are the unlettered   2:78
who know nothing of the Book except fantasy;
and truly *it is so.*
Then woe to those who write down the Book   2:79
with their own hands.
Then they say: This *is* from God
so that they shall exchange it for a little price;°
then woe to them for what
their hands write down;
and woe to them for what they earn!
They said: The fire shall never touch us   2:80
except for numbered days.°
Say: Have you taken to yourselves
a compact from God?

For God never breaks His compact;°
or you said about God what you know not?

2:81 Rather whoever earns an evil deed,
and his transgression encloses him,
then those *shall be* the Companions of the Fire;°
they, ones who shall dwell in it forever!

2:82 Those who have believed,
ones who have acted in accord with morality,
those *shall be* the Companions of the Garden;°
they, ones who shall dwell in it forever!

Sec. 10

*

2:83 *Recall* when We took a solemn promise
from the Children of Israel:
You shall not worship other than God
and *have* goodness to the ones who are *your* parents
to the kin and the orphans
and the needy;
speak with kindness to humanity;
perform the formal prayer;
and give the purifying alms.
Then you turned away except a few among you,
and you *were* ones who turned aside.

2:84 *Recall* when We took your solemn promise:
You shall not shed your blood,
nor drive yourselves out from your abodes;
then you were in accord,
and you bore witness.

2:85 Then there you were killing one another,
and driving out a group of people among you
from their abodes,
supporting one another against them
in sin and deep seated dislike;
and if they approach you as prisoners of war,
you redeem them,
yet their expulsion had been forbidden to you.°
What? You believe in some of the Book
and are ungrateful for some;°
then what *shall be* the recompense
of those who commit that among you

except degradation in this present life;°
and on the Day of Resurrection,
they shall be returned
to the hardest punishment;°
God is not One Heedless
of what you do.
They *are* those who bought this present life   2:86
for the world to come,°
so their punishment shall not be lightened,
nor shall they be helped.
*

Indeed We gave Moses the Book,   2:87
and We sent Messengers after him;°
We gave Jesus son of Mary
clear portents
and confirmed him with the hallowed Spirit.°
Is it not that whenever a Messenger drew near you
with what you yourselves yearned not for,
you grew arrogant;°
you denied a group of people,
and you killed a group of people?
They said: Our hearts are encased!°   2:88
Rather God cursed them for their ingratitude,
so little *is* what they believe!
Recall when a Book drew near to them from God,   2:89
establishing as true what *was* with them
—although before that they had asked for victory
over those who were ungrateful—
but when there drew near to them
what they recognized,
they were ungrateful for it.°
So may the curse of God
be on the ones who are ungrateful!
Miserable *is* that for which   2:90
they have sold out themselves
by being ungrateful
for what God sent forth—
resenting that God should send down of His grace
to whom He will of His servants;°

they drew the burden of anger—anger on anger;°
and for the ones who were ungrateful,
there is a despised punishment.

2:91 When it was said to them:
Believe in what God sent forth,
they said:
We believe in what was sent forth to us;
and they are ungrateful for what is beyond it,
while it *is* The Truth,
establishing as true what *is* with them;°
say: Why then would you kill
the Prophets of God before
if you were ones who believe?

2:92 Indeed Moses drew near to you
with clear portents
and yet you took to yourselves the calf
after him. •
You were ones who were unjust.

2:93 *Recall* when We took your solemn promise,
and We exalted the mount above you:
Take what We have given you firmly and hear!°
They said: We heard and we rebelled;
and they were steeped with the calf
in their hearts
because of their ingratitude.°
Say: Miserable is the command
of your belief if you are ones who believe.

2:94 Say: If the Last Abode with God
were one that is exclusively for you,
excluding others of humanity,
covet death if you would be ones who are sincere.

2:95 But they shall never covet it
for what their hands have put forward;°
and God *is* Knowing of the ones who are unjust.

2:96 Truly **you** shall find them
eager among humanity for this life;°
and of those who have associated partners *with God*,°
one of them wishes he would be given a long life,
a thousand years—

except this would not exempt him
from the punishment,
even if he be given a long life;°
and God *is* Seeing of what they do.

*

Say: Whoever is an enemy of Gabriel,   2:97
know that it was sent down through him to **your** heart
with the permission of God
establishing as true what *was* before it
and as a guidance and good tidings
for the ones who believe.
Whoever is an enemy of God and His angels,   2:98
His Messengers and Gabriel and Michael,
then truly God *is* an enemy
to the ones who are ungrateful.
Indeed We have sent forth to **you** Signs,   2:99
clear portents;°
and none are ungrateful for them
but the ones who disobey.
Is it not that whenever   2:100
they have made a contract—a compact,
a group of people among them repudiated it?°
Rather most of them believe not.
When a Messenger has drawn near to them   2:101
from God,
establishing as true what *was* with them,
a group of people among those
who were given the Book
repudiated the Book of God behind their backs
as if they knew not *what it was.*
They followed   2:102
what the satans recounted
during the dominion of Solomon;°
and Solomon was not ungrateful,
but the satans were ungrateful,
teaching humanity sorcery
and what was sent forth to the two angels
at Babylon—Harut and Marut;°
but neither of these two taught anyone

unless they said:
We *are* not but a test, so be not ungrateful;°
but they would learn from these two
how they would separate and divide
between a man and his spouse;°
but they would not hurt or profit anyone with it
except by the permission of God;°
and they would learn
what would injure them
and would not profit them;°
indeed they knew that whoever buys it,
for him *there is* no apportionment
in the world to come;°
and miserable indeed
was that for which they sold themselves—°
would that they had known!

2:103
If they had believed,
and had been Godfearing,
indeed their reward from God
would have been better—°
would that they had known!

*

2:104
O those who have believed!
Say not: Look at us,
but say: Wait for us and hear!°
For the ones who are ungrateful,
there *is* a painful punishment.

2:105
Neither those who are ungrateful
from among the People of the Book,
nor the ones who are polytheists
wish that any good should be sent down to you
from your Lord;°
but God singles out for His mercy
whom He will.°
God *is* Possessor of the Sublime Grace.

2:106
Whenever We abrogate a Sign
or cause *it* to be forgotten,
We bring better than it,
or similar to it;°

is Powerful over everything?
What? Know **you** not that God,   2:107
to Him *is* the dominion
of the heavens and the earth?°
Other than God, you *have*
neither protector nor helper.
Or would you want that you ask   2:108
your Messenger as Moses was asked before?°
Whoever takes ingratitude
in exchange for belief
then indeed has gone astray from the right way.
Many of the People of the Book wished   2:109
that after your belief they would return you
to the ones who are ungrateful
—out of jealousy within themselves—
even after The Truth has become clear to them;°
so pardon and overlook *them*
until God brings His command;°
truly God *is* Powerful over everything.
Perform the formal prayer   2:110
and give the purifying alms.°
Whatever good you put forward for yourselves,
you shall find it with God;°
truly God *is* Seeing of what you do.
They said: None shall enter the Garden   2:111
but one who is a Jew or a Christian;°
that *is* to fantasize.°
Say: Prepare your proof
if you are ones who are sincere.
Rather whoever has submitted his face to God,   2:112
as one who is a doer of good,
then for him his compensation *is* with his Lord;
and *there is* neither fear in them,
nor *shall* they feel remorse.

*   Sec. 14

The Jews said: 2:113
The Christians are not based on anything;
and the Christians said:

The Jews are not based on anything,
yet they both recount the Book;°
thus those who know not
have like sayings.°
So God shall give judgment between them
on the Day of Resurrection
about what they were at variance.

2:114 Who is he who does greater wrong
than he who prevents access
to the places of prostration to God
so His Name not be remembered in them,
and endeavors for their devastation?°
It was not for those to enter them
but as the ones who are fearful;°
for them *is* degradation in this present,
and for them
is a tremendous punishment in the world to come.

2:115 To God *belongs* the East and the West.°
So truly wherever you turn to,
then there *is* the Countenance of God;°
truly God is One Who Embraces, Knowing.

2:116 They said: God has taken to Himself a son;°
glory be to Him!°
Rather to Him *is*
whatever *is* in the heavens and the earth;°
all are ones who *are* morally obligated to Him,

2:117 Beginner of the heavens and the earth;°
and when He decrees a command,
then truly He only says to it: Be! And it is!

2:118 Those who know not said:
Why speaks not God to us
or a Sign approach us?°
Thus those who were before them said
the like of their sayings.•
Their hearts resemble one another;°
indeed We have made manifest the Signs
for a folk who are certain.

2:119 Truly We sent **you** with The Truth
as a bearer of good tidings and as a warner;°

19

and **you** shall not be asked
about the Companions of Hellfire.
The Jews shall never be well-pleased with **you**   2:120
nor the Christians
until **you** follow their creed;°
say: Truly the guidance of God,
that *is* The Guidance;°
but if **you** follow their desires
after what has drawn near to **you**
of knowledge;   •
other than God, **you** *have*
neither protector nor helper.
Those to whom We have given the Book   2:121
recount
with a true recounting;
those *are* the ones who believe in it;°
and whoever is ungrateful for it,
then they, those are the ones who are losers.
*

O Children of Israel!   2:122
Remember My divine blessing
with which I was gracious to you,
and that I gave you an advantage over the worlds.
Be Godfearing of the Day   2:123
when no soul shall give recompense for
another soul at all,
nor shall the equivalent be accepted from it,
nor shall intercession profit it,
nor shall they be helped.
When his Lord tested Abraham   2:124
with words then he fulfilled them;°
He said: Truly I am the One Who Makes **you**
a leader for humanity;°
he said: And of my offspring?°
He said: My compact is not attained by
the ones who are unjust.
When We made the House   2:125
a place of spiritual reward for humanity,
and a place of sanctuary:

Take the Station of Abraham to yourself
as a place of formal prayer;°
and We made a compact with Abraham
and Ishmael:
Purify My House
for the ones who circumambulate it,
and the ones who cleave to it,
and the ones who bow down,
and the ones who prostrate themselves.

2:126 When Abraham said: My Lord!
Make this land safe
and provide its people with fruits;
whoever of them have believed in God
and the Last Day;°
He said: Whoever is ungrateful,
I shall give him enjoyment for awhile;
then I shall compel him
to the punishment of the fire;°
and miserable is the Homecoming!

2:127 When Abraham elevated
the foundations of the House
with Ishmael *saying*:
Our Lord! Receive it from us.°
Truly **You**, **You** *are*
The Hearing, The Knowing.

2:128 Our Lord!
Make us the ones who submit to **You**
and of our offspring, a community
of the ones who submit to **You**;°
and cause us to see our devotional acts,
and turn to us in forgiveness;°
truly **You**, **You** *are*
The Compassioned
Accepter of Repentance.

2:129 Our Lord!
Raise **You** up from among them
a Messenger
who shall recount to them
Your Signs and teach them the Book

and wisdom and make them pure;°
truly **You, You** *are* The Almighty, The Wise.

*

Who shall shrink from
the creed of Abraham,
but he who fools himself?°
Truly We favored him in this present life;°
and truly in the world to come
he *shall be*
among the ones who are in accord with morality.
When his Lord said to him: Submit!°
He said: I have submitted
to the Lord of the worlds.
Abraham charged his sons to it
and Jacob:
O my sons!
Truly God has favored the way of life for you.
Then be not overtaken by death
except as ones who submit *to God.*
Or were you witnesses
when death attended Jacob?
When he said to his sons:
How shall you worship after me?
They said: We shall worship **your** God,
and the God of **your** fathers,
Abraham and Ishmael and Isaac,
The One God;
and we *are* ones who submit to Him.
That was a community that has passed away;°
for it *is* what it has earned,
and for you *is* what you have earned;°
and you shall not be asked
about what they were doing.
They said: Be you
ones who are Jews or Christians,
you would be truly guided;°
say: Rather the creed of Abraham
is that of a monotheist;°
and he was not

of the ones who are polytheists.

2:136 Say: We have believed in God,
and what has been sent forth to us,
and what was sent forth to Abraham,
Ishmael, Isaac, Jacob,
and the Tribes
and what was given Moses and Jesus,
and what was given the Prophets
from their Lord;
we separate and divide not
between anyone of them;
and we are the ones who submit to Him.

2:137 So if they have believed
the like of what you have believed,
then they were truly guided;°
but if they turned away,
then they *are* not but in breach;°
so God shall suffice for you against them;°
and He *is* The Hearing, The Knowing.

2:138 *Our* coloring *is* by God;°
and who is fairer at coloring than God?°
We *are* ones who are worshippers of Him.

2:139 Say: Would you argue with us about God
when He *is* our Lord and your Lord?
To us are our actions,
and to you are your actions;
and we *are*
the ones who are sincere and devoted to Him.

2:140 Or say you that Abraham, Ishmael,
Isaac, Jacob and the Tribes
were the ones who were Jews or Christians?°
Say: *Have* you greater knowledge or God?°
Who *is* he who does greater wrong
than he who keeps back testimony that *is* with him
from God?°
God *is* not One Heedless of what you do.

2:141 That was a community that has passed away;°
for it *is* what it has earned,
and for you *is* what you have earned;°

and you shall not be asked
about what they were doing.
***
*

The fools among humanity shall say:
What has turned them
from the direction of formal prayer
when they were toward it?°
Say: To God *belongs* the East and the West;°
He guides whom He will
to a straight path.
Thus We have made you
a middle community
that you may be witnesses to humanity,
and that the Messenger
be a witness to you;°
and We made the direction of the formal prayer
that you were towards
only so that We might know
who followed the Messenger
from him who turns about on his two heels;°
and truly it was grave,
except for those whom God has guided;°
and God would never waste your belief;°
truly God *is* The Gentle toward humanity,
The Compassionate.
We have indeed seen the going to and fro
of **your** face toward heaven;°
truly We shall turn **you** to
the direction of formal prayer
with which **you** shall be well-pleased;°
so turn **your** face to the direction
of the Masjid al-Haram;°
and wherever you shall be,
then turn your faces to its direction;°
and truly those who were given the Book
know that it *is* The Truth from their Lord;°
and God *is* not One Heedless of what you do.
Even if **you** were to bring all its Signs

to those who
were given the Book,
they would not heed
your direction of formal prayer;°
nor are **you** one who heeds
their direction of formal prayer;°
nor are some of them the ones who heed
the direction of the other's formal prayer;°
and if **you** were to follow their desires after

•   the knowledge that has been brought about to **you**,
then truly **you** would be
of the the ones who are unjust.

2:146   Those to whom We have given the Book
recognize it
as well as they recognize their sons,°
but truly a group of people among them
keep back The Truth while they know

2:147   *it is* The Truth from **your** Lord,°
so **you** be not of the ones who contest.

Sec. 18   *

2:148   Everyone has a direction
toward which he turns;°
so be forward in good deeds;°
wherever you shall be,
God shall bring you altogether;°
truly God *is* Powerful over everything.

2:149   From wherever **you** go forth
then turn **your** face to the direction
of the Masjid al-Haram;°
and truly *it is* The Truth from **your** Lord;°
and God *is* not One Heedless of what you do.

2:150   From wherever **you** go forth,
turn **your** face
to the direction of the Masjid al-Haram;°
and wherever you shall be,
then turn your faces to the direction of it
so that there is
no disputation from humanity against you;
but for those who do wrong,

then dread them not, but dread Me
that then I may fulfill
My divine blessing on you
so that perhaps you would be truly guided,
even as We have sent to you a Messenger   2:151
from among you
who recounts Our Signs to you,
and makes you pure
and teaches you the Book and wisdom
and teaches you what you were not knowing.
So remember Me and I shall remember you;   2:152
and give thanks to Me
and be not ungrateful!
*   **Sec. 19**

O those who have believed!   2:153
Pray for help with patience and formal prayer;°
truly God *is* with the ones who remain steadfast.
Say not about those who were slain   2:154
in the way of God: *They are* lifeless.°
Rather they are living,
but you are not aware.
We shall indeed try you   2:155
with something of fear and hunger,
and diminution of wealth and lives,
and fruits;°
but give good tidings
to the ones who remain steadfast,
those who, when an affliction lights on them,   2:156
they say: Truly we *belong* to God,
and truly we are the ones who return to Him.°
Blessings shall be sent on them   2:157
from their Lord and mercy;°
and those, they are the ones who are truly guided.
Truly Safa and Marwa   2:158
are among the waymarks of God;°
so whoever makes the pilgrimage to Mecca
to the House,
or visits *the House*,
there is no blame on him

that he walk quickly between the two;°
and whoever volunteers good,
then truly God *is* One Responsive, Knowing.

2:159
Truly those who keep back
what We have sent forth
of the clear portents and guidance,
after We have made it manifest to humanity
·
in the Book—
those, God curses them,
and the ones who curse, curse them.

2:160
But those who repent
and make things right
and make things manifest,
those, I shall turn in forgiveness to them;°
and I am The Compassioned
Accepter of Repentance.

2:161
Truly those who are ungrateful
and die while they are ones who are ungrateful,
those, on them is the curse of God,
and the angels and humanity one and all.

2:162
They are ones who shall dwell in it forever;°
the punishment shall not be lightened for them,
nor shall they be given respite.

2:163
Your God is One God;°
there *is* no god but He,
The Merciful, The Compassionate.

Sec. 20
*

2:164
Truly the creation
of the heavens and the earth,
and the alteration
of the nighttime and the daytime,
and the boats that run on the sea,
with what profits humanity,
and what God sent forth from heaven of water,
and gave life to the earth after its death,
and disseminated on it all moving creatures;
and diversified the winds,
and the clouds that are caused to be subservient
between heaven and earth

are Signs for a folk who *are* reasonable.
Among humanity *are some*   2:165
who take to themselves rivals besides God,
loving them like they cherish God;°
but those who have believed are stauncher
in cherishing God;°
and if those who do wrong
might see, when they see the punishment,
that all strength *belongs* to God,
and truly God *is* Severe in punishment.
Then they would clear themselves,   2:166
those who were followed,
from those who followed them—
and they would see the punishment
and their relation would be cut asunder.
those that followed would say: 2:167
Would that there would be a return again for us,
then we would clear ourselves from them
as they have cleared themselves from us;°
thus God shall cause them to see their actions
with regret;°
and they shall never be ones who go forth
from the fire.
                          *   Sec. 21

O humanity!   2:168
Eat of what is in and on the earth,
what is wholesome,   •
and follow not the steps of Satan;°
truly he *is* a clear enemy to you.
Truly he commands you   2:169
to evil and depravity,
and that you say about God
what you know not.
When it is said to them: 2:170
Follow what God has sent forth
they say: Rather we shall follow
what we discovered our fathers following.°
What! Even if their fathers
were not at all reasonable

nor were they truly guided?

The parable of those who are ungrateful
is like the parable of those who cry out
to what hears not
except shouting and pleading,°
unwilling to hear, to speak, to see,
they are not reasonable.

2:172 O those who have believed!
Eat of what is good
that We have provided you and give thanks to God
if it is He whom you worship.

2:173 Truly He has forbidden you carrion,
blood and the flesh of swine,
and what has been hallowed to other than God;°
but whoever is driven by necessity,
without being one who desires,
and not one who is turning away,
then no sin shall be on him;°
truly God is Forgiving, Compassionate.

2:174 Truly those who keep back
what God has sent forth of the Book,
• and exchange it for a little price,
they consume into their bellies
not but fire;
God shall not speak to them
on the Day of Resurrection,
nor shall He make them pure;
and for them shall be a painful punishment.

2:175 Those are they who bought misjudgment
for guidance
and punishment for forgiveness,°
how they are the ones who remain steadfastly
in the fire!

2:176 That is because God has sent down
the Book with The Truth.°
Truly those who are at variance
about the Book
are in a wide breach.

Sec. 22 *

It is not virtuous conduct   **2:177**
that you turn your faces
towards the East or the West,
but virtuous conduct is
to have believed in God
and the Last Day
and the angels and the Book
and the Prophets;°
to have given wealth out of cherishing Him
to the kin and the orphans
and the needy and the traveler of the way
and one who seeks and for *freeing* a bondsperson;
to perform the formal prayer,
to give the purifying alms,
to be ones who live up to their compact
when they make a contract;°
who are the ones who remain steadfast
in desolation and tribulation
and at the time of danger;°
they, those have been sincere;°
and they, those *are* the ones who are Godfearing!
O those who have believed!   **2:178**
Reciprocation is prescribed for you
for the slain;°
the freeman for the freeman,
the servant for the servant,
the female for the female;°
but whoever is forgiven
a thing by his brother,
the pursuing
should be as one who is honorable,
and the remuneration *be* with kindness;°
that *is* a lightening from your Lord,
and a mercy;°
and he who commits aggression after that,
for him *is* a painful punishment.
There is the saving of life for you in reciprocation,   **2:179**
O you who have intuition,
so that perhaps you would be Godfearing.

2:180   *It is* prescribed for you

It is prescribed for you
when death attends anyone of you,
if he leave goods,
that he bequeath to the ones who are *his* parents
and nearest kin as one who is honorable;°
an obligation for the ones who are Godfearing.

2:181 Then whoever substituted it after he has heard it,
truly the sin of it is on those who substitute it;°
truly God *is* Hearing, Knowing.

2:182 Then whoever fears from
one who makes a testament
a swerving from the right path or sinning,
and makes things right between them,
there is no sin on him.°
Truly God *is* Forgiving, Compassionate.

Sec. 23

*

2:183 O those who have believed!
Prescribed for you is formal fasting
as it was prescribed
for those before you
so that perhaps you would be Godfearing.

2:184 *Fasting is prescribed for* numbered days;°
then whoever among you is sick
or on a journey,
then a period of other days;°
and for those who can,
a redemption of food for the needy;°
and whoever volunteers good,
it is better for him,°
but that the formal fast *is* best for you,°
if you were to know.

2:185 The month of Ramadan
is one in which the Quran was sent forth
as a guidance for humanity,
with clear portents of the guidance,
and the Criterion between right and wrong;°
so whoever of you bears witness to the month,
then he should formally fast it;°
and whoever is sick or on a journey,

then a period of other days;°
God wants ease for you,
and wants not hardship for you,
so that you complete the period,
and that you magnify God,
because He guided you
so that perhaps you would give thanks.
When My servants ask **you** about Me,   2:186
then truly I am near;°
I answer the call of one who calls
when he calls to Me;°
so they should respond to Me and believe in Me
so that perhaps they shall be on the right way.
It is permitted for you   2:187
on the night of formal fasting
to have intercourse with your wives;
they (f) *are* a garment for you
and you *are* a garment for them (f);°
God knew
that you had been dishonest to yourselves,
so He turned in forgiveness to you
and pardoned you;°
so lie with them (f)
and be looking for what God has prescribed for you;°
and eat and drink
until the white thread become clear to you
from the black thread at dawn;°
then fulfill the formal fast until night,°
and lie not with them (f)
when you *are* ones who cleave   •
to the places of prostration;°
these *are* the ordinances of God,
keep well within them;°
thus God makes His Signs manifest to humanity
so that perhaps they would be Godfearing.
Consume not your wealth   2:188
among yourselves in falsehood,
nor let *it* down to the ones who are judges
so that you consume a group of people's

wealth among humanity in sin
while you know.

*

2:189   They ask **you** about the new moons;°
say: They *are* times appointed for humanity
and for the pilgrimage to Mecca;°
it is not virtuous conduct that you approach
houses from the back
but virtuous conduct is to be Godfearing;°
and approach houses from their *front* doors;°
and be Godfearing of God
so that perhaps you would prosper.

2:190   Fight in the Way of God those who fight you,
but commit not aggression;°
truly God loves not the ones who are aggressors.

2:191   Kill them wherever you come upon them
and drive them out from wherever
they have driven you out,°
for persecution *is* more grave than killing;°
but fight them not near
the Masjid al-Haram
unless they fight you in it;°
but if they fight you, then kill them;°
thus *this is* the recompense
for the ones who are ungrateful.

2:192   But if they refrain,
then truly God *is* Forgiving, Compassionate.

2:193   Fight them until there be no persecution
and the way of life becomes for God;°
then if they refrain,
there is to be no deep seated dislike
except against the ones who are unjust.

2:194   The Sacred Month for the Sacred Month
and reciprocation for sacred things;°
so whoever commits aggression against you°
commit aggression against him likewise
as he has committed aggression against you;°
and be Godfearing
and know God *is* with the ones who are Godfearing.

Spend in the way of God,   2:195
and cast not *yourselves* by your own hands
into deprivation,
and do good;
truly God loves the ones who are doers of good.
Fulfill the pilgrimage to Mecca   2:196
and the visit for God;°
and if you are restrained,
then whatever is feasible of sacrificial gifts;°
and shave not your heads
until the sacrificial gift reaches its place;°
and whoever is sick among you,
or has an injury of his head,
then a redemption by formal fasting
or charity or a ritual sacrifice;°
and when you are safe,
then whoever takes joy in the visit
and the pilgrimage to Mecca
then whatever is feasible of a sacrificial gift;°
and whoever finds not the *means,*
then formal fasting for three days
during the pilgrimage to Mecca
and seven when you have returned;°
that *is* ten complete;
that *is* for those whose people
are not ones who are present
at the Masjid al-Haram;°
and be Godfearing and know that God
is Severe in repayment.

*   Sec. 25

The pilgrimage to Mecca *is* in known months,°   2:197
and whoever undertakes the duty
of pilgrimage to Mecca in these,
then *there is* no intercourse
nor disobedience nor dispute
during the pilgrimage to Mecca;°
and whatever you accomplish of good
God knows it;°
and take provision;

then truly the best ration is Godfearingness;°
so be Godfearing *of Me*
O you who have intuition!

2:198 There is no blame on you
that you should be looking for
the grace of your Lord;°
and when you press on from Arafat,
then remember God at the Sacred Monument;°
and remember Him, for He has guided you,
although you were before this
indeed of the ones who had gone astray.

2:199 Then press on from where humanity presses on
and ask God for forgiveness;°
truly God *is* Forgiving, Compassionate.

2:200 When you have satisfied
your devotional acts,
then remember God
like *your* remembrance of your fathers
or a stauncher remembrance;°
and among humanity is he who says:
Our Lord! Give to us in the present!
For him,
there is no apportionment in the world to come!

2:201 Among them *is* he who says:
Our Lord! Give us benevolence in the present,
and benevolence in the world to come,
and protect us from the punishment of the fire!

2:202 Those, for them *is* a share
of what they earned;°
and God is Swift at reckoning.

2:203 Remember God during the numbered days;°
then whoever hastens on in two days,
there is no sin on him;°
and whoever remains behind,
there is no sin on him;°
and for whoever *is* Godfearing,°
be Godfearing of God,
and know that to Him you shall be assembled.

2:204 Among humanity

is he whose sayings impress **you**
about this present life,
and he calls to God to witness
what is in his heart,
yet he is most stubborn in altercation.
When he turns away,   2:205
he hastens about the earth
so that he make corruption in and on it,
and he causes the cultivation and stock to perish;°
and God loves not corruption.
When it is said to him: 2:206
Be Godfearing of God!
Renown takes him to sin,°
so hell is enough for him!°
Indeed a miserable Final Place!
Among humanity *is* he who sells himself   2:207
looking for the good pleasure of God;°
and God *is* Gentle with *His* servants.
O those who have believed!   2:208
Enter in peacefulness collectively,
and follow not the steps of Satan;°
truly he *is* a clear enemy to you.
But if you back slide   2:209
after the clear portents have drawn near to you,
know indeed God *is* Almighty, Wise.
Look they for   2:210
nothing but that God should approach them
in the over shadowing
of cloud shadows with the angels?
The command is decided,°
and commands shall be returned to God.

*   Sec. 26

Ask the Children of Israel   2:211
how many Signs, clear portents, We gave them;°
and whoever substitutes
the divine blessing of God,
after it has drawn near to him,
then truly God *is* Severe in repayment.
Made to appear pleasing   2:212

to those who are ungrateful *is* this present life,
and they deride those who have believed. •
But those who are Godfearing
shall be above them on the Day of Resurrection;°
and God provides
for whomever He will without reckoning.

2:213   Humanity was of one community,
then God raised up the Prophets
as ones who give good tidings
and ones who warn;
and with them He sent forth the Book,
with The Truth
to give judgment among humanity
about what they were at variance;°
none were at variance in it
except those who were given it
after clear portents had drawn near to them
because of their insolence to one another;°
then God guided those who had believed
to The Truth about what they were at variance
with His permission,°
and God guides whom He will
to the straight path.

2:214   Or assumed you that you should enter the Garden
while there has not come
the like of those who passed away before you?°
They were afflicted with desolation, tribulation,
and were so convulsed that
the Messenger
and those who have believed with him said:
When *shall be* the help of God?°
Truly the help of God *is* Near.

2:215   They ask **you** what they should spend;°
say: Whatever thing you spend for good
is for the ones who are *your* parents,
the nearest kin, the orphans, the needy
and the traveler of the way;°
whatever good you accomplish,
then truly God *is* Knowing of it.

Prescribed for you is fighting
although it shall be disliked by you;°
and perhaps you dislike a thing,
and it *is* good for you;°
and perhaps you love a thing,
and it *is* worse for you;°
and God knows, and you know not.

*

They ask **you**

about the Sacred Month and fighting in it;°
say: Fighting in it is deplorable,°
but barring from the way of God
and being ungrateful to Him
and *to bar from* the Masjid al-Haram
and to expel people from it
are more deplorable with God;°
and persecution *is* more deplorable than killing;°
they cease not to fight you
until they turn you away from your way of life,
if they are able;°
and whoever of you goes back on his way of life,
and dies while he *is* one who is ungrateful,
those, their actions are fruitless
in the present and in the world to come;°
and those *shall be* the Companions of the Fire;°
they are ones who shall dwell in it forever.

Truly those who have believed,

those who have migrated
and have struggled in the way of God,
those have hope for the mercy of God,°
and God *is* Forgiving, Compassionate.

They ask **you** about intoxicants and gambling;°

say: In both of them there is a deplorable sin
and profit for humanity,
but their sin *is* more deplorable
than what *is* profitable;°
they ask you how much they should spend;
say: *What is* extra;°
thus God makes manifest His Signs to you

2:220
so that perhaps you would reflect
on the present and the world to come;°
and they ask **you** about orphans;°
say: Making things right for them is best;°
and if you intermix with them,
then they *are* your brothers;°
God knows the ones who make corruption
from the ones who make things right;°
and had God willed,
He would have overburdened you;°
truly God *is* Almighty, Wise.

2:221
Marry not the ones who are female polytheists
until they (f) believe.°
The one who is a believing female bond servant
is better than the one who is a female polytheist
although she impresses you;°
and wed not to the ones who are male polytheists
until they (m) believe;
and one who is a believing male bond servant
is better than the one who is a male polytheist
although he impresses you;°
those call you to the fire;°
but God calls to the Garden and to forgiveness
with His permission;
and He makes manifest His Signs to humanity
so that perhaps they would recollect.

Sec. 28
                          *

2:222
They ask **you** about menstruation;°
say: It is an impurity,
so withdraw from your wives during menstruation;°
come not near them (f) until they become pure;°
and then when they (f) are purified,
approach them as God commanded you;°
truly God loves the ones who turn in repentance,
and loves the ones who keep themselves clean.

2:223
Your wives *are a place* of cultivation for you°
so approach your cultivation as you willed;°
and put forward for your souls;°
and be Godfearing of God

and know that you *shall be*
the ones who encounter Him;°
and give good tidings to the ones who believe.
Make God not an obstacle   2:224
through your sworn oaths
to your being good and being Godfearing
and making things right among humanity;°
and God *is* Hearing, Knowing.
God shall not take you to task   2:225
for idle talk in your sworn oaths,
but He shall take you to task
for what your hearts have earned;°
and God *is* Forgiving, Forbearing.
For those who vow abstinence from their wives,   2:226
await a period of four months;°
then if they change their minds,
truly God *is* Hearing, Knowing.
If they resolve on setting *them* (f) free,   2:227
then truly God *is* Forgiving, Knowing.
Divorced women shall await by themselves   2:228
three menstrual periods,°
and it is not lawful for them
that they keep back
what God has created in their wombs
if they were to believe in God and the Last Day;°
their mates *have* better right
to come back during that period
if they wanted to make things right;°
and for them (f)
the like of what is on them (f),
as one who is honorable;°
and men *have* a degree above them (f);°
and God *is* Almighty, Wise.
                          *   Sec.29
Setting free *may be said* twice,   2:229
then an honorable *continuing* to hold fast to them
or letting them go with kindness;°
and it is not lawful for you
that you take anything

of what you have given them (f)
unless they both fear
that they both shall not perform
within the ordinances of God;°
and if you fear that they both shall not perform
within the ordinances of God,
then no blame on either of them
in what she offers as redemption for that;°
these are the ordinances of God,
so commit not aggression;°
and whoever violates the ordinances of God,
then they, those *are* the ones who are unjust.

2:230 If he divorces her *finally*,
then she is not lawful to him after that,
until she marries a spouse other than him;°
yet if he divorces her irrevocably,
there *is* no blame on them
if they return to one another,
if both of them think that
they shall perform within the ordinances of God;°
and these *are* the ordinances of God;
He makes them manifest for a folk who know.

2:231 When you divorce wives,
and they (f) *are about to* reach their (f) term,
then hold them (f) back honorably
or set them (f) free honorably;°
but hold them (f) not back by injuring them
so that you commit aggression,°
and whoever commits that,
then indeed he does wrong to himself;°
and take not the Signs of God to yourselves
in mockery;°
remember the divine blessing of God
on you and what He sent forth to you
of the Book and wisdom;
He admonishes you with it;°
and be Godfearing *of God*
and know that God *is* Knowing of everything.

Sec. 30 *

When you *revocably* divorce wives, 2:232
and they (f) reach their (f) term,
then place not difficulties for them (f)
that they (f) *re*-marry their (f) *former* spouses
when they agree honorably among themselves;°
this is admonished for him
among you who believe in God
and the Last Day;°
that is pure and purer for you;°
and God knows and you know not.
The ones who are mothers 2:233
shall breast feed their (f) children
as one who completes two years,°
for those who wanted to fulfill breast feeding;°
and on him to whom a child is born
is their (f) provisions
and their (f) clothing as one who is honorable;°
no soul is placed with a burden
except to its capacity;°
neither the one who is a mother should be pressed
for her child
nor he to whom a child is born for his child;
and on one who is an inheritor
is the like of that;°
but if they both wanted weaning
by them agreeing together and after consultation,
then there is no blame on either of them;°
and if you wanted
to seek wet-nursing for your child,
then there is no blame on you if you hand over
what you give
as one who is honorable;°
and be Godfearing of God
and know that God *is* Seeing of what you do.
Those of you whom death calls to itself, 2:234
forsaking spouses (f),
they (f) shall await by themselves (f)
four months and ten;°
and when they (f) reach their (f) term,

42

then there is no blame on you
in what they (f) accomplish for themselves (f)
as ones who are honorable;
God *is* Aware of what you do.

There is no blame on you
in what you offered with it
of a proposal to women,
or for what you hide in yourselves;°
God knows that you,
truly shall remember them (f),
but appoint not with them (f) secretly,
unless you say a saying
as one who is honorable;°
and resolve not on the knot of marriage
until the term prescribed is reached;°
and know that God knows
what is within yourselves
so be fearful of Him,°
and know that God is Forgiving, Forbearing.

*

There is no blame on you if you divorce wives
whom you have not touched,
nor undertaken a duty towards them (f);°
make provisions for them (f);°
for one who is wealthy
—according to his means—
and for one who is needy
—according to his means—
with an honorable sustenance;°
an obligation on one who is a doer of good.

If you divorce them (f)
before you touch them (f),
and indeed you have undertaken the duty
of a dowry portion for them (f),
then half of what you have undertaken as a duty,
unless they (f) pardon it,
or it is pardoned by him
in whose hand *is* the marriage knot;
yet that you should pardon

is nearer to Godfearingness;
forget not grace with each other.
Truly God *is* Seeing of what you do.
Be watchful of the formal prayers   2:238
and the middle formal prayer.
Stand up
as ones who are morally obligated to God.
If you fear,   2:239
then on foot or as one who is mounted;°
and when you are safe,
then remember God
for He has taught you
what you knew not.
Those whom death calls to itself,   2:240
forsaking spouses,
shall bequeath for their spouses
sustenance for a year
without expulsion,°
but if they (f) go forth themselves,
there is no blame on you
in what they (f) accomplish for themselves
as ones who are honorable;°
and God *is* Almighty, Wise.
There shall be for divorced women   2:241
an honorable sustenance;°
this is an obligation on the ones who are Godfearing.
Thus God makes His Signs manifest to you   2:242
so that perhaps you would be reasonable.
                        *   Sec. 32

Have **you** not considered those who went forth   2:243
from their abodes
while there were thousands of them,
fearful of death?
God said to them: Die!
Then He gave them life;°
truly God *is* Possessor of Grace for humanity,
but most of humanity gives not thanks.
So fight in the Way of God   2:244
and know that God *is* Hearing, Knowing.

Who is he who shall lend God a fair loan
so that He shall multiply it for him manifold?°
God seizes and extends
and you shall be returned to Him.
Have **you** not considered the Council
of the Children of Israel after Moses
when they said to a Prophet of theirs:
Raise up a king for us?
We shall fight in the way of God;°
he said:
Perhaps if fighting is prescribed for you,
you would not fight?°
They said: Why should we not fight
in the way of God
when we have been driven out
of our abodes with our children?°
But when fighting was prescribed for them,
they turned away, except for a few of them;°
and God *is* Knowing of the ones who are unjust.
Their Prophet then said to them:
Truly God has raised up Saul for you as king;°
they said: How would it be for him
to *have* dominion over us
when we *have* better right to dominion than he,
as he has not been given plenty of wealth?°
He said: Truly God has favored him over you
and has increased him
in knowledge and stature;°
and God gives His dominion to whom He will;°
and God *is* One Embracing, Knowing.
Their Prophet then said to them:
Truly a Sign of his kingship
is that the Ark of the Covenant
would approach you there;
in it *is* tranquility from your Lord,
and a relic
of what the people of Moses left,
and the people of Aaron;
and the angels shall carry it;°

truly in that is a Sign for you
if you are the ones who believe.

*

So when Saul set forth with his army
he said: Truly God is One Who Tests you
with a river;
so whoever drinks of it, he is not of me,
and whoever tastes it not, indeed he is of me,
except he who scoops up with a scoop of his hand;°
yet they drank of it but a few of them;°
so when he crossed it,
he and those who had believed with him,
they said: *There is* no energy for us today
against Goliath and his armies;°
those who thought that they would be
the ones who encounter God said:
How often has a faction of a few
vanquished a faction of many
with the permission of God?°
God *is* with the ones who remain steadfast.
So when they departed
2:250
against Goliath and his army
they said: Our Lord! Pour out patience on us,
and make our feet firm;
help us against the ones who are ungrateful.
So they put them to flight
2:251
with the permission of God,
and David killed Goliath;
and God gave him the kingship and wisdom,
and taught him of what He will;°
had God not driven men back
—some by means of some others—
the earth would have indeed gone into ruin,
but God *is* Possessor of Grace to the worlds.
These are the Signs of God
2:252
that We recount to **you** in Truth;°
truly **you** *are*
of the ones who have been sent.

***

Part 3

These *are* the Messengers—
We have given advantage
to some of them over others. •
Of them are those to whom God spoke,°
while some of them He exalted in degree,°
and We gave Jesus son of Mary clear portents
and confirmed him with the hallowed Spirit;°
and had God willed it, those after them
would not have fought one another
after the clear portents had drawn near to them,
except they were at variance,
and some of them have believed,
and some of them are ones who are ungrateful;°
and had God willed,
they would not have fought one another,
but God accomplishes what He wants.

*

O those who have believed!
Spend of what We have provided you
before that day approaches
when there is neither trading in it
nor friendship, nor intercession;°
and the ones who are ungrateful,
they are the ones who are unjust.

God! There is no god but He;
The Living, The Eternal;°
neither slumber takes Him nor sleep;°
to Him *belongs* whatever *is* in the heavens
and whatever *is* in and on the earth;°
who is he that would intercede with Him
except with His permission?°
He knows what *is* in front of them
and what *is* behind them;°
and they shall never comprehend
anything of His knowledge,
but what He willed;°
His seat encompasses
the heavens and the earth,°
and He is not hampered by their safe keeping,°

and He *is* The Lofty, The Sublime.
There is no compulsion in the way of life;°

indeed right judgment
has become clear from error;°
so whoever disbelieves in false deities
and believes in God, indeed
holds fast with the most firm handhold,
unbreakable;°
and God *is* Hearing, Knowing.
God *is* The Protector of those who have believed.

He brings them out
from the shadows into the light;°
and those who are ungrateful,
their protectors are false deities;
they bring them out
from the light into the shadows;°
those *shall be* the Companions of the Fire;°
they *are* the ones who shall dwell in it forever.

*

Have **you** not considered him

who argued with Abraham about his Lord
because God had given him dominion?
When Abraham said:
My Lord *is* He Who gives life and causes to die,
he said: I give life and cause to die;°
Abraham said:
Truly God brings the sun from the East,
so shall **you** bring it from the West?
Then he who was ungrateful was dumfounded;°
and God guides not the unjust folk.
Or like the one who passed by a town,

and it had fallen down into ruins;°
he said: How shall God give life to this
after its death?°
So God caused him to die for a hundred years;°
then He raised him up,°
He said:
How long have **you** lingered in expectation?°
He said: I have lingered in expectation

for a day or some part of a day;°
He said: Rather **you** have lingered in expectation
a hundred years;
then look at your food and drink,
they are not spoiled;°
and look at **your** donkey.
We have made **you** a Sign
for humanity;°
and look at the bones, how We set them up,
then clothe them with flesh;°
so when it became clear to him he said:
I know that God *is* Powerful over everything.

2:260
When Abraham said:
My Lord! Cause me to see
how **You** give life to the dead;°
He said: Shall **you** not believe?°
He said: Yea, indeed!
But so that my heart may be at rest;°
He said: Then take four birds
and twist them to **yourself**,
and lay a part of them on every mountain;
then call to them.
They shall approach you coming eagerly,°
and know that God *is* Almighty, Wise.

Sec. 36

*

2:261
A parable of those who spend their wealth
in the way of God
is like a parable of a grain
that puts forth seven ears of wheat;
in every ear of wheat, a hundred grains;°
so God multiplies for whom He will;°
God *is* One Who Embraces, Knowing.

2:262
Those who spend their wealth
in the way of God,
then pursue not what they spent
·
with reproachful reminders nor injury,
the compensation for them *is* with their Lord;
then *there is* neither fear in them
nor *shall* they feel remorse.

49

An honorable saying
with forgiveness
is better than charity
that *is* succeeded by injury;°
and God *is* Sufficient, Forbearing.

O those who have believed!
Render not untrue your charities
with reproachful reminders nor injury
like those who spend of their wealth
to show off to humanity
and believe not in God and the Last Day;°
His parable *is* like the parable of a smooth rock;
over *it is* earthy dust;
a heavy downpour lights on it
and leaves it bare;°
they *have* no power over anything
for what they have earned;°
God guides not the ungrateful folk.

But the parable
of those who spend their wealth
looking for the good pleasure of God
to confirm their souls
is like the parable of a garden on a hillside
when a heavy downpour lights on it;
then it gives its harvest double;
and even if a heavy downpour lit not on it,
then a dew;°
and God *is* Seeing of what you do.

Would anyone of you wish to have
a garden of date palm trees
and grapevines
beneath which rivers run
with every kind of fruit in it?
Then old age lights on him,
and he has weak offspring;
then a whirlwind lights on it
in which there is a fire
and it is consumed?°
Thus God makes manifest His Signs for you

so that perhaps you would reflect.

*

2:267

O those who have believed!
Spend of what *is* good that you have earned,
and of what We have brought out for you
from the earth;°
and aim not at getting the worst of it to spend;
and you would not be the ones who take it
except that you close an eye to it,°
and know that God *is* Sufficient,
Worthy of Praise.

2:268

Satan threatens you with poverty,°
and commands you to depravity;
whereas God promises you His forgiveness
from Himself and His grace;°
and God *is* One Who Embraces, Knowing.

2:269

He gives wisdom to whom He will,°
and whomever *is* given wisdom,
then indeed has been given much good;°
yet none recollects but those who have intuition.

2:270

Whatever of contributions you spend
or vows that you may vow,
truly God knows it;°
and *there is no* helper for the ones who are unjust.

2:271

If you show your charity, then how bountiful it *is;*°
but if you conceal it and give it to the poor,
that *would be* better for you;°
this would absolve you of some of your evil deeds;°
and God *is* Aware of what you do.

2:272

Their guidance is not on **you**,
for God guides whomever He will;°
and whatever of good you spend,
it is for yourselves;°
and spend not
except looking for the countenance of God;°
and whatever of good you spend,
your account shall be paid to you in full,
and wrong shall not be done to you.

2:273

Spend for the poor, those who are restrained

in the way of God,
and are not capable of traveling on the earth;
one who is ignorant assumes them to be rich
because of their reserve;
you shall recognize them by their mark;
they ask not persistently of humanity;°
and whatever of good you spend,
then truly God *is* Knowing of that.

*

Those who spend their wealth

by nighttime and daytime, secretly or in public,
indeed for them, their compensation
proceeds from their Lord;
then *there is* neither fear in them,
nor *shall* they feel remorse.
Those who consume usury

shall not arise,
except as one arises
whom Satan has prostrated by touch;°
that *is* because they said:
Truly trading *is* like usury;
and God permitted trading and forbade usury;°
so whoever draws near an admonishment
from his Lord and refrains,
for him *is* what is past;
and his command *is* with God;°
but those who revert,
those *shall be* the Companions of the Fire;°
they, ones who shall dwell in it forever!
God eliminates usury

and He makes charity greater;°
and God loves not
any sinful ingrate.
Truly those who have believed,

ones who have acted in accord with morality,
and perform the formal prayer,
and give the purifying alms,
for them, their compensation *is* with their Lord,
and *there is* neither fear in them

nor *shall* they feel remorse.

O those who have believed!
Be Godfearing of God,
and forsake what remains of usury
if you are ones who believe.

But if you accomplish it not,
then take notice of war from God,
and His Messenger;°
yet if you repent,
you shall *have* your principal capital,
doing no wrong nor shall wrong be done to you.

If *a debtor* is in adversity, then a respite
until a time of ease and prosperity;°
but *it is* better for you that you be charitable,°
if you were to know.

Be Godfearing of a Day
when you shall be returned to God;°
then every soul shall be paid its account in full
for what it has earned
and wrong shall not be done to them.

Sec. 39 *

2:282 O those who have believed!
When you contract a debt for a determined term,
then write it down;°
and *have* a scribe write it down between you
justly;°
and a scribe should not refuse to write down
as God has taught him;
so have him write down,
and have the debtor dictate,
he being Godfearing of God, his Lord,
and diminish nothing out of it,°
but if the debtor be mentally deficient,
or weak
or not able to dictate himself,
then have his protector dictate justly;°
and *have* two witnesses witness
from among your men;°
or if there are not two men,

then a man and two women,
from those with whom you are well-pleased
as witnesses so that if one of the two goes astray,
then the other one of the two shall remind;°
and the witnesses should not refuse
when they are called;°
and grow not weary that you write it down,
be it small or great, with its term;°
that *is* more equitable with God,
and more upright for witnessing,
and likelier not to be in doubt;°
unless it be a trade you transfer *at the time,*
giving and taking between yourselves;
there is no blame on you
if you not write it down;°
and *have* witnesses when you *have* a transaction;°
and *have* neither scribe nor witness be pressed;°
and if you accomplish that,
then *it is* disobedience;°
so be Godfearing of God;°
God teaches you;°
and God *is* Knowing of everything.
If you are on a journey
and find no scribe,
then a guarantee that *is* held in your hand;°
but if any of you entrust to another,
then *have* the one who is trusted
give back his trust,
and he be Godfearing of God, his Lord;°
and keep not back witnessing;°
and truly he who keeps back,
he, his heart shall be one that is perverted;°
and God *is* Knowing of what you do.

*

To God *belongs* what *is* in the heavens,
and in and on the earth;°
whether you show what *is* within yourself,
or conceal it,
God shall make a reckoning with you for it;°

2:283

Sec. 40

2:284

He shall forgive whom He will,
and He shall punish whom He will;°
and God *is* Powerful over everything.

2:285

The Messenger has believed in
what has been sent forth to him
from his Lord *as do* the ones who believe;°
all have believed in God, His angels,
His Books and His Messengers:
We separate and divide not
among anyone of His Messengers;°
and they said: We heard and we obeyed;°
so grant **Your** forgiveness, Our Lord!
To **You** *is* the Homecoming.

2:286

God places not a burden
on a soul beyond its capacity;°
for it *is* what it has earned
and against it *is* what it deserves;°
Our Lord!
Take us not to task
if we forget or make a mistake;°
our Lord!
Load not on us a severe test
like that which **You** have burdened those before us;°
our Lord!
Burden us not such that we *have* no power for it;°
and pardon us and forgive us,
and *have* mercy on us;°
You are One Who Protects
so help us over the ungrateful folk.

*

CHAPTER 3
THE FAMILY OF IMRAN (*Āl-i-ʿImrān*)

In the Name of God,

Sec. 1

The Merciful, The Compassionate

3:1

Alif Lām Mīm;

3:2

God! *There is* no god but He,
The Living, The Eternal.

3:3

He sent down to **you** the Book with The Truth

55

establishing as true what *was* before it;
and He has sent forth
the Torah and the Gospel
before this as a guidance for humanity;   3:4
and He has sent forth
the Criterion between right and wrong;°
truly those who are ungrateful
for the Signs of God,
for them *is* a severe punishment;°
God *is* Almighty, the Possessor of Requital.
Truly God, nothing is hidden from Him   3:5
in or on the earth nor in heaven.
It is He Who forms you in the wombs   3:6
how He will;°
there is no god but He, Almighty, Wise.
It is He who has sent forth to **you** the Book;   3:7
in it are definitive Signs;
they are the essence of the Book
and others are ambiguous;°
then those whose hearts are swerving,
they follow what *is*
susceptible to different interpretations,
looking to dissent,
and looking for an interpretation;°
and none knows its interpretation except God;
the ones who are firmly rooted in knowledge say:
We have believed in it
as all is from our Lord;°
and none recollects but those who have intuition.
Our Lord!   3:8
Cause our hearts not to swerve
after **You** have guided us
and bestow on us mercy
from that which proceeds from **Your** Presence;°
truly **You, You** alone *are* The Giver.
Our Lord!   3:9
Truly **You** are One Who Gathers
humanity on a Day
in which *there is* no doubt;°

truly God breaks not His solemn declaration.

*

3:10
> Truly those who are ungrateful,
> their wealth nor their children
> shall not avail them
> against God at all;°
> and they, those shall be fuel for the fire

3:11
> similar to the custom of the people of Pharaoh
> and those before them;°
> they denied Our Signs
> and so God took them because of their impiety;°
> and God *is* Severe in repayment.

3:12
> Say to those who are ungrateful:
> You shall be vanquished,
> and are to be assembled into hell,°
> a miserable Final Place.

3:13
> Indeed there was a Sign for you
> in the two factions who met each other;°
> one faction to fight in the way of God,
> and the other as ones who are ungrateful,
> whom, in their view,
> they saw as twice with their eyes;°
> but God confirms with His help whom He will;°
> truly in this *is* a lesson
> for those who have insight.

3:14
> Made to appear pleasing to humanity
> *is* the cherishing
> of what they *have* an appetite for:
> Women and children,
> and heaped up heaps
> of gold and silver,
> and branded horses and flocks,
> and tilled land;°
> that *is* the enjoyment of this present life;°
> but God, with Him
> *is* the goodness of the Excellent Abode.

3:15
> Say: Shall I tell you of better than that?°
> For those who are Godfearing,
> with their Lord

are Gardens beneath which rivers run;
they *are* ones who shall dwell in them forever
with purified spouses
and contentment from God;°
and God *is* Seeing *His* servants.

Those who say: 3:16
Our Lord!
Truly we have believed,
so forgive us our impieties
and protect us from the punishment of the fire:

The ones who remain steadfast,   3:17
the ones who are sincere,
the ones who are morally obligated,
the ones who are expenders,
and the ones who ask for forgiveness
at the breaking of day.

God bears witness that *there is* no god but He,   3:18•
as do the angels and those who have knowledge,
the ones who uphold equity;°
there is no god but He,
The Almighty, The Wise.

Truly the way of life with God   3:19
is submission *to the Will of God;*°
because of insolence among themselves
those who had been given the Book
were at variance
only after knowledge
had drawn near to them;°
and whoever is ungrateful for the Signs of God,
then truly God *is* Swift in reckoning.

So if they argue with **you**, say: 3:20
I have submitted my face to God
as *have* those who follow me;°
say to those who were given the Book
and to the unlettered:
Have you submitted?°
If they have submitted,
then indeed they are truly guided;°
but if they turn away, then

truly on **you** *is* not but delivering the message;°
and God *is* Seeing of *His* servants.

       *

3:21   Truly those who are ungrateful for the Signs of God,
and kill the Prophets without right,
and kill those who command to equity
from among humanity,
then give them the good tidings
of a painful punishment.

3:22   Those *are* they whose actions have been fruitless
in the present and the world to come;
and for them *there is* no one who helps.

3:23   Have **you** not considered those who were given
a share of the Book?
They are called to the Book of God
to give judgment among them;
then a group of people turns away,
and they *are* the ones who turn aside.

3:24   That *is* because they said:
The fire shall not touch us
except for numbered days;°
and they have been deluded in their way of life
by what they used to devise.

3:25   How then *shall it be*
when We shall gather them together
on a Day in which *there is* no doubt,
and every soul shall have its account paid in full
for what it has earned,
and wrong shall not be done to them?

3:26   Say: O God!
One Who is Sovereign of Dominion,
You give dominion to whom **You** will
and **You** tear away dominion
from whom **You** will;
and **You** render powerful whom **You** will
and **You** abase whom **You** will;°
in **Your** hand *is* the good;°
truly **You** *are* Powerful over everything.

3:27   **You** cause the nighttime to be interposed

into the daytime,
and **You** cause the daytime to be interposed
into the nighttime;°
and **You** bring out the living from the dead
and **You** bring out the dead from the living;°
and **You** provide to whomever **You** will
without stint.
The ones who believe should not take to themselves   3:28
the ones who are ungrateful
for protectors
instead of the ones who believe;°
for whoever accomplishes that,
he is not with God in anything,
unless it is because of your Godfearingness
that you are being cautious toward them;°
God cautions you of Himself;°
and to God *is* the Homecoming.
Say: Whether you conceal   3:29
what *is* in your breasts
or show it
God knows it;°
and He knows whatever *is* in the heavens
and whatever *is* in and on the earth;°
and God *is* Powerful over everything.
On the Day when every person shall find   3:30
what is to be brought forward of good;°
and what one did of evil,°
each shall truly wish that
there would be between this and between that
a long space of time;°
God cautions you of Himself;°
and God *is* Gentle to the servants.
                    *   Sec. 4
Say: If it be that you love God, then follow me,   3:31
and God shall love you and forgive you
your impieties;°
God *is* Forgiving, Compassionate.
Say: Obey God and the Messenger;°   3:32
but if they turn away,

then truly God loves not
the ones who are ungrateful.

3:33 Truly God favored Adam, Noah,
the people of Abraham,
and the people of Imran above *all* the worlds,

3:34 some *are* of one another's offspring;°
and God *is* The Hearing, The Knowing;°

3:35 when the wife of Imran said:
My Lord!
I have vowed to **You**
what is in my womb
in dedication
so receive this from me;°
truly **You, You** *are*
The Hearing, The Knowing.

3:36 Then when she brought forth her baby she said:
My Lord! Truly I have brought her forth,
a female baby;°
and God *has* greater knowledge
of what baby she brought forth;°
and the male is not like the female!°
Truly I have named her Mary
and truly I commend her to **Your** protection
with her offspring from the accursed Satan.

3:37 So her Lord received her
with the very best acceptance;
and her bringing forth
to develop with the very best;
and Zechariah took charge of her;°
whenever Zechariah entered on her
in her sanctuary,
he found her with provisions;°
he said: O Mary! From where *is* this for **you** (f)?°
She said: This *is* from God;°
truly God provides to whom He will
without reckoning.

3:38 Then Zechariah called to his Lord;°
he said: My Lord!
Bestow on me

from that which proceeds from **Your** Presence;°
good offspring; truly **You** *are* hearing supplication.
Then the angels proclaimed to him,   3:39
while he was one who stood invoking blessings
in the sanctuary: •
Truly God gives **you** good tidings of John
—establishing the word of God as true—
a noble man, chaste and a Prophet,
among the ones who are in accord with morality.
He said: My Lord!   3:40
How is it I shall have a boy
when I have reached old age,
and my wife *is* a barren woman?°
He said: Thus God accomplishes
what He will.
He said: My Lord!   3:41
Assign a Sign for me.°
He said: **Your** Sign
is that **you** shall not speak
to humanity for three days, except by gesture;°
remember **your** Lord frequently,
and glorify in the evening and early morning.
*   **Sec. 5**

When the angels said: 3:42
O Mary! Truly God has favored **you** (f),
and purified **you** (f),
and has favored **you** (f)
above women of the world.
O Mary! **You** are morally obligated to **your** (f) Lord;   3:43
prostrate **yourself** (f),
and bow down (f) with the ones who bow down.
These *are* tidings from the unseen   3:44
that We reveal to **you**.°
You were not present with them
when they cast their pens
as to which of them would take control of Mary;
nor were **you** present with them
when they strove against one another.
When the angels said: O Mary!   3:45

Truly God gives you (f) good tidings
of a word from Him
whose name is Messiah
—Jesus son of Mary—
well-esteemed in the present
and the world to come;
and of the ones who are brought near.

3:46 He shall speak to humanity from his cradle,
and in his manhood, and *be* among
the ones who are in accord with morality.

3:47 She said: My Lord! From where shall I *have* a child
when no mortal has touched me?°
He said: Thus God
creates whatever He will;°
when He decrees a command,
truly He only says to it: Be! And it is!

3:48 He shall teach him the Book and wisdom
and the Torah and the Gospel,°

3:49 *to be* a Messenger to the Children of Israel *saying:*
I have drawn near to you

• with a Sign from your Lord:°
I shall create for you out of clay
a likeness of a bird;
then I shall breathe into it,
and it shall become a bird
with the permission of God;°
and I shall cure one who is blind from birth,
and the leper,
and shall give life to dead mortals
with the permission of God;°
and I shall tell you what you have eaten,
and what you store up
in your houses;°
truly in that is a Sign for you
if you are the ones who believe.°

3:50 Establishing as true
what was before me of the Torah,
permitting to you
some of what had been forbidden to you;°

and I draw near to you
with a Sign from your Lord;
so be Godfearing of God and obey Me.
Truly God *is* my Lord and your Lord,   3:51
so worship Him;°
this *is* a straight path.
But when Jesus was conscious   3:52
of their ingratitude, he said:
Who shall be my helpers to God?°
The disciples said: We shall be helpers of God;
we have believed in God
and bear **you** witness that we *are* ones who submit.
Our Lord! We have believed in what   3:53
You have sent forth,
and we follow the Messenger,
so write us down
with the ones who bear witness;
and they planned and God planned;°   3:54
and God *is* the Best of one who plans.
*   Sec. 6

When God said: O Jesus!   3:55
I *shall be* the One Who Gathers **you**,
and I *shall be* One Who Elevates **you**
toward Myself,
and the One Who Purifies **you**
from those who are ungrateful,
and I *shall be* One Who Makes those who follow **you**
above those who are ungrateful
until the Day of Resurrection;°
then you shall return to Me
and I shall give judgment among you
about what you were at variance.
As for those who are ungrateful,   3:56
then I shall punish them
with a severe punishment
in the present and the world to come;
and for them *there is* no one who helps.
As to those who have believed,   3:57
and the ones who have acted in accord with morality,

then He shall pay them their full compensation;°
and God loves not the ones who are unjust.

3:58   This We recount to **you**
of the Signs and the wise reminder.

3:59   Truly the parable of Jesus with God
is like the parable of Adam;°
He created him from earthy dust
then said to him: Be! And he was!

3:60   The Truth *is* from **your** Lord
so be **you** not the ones who contest.

3:61   To whoever argues with **you** about it
after what has drawn near to **you**
of knowledge, say: Approach now!
We call to our sons and your sons,
and our women and your women,
and ourselves and yourselves;
and then we shall humbly supplicate
and we lay the curse of God on the ones who lie.

3:62   Truly this *is* a narrative of The Truth;°
and *there is* no god but God;°
and truly God, He *is* The Almighty, The Wise.

3:63   If they turn away,
then truly God *is* Knowing
of the ones who make corruption.

Sec. 7   *

3:64   Say: O People of the Book!
Approach now
to a word common between us and between you
that we worship none other than God,
and we make no partner with Him,
and some of us take not others as lords
other than God;°
and if they turn away, then say:
Bear witness that we are ones who submit.

3:65   O People of the Book!
Why argue with one another about Abraham,
while neither the Torah nor the Gospel
were sent forth until after him;°
shall you not be reasonable?

Behold! You are those who argue   3:66
about what you *have* knowledge;
why then argue with one another
about what you *have* no knowledge?°
God knows and you know not.
Abraham was neither a Jew nor a Christian,   3:67
but he was a monotheist—one who submits;
he was not of
the ones who are polytheists.
Truly those of humanity closest to Abraham   3:68
are those who followed him
and this Prophet and those who have believed;°
and God *is* Protector of the ones who believe.
A section of the People of the Book wished   3:69
they would cause you to go astray;
and they cause none to go astray
except themselves, yet they are not aware.
O People of the Book!   3:70
Why be ungrateful for the Signs of God
while you bear witness?
O People of the Book!   3:71
Why confuse you truth with falsehood
and keep back The Truth while you know?
*   Sec. 8

A section of the People of the Book said: 3:72
Believe in what was sent forth
to those who believe
at the beginning of the daytime,
and disbelieve at the last *of the day*
so that perhaps they would return *to disbelief.*
Believe no one   3:73
except one who heeds your way of life;
say: Truly guidance *is* guidance from God,
and *believe not* that anyone be given the like
of what have been given
so that he may argue with you
before your Lord;°
say: Truly the grace *is* in the hand of God.
He gives it to whomever He will;°

God *is* One Who Embraces, Knowing.

3:74　　He singles out for His mercy whom He will;°
and God *is* Possessor of Sublime Grace.

3:75　　Among the People of the Book
is one who, if **you** entrust him
with a hundredweight,
He would give it back to **you**;
and among them *is* one who,
if **you** entrust him with a dinar,
he would not give it back to **you**
unless **you** were to stand persistently over him;°
that *is* because they say:
There is no *moral duty* for us as to the unlettered;
and they lie against God
while they know.

3:76　　Rather whoever lives up to his compact
and *is* Godfearing
then truly God loves the ones who are Godfearing.

3:77　　Truly those who exchange
the compact of God,
and their sworn oaths
for a little price,
there is no apportionment for them
in the world to come;
God shall neither speak to them,
nor look on them
on the Day of Resurrection,
nor shall He make them pure;
and for them is a painful punishment.

3:78　　Truly among them *is* a group of people
who distort their tongues with the Book
so that you assume it is from the Book,
yet it is not from the Book;
and they say: It is from God,
yet it is not from God,
and they say a lie against God
while they know.

3:79　　It is not for a mortal
that God should give him the Book

and critical judgment and the prophethood,
and then he say to humanity:
Be you servants of me instead of God;
but *he should say*: Be you masters,
in that you teach the Book,
and in that you study it.

•

Nor would He command you to take to yourselves   **3:80**
the angels and the Prophets as lords;°
would He command you to ingratitude
after you were the ones who submit?

*

Sec. 9

When God took a solemn promise   **3:81**
about the Prophets:
Because I have given you the Book and wisdom,
should a Messenger draw near to you,
establishing as true what *is* with you,
you shall believe in him, and you shall help him;°
He said: Are you in accord
and shall you take on My severe test?°
They said: We are in accord with it;°
He said: Then bear witness
and I shall be One Who Bears Witness with you.
Then whoever turns away after this,   **3:82**
they, those are the ones who disobey.
Desire they other than the way of life from God   **3:83**
while to Him submits
whatever *is* in the heavens and the earth
willingly or unwillingly,
and they shall be returned to Him?
Say: We have believed in God   **3:84**
and what has been sent forth to us,
and what was sent forth to Abraham,
Ishmael, Isaac, Jacob
and the Tribes
and what was given to Moses and Jesus
and the Prophets from their Lord;
we separate and divide not
between anyone of them,
and we are the ones who submit to Him.

3:85
Whoever be looking for
a way of life other than submission,
it shall not be accepted from him;
and he, in the world to come,
shall be of the ones who are losers.

3:86
How shall God guide a folk
who are ungrateful after their belief?
They bore witness
to The Truth of the Messenger
after clear portents had drawn near to them;°
and God guides not
the unjust folk.

3:87
Those, their recompense
is the curse of God on them,
and of the angels and of humanity, one and all,

3:88
ones who shall dwell in it forever.
The punishment shall neither be lightened
for them nor shall they be given respite,

3:89
except those who, after they repent,
make things right,
for truly God *is* Forgiving, Compassionate.

3:90
Truly those who are ungrateful after their belief,
and then add to their ingratitude,
their remorse shall never be accepted;
they, those are the ones who have gone astray.

3:91
Truly those who are ungrateful,
and die as the ones who are ungrateful,
the earth, full of gold, shall not be accepted
from anyone of them if offered for ransom;°
those, for them, *is* a painful punishment
and for them *there is* no one who helps;

3:92
you shall never attain virtuous conduct
until you spend of what you love;°
and whatever thing you spend,
God *is* Knowing of it.

Part 4

Sec. 10

***

*

3:93
All food was allowed to the Children of Israel,
except what Israel forbid itself

before the Torah was sent down;°
say: Then approach with the Torah
and recount it
if you are ones who are sincere.
Then whoever devised lies against God   **3:94**
after that,
then they, those are the ones who are unjust.
Say: God is Sincere;°   **3:95**
so follow the creed of Abraham
—a monotheist—
and he was not
among the ones who were polytheists.
Truly the first House to be set in place   **3:96**
for humanity *is* at Bekka,
blessed,
and a guidance for the worlds.
In it are clear portents, Signs,   **3:97**
and the Station of Abraham;
and whoever enters it
is one who is in safety;°
and the pilgrimage to the House in Mecca
is a duty to God on humanity
for those who are able to travel the way to it;°
and whoever should be ungrateful,
truly God is Independent of the worlds.
Say: O People of the Book!   **3:98**
Why be ungrateful for the Signs of God
when God is Witness over what you do?
Say: O People of the Book!   **3:99**
Why bar you those who have believed
from the way of God,
desiring crookedness when you were witnesses?°
God is not One Heedless of what you do.
O those who have believed!   **3:100**
If you obey a group of people
of those who were given the Book,
they shall turn you away after your belief
and *become* ones who are ungrateful.
Why would you be ungrateful   **3:101**

when the Signs of God are recounted to you,
and His Messenger is among you?°
Whoever cleaves firmly to God
is then guided to a straight path.

*

3:102   O those who have believed!
Be Godfearing of God as it is His right
that He should be feared,
and die not except
as ones who submit.

3:103   Cleave firmly to the rope of God altogether,
and be not split up;°
remember the divine blessing of God on you
when you were enemies,
then He brought your hearts together,
and you became, by His divine blessing, brothers;
and you were on the brink of an abyss
of the fire,
and you were saved from it by Him;°
thus God makes manifest to you His Signs,
so that perhaps you would be truly guided.

3:104   There may be from among you a community
who calls to good,
commands to what is moral,
and prohibits what is immoral;°
and those, they *are* the ones who prosper.

3:105   Be not like those who had split up
and were at variance
after the clear portents had drawn near them;°
•   and those, for them *is* a tremendous punishment,

3:106   on a Day *when* faces shall brighten,
and faces shall become clouded over;°
as for those whose faces become clouded over:
Are you ungrateful after your belief?
Then experience the punishment
for what you were ungrateful.

3:107   As for those whose faces brightened,
they are in the mercy of God;
they, ones who shall dwell in it forever.

71

These are the Signs of God;   3:108
We recount them to **you** in Truth;°
and God wants no injustice in the worlds.
To God *belongs* whatever *is* in the heavens   3:109
and whatever *is* in and on the earth.°
To God all commands are returned.

*

You were the best community   3:110
brought out for humanity;
you command to what is moral,
and prohibit what is immoral,
and believe in God;°
had the People of the Book believed,
it would have been better for them;°
among them *are* the ones who believe,
but most of them *are* the ones who disobey.
They never injure you but a little hurt;°   3:111
and if they fight you,
they shall turn their backs on you;
then they shall not be helped.
Abasement has been stamped on them   3:112
wherever they are come upon,
except *those* with a link to God
and a link to humanity,
and they have drawn the burden
of the anger of God,
and wretchedness shall be stamped on them;°
that *is* because, truly they are ungrateful
for the Signs of God
and kill the Prophets without right;°
that *is* because they would rebel,
and were committing aggression.
They are not all the same;°   3:113
among the People of the Book
is a community of ones who are upstanding;
they recount the Signs of God
in the night watch of the night,
and they prostrate.
They believe in God and the Last Day;   3:114

they command what is moral,
and prohibit what is immoral;
and they compete with one another
in good deeds;
those *are* among
the ones who are in accord with morality.

3:115 Whatever good they accomplish
shall never go unappreciated;°
and God *is* Knowing
of the ones who are Godfearing.

3:116 Truly those who are ungrateful,
neither shall their wealth nor their children
avail them
against God at all;°
those *shall be* the Companions of the Fire;°
ones who shall dwell in it forever.

3:117 The parable of what they spend
in this present life
is like the parable of a freezing wind
that lights on the cultivation of a folk
who did wrong to themselves
and it caused it to perish;°
and God did not wrong them,
but they did wrong themselves.

3:118 O those who have believed!
Take not to yourselves as close friends
other than yourselves;
they stop at nothing to ruin you;
they wish for you to fall into misfortune;
their hatred shows itself from their mouths;
and what their breasts conceal is greater;°
indeed We have made manifest to you the Signs°
if you are reasonable.

3:119 Behold! You are those who love them,
but they love you not;
and you have believed in the Book, all of it.
When they meet you
they say: We believe;
but when they go privately,

they bite the tips of their fingers at you in rage;°
say: Die in your rage!°
Truly God *is* Knowing
of what *is* within your breasts.
If you are touched with benevolence, 3:120
it raises anger in them,
but if an evil deed lights on you,
they are glad about it;°
but if you patiently endure,
and are Godfearing,
their cunning shall not injure you at all;
truly God *is* One Who Encloses what they do.
*

When **you** set forth in the early morning 3:121
from **your** family
to place the ones who believe
in their positions for fighting,°
God *is* Hearing, Knowing
when two sections of yours 3:122
were about to lose heart,
even though God *had been* their Protector;°
let the ones who believe put their trust in God.
Indeed God helped you at Badr 3:123
when you *were* humiliated in spirit;°
so be Godfearing of God
so that perhaps you would give thanks.
When **you** said to the ones who believe: 3:124
Shall it not suffice you
that your Lord reinforces you
with three thousand angels that are sent forth?
Rather° 3:125
if you patiently endure and are Godfearing,
and they approach you instantly,
your Lord shall reinforce you
with five thousand angels,
ones who are sweeping on.
God made this not but as good tidings to you; 3:126
with it your hearts shall be at rest;°
and *there is* no help

except from God,
The Almighty, The Wise.

3:127 He shall cut off a selection
of those who are ungrateful
or suppress them so they turn about
as ones who are frustrated.

3:128 It is none of **your** affair at all
whether He turns to them in forgiveness
or He punishes them;
for truly they are ones who are unjust.

3:129 To God *belongs* whatever *is* in the heavens
and whatever *is* in and on the earth;°
He forgives whom He will
and punishes whom He will;°
God *is* Forgiving, Compassionate.

Sec. 14
*

3:130 O those who have believed!
Consume not usury,
what is to be doubled and redoubled;°
and be Godfearing of God
so that perhaps you would prosper.

3:131 Be Godfearing of the fire
that is prepared for the ones who are ungrateful.

3:132 Obey God and the Messenger,
so that perhaps you would find mercy.

3:133 Compete with one another for forgiveness
from your Lord and for a Garden whose depth
is as the heavens and the earth

· prepared for the ones who are Godfearing,

3:134 those who spend
in gladness and tribulation,
the ones who choke their rage
and the ones who pardon humanity;°
God loves the ones who are doers of good.

3:135 Those who, when they commit
an indecency, or do wrong to themselves,
they remember God,
and ask for forgiveness for their impieties.
Who forgives their impieties except God?

Who persists not
in what they have accomplished while they know?
Those, their recompense is forgiveness   3:136
from their Lord
and Gardens beneath which rivers run;
they, ones who shall dwell in them forever;°
and how bountiful is the compensation
for the ones who work!°
Customs have passed away before you   3:137
so journey on the earth
and look on how the Ultimate End
was of the ones who denied.
This *is* a clear explanation for humanity;   3:138
a guidance and an admonishment
for the ones who are Godfearing.
Be not feeble nor feel remorse;   3:139
you *shall be among* the lofty ones
if you are ones who believe.
If a wound afflicts you,   3:140
a similar wound has afflicted that folk;
and these *are* days We rotate among humanity
so that God may know
those who have believed,
and take witnesses to Himself from among you;°
God loves not the ones who are unjust;
and so that God may prove   3:141
those who have believed,
and eliminate the ones who are ungrateful.
Or assumed you that you would enter   3:142
the Garden while God has not yet known
those who struggled among you,
nor known the ones who remained steadfast?
Truly you were to covet death   3:143
before you met it;
now you have seen and looked on it.

*   Sec. 15

Muhammad is nothing but a Messenger;   3:144
indeed Messengers have passed away before him.°
Then if he should die or be slain,

shall you turn about on your heels?°
He who turns about on his heels
shall not injure God at all;°
and God shall give recompense
to the ones who are thankful.

3:145 It is not for any soul to die
except with the permission of God,
prescribed as what is appointed;°
and whoever wants a reward for good deeds
in the present,
We shall give him that;°
and whoever wants a reward for good deeds
in the world to come,
We shall give him that;°
and We shall give recompense
to the ones who are thankful.

3:146 How many a Prophet there has been
and with him many thousands have fought,
but none became feeble
for what lighted on them
in the way of God,
nor were they weakened,
nor were they to give in;°
and God loves the ones who remain steadfast.

3:147 Their saying was nothing but that they said:
Our Lord! Forgive us our impieties
and our excessiveness in our affair;
make our feet firm,
and help us against the folk,
the ones who are ungrateful.

3:148 So God gave them a reward for good deeds
in the present
and the fairest reward for good deeds
in the world to come;°
God loves the ones who are doers of good.

Sec. 16   *

3:149 O those who have believed!
If you obey those who are ungrateful,
they shall shove you back on your heels,

and you shall turn about
as the ones who are losers.
But God *is* One Who Protects you;°   3:150
and He *is* the Best of ones who help.
We shall cast alarm into the hearts   3:151
of those who are ungrateful
because they made partners *with God*,
and He has not
sent down any authority for it;°
their place of shelter is the fire.°
Miserable is the place of lodging
of the ones who are unjust.
Indeed God has been sincere   3:152
in His promise to you
when you blasted them
with His permission;°
until you lost heart,
and you contended with one another
about the command;
you rebelled
after He had caused you to see
what you longed for;°
among you are those who want the present,
and among you are those who want
the world to come;°
then He turned you away from them
so as to test you;°
and indeed He pardoned you;°
and God *is* Possessor of Grace
for the ones who believe.
When you mount up,   3:153
not attentive to anyone,
and the Messenger was calling to you
from the rear,
then He repaid you, lament for lament,
so that you neither feel remorse
for what had slipped away from you,
nor for what has lighted on you;°
and God *is* Aware of what you do.

Then He sent forth safety for you after lament;
sleepiness overcame a section of you;°
while another section caused themselves grief,
supposing of God unjustifiably
a thought out of the Age of Ignorance;°
they say:
Have we a part in the command?°
Say: The command *is* entirely from God;°
they conceal within themselves
what they show not to **you**;°
they say: If we were to have had
any part in the command,°
we would not have been killed here;°
say: Even if you had been in your houses,
those it prescribed be slain would have departed
for the Final Place of sleeping;°
so that God may test what *is* in your breasts
and He may prove
what *is* in your hearts;°
and God *is* Knowing what is in the breasts.

3:155
·

Truly those of you who turned away
the day two multitudes met one another,
truly Satan alone caused them to slip back
for some of what they had earned;°
but indeed God pardoned them;°
truly God *is* Forgiving, Forbearing.

Sec. 17

3:156

*

O those who have believed!
Be not like those who were ungrateful,
and who said of their brothers
when they were traveling through the earth,
or were ones who were combatants:
If they had been with us
neither would they have died,
nor would they have been slain;°
so that God makes it a cause of regret
in their hearts;°
but God gives life and causes to die;°
and God *is* Seeing of what you do.

If indeed you are slain
in the way of God or die,
indeed forgiveness and mercy from God
are better than what they gather.

If indeed you die or are slain,
it is surely to God you shall be assembled.

It is by the mercy of God
that **you** were gentle to them;°
and had **you** been hard, harsh of heart,
they would have spread away from around **you**;°
so pardon them,
and ask for forgiveness for them,
and consult them in the affair;°
but when **you** are resolved,
then put **your** trust in God;°
truly God loves the ones who trust in Him.

If God helps you, then none *shall be*
one who is a victor over you;°
but if He withdraws His help from you,
then who is there to help you after Him?°
In God let the ones who believe
put their trust.

It is not for a Prophet
that he defraud;°
and whoever defrauds,
what he had defrauded shall approach him
on the Day of Resurrection;°
then the account shall be paid in full
of every person
for what he has earned,
and they shall not be wronged.

What? Is he who follows
the contentment of God
like one who draws the burden
of the displeasure of God
and whose place of shelter is hell?°
A miserable Homecoming!

They have degrees with God;°
and God *is* Seeing of what they do.

3:164   Indeed God showed grace
to the ones who believed
when he raised up a Messenger
among them from themselves
who recounted His Signs to them
and made them pure
and taught them the Book and wisdom
as before that they had gone clearly astray.

3:165   Why, when an affliction lights on you,
while you had lighted twice its like on them,
said you: Where is this from?°
Say: It is from yourselves;°
truly God *is* Powerful over everything.

3:166   That which lighted on you on the day
when the two multitudes met one another
was with the permission of God
that He might know the ones who believe,

3:167   and that He might know the hypocrites.°
It was said to them: Approach now!
Fight in the way of God or drive back!°
They said: Had we known
there would be fighting,
we would have surely followed you;°
on that day they were nearer to ingratitude
than to belief;°
they say with their mouths
what was not in in their hearts;°
and God *has* greater knowledge
of what they keep back.

3:168   Those who said to their brothers
while they sat back:
Had they obeyed us,
they would not have been slain;°
say: Then drive off death from yourselves,
if you are the ones who are sincere.

3:169   Assume not those who are slain
in the way of God to be lifeless;°
but they are living,
and they are provided for near their Lord,

glad in what God has given to them
of His grace,
rejoicing at the good tidings;
for those who have not joined them,
but are behind
that *there is* neither fear in them,
nor *shall* they feel remorse.
They rejoice at the good tidings
of the divine blessing from God,
and His grace
and that God shall never
waste the compensation
of the ones who believe.

*

Those who responded to God
and the Messenger
after wounds had lighted on them,°
for those of them who did good
and were Godfearing,
there is a sublime compensation.°
Those to whom humanity said:
Truly humanity has gathered against you
so dread them;
but *this only* increased them in belief,
and they said: God is enough for us,
and how excellent *is He*, The Trustee.
So they turned about
with divine blessing from God and grace;
evil afflicts them not,
and they followed the contentment of God;
and God *is* Possessor of Sublime Grace.
It is not but Satan who frightens you
with his protectors;°
so fear them not, but fear Me
if you are the ones who believe.
Let not those who compete with one another in
ingratitude grieve **you**.°
Truly they shall never injure God at all;°
God wants to assign no allotment for them

3:170

3:171

Sec. 18

3:172

3:173

3:174

3:175

3:176

in the world to come;°
and for them *is* a tremendous punishment.

3:177   Truly those who have bought ingratitude
for belief
shall never injure God at all;
and for them *shall be* a painful punishment.

3:178   Those who are ungrateful should not assume
that the indulgence We grant to them
is better for themselves.°
We only grant indulgence to them
so that they may add sin;°
and for them is a despised punishment.

3:179   It is not that God shall forsake
the ones who believe in what you are in
until He differentiates
the bad from what is good;°
and God shall not inform you about the unseen,
but God elects from His Messengers
whom He will;°
so believe in God and His Messengers;°
and if you believe and are Godfearing,
then for you *there is* a sublime compensation.

3:180   But as for those who are misers, let them not assume
that what God has given them of His grace
is better for them;°
rather it is worse for them;°
hung around their necks
on the Day of Resurrection
is that with which they were miserly,°
and to God *is* the heritage
of the heavens and the earth;°
and God is Aware of what you do.

*

Sec. 19

3:181   Indeed God has heard the saying
of those who said:
Truly God is poor and we are rich. •
We shall write down what they have said,
and their killing of the Prophets without right;
and We shall say:

Experience the burning punishment!
That is for what your hands have put forward,   3:182
and because God is never unjust to His servants.°
Those who say: 3:183
Truly God has made a compact with us
that we not believe in a Messenger,
until He approaches with a sacrifice
to be consumed by the fire;°
say: Surely Messengers before me brought about
clear portents to you,
and even of what you speak;
why have you killed them
if you are the ones who are sincere?
But if they have denied **you**,   3:184
so Messengers before **you** were denied
who drew near with clear portents,
and the Psalms and the illuminating Book.
Every soul is one that experiences death;°   3:185
then your compensation shall be paid in full
on the Day of Resurrection;°
whoever is extracted from the fire,
and is caused to enter the Garden,
has indeed won a triumph;°
what *is* this present life,
but the enjoyment of delusion?
You shall certainly be tried   3:186
with your wealth and yourselves;
and you shall certainly hear much *that is* hurtful
from those who were given
the Book before you,
and those
who have associated partners *with God,*°
but if you patiently endure,
and be Godfearing,
truly that is of the commands to constancy.
When God took a solemn promise   3:187
from those who were given the Book:
You shall make it manifest to humanity
and keep it not back;

but they repudiated it behind their backs,
and exchanged it for a little price;°
and how miserable is what they buy!

3:188 Assume not that those
who are glad for what they have brought,
and *who* love to be praised
for what they have not accomplished—
assume not that they shall be kept safe
from the punishment;°
for them, a painful punishment.

3:189 To God *belongs* the dominion
of the heavens and of the earth;°
and God *is* Powerful over everything.

Sec. 20

*

3:190 Truly in the creation
of the heavens and of the earth,
and the alteration of nighttime and daytime,
truly there *are* Signs
for those who have intuition,

3:191 those who remember God
while upright and sitting and on their sides
and reflect on the creation
of the heavens and of the earth;
our Lord!
You have not created this in vain.
Glory be to **You**!
Then protect us
from the punishment of the fire.

3:192 Our Lord!
Whomever **You** cause to enter the fire,
then **You** have covered him with shame;°
and for the ones who are unjust,
there are no helpers.

3:193 Our Lord!
Truly we have heard
one who calls out a cry for belief:
Believe in your Lord!
We have believed;
our Lord!

Forgive **You** our impieties
and absolve us of our evil deeds,
and gather us to **You** with the pious.
Our Lord!   3:194
Give us what **You** have promised us
through **Your** Messengers,
and cover us not with shame
on the Day of Resurrection;°
truly **You** shall never
break **Your** solemn declaration.
Their Lord responded to them: 3:195
I waste not the actions of ones who work
among you, male or female;°
each one of you *is* as the other;°
so those who migrated
and were driven out from their abodes
and were afflicted with torment on My way,
and who fought and were slain,
I shall indeed absolve them of their evil deeds;
I shall certainly cause them to enter
into Gardens beneath which rivers run;
a reward for good deeds from God;°
and God, with Him
is the goodness of rewards for good deeds.
The ones who go to and fro should not delude **you**   3:196
among those who are ungrateful in the land.
A little enjoyment;   3:197
then their place of shelter is hell;°
a miserable Final Place.
But those who are Godfearing of their Lord,   3:198
for them *shall be* Gardens
beneath which rivers run,
ones who shall dwell in them forever,
a welcome from God;°
and what is with God
is best for the pious.
Truly among the People of the Book   3:199
are those who believe in God,
and what was sent forth to you,

and what was sent forth to them,
ones who are humbled towards God;
they exchange not the Signs of God
for a little price;°
those, for them their compensation
is with their Lord;°
and truly God is Swift in reckoning.

3:200 O those who have believed!
Be patient and excel in patience,
and be steadfast,
and be Godfearing of God
so that perhaps you would prosper.

*

CHAPTER 4
WOMEN (*al-Nisāʾ*)

In the Name of God,

Sec. 1 The Merciful, The Compassionate
4:1 O humanity!
Be Godfearing of your Lord
Who created you from a single soul,
and from it created its spouse,
and from them both disseminated
many men and women.°
Be Godfearing of God;
through Him you question one another
and blood relations.°
Truly God watches over you.

4:2 Give the orphans their property;°
and take not in exchange
the bad for what is good;°
and consume not their property
with your own property.°
Truly this is criminal, a hateful sin.

4:3 If you fear that you shall not be equitable
with the orphans,
marry who seems good to you of the women,
two, three or four;°
but if you fear you shall not be just,

87

then one or what your right hands possess;°
that is likelier
so that you shall not *have* injustice.
Give wives their marriage portion   4:4
as a spontaneous gift,°
but if truly they (f) are pleased to offer
anything of it to you on their own,
consume it with wholesome appetite.
Give not the mentally deficient your wealth   4:5
that God has assigned to you for them,
but provide for them from it and clothe them,
and speak to them honorable sayings.
Test the orphans   4:6
when they reach the *age for* marriage;
then if you observe them
to be of right judgment,
release their property to them;°
and consume it not excessively and hastily,
for they shall develop;°
and whoever is rich let him have restraint;°
and whoever is poor,
then he consume as one who is honorable;°
and when you release their property to them,
call witnesses over them;°
and God suffices as a Reckoner.
For men *is* a share of what is left by   4:7
the ones who are *his* parents and nearest kin;
and to women *is* a share of what is left by
the ones who are *her* parents and nearest kin,
whether it be little or much;°
a share of what is apportioned.
When the division   4:8
is attended by kin,
the orphans and the needy,
then provide for them out of it,
and speak to them honorable sayings.
Let those dread like   4:9
those who may leave behind weak offspring
would fear for them;

let them be Godfearing of God,
and let them speak appropriate sayings.

Truly those who consume
the wealth of orphans with injustice,
consume nothing but fire into their bellies;°
and soon they shall roast in a blaze.

God enjoins you concerning your children;
for the male, the like allotment of two females;°
and if there be more than two females,°
then for them two-thirds of what he leaves;
but if she be alone, then for her is half;°
and for one's parents, for each one of them
a sixth of what he leaves if he has a child;°
but if he has no children,
and his parents inherit,
then a third to his mother;°
but if he has a brother
then a sixth for his mother°
after any bequest
he shall enjoin or any debt;°
your parents or your children,
you are not informed which of them
is nearer to you in profit;°
this is a duty to God;°
truly God has been Knowing, Wise.

For you *is* a half of what your spouses leave
if they (f) *have* no child;°
but if they (f) *have* a child,
then for you is a fourth of what they (f) leave°
after any bequest which
they shall bequeath or any debt;°
and for them (f) a fourth of what you leave
if you *have* no children;°
and if you *have* children,
then for them (f) *is* an eighth of what you leave
after any bequest
which you bequeath or any debt;°
and if a man or a woman has

no direct heirs, but indirect heirs,
and has a brother or sister,
then for each one of them (f) a sixth;°
but if there are more than that,
then they are the ones who associate in a third°
after any bequest which one bequeaths
or any debt without being one who presses *the heirs;*°
this is the enjoinment from God;°
and God *is* Knowing, Forbearing.
These *are* the ordinances of God;°   4:13
and whoever obeys God and His Messenger,
he shall be caused to enter Gardens
beneath which rivers run,
ones who shall dwell in them forever;°
and that is the winning the sublime triumph.
But whoever rebels *against* God   4:14
and His Messenger and violates His ordinances,
He shall cause him to enter fire,
one who shall dwell in it forever;
and he shall *have* a despised punishment.

*   Sec. 3

Those among your wives   4:15
who approach indecency,
four of you must testify against them (f);°
then if they bear witness,
hold them (f) back in their houses
until death gathers them (f) to itself,
or God makes a way for them (f).
Those two who among you approach that,   4:16
then penalize them both;°
but if they repent and make things right,
then leave them alone;°
truly God is Accepter of Repentance,
Compassionate.
Truly the turning of God in forgiveness   4:17
is for those who do evil in ignorance,
and then repent shortly;
then those *are* whom God turns to in forgiveness;°
God has been Knowing, Wise.

4:18   But remorse is not for those who
do evil deeds,°
until when one of them is attended by death,
he says: Truly I repent now;
nor for those who die
while they are the ones who are ungrateful;°
for those
We have made ready
a painful punishment.

4:19   O those who have believed!
It is not lawful for you
that you inherit women unwillingly;°
and place not difficulties for them (f)
so that you go off with
some of what you have given them (f),
unless they approach a glaring indecency;°
live as one who is honorable with them (f);°
and if you dislike them (f)
perhaps you dislike something
in which God has made much good.

4:20   But if you wanted
to exchange your spouse
in place of another spouse,
and you have given one of them (f)
a hundredweight, take not anything from it;°
would you take it
by false charges to harm her reputation
and in clear sin?

4:21   How would you take it
when one of you have had intercourse
with another
and they have taken from you
an earnest solemn promise?

4:22   Marry not
women whom your fathers married,
unless it was in the past;°
truly it is an indecency and repugnant,
and how evil a way!

Sec. 4   *

Forbidden to you are your mothers,
daughters and your sisters,
your paternal and maternal aunts,
the daughters of your brothers,
the daughters of your sisters,
your foster mothers, those who suckled you,
your sisters through fosterage,
the mothers of your wives,
and your stepdaughters, those who are in your care
from the wives, those with whom you have lain—
but if you have not yet lain with them,
it is no blame on you—
and the wives of your sons
who are of your loins;
and that you should not have two sisters together
unless it be from the past;°
truly God has been Forgiving, Compassionate;

***

and the ones who are married women,

except those whom your right hands possess;°
this is prescribed by God for you;°
and permitted to you
are those who are beyond these
so that with your wealth you be looking for
wedlock,
not as ones who are licentious;°
for what you enjoy of it from them (f),
give them (f) their bridal due
as their dowry portion;°
and *there is* no blame on you
for what you agree on among yourselves
after the duty;°
truly God has been Knowing, Wise.
Whoever of you has not the affluence

to be able to marry
the ones who are free, chaste female believers,
then from those whom your right hands possess
of moral female believers;°
and God *has* greater knowledge

about your belief;°
you are one from another,°
so marry them (f) with their people's permission,
and give them (f) their bridal due
as one who is honorable,
they being the ones who are free, chaste females,
neither ones who are licentious
nor ones who takes lovers to themselves;°
and when in wedlock,
if they (f) *are*
ones who approach indecencies,
then on them is half the punishment
of the ones who are free, chaste females;°
that is for those who dread
fornication among you;°
but that you patiently endure is better for you;°
God *is* Forgiving, Compassionate.

*

Sec. 5

4:26   God wants to make manifest to you
and to guide you
to customs of those who *were* before you,
and to turn to you in forgiveness;°
and God *is* Knowing, Wise.

4:27   God wants to turn to you in forgiveness;
but those who follow their lusts want you
to turn against *God* in a serious deviation.

4:28   God wants to lighten the burden on you
for the human being was created weak.

4:29   O those who have believed!
Consume not your wealth
among you with falsehood;
except that it be a transaction
of agreeing together among you;°
and kill not one another;°
truly God is Compassionate to you.

4:30   But whoever accomplishes that
through deep seated dislike and injustice,
truly We shall scorch him in a fire;°
and that is easy for God.

If you avoid major sins,   4:31
from which you have been prohibited,
We shall absolve you of your minor sins,
and cause you to enter a generous gate.
Covet not what God has given as advantage   4:32
to some of you over others;°
for men a share of what they deserve;°
and for women a share of what they (f) deserve;°
and ask God for His grace;°
truly God has been Knowing of everything.
To everyone We assigned   4:33
one who protects what
the ones who are one's parents and nearest kin leave;°
and those with whom
you have made an agreement with a sworn oath,
then give them their share;°
truly God is Witness over everything.

*   Sec. 6

Men are supporters of wives   4:34
because God has given some of them an advantage
over others
and because they spend of their wealth.°
So the ones (f) who are in accord with morality
are the ones (f) who are morally obligated,
the ones (f) who guard the unseen
of what God has kept safe.°
But those (f) whose resistance you fear,
then admonish them (f)
and abandon them (f) in their sleeping place
then go away from them (f);°
and if they (f) obey you,
surely look not for any way against them (f);°
truly God is Lofty, Great.
If you fear a breach between the two,   4:35
then raise up an arbiter from his people
and an arbiter from her people;
if they both want to make things right,
God shall reconcile it between the two;°
truly God has been Knowing, Aware.

94

Worship God,
and associate no partner *with Him;*°
be kind to the ones who are *your* parents
and to kin and the orphans and the needy
and to the neighbor who *is* a stranger
and the neighbor who *is* kin
and to the companion by your side
and the traveler of the way
and whom your right hands possess;°
truly God loves not
ones who are proud, boastful,

those who *are* misers,
and command humanity to miserliness,
and keep back what God has given them
of His grace.°
We have made ready
for the ones who are ungrateful
a despised punishment,

and those who spend their wealth
to show off to humanity,
and believe
neither in God nor in the Last Day;°
and to whomever Satan is a comrade,
then how evil a comrade!

What would be for them
had they believed in God and the Last Day
and spent of what God has provided them?°
God has been Knowing of them.

Truly God does not wrong
even the weight of an atom;°
and if there is benevolence,
He multiplies it,
and gives that which proceeds from His Presence
a sublime compensation.

How then *shall it be*
when We have brought about from each community
a witness,
and We have brought **you** about
as witness to these?

On a Day those who are ungrateful
and rebel against the Messenger
shall wish the earth would be shaped over them;
but they shall not keep back
discourse from God.

*

O those who have believed!
Come not near the formal prayer
when you *are* intoxicated
until you know what you are saying,
nor defiled except as one who journeys
until you have washed yourselves;°
but if you are sick or one who journeys,
or one of you draws near from the privy,
or you have come into sexual contact
with your wives,
and you find no water,
then aim at getting wholesome, dry earth
and wipe your faces and your hands;°
truly God is Pardoning, Forgiving.
Have **you** not considered
those who were given
a share of the Book?
They exchange misjudgment,
and they want you to go astray from the way.
But God *has* greater knowledge
of your enemies;°
and God suffices as a protector,
and God suffices as a helper.
Among those who have become Jews
are those who tamper with words out of context;
and they say: We heard and we rebelled
and: Hear—
without being caused to be heard;
and: Look at us—
distorting their tongues,
and discrediting the way of life;°
and if they had said: We heard and we obeyed
and: Hear **you** and: Look on *us,*

it would have been better for them
and more upright;
but God cursed them for their ingratitude;
so they believe not, except a few.

4:47   O those who have been given the Book!
Believe in what We have sent down,
establishing as true what *was* with you,
before We obliterate faces,
and turn them away, turning them backwards
or curse them
as We cursed the Companions of the Sabbath;°
and the command of God
is what is to be accomplished.

4:48   Truly God forgives not
that any partner be ascribed to Him,
but He forgives other than that
to whomever He will.°
Whoever ascribes partners unto God,
indeed he has devised a serious sin.

4:49   Have **you** not considered
those who make themselves *seem* pure?°
Rather God makes pure whom He will;
wrong shall not be done to them
as much as a date-thread.

4:50   Look on how they devise a lie against God;°
and it suffices as clear sin.

Sec. 8   *

4:51   Have **you** not considered
those who were given a share of the Book?
They believe in false gods and false deities.
They say to those who are ungrateful:
These are better guided
than those who have believed in the way!

4:52   Those are they whom God cursed;°
and for whomever God curses,
then **you** shall not find a helper for him.

4:53   Or *have* they a share in the dominion?
Then they would not give humanity
even a speck on a date stone.

Or are they jealous of humanity   **4:54**
for what God gave them of His grace?°
Indeed We gave the people of Abraham
the Book and wisdom,
and We gave them a sublime dominion.
Among them are those who have believed in it,   **4:55**
and among them are those who barred it.°
Hell suffices for a blaze.
Truly those who are ungrateful for Our Signs,   **4:56**
We shall scorch them in a fire;
as often as their skins are wholly burned,
We shall substitute with other skins
so that they shall experience the punishment;°
truly God has been Almighty, Wise.
Those who have believed,   **4:57**
and the ones who have acted in accord with morality,
We shall cause them to enter into Gardens
beneath which rivers run,
ones who shall dwell in them forever, eternally;°
for them in it shall be purified spouses;°
and We shall cause them to enter
into plenteous shady shadow.
Truly God commands you   **4:58**
to give back trusts to the people;
and when you give judgment
between humanity, give judgment justly;°
truly how excellent God admonishes you of it;°
truly God has been Hearing, Seeing.
O those who have believed!   **4:59**
Obey God and obey the Messenger,
and ones in command among you;°
then if you contend with one another
in anything,
refer it to God and the Messenger
if you believe in God and the Last Day;°
that is better and a fairer interpretation.
                              *   **Sec. 9**

Have **you** not considered   **4:60**
those who claim that they have believed

in what has been sent forth to **you**,
and what was sent forth before **you**?
They want to take
their disputes to another for judgment
—to false deities—
in whom they have been commanded
to disbelieve,
but Satan wants to cause them to go astray
—a far wandering astray.

4:61　　When it was said to them:
Approach now to what God sent forth
and *approach now* to the Messenger,
you have seen the ones who are hypocrites
barring **you** with hindrances.

4:62　How then shall it be when they are lighted on
by an affliction
for what their hands put forward?
Then they draw near to **you** swearing by God:
Truly we wanted
nothing but kindness and conciliation!

4:63　　They, those *are* of whom God knows
what is in their hearts,
so turn aside from them,
and admonish them,
and speak to them about themselves
with eloquent sayings.

4:64　　Never have We sent a Messenger,
but he is to be obeyed
with the permission of God;°
and if when they do wrong themselves,
they draw near to **you**,
and ask for the forgiveness of God,
and the Messenger asks for forgiveness for them,
they shall surely have found God
Accepting Repentance, Compassionate.

4:65　　But no! By **your** Lord!
They shall not believe
until they make **you** a judge
in the disagreement between them;

then find within themselves no impediment
in what **you** have decided
and surrender in submission.
But if We had prescribed for them   4:66
that you kill your souls
or: Go forth from your abodes,
they would not have accomplished it,
but a few of them;
yet had they accomplished
what they were admonished *for,*
it would have been better for them
and a stauncher confirmation.
Then We would have given them   4:67
from that which proceeds from Our Presence
a sublime compensation.
We would have guided them   4:68
on a straight path.
Whoever obeys God and the Messenger,   4:69
those *are* to whom
God has been gracious
among the Prophets and just persons,
and the witnesses,
and the ones who are in accord with morality.°
How excellent they are *as* allies!
That is the grace from God;°   4:70
and God has sufficed as The Knowing.
                            *   Sec. 10

O those who have believed!   4:71
Take your precautions
and move forward in companies of men
or move forward altogether.
Truly among you   4:72
is he who lingers behind;
then should an affliction light on you, he says:
Indeed God has been gracious to me
that I witnessed them not.
If the grace of God lights on you,   4:73
he would say,
as if there had never been

any affection between you and between him:
Would that I had been with them
so that I would have won a triumph,
a sublime triumph!

4:74 Let those fight in the way of God
who sell this present life for the world to come;°
and whoever fights in the way of God
and then is slain or vanquished,
We shall give him a sublime compensation.

4:75 Why should you not fight
in the way of God and for
ones taken advantage of because of their weakness
among the men and the women
and the children who say:
Our Lord! Bring us out from this town
whose people are the ones who are unjust,
and assign to us a protector
from that which proceeds from **Your** Presence,
and assign for us a helper
from that which proceeds from **Your** Presence.

4:76 Those who have believed, fight in the way of God;°
and those who are ungrateful
fight in the way of the false deity;
so fight the protectors of Satan;°
truly the cunning of Satan has been weak.

Sec. 11 *

4:77 Have **you** not considered
those when it was said to them:
Limit your hands *from warfare*,
and perform the formal prayer
and give the purifying alms?
But when fighting was prescribed for them,
there was a group of people among them
dreading humanity,
even as they would dread God
or with a more severe dread;°
and they said:
Our Lord!
Why have **You** prescribed fighting for us?

101

Why have **You** not postponed it
for another near term for us?°
Say: The enjoyment of the present is little,
and the world to come *is* better
for whomever is Godfearing,
and you shall not be wronged
as much as a date-thread.
Wherever you shall be,   4:78
death shall overtake you,
even if you are in imposing towers;°
and if benevolence lights on them,
they say: This *is* from God;°
and if an evil deed lights on them,
they say: This *is* from **you**;°
say: All *is* from God;°
so what *is* with that folk
that they understand hardly any discourse?
Then whatever of benevolence lights on **you**   4:79
is from God;°
and whatever evil deeds light on **you**
then *is* from **yourself**;°
and We have sent **you**
to humanity as a Messenger;°
and God has sufficed as Witness.
Whoever obeys the Messenger   4:80
has indeed obeyed God;°
and whoever turns away,
then We have not sent **you**
as a guardian over them.
They say: Obedience!   4:81
But when they depart from **you**,
a section of them spend the night planning
on other than what **you** say;°
and God records
what they spend the night planning;°
so turn aside from them,
and put **your** trust in God.°
God has sufficed as Trustee.
Meditate they not on the Recitation?°   4:82

Had it been from other than God,
certainly they would have found in it
many contradictions.

4:83 Whenever draws near them
a command of security or fear,
they broadcast it;°
but had they referred it to the Messenger,
and to those in command among them,
they would have known it,
those who investigate from among them;°
and were it not for the grace of God on you
and His mercy,
certainly you would have followed Satan,
except a few.

4:84 So fight **you** in the way of God;°
you are not placed with a burden
except for **yourself**;°
and encourage the ones who believe°
so that perhaps God
shall limit the might of those who are ungrateful;°
and God *is* Stauncher in might
and Stauncher in punishing.

4:85 Whoever intercedes
with an intercession of benevolence,
he shall *have* a share of it;°
and whoever intercedes
with an intercession for bad deeds,
he shall *have* a like part of it;°
God has been One Who Oversees everything.

4:86 When you are greeted with a greeting,
then give greetings fairer than that
or return *the same* to them;°
truly God has been a Reckoner over everything.

4:87 God, there is no god but He.°
He shall certainly gather you
on the Day of Resurrection;
there is no doubt about it;°
and who is one who is more sincere
in discourse than God?

Then what *is it* for you *that you be*
two factions concerning the ones who are hypocrites
when God overthrew them
for what they had earned?°
Are you wanting to guide
whom God has caused to go astray?°
Whomever God causes to go astray,
you shall never find for him a way.
They wished for you to be ungrateful
as they are ungrateful
so that you become equals;°
so take not to yourself protectors from them
until they migrate in the way of God;°
but if they turn away,
then take them and kill them
wherever you find them;°
and take to yourself from them
neither protector nor helper,
except those who reach out to a folk
who between you and between them
is a solemn promise,
or those who draw near to you
with their breasts reluctant
to fight you or to fight their own folk.°
Had God willed,
He would have given them authority over you,
and they would have fought you;°
so if they withdraw from you
and fight you not,
and give a proposal of surrender to you,
then God has not assigned
any way to you against them.
You shall find others
who want that they be safe from you,
and that they be safe from their folk;
yet whenever they are returned
to temptation,
they relapse into it;°

so if they withdraw not from you,
nor give a proposal of surrender to you,
and limit not their hands,
then take them and kill them
wherever you come on them;°
and those, We have made for you
a clear authority against them.

*

4:92   It is not for the ones who believe
to kill one who believes unless by error;°
and whoever kills one who believes by error
should let go of a believing bond person,
and hand over blood-money to his family
unless they be charitable;°
and if one be of the enemy folk of yours
and he *be* one who believes
then there *should be* the letting go
of a believing bond person;°
and if he be of a folk
who between you and between them
there is a solemn promise,
then blood-money *should be* handed over
to the family,
and a believing bond person *should be* let go;°
but whoever find not the means,
then formally fast for two successive months
as a penance from God;°
and God is Knowing, Wise.

4:93   Whoever kills one who believes
as one who is willful,
then his recompense *is* hell,
one who shall dwell in it forever,
and God shall become angry with him,
and curse him,
and He has prepared for him
a tremendous punishment.

4:94   O those who have believed!
When you travel in the way of God,
then it *should* become clear

you say not to whomever
gives you a proposal of peace:
You are not one who believes,
looking for advantage in this present life;
with God *is* much gain;°
thus you were before like this,
but then God showed grace to you so be clear;°
truly God has been Aware of what you do.

Not on the same level *are*   4:95
the ones who sit at home among the ones who believe
—other than those who *are* disabled—
with the ones who struggle in the way of God
with their wealth and their lives;°
God has given advantage to the ones who struggle
with their wealth and their lives
by a degree over the ones who sit at home;°
yet to each God has promised fairness;°
and God has given advantage
with a sublime compensation
to the ones who struggle
over the ones who sit at home,
degrees from Him and forgiveness and mercy;°   4:96
and God has been Forgiving, Compassionate.

*   Sec. 14

To those whom the angels gather to themselves   4:97
—ones who are unjust to themselves—
they shall say: In what condition were you?°
They shall say: We were
taken advantage of because of our weakness
on the earth;°
they shall say:
Was the earth of God not wide enough
to migrate in it?°
Then for those, their place of shelter shall be hell;°
how evil a Homecoming!
Except   4:98
ones taken advantage of because of the weakness
of the men and the women and the children
who are neither capable of accessing some means,

nor are they truly guided to the way.

Then those perhaps God shall pardon them.°
God has been Pardoning, Forgiving.

Whoever migrates in the way of God
shall find in and on the earth
many places of refuge and plenty;°
and whoever goes forth from his house
as one who emigrates to God
and His Messenger
and death overtakes him,
certainly his compensation shall fall on God;°
truly God has been Forgiving, Compassionate.

Sec. 15 *

4:101 When you travel on the earth,
there is no blame on you
in shortening the formal prayer
if you fear persecution
from those who are ungrateful;°
truly the ones who are ungrateful
are a clear enemy to you.

4:102 When **you** are among them,
performing the formal prayer with them,
let a section of them stand up with **you**,
taking their weapons;
and when they have prostrated,
then let them *move* behind you,
and then let another section approach
who has not yet formally prayed;
let them formally pray with **you**
taking their precaution
and their weapons;°
those who are ungrateful
wished for you to be heedless of your weapons,
and sustenance;
then they shall turn against you a single turning;°
but there is no blame on you
if you are troubled because of rain
or you are sick
that you lay down your weapons;°

but take for yourselves precaution!°
God has prepared for the ones who are ungrateful
a despised punishment.
When you have satisfied the formal prayer,   4:103
then remember God
when upright and sitting and on your sides;°
and then when you are secure,
perform the formal prayer;°
truly the formal prayer is a timed prescription,
for the ones who believe.
Be not feeble in looking for that folk;°   4:104
if you are suffering,
they also are suffering as you are suffering;°
yet you hope from God
that for which they hope not;°
and God has been Knowing, Wise.
                    *   Sec. 16

Truly We have sent forth to **you** the Book   4:105
with The Truth
so that **you** shall give judgment
among humanity
by what God has caused **you** to see;°
be **you** not an adversary
for ones who are traitors.   •
Ask God for forgiveness;°   4:106
truly God has been Forgiving, Compassionate.
Dispute not   4:107
for those who are dishonest to themselves;°
truly God loves not
someone who is a sinful betrayer.
They conceal themselves from humanity,   4:108
but they conceal themselves not from God,
as He is with them when they spend the night
with sayings with which He is not well-pleased;°
and God is One Who Encloses what they do.
Behold! You are those who disputed for them   4:109
in this present life;
but who shall dispute with God for them
on the Day of Resurrection,

or who shall be a trustee over them?

Whoever does evil or does wrong to himself,
and then asks for forgiveness from God
shall, truly find God
Forgiving, Compassionate.

4:111 Whoever earns a sin,
truly he earns it not but against himself;°
and God has been Knowing, Wise.

4:112 Whoever earns a transgression or a sin,
and then accuses an innocent one
has indeed laid a burden on himself
of false charges that harm another's reputation,
a clear sin.

Sec.17 *

4:113 Were it not for the grace of God on **you**
and His mercy,
a section of them
was about to do something
that would cause **you** to go astray.°
But they caused none to go astray
but themselves;°
and they injured **you** not at all;°
and God has sent forth to **you**
the Book and wisdom and has taught **you**
what you knew not;°
and sublime is the grace of God on **you**.

4:114 No good *is there*
in most of their conspiring secretly
except *for* him who commands charity
as one who is honorable,
or makes things right between humanity;°
and whoever accomplishes that
—looking for the good pleasure of God—
then We shall give him a sublime compensation.

4:115 But whoever makes a breach
with the Messenger
after the guidance has become clear to him,
and follows a way other than that
of the ones who believe,

We shall turn him away from
what he has turned to,
and We shall scorch him in hell;°
and how evil a Homecoming!

*

Truly God forgives not
that any partner be ascribed to Him;
He forgives other than that
whomever He will;°
and whoever makes partners with God,
then has gone astray, a wandering far astray.
They call to other than Him,
none else but female gods
and they call to none else than the rebellious Satan
whom God cursed.•
Satan said:
Truly I shall take to myself of **Your** servants
a share of what is apportioned;
I shall cause them to go astray;
truly I shall fill them with false desires.
I shall command them,
then they shall slit the ears of the flocks.
I shall command them
then they shall alter the creation of God.°
Whoever takes Satan to himself
for a protector other than God,
truly he has lost a clear loss.
He promises them
and fills them with false desires;°
and Satan promises them nothing but delusion.
Those, their place of shelter *shall be* hell;
they shall find no way to escape from it.
But those who have believed,
the ones who have acted in accord with morality,
We shall cause them to enter Gardens
beneath which rivers run,
ones who shall dwell in them forever, eternally;°
the promise of God is true;°
and who *is* One More Sincere

4:116

4:117

4:118

4:119

4:120

4:121

4:122

in speech than God?

It shall be neither after your fantasies
nor the fantasies of the People of the Book;°
whoever does evil
shall be given recompense for it,
and he shall find for himself
neither protector nor helper
other than God.

4:124 Whoever *be*
among the ones who act in accord with morality
—whether male or female—
and is one who believes,
then those shall enter the Garden,
and wrong shall not be done to them,
even a speck on a date stone.

4:125 Who is fairer in the way of life
than he who has submitted his face to God,
and one is a doer of good,
and follows the creed of Abraham,
—a monotheist?°
God took Abraham to Himself as a friend.

4:126 To God *is* whatever *is* in the heavens
and whatever *is* in and on the earth;°
and God is One Who Encloses everything.

Sec. 19 *

4:127 They ask **you** for advice about women;°
say: God pronounces to you about them (f)
and what is
recounted to you in the Book
about female orphans
to whom (f) you give not
what was prescribed for them (f)
and yet you prefer
that you marry them (f); and about
children taken advantage of because of their weakness
that you stand up for orphans with equity;°
and whatever you accomplish of good,
God is Knowing of it.

4:128 If a wife fears resistance from her mate,

no blame on either of them
that they make things right between the two,
that there be reconciliation;°
and reconciliation is better.°
Souls are prone to stinginess,°
but if you do good and are Godfearing,
then truly God is Aware of what you do.
You shall never be able to be just between wives,   4:129
even if you are eager;
but incline not with total inclination *away from* her,
forsaking her as if she be one who is in suspense;°
but if you make things right,
and are Godfearing,
then indeed He is Forgiving, Compassionate.
If the two split up,   4:130
God shall enrich them from all His plenty;°
and God is One Who Embraces, *and is* Wise.
To God *belongs* whatever *is* in the heavens,   4:131
and whatever *is* in and on the earth;°
and indeed We have charged
those who were given the Book before you
to be Godfearing of God.°
If you are ungrateful,
truly to God *is* whatever *is*
in the heavens
and whatever *is* in and on the earth;°
and God is Sufficient, Worthy of Praise.
To God *belongs* whatever *is* in the heavens   4:132
and whatever *is* in and on the earth;°
and God suffices as a Trustee.
If He will, He shall cause you to be put away   4:133
—O humanity—
and arrive with others.°
Over that God is Powerful.
Whoever wants a reward for good deeds   4:134
in the present
then with God *is* The Reward for good deeds
in the present

and in the world to come;°
and God is Hearing, Seeing.

*

4:135   O those who have believed!
Be one who is staunch in equity,
witnesses for God
even against yourselves
or ones who are *your* parents or nearest of kin;°
whether rich or poor,
for God *is* Closer to both *than you are;*°
so follow not your desires
that you become unbalanced;°
and if you distort or turn aside,
then truly God is Aware of what you do.

4:136   O those who have believed!
Believe in God and His Messenger,
and the Book which He has sent down
to His Messenger,
and the Book which He has sent forth before;°
and whoever is ungrateful to God and His angels,
His Books and His Messengers,
and the Last Day,
has then indeed gone astray,
a wandering far astray.

4:137   Truly those who have believed,
and then are ungrateful,
and then believe, and again are ungrateful
and add to ingratitude,
neither shall God forgive them
nor guide them on the way.

4:138 Give good tidings to the ones who are hypocrites
•   that truly for them is a painful punishment,
4:139   those who take to themselves
the ones who are ungrateful as their protectors
instead of the ones who believe!°
Are they looking for renown with them?
Truly all renown *belongs* to God.

4:140   Indeed He has sent down to you
in the Book

that when you hear
the Signs of God being unappreciated
and ridiculed, then sit not with them
until they discuss in conversation
about other than that
or else, you *shall be* like them;°
truly God *is* One Who Shall Gather
the ones who are hypocrites
and the ones who are ungrateful altogether in hell.
Those who lie in wait for you,°

if there is a victory from God for you,
they would say: Were we not with you?
If the ones who are ungrateful *have* a share,
they would say: Have we not gained mastery
over you and secured you
from the ones who believe?°
God shall give judgment among you
on the Day of Resurrection;°
God shall never assign the ones who are ungrateful
any way over the ones who believe.

*

Truly the ones who are hypocrites

seek to deceive God,
but it is He, He is The One Who Deceives them;
and when they stand up for formal prayer
they stand up lazily to show off to humanity,
and they remember not God but a little
as ones who are wavering

between *this and* that,
neither with these, nor with those;°
and whom God causes to go astray,
you shall never find any way for him.
O those who have believed!

Take not to yourself the ones who are ungrateful
as protectors instead of the ones who believe.°
Want you to assign to God
clear authority against yourselves?
Truly the ones who are hypocrites

shall be in the lowest, deepest reaches of the fire;

•
4:146
and **you** shall not find for them any helper
except those who repent
and make things right
and cleave firmly to God
and make their way of life sincerely for God;
then those are with the ones who believe;°
and God shall give the ones who believe
a sublime compensation.

4:147 What would God accomplish by your punishment
if you have given thanks to Him
and have believed in Him?°
God has been One Responsive, Knowing.

Part 6

***

4:148
God loves not
the open publishing of evil sayings
except *by him* who has been wronged;
God has been Hearing, Knowing.

4:149
If you show good,
or conceal it or pardon evil,
then truly God has been Pardoning, Powerful.

4:150
Truly those who *are* ungrateful to God
and His Messengers,
and they want to separate and divide
between God and His Messengers,
they say: We believe in some
and we disbelieve in others;
they want to
take themselves to a way between that.

4:151 They, those in truth *are* the ones who are ungrateful.
We have made ready for the ones who are ungrateful
a despised punishment.

4:152
Those who have believed in God
and His Messengers,
they separate and divide not
between any one of them,
those, He shall give them their compensation;
and God has been Forgiving, Compassionate.

Sec. 22

*

4:153
The People of the Book ask **you**

to send down to them a Book from heaven;°
indeed they had asked Moses
for greater than that;
they had said: Cause us to see God publicly;
so a thunderbolt took them
for their injustice;°
then they took the calf to themselves
after what had drawn near to them
of clear portents;
even so We pardoned that;°
and We gave Moses a clear authority.
We exalted the mount above them   4:154
for their solemn promise;
and We said to them:
Enter the door as ones who prostrate themselves,
and We said to them:
Disregard not the Sabbath!
We took from them
an earnest solemn promise;
then because of their breaking   4:155
their solemn promise,
their ingratitude for the Signs of God,
their killing the Prophets without right,
their saying: Our hearts are encased,°
rather God has set a seal on them
for their ingratitude,
so they believe not except a few—
and for their ingratitude,   4:156
and their saying against Mary
serious, false charges to harm her reputation,
and for their saying: 4:157
We have killed the Messiah,
Jesus son of Mary,
the Messenger of God;
yet they killed him not, nor they crucified him;
but a likeness was shown to them;°
and truly those who were at variance about him
are in uncertainty about him;°
they have no knowledge about him,

but *are* pursuing an opinion;°
and certainly they killed him not.

4:158   Rather God exalted him to Himself;°
and God has been Almighty, Wise.

4:159   *Yet there is* none among the People of the Book
but shall surely believe in him before his death;°
and on the Day of Resurrection
he shall be a witness against them.

4:160   So for the injustice
of those who had become Jews,
We forbade them what was good
that had been permitted to them
and for their barring many from the way of God

4:161   and for their taking usury
although they had been prohibited from it
and for their consuming the wealth
of humanity with falsehood,°
We have made ready
a painful punishment
for the ones who are ungrateful among them.

4:162   But the ones who are firmly rooted in knowledge
among them and the ones who believe,
they believe in what has been sent forth to **you**
and what was sent forth before **you**;°
they *are* the ones who perform the formal prayer;°
they *are* the ones who give the purifying alms,
and the ones who believe in God and the Last Day;
those, We shall be ones who give them
a sublime compensation.

Sec. 23   *

4:163   Truly We have revealed to **you**
as We had revealed to Noah
and the Prophets after him.°
We revealed to Abraham, Ishmael,
Isaac, Jacob, the Tribes,
Jesus, Job,
Jonah, Aaron and Solomon;°
and We gave David the Psalms

4:164   and Messengers

We have already related to **you** before,
and Messengers We have not related to **you**.°
God spoke directly to Moses.°
Messengers *are* the ones who give good tidings,   4:165
and the ones who warn,
so that humanity
has no disputation against God
after the Messengers;°
God has been Almighty, Wise.
God bears witness   4:166
to what He has sent forth to **you**;
He has sent it forth with His knowledge;°
the angels *also* bear witness;°
and God has sufficed as witness.
Truly those who are ungrateful,   4:167
and bar others from the way of God,
they have indeed gone astray,
a wandering far astray.
Truly those who are ungrateful and do wrong,   4:168
God shall neither forgive them,
nor guide them to a road
except the road *to* hell,   4:169
ones who shall dwell in it forever, eternally.°
That is easy for God.
O humanity!   4:170
Indeed the Messenger has drawn near to you
with The Truth from your Lord;
so believe, *it is* better for you;°
but if you are ungrateful,
then truly to God *belongs* whatever *is* in the heavens
and the earth;°
and God has been Knowing, Wise.
O People of the Book!   4:171
Go not beyond the limits in your way of life,
and say not about God but The Truth:°
That the Messiah, Jesus son of Mary,
was a Messenger of God
and His word that He cast to Mary
and a Spirit from Him;°

so believe in God and His Messengers;°
and say not: Three;°
to refrain *from it is* better for you;°
there is not but One God!°
Glory be to Him that He should *have* a son! •
To Him *belongs* whatever *is* in the heavens
and whatever *is* in and on the earth;°
and God suffices as a Trustee.

*

4:172   The Messiah shall never disdain
that he be a servant of God,
nor the angels brought near *to Him;*°
and whoever disdains worshipping Him,
and grows arrogant,
He shall assemble them altogether to Himself.

4:173   Then as for those who have believed,
the ones who have acted in accord with morality,
then He would pay their account in full,
and increase His grace for them;°
but as for those who disdained
and grew arrogant,
He shall punish them
with a painful punishment;
other than God, they shall find
neither protector nor helper.

4:174   O humanity!
Indeed there has drawn near to you
proof from your Lord;
and We have sent forth to you a clear light.

4:175   So for those who have believed in God,
and cleave firmly to Him,
then He shall cause them to enter
mercy from Him and grace,
and guide them to Himself
on a straight path.

4:176   They ask **you** for advice;
say: God pronounces to you
about indirect heirs;°
if a man perishes *and* he has no child,

but he has a sister,
then for her is half of what he leaves;°
and he shall be one who is her inheritor
if she has no children;°
and if there are two *sister*s
then for them (f), two-thirds of what he leaves;°
and if there are brothers and sisters,
then the male shall *have*
the same allotment as two females;°
God makes manifest to you so that you go not astray;°
God is Knowing of everything.

CHAPTER 5
THE TABLE SPREAD WITH FOOD (*al-Māʾidah*)

In the Name of God,   Stage 2
The Merciful, The Compassionate   Sec. 1
O those who have believed!   5:1
Live up to your agreements:°
Permitted to you *are* flocks of animals
except what is *now* recounted to you:
You are not permitted hunting
while you *are* in pilgrim sanctity;°
truly God gives judgment how He wants.
O those who have believed!   5:2
Profane not the Waymarks of God,
nor the Sacred Month nor the sacrificial gift,
nor the garlanded,
nor the ones who are bound for
the Masjid al-Haram
who are looking for
grace from their Lord and contentment;°
and when you have left your pilgrim sanctity,
then you shall hunt;°
let not your detestation of a folk
who barred you from the Sacred House
move you to commit aggression.•
Cooperate with one another in virtuous conduct,

and Godfearingness;°
cooperate not with one another
in sin and deep seated dislike;°
be Godfearing of God;°
truly God *is* Severe in repayment.

5:3 Forbidden to you are carrion
and blood and flesh of swine
and what has been hallowed to other than God;
and the strangled beast
and one that has been beaten to death
and one that has fallen to its death
and one gored to death
and one eaten by a beast of prey
—but what you slay lawfully—
and those slaughtered to fetishes,
and those you partition by divining arrows;°
that is disobedience.°
Today those who are ungrateful have given up hope
because of your way of life;
so dread not them but dread Me;°
today I have perfected your way of life for you,
and I have fulfilled My divine blessing on you,
and I am well-pleased with
submission for your way of life;°
but whoever is driven by necessity due to famine,
• not one who is inclined to sin,
then truly God *is* Forgiving, Compassionate.

5:4 They ask **you** what is to be permitted to them;°
• say: Permitted to you *is* what is good,
and what you have *taught* to hunting creatures,
as one who teaches hunting dogs,
you teach them of what God has taught you;°
so you shall eat of what they seize for you,
but remember the Name of God over it;°
and be Godfearing of God;
truly God *is* Swift in reckoning.

5:5 Today what is good is permitted to you;°
the food of those who have been given the Book
is allowed to you;

and your food is allowed to them;°
likewise the ones who are free, chaste
from among the believing females
and the ones who are free, chaste females
among those who have been given the Book
before you,
when you have given the bridal due
to the ones (f) in wedlock,
not as one who is licentious,
or as one who takes lovers to oneself;°
and whoever is ungrateful after belief,
indeed his actions shall be fruitless;
and in the world to come,
he shall be of the ones who are losers.

*

O those who have believed!
When you stand up for the formal prayer,
then wash your faces
and your hands up to the elbows;
and wipe your heads and your feet
up to the ankles;°
but if you are defiled, then purify yourself.°
If you are sick or on a journey,
or one of you has drawn near
from the privy,
or you have come into sexual contact
with your wives,
and you find no water,
then aim at getting wholesome, dry earth
and wipe your faces and hands with it;°
God wants not
to make any impediment for you,
and He wants you to be purified,
and to fulfill His divine blessing on you
so that perhaps you would give thanks.
Remember the divine blessing of God on you,
and His solemn promise
that he made as a covenant with you by it
when you said:

We heard and we obeyed;°
and be Godfearing of God;°
truly God is Knowing what *is* in the breasts.

5:8
O those who have believed!
Be the ones who are staunch
as witnesses to equity for God;°
and let not detestation for a folk move you
from dealing justly;°
be just, that is nearer to Godfearingness;°
and be Godfearing of God;°
truly God *is* Aware of what you do.

5:9
•
God has promised those who have believed,
the ones who have acted in accord with morality,
that for them *is* forgiveness,
and a sublime compensation.

5:10
Those who are ungrateful,
and deny Our Signs,
those *shall be* the Companions of Hellfire!

5:11
O those who have believed!
Remember the divine blessing of God on you
when a folk were
about to extend their hands against you,
but He limited their hands from you;°
and be Godfearing of God;°
and in God let the ones who believe put their trust.

Sec. 3
*

5:12
Truly God took a solemn promise
from the Children of Israel;°
and We raised up among them twelve chieftains;°
God said: I am with you;°
certainly if you perform the formal prayer,
and give the purifying alms,
and believe in My Messengers,
and you support them,
and you lend God a fair loan,
I would certainly absolve you of your evil deeds,
and I would certainly cause you to enter
into Gardens
beneath which rivers run;°

but whoever among you is ungrateful after this,
indeed he has gone astray
from the way of the right path.
Then for their breaking 5:13
their solemn promise,
We cursed them,
and We made their hearts ones that are hard;°
they tampered with the words
out of their contexts; •
they have forgotten an allotment
of what they had been reminded;°
you shall not cease to peruse their treachery
except a few of them;°
yet overlook and pardon them.°
Truly God loves one who is a doer of good.
From those who said: We are Christians, 5:14
We took their solemn promise,
but they have forgotten an allotment
of what they had been reminded,
so We incited enmity and hatred among them
until the Day of Resurrection;°
and God shall tell them
of what they had been crafting.
O People of the Book! 5:15
Indeed Our Messenger has drawn near to you,
making manifest to you
much of what you were to conceal of the Book,
and pardons much;°
indeed from God has drawn near to you
a light and a clear Book.
God guides with it whoever 5:16
follows His contentment
to ways of peace;
He brings them out
from the shadows into the light
with His permission,
and He guides them to a straight path.
Indeed they are ungrateful who *have* said: 5:17
Truly God *is* the Messiah, the son of Mary;°

say: Who then has sway over God at all?
Had He wanted, He would have caused to perish
the Messiah son of Mary and his mother.
Whatever is in and on the earth altogether;°
all *belongs* to God: Dominion of the heavens
and the earth and what is between the two;°
He creates what He will;°
and God *is* Powerful over everything.

5:18 The Jews and Christians said:
We *are* the sons of God and His beloved;°
say: Why then punishes He your impieties?°
Rather you are but mortals of His creating;°
He forgives whom He will,
and He punishes whom He will;°
and to God *belongs* the dominion
of the heavens and the earth,
and what *is* between the two;°
and to Him *is* the Homecoming!

5:19 O People of the Book!
Indeed Our Messenger has drawn near to you;
He makes manifest to you,
after an interval without Messengers,
so that you say not: There has drawn near to us
• neither a bearer of good tidings, nor a warner;
indeed *there* has drawn near to you
a bearer of good tidings and a warner;°
and God *is* Powerful over everything.

Sec. 4 *

5:20 When Moses said to his folk:
O my folk!
Remember the divine blessing of God on you
when He assigned Prophets among you,
and assigned kings and gave you
what He had not given to anyone of the worlds.

5:21 O my folk!
Enter the earth that is sanctified
which God has prescribed for you,
and go not back, turning backward
for then you shall turn about

as the ones who are losers.
They said: O Moses!   5:22
Truly in it *is* a haughty folk,
and we shall never enter it
until they go forth from it;
but if they go forth from it,
then we shall certainly be ones who enter.
Two men of those who feared,   5:23
to whom God had been gracious, said:
Enter on them through the door!
When you enter it,
you shall certainly be ones who are victors;°
and put your trust in God
if you are ones who believe.
They said: O Moses!   5:24
We shall never ever enter it
as long as they *are* in it;°
so **you** and **your** Lord, you two go and fight;
we are here, ones who sit at home.
He said: O my Lord!   5:25
I control no one but myself and my brother;°
so separate between us
and between the disobedient folk.
He said: Truly it shall be forbidden to them   5:26
^for forty years^;
they shall wander about the earth;°
so grieve not for the disobedient folk.

*

    Sec. 5

Recount **you** to them   5:27
The Truth of the tiding of the two sons of Adam
when they both brought near a sacrifice,
and it was received from one of them,
but was not received from the other;
he said: I shall indeed kill **you**;°
he said: Truly God receives
only from the ones who are Godfearing,
even if **you** were one who extends out **your** hand   5:28
against me so that **you** would kill me,
I shall not be one who stretches out my hand

against **you** so that I kill **you**;°
I fear God, the Lord of the worlds.

5:29 Truly I want **you** to draw the burden
of my sin and **your** sin
to become
among the Companions of the Fire;°
that *is* the recompense of the ones who are unjust.

5:30 Then his soul prompted him
to kill his brother,
and he killed him,
and by that became among the ones who are losers.

5:31 Then God raised up a raven
to scratch the earth causing him to see how
he might cover up the naked corpse of his brother;°
he said: Woe to me!
Am I unable to be like this raven
and cover up the naked corpse of my brother?°

• Then he was among the ones who are remorseful.

5:32 On account of that,
We prescribed for the Children of Israel
that whoever kills a person,
except *in retribution* for another person,
or because of corruption in and on the earth,
it shall be as if he had killed all of humanity;°
and whoever gives life to one it shall be
as if he had given life to all of humanity;°
and indeed our Messengers drew near to them
with clear portents,
yet truly many of them after that
were ones who were excessive in and on the earth.

5:33 The only recompense for those who war
against God and His Messenger
and hasten about corruption in and on the earth
is that they be killed
or they be crucified
or their hands and their feet be cut off
alternately
or they be expelled from the region;°
that for them *is* their degradation

in the present;°
and in the world to come,
there is a tremendous punishment for them,   •
except for those who repent   5:34
before you overpower them;°
so know that God *is* Forgiving, Compassionate.

*   Sec. 6

O those who have believed!   5:35
Be Godfearing of God,
and be looking for an approach to Him,
and struggle in His way
so that perhaps you would prosper.
Truly those who are ungrateful,   5:36
if they *had* all that *is* in and on the earth
and the like of it with as much again
so that they would offer it as ransom for themselves
from the punishment on the Day of Resurrection,
it shall not be accepted from them;°
and for them *is* a painful punishment;
they would want to go forth from the fire,   5:37
but they shall never be the ones who go forth from it;
and for them is an abiding punishment.
As for the one who is a male thief,   5:38
and the one who is a female thief,
then sever their hands as recompense
for what they have earned,
an exemplary punishment from God;°
and God is Almighty, Wise.
But whoever repents after his injustice   5:39
and makes things right,
then truly God shall turn to him in forgiveness;°
truly God *is* Forgiving, Compassionate.
Know **you** not that to God, to Him   5:40
belongs the dominion of the heavens and the earth?
He punishes whom He will,
and He forgives whom He will;°
and God *is* Powerful over everything.
O Messenger! Let them not grieve **you**   5:41
for those who compete with one another

128

in ingratitude,
among those who said: We have believed
with their mouths while their hearts believed not;
^and among those who have become Jews,°^
the ones who hearken to lies,
the ones who hearken to the other folks
who have never approached **you**;°
they tamper with the words out of context;
they say: If you are given this, then take it,
but if you are not given this, beware!°
For whomever God wants to test,
you shall never have sway against God at all;°
those are they whose
hearts God wants not to purify;°
for them in the present is degradation;°
and for them in the world to come
is a tremendous punishment.

5:42
The ones who hearken to lies,
the ones who devour the wrongful,°
if they draw near to **you**,
then give judgment among them
or turn aside from them;°
and if **you** turn aside from them,
they shall never injure **you** at all;°
and if **you** give judgment,
then give judgment among them with equity;°
truly God loves the ones who are equitable.

5:43
How shall they make **you** their judge
while the Torah *is* with them
wherein *is* the determination of God;
yet after that they turn away?°
Those *are* not the ones who believe.

Sec. 7
*

5:44
Truly We have sent forth the Torah
wherein *is* guidance and light;°
the Prophets who had submitted
gave judgment with it
for those who had become Jews
as had the rabbis and learned Jewish scholars,

because it had been committed to their keeping
—the Book of God—
and they were witnesses to it;°
so dread not humanity, but dread Me,
and exchange not My Signs for a little price;°
and whoever gives not judgment
by what God has sent forth,
they, those are the ones who are ungrateful.

We prescribed for them in it: **5:45**
A life for a life
and an eye for an eye
a nose for a nose and an ear for an ear
and a tooth for a tooth
and for injuries to the body, reciprocation;°
but whoever is charitable,
it shall be an expiation for him;°
and whoever gives judgment not
by what God sent forth,
then they, those *are* the ones who are unjust.

We sent in their footsteps   **5:46**
Jesus son of Mary establishing as true
what had been before him in the Torah;°
and We gave him the Gospel
in which is guidance and light,
and establishing as true
what *was* before him in the Torah,
and a guidance and an admonishment
for the ones who are Godfearing.

Let the People of the Gospel give judgment   **5:47**
by what God has sent forth in it;°
and whoever gives judgment not
by what God has sent forth,
then they, those are the ones who disobey.

We have sent forth the Book to **you**   **5:48**
with The Truth,
establishing as true what *was* before it
of the Book
and one who preserves it;°
so give judgment among them

by what God has sent forth;°
and follow not their desires
against The Truth that has drawn near to **you**;°
for each among you We have made
a divine law and an open road;°
and had God willed,
He would have made you one community
to try you with what He gave you;°
so be forward in good deeds;
to God *is* your return altogether,
then He shall tell you
about what you were at variance.

5:49 Give judgment between them
by what God has sent forth,
and follow not their desires,
and beware of them so that they tempt **you** not
from some of what God has sent forth to **you**;°
and if they turn away,
then know that God only wants
that He light on them for some of their impieties;°
and truly many within humanity
are ones who disobey.

5:50 Are they looking for a determination of ignorance?°
Who *is* more fair than God *in* determination
for a folk that are certain?

Sec. 8
*

5:51 O those who have believed!
Take not to yourselves
Jews and Christians
as protectors. •
Some of them are protectors of one another;°
whoever among you turns away to them,
then he *is* of them;°
truly God guides not the unjust folk.

5:52 **You** see those
in whose hearts *is* a sickness
competing with one another.
They say: We dread that a turn of fortune
should light on us;°

so perhaps God advances a victory
or a command from Him?
Then they shall become
—from what they kept secret within themselves—
ones who are remorseful.

Those who have believed shall say: 5:53
What? Are they those who swore an oath by God,
the most earnest of sworn oaths,   ·
that they *were* with you?°
Their actions are fruitless;
they have become ones who are losers.

O those who have believed!   5:54
Whoever of you goes back on his way of life,
God shall bring a folk that He loves,
and that love Him,
humble-spirited towards the ones who believe,
disdainful towards the ones who are ungrateful;
they struggle in the way of God,
and they fear not the reproach
of the ones who are reproachers;°
that *is* the grace of God;
He gives it to whom He will;°
and God *is* One Who Embraces, Knowing.

Your protector *is* not but God and His Messenger   5:55
and those who have believed,
and those who perform the formal prayer,
and give the purifying alms,
and they *are* the ones who bow down.

Whoever turns in friendship   5:56
to God and His Messenger
and those who have believed,
behold the Party of God;
they *are* the ones who are victors.

*   Sec. 9

O those who have believed!   5:57
Take not to yourselves those who take
your way of life
in mockery and as a pastime
from among those who have been given

132

the Book before you,
nor the ones who are ungrateful,
as protectors.°
Be Godfearing of God
if you are ones who believe.

5:58   When you cry out for formal prayer,
they take it to themselves
in mockery and as a pastime.°
That is because
they *are* a folk who are not reasonable.

5:59   Say: O People of the Book!
Are you taking your revenge on us
because we have believed in God
and what has been sent forth to us
and what was sent forth before
while most of you are the ones who disobey?

5:60   Say: Shall I tell **you**
of worse than that as a reward from God?°
He whom God has cursed
and with whom He is angry;
He made some of them into apes and swine,
and those who worshiped false deities,°
those *are* worse situated
and ones who have gone further astray
from the way.

5:61   When they drew near to you they said:
We have believed,
yet they enter with ingratitude;
and they indeed go forth with it;°
God *has* greater knowledge
of what they are keeping back.

5:62   **You** see many of them
competing with one another
in sin and deep seated dislike
and in consuming the wrongful;°
what they have been doing is miserable.

5:63   Why have the rabbis and learned Jewish scholars
not prohibited their sayings of sin
and their consuming the wrongful?°

Miserable is what they have been crafting.
The Jews have said:
The hand of God is one that is restricted!°
Restricted are their hands!
Cursed be they for what they said. •
Rather His hands are ones that are stretched out:
He spends how He will;°
and certainly many of them shall be increased
by what has been sent forth to **you**
from **your** Lord
in defiance and ingratitude;°
and We have cast among them
enmity and hatred
until the Day of Resurrection;°
whenever they kindle a fire of war,
God extinguishes it,°
and they hasten about
corrupting in and on the earth;°
God loves not the ones who make corruption.
If the People of the Book had believed 5:65
and had been Godfearing,
certainly We would have absolved them
from their evil deeds
and caused them to enter into Gardens of Bliss.
If they had adhered to 5:66
the Torah and the Gospel,
and what was sent forth to them from their Lord,
they would certainly have eaten
from above them and from beneath their feet;°
among them is a community
of the ones who are moderate,°
but *as for* many of them,
how evil *are* the things they do.
*
Sec. 10

O Messenger! 5:67
State what has been sent forth to **you**
from **your** Lord;°
for if **you** were not to accomplish it,
then **you** shall not have stated His message;°

and God shall save **you** from the harm of humanity;°
truly God guides not
the ungrateful folk.

5:68　Say: O People of the Book!
You are not based on anything
until you adhere to the Torah and the Gospel
and what was sent forth to **you**
from **your** Lord;°
certainly many of them shall be increased
by what was sent forth to you from your Lord
in defiance and ingratitude;°
so grieve not for the ungrateful folk.

5:69　Truly those who have believed,
those who became Jews, Sabaeans
and Christians—
whoever has believed in God and the Last Day,
one who has acted in accord with morality,
then *there is* neither fear in them
nor *shall* they feel remorse.

5:70　Indeed We took a solemn promise
from the Children of Israel,
and We sent to them Messengers;°
whenever a Messenger drew near to them
with what they yearned not for,
a group of people
would deny them,
and a group of people
would kill them.

5:71　They assumed there would be no test;
they were in darkness and unhearing,
then God turned to them in forgiveness,
but again, many of them
were in darkness and unhearing;°
God *is* Seeing of what they do.

5:72　Yet they are ungrateful, those who said:
Truly God *is* He, the Messiah, son of Mary;°
but the Messiah said: O Children of Israel!
You worship God, my Lord and your Lord;°
truly whoever makes partners with God,

135

then God has forbidden the Garden to him;
and his place of shelter *is* the fire;°
and for the ones who are unjust,
there are no helpers.
Yet ungrateful are those who said: 5:73
Truly God *is* the third of three. •
While *there is* no god but One God.°
If they refrain not
from what they say,
there shall afflict those who are ungrateful
among them, a painful punishment.
Shall they not then turn to God for forgiveness   5:74
and ask for His forgiveness?°
God *is* Forgiving, Compassionate.
The Messiah, son of Mary,   5:75
was nothing but a Messenger;
indeed Messengers had passed away before him;
and his mother was a just person (f);°
they both would eat food;°
look upon how We make manifest
the Signs to them;
then look on how misled they are!
Say: Worship you other than God   5:76
what has no control to either hurt nor profit you?°
God, He *is* The Hearing, The Knowing.
Say: O People of the Book!   5:77
Go not beyond The Truth of your way of life
and follow not the desires of a folk
who have indeed gone astray before;
and they caused many to go astray,
and they *themselves* have gone astray
from the Right Way.

*   Sec. 11

Cursed were those who were ungrateful   5:78
among the Children of Israel
by the tongue
of David and that of Jesus son of Mary;°
that *was* because they would rebel,
and they were committing aggression.

5:79	They forbade not one another
	from the immorality they accomplished;°
	miserable was what they were accomplishing!
5:80	**You** see many of them
	turning away to those who were ungrateful;°
	miserable is what they were putting forward
	for themselves
	so that God became displeased with them,
	and in their punishment they *are*
	ones who shall dwell in it forever.
5:81	If they had believed in God and the Prophet
	and what had been sent forth to him,
	they would not have taken them to themselves
	as protectors,
	but many of them are ones who disobey.

Part 7

***

5:82	Indeed **you** shall find
	the hardest of humanity in enmity
	to those who have believed are the Jews,
	and those who have associated partners *with God;*°
	and indeed **you** shall find the nearest of them
	in affection to those who have believed
	are those who said: We are Christians;°
	that is because
	among them are priests and monks
	and they grow not arrogant.
5:83	When they heard
	what has been sent forth to the Messenger,
	you see their eyes overflow with tears
	because they have recognized The Truth;°
	they say: Our Lord! We have believed,
	so write us down with the ones who bear witness.
5:84	Why should we not have believed in God
	and in what has drawn near to us of The Truth?
	We are desirous that Our Lord
	would cause us to enter among the folk—
	ones who are in accord with morality.
5:85	Then God repaid them for what they said—
	gardens beneath which rivers run;

they are ones who shall dwell in them forever;°
and that *is* the recompense
of the ones who are doers of good;
but those who are ungrateful
and denied Our Signs,
those *shall be* the Companions of Hellfire.

*

O those who have believed!
Forbid not what is good
that God has permitted to you,
and commit not aggression;°
truly God loves not the ones who are aggressors.
Eat of what God has provided you,
the lawful and what is good;°
and be Godfearing of God
in Whom you *are* ones who believe.
God shall not take you to task
for what *is* idle talk in your sworn oaths,
but He shall take you to task for the
sworn oaths you have made as an agreement;°
and its expiation *is* the feeding of ten needy
of the average of what you feed your *own* people
or clothing them or letting go of a bond person;°
but whoever finds not *the means*
then formal fasting for three days;°
that *is* the expiation for your sworn oaths
when you have sworn them;°
and keep your sworn oaths safe;°
thus God makes manifest His Signs to you
so that perhaps you would give thanks.
O those who have believed!
Indeed intoxicants, gambling, fetishes,
and divining arrows are of the disgraceful
actions of Satan; then avoid them
so that perhaps you would prosper.
Indeed Satan wants that
he precipitate enmity and hatred between you
through intoxicants and gambling,
and bar you from the remembrance of God,

and from formal prayer;°
shall you then *be* the ones who desist?

5:92 Obey God and obey the Messenger
and beware;°
but if you turn away,
then know what *is* on Our Messenger
is not but the clear delivery of Our message.

5:93 There is no blame for those who have believed,
the ones who have acted in accord with morality,
in regard to what they have tasted
as long as they have been Godfearing
and have believed and *are*
the ones who have acted in accord with morality;
and, again, they have been Godfearing
and have believed;
again, they have been Godfearing and do good;°
and God loves the ones who are doers of good.

Sec. 13 *

5:94 O those who have believed!
Certainly God shall try you
with something of the game
that your hands and your lances attain
so that God may know
who fears Him in the unseen;°
then whoever commits aggression after that,
for him *is* a painful punishment.

5:95 O those who have believed!
Kill not game when you *are in* pilgrim sanctity;°
and whoever of you kills it as one who is willful,
then the recompense *is*
the like of what he killed of flocks,
as the judgment given by two just owners
among you *shall be*
a sacrificial gift, one that reaches the Kabah,
or the expiation of food for the needy,
or the equivalent of that in formal fasting
so that he certainly experiences
the mischief of his conduct;°
God pardons what is past;°

but whoever reverts to it,
then God shall requite him;°
and God *is* Almighty, Possessor of Requital.
The game of the sea is permitted to you,   **5:96**
and the food of it as sustenance for you,
and for a company of travelers;°
but forbidden to you is the game of dry land
so long as you are in pilgrim sanctity;°
and be Godfearing of God
to Whom you shall be assembled.
God has made the Kabah the Sacred House,   **5:97**
maintaining *it* for humanity
and the Sacred Month and the sacrificial gift
and their garlands;°
that *is* so that you shall know that God knows
whatever *is* in the heavens,
and whatever *is* in and on the earth,
and that God *is* Knowing of everything.
Know that God *is* Severe in repayment   **5:98**
and that God *is* Forgiving, Compassionate.
What *is* with the Messenger   **5:99**
is not but the delivery of the message;°
and God knows whatever you show,
and whatever you keep back.
Say: Not on the same level *are*   **5:100**
the bad and what is good even though
the prevalence of the bad impresses **you**;°
so be Godfearing of God,
O you who have intuition,
so that perhaps you would prosper.
*   **Sec. 14**

O those who have believed!   **5:101**
Ask not about things
that if they were shown to you
would upset you;
yet if you were to ask about these
at the time the **Quran** is being sent down,
they shall be shown to you;
God has pardoned that;°

140

for God *is* Forgiving, Forbearing.

5:102 Indeed a folk asked about them before you,
and then they became
ones who were ungrateful for them.

5:103 God has not made the thing *called* Bahirah,
• nor Saibah, nor Wasilah, nor Hami,
but those who were ungrateful
devise lies against God;°
and most of them are not reasonable.

5:104 When it was said to them:
Approach now to what God has sent forth,
and to the Messenger, they said:
Enough *is* what we found our fathers *had*.°
What? Even though their fathers knew nothing,
nor were they truly guided?

5:105 O those who have believed!
Upon you *is the* charge of your 'self';°
one who goes astray injures you not
if you are truly guided;°
to God *is* the return of you all;
then He shall tell you what you were doing.

5:106 O those who have believed!
Have testimony between you
when death attends anyone of you;
at the time of bequeathing,
two possessors of justice from among yourselves
or two others from among others,
if you are traveling through the region,
and the affliction of death lights on you;°
you shall detain them both after the formal prayer;
they shall swear by God
and if you be in doubt about them, *they shall say*:
We shall not exchange it for a price,
• even if it were kin;
and we shall not keep back testimony of God;
truly we then would be among
the ones who are perverted.

5:107 Then if it is ascertained
that the other two merited an accusation of sin,

then two others shall stand up in their station
from among the most deserving two,
those who are nearest in kinship,
and they both swear an oath by God *saying*:
Our testimony has a better right
than the testimony of the other two,
and we have not committed aggression,
for then truly
we would be of the ones who are unjust.
That *is* likelier that they bring testimony   5:108
in proper form,
or they fear
that their sworn oaths shall be repelled
after the others' sworn oaths;°
so be Godfearing of God and hear;°
and God guides not the disobedient folk.

*

Sec. 15

On a Day when God   5:109
shall gather the Messengers
and shall say: What was your answer?°
They shall say: We *have* no knowledge;°
truly **You**, **You** alone *are*
Knower of the unseen.
When God said: O Jesus son of Mary!   5:110
Remember My divine blessing on **you**,
and on the one who was **your** mother,
when I confirmed you with the hallowed Spirit
so that **you** spoke to humanity
from the cradle and in manhood;°
and when I taught **you** the Book and wisdom,
and the Torah and the Gospel;°
and when **you** created from clay
the likeness of a bird with My permission;°
and **you** breathed into it,
and it became a bird with My permission;°
and **you** cured one blind from birth,
and the leper with My permission;°
and when **you** brought out the dead,
with My permission;°

142

and when I limited the Children of Israel from **you**
when **you** had drawn near to them
with clear portents,
and those who are ungrateful among them said:
This *is* nothing but clear sorcery.
When I inspired the disciples:
Believe in Me and My Messenger;
they said: We have believed
and bear witness that we are the ones who submit.
When the disciples said: O Jesus son of Mary!
Is **your** Lord able to send down to us
a table spread with food from heaven?°
He said: Be Godfearing of God
if you are the ones who believe.
They said: We want that we eat of it
so that our hearts be at rest,
and we know that **you** have been sincere to us
and that we are the ones who bear witness to that.
Jesus son of Mary said: O God! Our Lord!
Send forth for us a table spread with food
from heaven that it shall be a festival
for the first and the last of us
and a Sign from **You**;°
and provide us
and **You** *are* the Best of one who provides.
God said:
Truly I am One Who Sends Down to you;°
but whoever is ungrateful after that among you,
then I shall punish him with a punishment
that I have not punished anyone within the worlds.

*

When God said: O Jesus son of Mary!
Say **you** to humanity:
Take me and my mother to yourselves
other than God?°
He would say: Glory be to **You**!
It was not for me that I say
what I *have* no right;°
if I had said it then indeed

143

You would have known it;°
You know what *is* in my soul
and I know not what is in **Your** Soul;°
truly **You**, **You** *are* Knower of the unseen.
I said nothing to them   5:117
except what **You** have commanded me:
Worship God, my Lord and your Lord;°
and I was witness for them
so long as I stood persistently among them;°
but when **You** have gathered me to **Yourself**,
You Yourself watched over them;°
truly over everything **You** *are* Witness.
If **You** were to punish them,   5:118
truly they *are* **Your** servants;°
and if **You** were to forgive them
truly **You**, **You** *are* The Almighty, The Wise.
God would say: 5:119
This Day the ones who are sincere shall profit
from their sincerity;°
for them *are* Gardens beneath which rivers run,
ones who shall dwell in them forever, eternally;°
God is well-pleased with them
and they are well-pleased with Him;°
that *is* the winning the sublime triumph.
To God *belongs* the dominion of the heavens   5:120
and the earth and whatever is in and on them.°
He *is* Powerful over everything.

CHAPTER 6
THE FLOCKS (*al-An'ām*)

In the Name of God,
The Merciful, The Compassionate   Sec. 1
The Praise *belongs* to God   6:1
Who created the heavens and the earth,
and made the shadows and the light;°
yet those who are ungrateful to their Lord
equate *others to Him*.
It is He Who created you from clay,   6:2

then decided a term;°
a term determined by Him;°
and yet you contest.

6:3 He *is* God in the heavens
and in and on the earth;°
He knows your secret
and what you openly publish;
and He knows whatever you earn.

6:4 Not a Sign arrives for them
from the Signs of their Lord
but they are
ones who used to turn aside from it.

6:5 Indeed they had denied The Truth
when it drew near to them;°
but soon tidings shall arrive for them
of what they were ridiculing.

6:6 Have they not considered how many
a generation before them We caused to perish?
We had established them firmly
in and on the earth
such as We *have* not firmly established for you;
We sent abundant rain from heaven,
We made rivers run beneath them;
so We caused them to perish for their impieties,
and We caused other generations to grow after them.

6:7 Had We sent down to **you**
a Book on parchment
for then they would have stretched towards it
with their hands;
surely those who are ungrateful would have said:
This *is* nothing but clear sorcery.

6:8 They say:
Why has an angel not been sent forth to him?°
Yet had We sent forth an angel
the command would have been decided;
truly no respite would have been given to them.

6:9 Had We made him an angel,
truly We would have made him as a man,
and We would have certainly confused them

when they *were already* confused.
Indeed Messengers were ridiculed

before **you**,
but those who derided them were surrounded
by what they were ridiculing.

*

Say: Journey on the earth, then look on

how was the Ultimate End of the ones who denied.
Say: To whom *is*

whatever is in the heavens and the earth?°
Say: To God.°
He has prescribed for Himself mercy;°
He shall truly gather you
on the Day of Resurrection
in which *there is* no doubt;°
those who have lost themselves;
truly they shall not believe.
To Him *is*

whatever inhabits the nighttime and the daytime;°
and He *is* The Hearing, The Knowing.
Say: Shall I take to myself a protector

other than God,
The Originator of the heavens and the earth?
It is He who feeds and He who is never fed;°
say: Truly I have been commanded
to be the first who has submitted;°
and be **you** not
among the ones who are polytheists.
Say: Truly I fear if I rebel against my Lord,

the punishment of the tremendous Day!
He who is turned away from it,

then indeed He had mercy on him.°
That *is* the winning the clear triumph.
If God touches **you** with evil,

then no one shall remove it but He;°
and if He touches **you** with good,
then He *is* Powerful over everything.
He *is* The Omniscient over His servants;°

and He *is* the The Wise, The Aware.

Say: What thing *is* greatest in testimony?°
Say: God *is* Witness between me and you;°
and this **Quran** has been revealed to me
that I shall warn you with it,
and whoever it shall reach;°
truly are you bearing witness
that *there are* other gods besides God?°
Say: I bear not *such* witness;°
say: Truly He *is* not but One God,
and I truly *am* free
of whatever partner you ascribe *unto Him.*

6:20 Those to whom We have given the Book
recognize it as they recognize their sons. •
But they, those who have lost themselves,
they believe not.

Sec. 3
*

6:21 Who *is* he who does greater wrong
than he who devises a lie against God
or denies His Signs?°
Truly one who is unjust shall not prosper.

6:22 We shall assemble them altogether
on a Day;
then We shall say
to those who have associated partners *with God*:
Where *are* your associates whom you used to claim?

6:23 Then their dissent shall not be
but that they would say: By God! Our Lord!
We were not ones who were polytheists.

6:24 Look on how they have lied against themselves;°
and what they used to devise
has taken them astray.

6:25 Among them *are* those who listen to **you**;°
but We have made sheaths *over* their hearts
so that they not understand it,
and in their ears *is* a heaviness;°
and although they were to see every Sign,
they would not believe in it;°
when they drew near to **you**,
they dispute with **you**

and those who are ungrateful say:
This is nothing but fables of the ancient ones.
They prohibit others from it;   6:26
they withdraw aside from it;°
even though they cause not to perish
any except themselves, but they are not aware.
If **you** would see   6:27
when they are stationed by the fire,
they shall say: Would that we might be returned.
Then we would not deny the Signs of our Lord,
and we would be among the ones who believe.
Rather it has now been shown to them   6:28
what they used to conceal before;°
and even if they were returned,
they would revert to
what they were prohibited,
and they are indeed ones who lie.
They have said: This *is* nothing but our present life,   6:29
and we *are* not ones who are raised up.
If **you** would see   6:30
when they are stationed before their Lord,°
He would say: Is this not The Truth?°
They would say: Yea, by Our Lord;°
He would say: Then experience the punishment
for what you were ungrateful.
                        *   Sec. 4

Those who have denied,   6:31
they have indeed lost the meeting with God;°
when the Hour suddenly draws near to them,
they would say: What a regret for us
that we neglected in it!
They shall carry heavy loads on their backs;°
how evil is what they bear!
This present life *is*   6:32
nothing but a pastime and diversion;°
the Last Abode *is* better
for those who are Godfearing;°
shall you not be reasonable?
We know indeed that what they say grieves **you**;°   6:33

then truly they deny not **you**,
it is the Signs of God that ones who are unjust negate.

6:34 Messengers indeed before **you** were denied
yet they endured patiently
despite that they were denied;
they were afflicted with torment
until Our help approached them;°
and *there is* no one who shall change
the words of God;°
indeed has drawn near to **you**
some of the tidings of the ones who were sent.

6:35 If their turning aside is troublesome to **you**,
then if **you** *are* able,
look for a hole in the earth
or a ladder to heaven
so that **you** bring them some Sign;°
had God willed,
He would have gathered them to the guidance,°
so **you** be not among the ones who are ignorant.

6:36 Truly those who hear, respond.•
As for the dead, God shall raise them up;
then they shall be returned to Him.

6:37 They said:
Why has a Sign not been sent down to him
from his Lord?°
Say: Indeed God *is* One Who Has Power
over what Sign He sends down,
but most of them know not.

6:38 *There is* no moving creature
in or on the earth
no fowl that flies with its wings
but they are communities like yours;°
We have not neglected anything in the Book;°
then they shall be assembled to their Lord.

6:39 Those who deny Our Signs
are unwilling to hear and *unwilling* to speak,
in the shadows;°
whomever God will, he causes to go astray;
and whomever He will,

He lays on a straight path.
Say: Have you yourselves considered?   6:40
If the punishment of God approaches you
or the Hour,
would you call to any other than God
if you were ones who were sincere?
Rather to Him alone you shall call;   6:41
He shall remove
that for which you call to Him
if He had willed
and you shall forget
whatever partner you ascribe *unto Him*.
*
Sec. 5

Indeed We have sent to communities   6:42
that were before **you**,
then We got hold of them
with desolation and tribulation
so that perhaps they would lower themselves.
Why then when Our might drew near to them   6:43
they lowered not themselves?
But their hearts had become hard,
and Satan had made what they were doing
appear pleasing to them.
So when they forgot   6:44
about what they had been reminded,
We opened the doors of everything to them.
When they were glad
with what they had been given,
We suddenly took them;
then they, they *were* ones seized with despair.
So the last remnant of the folk   6:45
who did wrong was cut off.°
The Praise *belongs* to God,
Lord of the worlds.
Say: Have you yourselves considered?   6:46
If God took your ability to hear and your sight,
and set a seal on your hearts;
what god other than God
would restore these to you?°

Look on how We diversify the Signs,
yet they draw aside.

6:47   Say: Have you yourselves considered?
If the punishment of God approached you
suddenly or publicly,
shall anyone be caused to perish
except the unjust folk?

6:48   We send not the ones who are sent
except as ones who give good tidings
and the ones who warn;°
so whoever has believed and made things right,
then *there is* neither fear in them,
nor *shall* they feel remorse.

6:49   But those who deny Our Signs
shall be afflicted by the punishment
because they were disobedient.

6:50   Say: I say not to you
that I *have* the treasures of God,
nor that I know the unseen,
nor say I to you that I am an angel;°
I follow not but what is revealed to me;°
say: Are they on the same level:
Those *unwilling* to see and those *willing* to see?°
Shall you then not reflect?

Sec. 6   *

6:51   Warn with it those who fear
•   when they shall be assembled to their Lord;
other than He, they *have*
neither protector nor intercessor
so that perhaps they would be Godfearing.

6:52   Drive not away those who call to their Lord
in the morning after the formal prayer,
and the evening, wanting His countenance;°
their reckoning is not on **you** at all,
and **your** reckoning is not on them at all;
if **you** should drive them away,
then you would become
of the ones who are unjust.

6:53   Even so We tried some of them by others

that they should say:
Are those the ones to whom God has shown grace
from among us?°
Has not God greater knowledge
of the ones who are thankful?
When those who believe in Our Signs   6:54
draw near to **you**
say: Peace *be* to you;°
your Lord has prescribed mercy for Himself;°
so that anyone of you who did evil in ignorance
and then repented after that
and made things right,
truly He *is* Forgiving, Compassionate.
Thus We explain Our Signs distinctly   6:55
so that the way is indicated
for the ones who are sinners.
                        *   Sec. 7

Say: I am prohibited from worshipping   6:56
those whom you call to other than God;°
say: I shall not follow your desires,   •
for then I would have gone astray
and *would not be* of the ones who are truly guided.
Say: I am a clear portent from my Lord,   6:57
but you have denied it;°
I *have* not of that for which you are impatient;°
the determination *is* from God;°
He relates The Truth;°
and He is the Best of
the ones who distinguishes truth from falsehood.
Say: Truly if I had   6:58
that for which you are impatient,
the command would have been decided
between me and between you;°
and God *has* greater knowledge
of the ones who are unjust.
With Him *are* the keys of the unseen;   6:59
none knows them but He;°
and He knows whatever is on dry land
and in the sea.°

Not a leaf descends but He knows it,
nor a grain in the shadows of the earth,
nor fresh nor dry but *it is* in a clear Book.

6:60 It is He Who gathers you to Himself by nighttime,
and He knows what you are busy with by daytime;
then He raises you up in it
so that the determined term
is decided;°
then to Him *is* your return;
then He shall tell you of what you were doing.

*

Sec. 8

6:61 He is The One Who Is Omniscient
over His servants;°
and He sends over you recorders;
when death draws near to anyone of you,
Our messengers gather him to themselves,
and they neglect not.

6:62 Then they are returned to God,
One Who Protects, The True;°
the determination *belongs* to Him?
He *is* The Swiftest of ones who reckon.

6:63 Say: Who delivers you from the shadows
of dry land and sea?
You call to Him
humbly and inwardly:
If He rescues us from this,
we shall be of the ones who are thankful.

6:64 Say: It is God Who delivers you from them
and from every distress,
yet then you ascribe partners *to Him*?

6:65 Say: He *is* One Who Has Power to raise up
on you a punishment from above you,
or from beneath your feet,
or to confuse you as partisans,
and to cause some of you to experience
the violence of one another;°
look at how We diversify the Signs
so that perhaps they would understand!

6:66 **Your** folk have denied it

although it *is* The Truth;°
say: I am not a trustee over you.
For every tiding *there is* an appointed time°

and soon you shall know it.
When **you** see

those who are engaged in idle talk about Our Signs,
then turn aside from them
until they discuss in conversation other than that;°
or if Satan should cause **you** to forget,
then after being mindful, sit not
with the unjust folk.
There is nothing on those who are Godfearing

of their reckoning,
but to be mindful
so that perhaps they would be Godfearing.
Forsake those who take to themselves

their way of life
as a pastime and as a diversion,
and whom this present life has deluded;°
remind with this
so that a soul should not be given up to destruction
for what it has earned;
other than God, they *have*
neither protector, nor intercessor;
and even if it be an equitable equivalent,
it shall not be taken from him;°
those *are* they who are given up to destruction
for what they have earned;°
for them is a drink of scalding water
and a painful punishment
because they were ungrateful.

*

Say: Shall we call to other than God,

what can neither hurt nor profit us?
Are we to be repelled on our heels
after God has guided us
like one whom the satans lured,
bewildered in and on the earth
although he has companions that call him

to guidance *saying*:
Approach us!
Say: Truly the guidance of God *is* The Guidance;°
and we have been commanded to submit
to the Lord of the worlds,

6:72 and perform the formal prayer
and be Godfearing of Him;°
and *it is* He to Whom you shall be assembled.

6:73 *It is* He Who created
the heavens and the earth with The Truth;°
and on a day He says: Be! And it is!°
His saying *is* The Truth;°
and His *is* the kingship on a Day
when the trumpet shall be blown;°
He is One Who Has Knowledge
of the unseen and the visible;
and He *is* The Wise, The Aware.

6:74 When Abraham said to his father Azar:
Take **you** idols to *yourself as* gods?°
Truly I see **you** and **your** folk
clearly wandering astray.

6:75 Thus We caused Abraham to see
the kingdom of the heavens and the earth
so that he would be of the ones who are certain.

6:76 So when night outspread over him,
he saw a star;°
and he said: This *is* my Lord;°
but when it set, he said: I love not what sets.

6:77 When he saw the rising moon,
he said: This *is* my Lord;°
but when it set, he said:
If my Lord guides me not,
surely, I shall be among
the folk gone astray.

6:78 When he saw the rising sun,
he said: This is my Lord; this is greater!°
But when it set, he said: O my folk!
I am truly free
from the partners you ascribe *unto Him.*

155

Truly I have turned my face as a monotheist, **6:79**
to Him Who Originated
the heavens and the earth;°
and I am not of the ones who are polytheists.
His folk argued with him.° **6:80**
He said: You argue with me about God
while He has guided me?
I fear not the partners you ascribe *unto Him*;
unless my Lord will a thing;°
my Lord encompasses everything
in His knowledge;°
shall you not then recollect?
How should I fear **6:81**
what you associate as partners *to Him*
while you fear not
associating partners to God?
He has not sent down to you any authority;°
then which of the two groups of people,
if you know,
has better right to a place of sanctuary?°
Those who have believed, **6:82**
and have not confused their belief with injustice;
those, to them *belongs* the place of sanctuary;
and they *are* the ones who are truly guided.
* **Sec. 10**

That was Our disputation **6:83**
that We gave Abraham against his folk;°
We exalt in degrees whom We will;°
truly your Lord *is* Wise, Knowing.
We bestowed on him Isaac and Jacob,° **6:84**
each of them We guided;°
and Noah We guided before;°
and among his offspring *are* David and Solomon,
Job, Joseph, Moses and Aaron;°
and thus We give recompense
to the ones who are doers of good.
Zechariah, John, Jesus and Elias,° **6:85**
each of them *were*
of the ones who are in accord with morality.

6:86   Ishmael, Elisha, Jonah and Lot,°
to each We gave an advantage over the worlds.

6:87   From among their fathers
and their offspring and their brothers,°
We elected them, and We guided them
to a straight path.

6:88   That *is* the guidance of God;
He guides with it whom He will of His servants;°
and if they had associated partners *with Him*,
what they were doing was fruitless for them.

6:89   They *are* those to whom We gave the Book,
critical judgment and prophethood;°
so if these were ungrateful for them,
then indeed We have charged a folk with them
who shall never *be*
of the ones who are ungrateful for them.

6:90   Those *are* they whom God has guided;°
so imitate their guidance;°
say: I ask of you no compensation for it;°
it is not but for the worlds to be mindful.

Sec. 11   *

6:91   They measured not God
with His true measure when they said:
God has not sent forth anything to a mortal;°
say: Who sent forth the Book
that was brought forth by Moses
as a light and guidance for humanity?°
You have made it into parchments;
you show them some of it
and conceal much of it;°
although you were taught
what neither you yourselves knew
nor your fathers;°
say: God!°
Forsake them
playing, engaging in their idle talk.

6:92   This is a Book
that We have sent forth,
one that is blessed,

157

establishing as true what *was* before it,
and for you to warn the Mother of Towns,
and those around it;°
and those who believe in the world to come,
believe in it;°
they, they are watchful of their formal prayers.
Who *is* he who *is* more unjust
than he who devised lies against God,
or said: It was revealed to me,
when nothing was revealed to him;
or who said: I shall send forth
the like of what God has sent forth?°
If **you** would see
when the ones who do greater wrong
are in the perplexity of death
and the angels *are*
the ones who stretch out their hands *saying*:°
Relinquish your souls!°
Today you shall be given recompense
with the humiliating punishment
for what you used to say other than the rightful
about God;
and you grew arrogant towards His Signs.
Indeed you have drawn near to Us
one by one as We had created you the first time;
and you have left what
We had granted you behind your backs;°
We see not your intercessors with you,
those whom you claimed as associates with you;°
indeed *the bonds* between you
have been cut asunder;
and what you were claiming
has gone astray from you.
*

Then truly *it is* God *who is*
One Who Causes to Break Forth
the grain and the pit of a date;°
He brings out the living from the dead and *is*
The One Who Brings Forth the dead from the living;°

that is God!°
Then how truly are you mislead?

6:96 *He is* The One Who Causes to Break Forth
the morning dawn,
and He has made the night as a place of rest,
and the sun and the moon to keep count;°
that *is* the decree of The Almighty, The Knowing.

6:97 *It is* He Who has made the stars
so that you shall be truly guided by them
in the shadows of dry land and the sea;°
indeed We have explained distinctly
the Signs for a folk who know.

6:98 *It is* He Who caused you to grow
from a single soul,
then a temporary stay and a repository;°
indeed We have explained distinctly
the Signs for a folk who understand.

6:99 *It is* He Who sends forth
water from heaven;°
and then We bring out from it
every kind of bringing forth;
and We bring out herbs from it,
and We bring out from it thick-clustered grain;°
and from the date palm tree,
from the spathe of it,
thick clusters of dates drawn near,
and gardens of grapevines and the olives,
and the pomegranates,
resembling and not resembling one another;°
look on its fruit when it bears fruit,
and it ripens;°
truly in this *are* Signs for a folk who believe.

6:100 They have made as associates with God
the jinn although He has created them;°
and they falsely attributed to Him
sons and daughters without knowledge;°
glory be to Him!
Exalted is He above what they allege.

Sec. 13   *

He is The Originator   6:101
of the heavens and the earth;°
how would He *have* a son
when He has had no companion?°
He has created everything;°
and He *is* Knowing of everything?
That is God, your Lord;°   6:102
there is no god but He;°
the One Who is the Creator of everything;
so worship Him;°
for He is a Trustee over everything.
No sight apprehends Him   6:103
but He apprehends sight;°
and He *is* The Subtle, The Aware.
Indeed clear evidence has drawn near to you   6:104
from your Lord;°
so whoever perceives, *it* is for his own self;°
whoever is in darkness, *it* is against his own self;°
and I am not a guardian over you.
Thus We diversify the Signs   6:105
so that they shall say:
You have received instruction,
and that We shall make it manifest
for a folk who know.
Follow what has been revealed to **you**   6:106
from **your** Lord;°
there *is* no god but He;°
and turn aside from the ones who are polytheists.
If God had willed,   6:107
they would not have associated partners *with Him*;°
We have not made **you** a guardian over them,°
nor *are **you*** their trustee.
Offend not those who call to   6:108
other than God
so that they not offend God out of spite
without knowledge;°
thus We have made to appear pleasing
the actions of every community;°
then to their Lord is their return,

and then He shall tell them
what they were doing.

6:109   They swear by God
the most earnest sworn oaths
that if a Sign would draw near to them,
truly they would believe in it;°
say: The Signs *are* not but with God;
and what shall cause you to realize
that even if they were to draw near,
they would not believe?

6:110   We shall turn around and around
their minds and their sight
as they believed not in it the first time,
and We shall forsake them
in their defiance,
wandering *unwilling* to see.

***

Part 8

Sec. 14   *

6:111   Even if We had sent down angels to them,
and the dead had spoken to them,
and we had assembled everything against them
face to face,
yet they would not believe unless God will,
but most of them are ignorant.

6:112   Thus
We have made an enemy for every Prophet,
satans from among human kind and the jinn,
some of them reveal to others
ornamented sayings as a delusion;°
and if **your** Lord willed
they would not accomplish it;°
so forsake them and what they devise.

6:113   That minds shall bend towards it
of those who believe not in the world to come,
and that they shall be well-pleased with it;
and that they shall gain
what the ones who gain *gain*.

6:114   What? Shall I be looking for an arbiter other than God
while it is He Who has sent forth to you the Book,

one that is distinct?°
Those to whom We have given the Book,
they know that it is what
was sent down by **your** Lord with The Truth;°
so be **you** not among the ones who contest.
The word of **your** Lord has been completed
in sincerity and justice;°
there is no one who changes His words;°
and He *is* the The Hearing, The Knowing.
If **you** obey most of those on the earth,
they shall cause **you** to go astray
from the way of God;°
they follow nothing but opinion,
and they not but guess.
Truly **your** Lord *is* He Who
has greater knowledge of those who go astray
from His way;°
and He has greater knowledge
of the ones who are truly guided.
So eat of that over which
the Name of God has been remembered;
if you were ones who believe in His Signs.
Why should you not eat of that over which
the Name of God has been remembered,
when, indeed He has explained distinctly to you
what He has forbidden to you
unless you are driven by necessity to it?°
Truly many cause others to go astray
by their desires without knowledge;°
truly **your** Lord, He has greater knowledge
of the ones who are aggressors.
Forsake manifest sin and its inward *part;*°
truly those who earn sin,
they shall be given recompense
for what they were to gain.
Eat not of that over which
the Name of God has not been remembered over it;
truly this *is* disobedience;°
and truly the satans

6:115

6:116

6:117

6:118

6:119

6:120

6:121

shall reveal to their protectors
so that they dispute with you;°
and truly if you obeyed them,
you would be of the ones who are polytheists.

*

6:122   Is he who was lifeless and We gave him life,
and We made a light for him
by which he walks among humanity
like one who is in the shadows,
one who goes not forth from it?°
Thus it is made to appear pleasing to
ones who are ungrateful for what they were doing.

6:123   Thus We have made in every town
great ones among the ones who sin,
who plan in it;°
but they plan not but against themselves
although they were not aware.

6:124   When a Sign drew near to them they said:
We shall not believe until we are given
the like of what was given to Messengers of God. •
God has greater knowledge
where to assign His message;°
soon contempt from God,
shall light on those who sin
and a severe punishment
for what they were planning.

6:125   Whoever God wants, He guides him;
He expands his breast for the submission;°
and whoever He wants to cause to go astray,
He makes his breast tight, narrow
as if he were climbing up a difficult ascent;°
thus God assigns disgrace
on those who believe not.

6:126   This *is* the straight path of **your** Lord;°
We have explained distinctly
the Signs for a folk who recollect.

6:127   For them *is* an abode of peace
with their Lord;°
and He is their protector

because of what they were doing.
On a Day He shall assemble them altogether;   6:128
O assembly of the jinn!
You have made much of human kind;°
and their protectors among human kind would say:
Our Lord! Some of us have enjoyed some others,
and we reached our term
that **You** have appointed for us;°
He would say: The fire is your place of lodging,
ones who shall dwell in it forever,
except as God willed;
truly **your** Lord *is* Wise, Knowing.
Thus *that is how*   6:129
We made some of them friends,
who were
unjust to one another
because of what they were earning.
*   Sec. 16

O assembly of jinn and human kind!   6:130
Have not Messengers approached
from among yourselves
relating to you My Signs,
and warning you of the meeting of this, your Day?°
They would say: We bear witness against ourselves;°
they were deluded by the present life,
and they shall bear witness against themselves
that they were ones who were ungrateful.
That *is because* **your** Lord would never   6:131
cause towns to perish unjustly
while their people were ones who were heedless.
For everyone *there are* degrees   6132
for what they did;°
and **your** Lord *is* not
One Heedless of what they do.
Your Lord *is* The Sufficient, Possessor of the Mercy;°   6:133
if He will, He shall cause you to be put away,
and He shall make one a successor after you
of whomever He will,
just as He caused you to grow

from the offspring of other folk.

6:134　Truly what you are promised
shall surely come;°
and you shall not be ones who frustrate it.

6:135　Say: O my folk!
Act according to your ability;
truly I *too am* one who acts;°
then soon you shall know
for whom the Ultimate End
shall be the Abode;°
truly the ones who are unjust shall not prosper.

6:136　Truly they assigned to God
of the cultivation and flocks made numerous,
a share,
and they said in their claim: This is for God
and this is for our associates;°
but what was for their associates
reaches not out to God;°
while what was for God
reaches out to their associates.°
How evil is the judgment they give!

6:137　Thus
appearing pleasing to many
of the ones who are polytheists
is the killing of their children
by those whom they associate *with Him*
so that they deal them destruction,
and so that they confuse their way of life for them;°
and had God willed,
they would not have accomplished it;°
.　so forsake them and what they devise.

6:138　They said:
These flocks and cultivation are banned;
none should taste them, but whom we will,
so they claim
and *there are* flocks whose backs have been forbidden
and cattle over which they remember not
the Name of God,
a devising against Him;°

He shall give them recompense
for what they were devising.
They said: 6:139
What *is* in the bellies of these flocks
is exclusively for our males,
and is forbidden to our spouses (f);°
but if it is born dead,
then they are associates in it;°
He shall give recompense to them
for their allegations;°
truly He *is* Wise, Knowing.
Those who with foolishness kill their children 6:140
without knowledge,
they have certainly lost;
they forbid what God has provided them
in a devising against God;°
they certainly have gone astray,
and are not ones who are truly guided.
                    *   Sec. 17
It is He Who caused gardens to grow, 6:141
with latticework
and without latticework,
and the date palm trees,
and a variety of harvest crops,
and the olives and the pomegranates
resembling and not resembling one another;°
eat of the fruits when it bears fruit,
and give its due *on* the day of its reaping,
and exceed not all bounds;°
truly God loves not the ones who are excessive. •
Of the flocks *are some* as beasts of burden, 6:142
and some for slaughter;°
eat then of what God has provided you,
and follow not in the steps of Satan;°
truly he *is* a clear enemy. •
Eight diverse pairs;° 6:143
two of sheep
and two of goats;°
say: Has He forbidden the two males

or the two females?
Or what the wombs of the two females contain?°
Tell me with knowledge
if you *are* ones who are sincere.

Of the camels, two and of cows two;°
say: Has he forbidden the two males
or the two females
or what the wombs of the two females contain?°
Were you witnesses
when God charged you with this?°
Then who *is* he who does greater wrong
than he who devises a lie against God
to cause humanity to go astray
without knowledge?°
Truly God guides not the unjust folk.

*

Say: I find not in what has been revealed to me
that anything be forbidden to taste
except that it be carrion or blood shed
or the flesh of swine
for that certainly is a disgrace
or disobedience having been hallowed
to other than God;°
but whoever is driven by necessity
without being one who desires,
or one who turns away,
then truly your Lord
is Forgiving, Compassionate.

To those who became Jews,
We forbade every possessor of claws;°
and of the cow and the herd of sheep
We forbade them the fat,
except what their backs carry or entrails,
or what is mingled with bone;°
thus have we given them recompense
for their insolence;°
and We are truly One Who is Sincere.

If they deny **you**, say:
Your Lord is the Possessor of Encompassing Mercy;°

and His might is not to be repelled
from the sinning folk.
Those who have associated *with God* shall say: **6:148**
Had God willed,
we would not have associated partners *with God,*
nor our fathers,
nor would we have forbidden anything;°
thus those before them denied
until they experienced Our might;°
say: *Is there* any knowledge with you
that you can bring out to us?°
You follow not but opinion,
and you are not but guessing.
Say: God has the conclusive disputation;°   **6:149**
had God willed,
He would have guided you, one and all.
Say: Bring your witnesses   **6:150**
to bear witness that God has forbidden this;°
then if they bear witness,
bear you not witness with them;°
and follow **you** not the desires
of those who deny Our Signs,
and those who believe not in the world to come,
and they equate others with their Lord.

*

Sec. 19

Say: Approach now; I shall recount   **6:151**
what your Lord has forbidden you;°
that you not make any partner *with Him* at all;°
but kindness to the ones who are *your* parents;°
and kill not your children from want;°
We shall provide for you and for them;°
and come not near any indecencies
whether these be manifest or inward;°
and kill not a soul which God has forbidden
unless justifiably;°
this then He has charged you with
so that perhaps you would be reasonable.
Come not near the property of the orphan   **6:152**
except with what is fair

until *the orphan* reaches maturity and comes of age;°
and live up to the full measure and Balance
with equity;°
We shall not place a burden on any soul,
except to its capacity;°
and when you have said *something*,
be just even if *be* with kin;°
and live up to the compact of God;°
He has charged you with this
so that perhaps you would recollect.

•

6:153
That this is My straight way,
so follow it;°
and follow not ways
that shall split you up from His path;°
He has charged you with this
so that perhaps you would be Godfearing.

6:154
Then We gave Moses the Book
rendered complete for him who does good,
a decisive explanation of all things,
and as a guidance and mercy,
so that perhaps they would
believe in the meeting with their Lord.

Sec. 20

*

6:155
This Book We have sent forth
is blessed, so follow it and be Godfearing
so that perhaps you would find mercy,
and so that you not say:

6:156
The Book was only sent forth
to two sections before us;
and indeed we were
ones who were heedless of their study.

6:157
Or so that you say:
If the Book had been sent forth to us,
we would have been better guided than they;°
then indeed there have drawn near to you
clear portents from your Lord
and a guidance and a mercy;°
and who then *is* he who has done greater wrong
than he who has denied the Signs of God

169

and has drawn aside from them?°
We shall give recompense to those who draw aside
from Our Signs with the worst punishment
because they were drawing aside.
What! Are they looking on for nothing 6:158
but that the angels approach them,
or **your** Lord approach them,
or some Signs of **your** Lord approach them?°
On a Day that some of the Signs of **your** Lord
approach,
it shall not profit a soul to have belief
if he had not believed before,
nor earned good because of his belief;°
say: You watch and wait!
We *too* are the ones who are watching and waiting!
Truly those who separate and divide 6:159
their way of life and become partisans,
be **you** not *concerned* with them at all;°
certainly their affair is with God;
then He shall tell them
what they were accomplishing.
Whoever draws near with benevolence, 6:160
then for him, ten times the like of it;°
and whoever draws near with an evil deed
shall not be given recompense but with its like;
and wrong shall not be done to them.
Say: Truly my Lord has guided me 6:161
to a straight path;°
a truth-loving way of life,
the creed of Abraham, the monotheist;°
and he was not of
the ones who were polytheists.
Say: Truly my formal prayer, 6:162
and my ritual sacrifice,
and my living and my dying
are for God, Lord of all the worlds. •
He has no associate;° 6:163
and of this have I been commanded;
and I am the first of the ones who submit.

Say: *Is it* other than God
that I should desire as lord
while He is Lord of everything?°
Each soul shall earn only for itself;°
no soul laden shall bear another's heavy load;°
then to your Lord shall you return,
and He shall tell you
about what you were at variance.

It is He who has made you as
viceregents on the earth
and has exalted some of you above another
in degree that He might try you
with what He has given you;°
truly **your** Lord *is* Swift in repayment
and certainly Forgiving, Compassionate.

CHAPTER 7
THE ELEVATED PLACES (*al-A^crāf*)

In the Name of God,
The Merciful, The Compassionate

Alif Lām Mīm Ṣād;°

it is a Book that has been sent forth to **you**;
and so let there be no impediment in **your** breast
about it so that **you** shall warn with it
and so the ones who believe are mindful.

Follow what has been sent forth to you
from your Lord
and follow not protectors other than He,°
little you recollect!

How many towns We have caused to perish!
Our might drew near to them at night
or to the ones who sleep at noon!

There was no calling out
when Our might drew near to them
except that they said:
Indeed we were ones who were unjust.

Then We shall certainly ask those
to whom *Our Message* was sent,

and We shall certainly ask
the ones who were sent.
We shall relate to them with knowledge,
for We were never of the ones who are absent.
The weighing *on that* Day *shall be* The Truth;°
so ones whose balance becomes heavy,
then they, those *are* the ones who prosper.
But ones whose balance is made light
are those who have lost their souls
because they used to do wrong with Our Signs.
Indeed We established you firmly
on the earth,
and We made for you in it a livelihood;°
but little you give thanks.

*

We had created you, then formed you,
then We said to the angels:
Prostrate before Adam!
They prostrated except Iblis;
he was not of the ones who prostrated.
God said: What prevented **you**
from prostrating
when I commanded **you**?°
He said: I am better than he;
You have created me of fire,
while **You** have created him of clay.
He said: So get **you** down from this!
It is not for **you** to increase in pride in this;
then go forth;
truly **you** are
of the ones who are contemptible.
He said: Give me respite
until the Day they are raised up.
God said: Truly **you** are
of the ones who are respited.
He said: Because **You** have led me into error,
certainly I shall sit in ambush for them
on **Your** straight path.
Then I shall approach them

7:7

7:8

7:9

7:10

Sec. 2

7:11

7:12

7:13

7:14

7:15

7:16

•

7:17

from before them and from behind them,
and from their right and from their left;°
and **You** shall not find many of them
ones who are thankful.

7:18   He said: Go forth from this,
as one who is scorned,
as one who is rejected;°
whoever heeds **you** among them;
I shall certainly fill hell with you one and all.

7:19   O Adam!
Inhabit **you** and **your** spouse the Garden
and both eat from where you both have willed,
but *neither* of you come near this tree
or you both shall be of the ones who are unjust.

7:20   Satan whispered evil to them both
to show them both what was to be kept secret
from them both—their intimate parts—
and he said:
The Lord of both of you prohibited you both
from this tree
so that neither of you should become angels
nor become ones who shall dwell forever.

7:21   He swore an oath to them both that:
I am one who gives advice to both of you.

7:22   Then he led both of them on to delusion;°
and when they had both experienced of the tree,
their intimate parts were shown to themselves,
and they took to stitch together over themselves
the tree leaves of the Garden;°
and the Lord of both of them proclaimed to them:
Prohibited I not both of you from that tree,
and I said to you both:
Truly Satan is a clear enemy of you both.

7:23   They both said:
Our Lord! We have done wrong to ourselves;
and if **You** shall not forgive us,
and have mercy on us,
we shall certainly be of the ones who are losers.

7:24   He said: Get you down,

each of you an enemy of the other;°
and for you on the earth an appointed time,
and enjoyment for awhile.
He said: You shall live in it,

and you shall die in it,
and from it you shall be brought out.

*

O Children of Adam!

Indeed We have sent forth to you garments
to cover up your intimate parts and feathers;°
surely the garment of Godfearingness,

•

that is the best;°
that *is* one of the Signs of God
so that perhaps you would recollect!
O Children of Adam!

Let not Satan tempt you
as he drove your parents out of the Garden,
tearing off both of their garments from them
to cause them to see their intimate parts;°
truly he and his type sees you
whereas you see them not;°
truly We have made he and the satans
protectors of those who believe not.
When they had committed an indecency,

they said: We found our fathers on it,
and God has commanded us in it;°
say: Truly God commands not depravity.°
What? Say you about God what you know not?
Say: My Lord has commanded me to equity;°

and set your faces in every place of prostration,
and call to Him
sincerely and devotedly
in your way of life for Him.°
As He began you, you shall revert to Him.
A group of people He guided,

and a group of people realized their misjudgment;°
truly they took satans to themselves
as protectors instead of God,
and yet they assume that they were

ones who were truly guided.

O Children of Adam!
Take your adornment
to every place of prostration and eat and drink,
but exceed not all bounds;°
truly He loves not the ones who are excessive.

Sec. 4

*

7:32 Say: Who has forbidden the adornment of God
which He brought out for His servants,
and what is the good of His providing?°
Say: They *are* for those who have believed
during this present life,
and exclusively on the Day of Resurrection;°
thus We explain distinctly Our Signs
for a folk who know.

7:33 Say: Indeed my Lord has forbidden indecencies,
both those that are manifest,
and those that are inward,
and sin and insolence without right,
and the partners you ascribed unto God
when He has not sent down to you
any authority
and that you say about God what you know not.

7:34 For every community *there is* a term;°
and when their term draws near,
they shall not delay it by an hour°
nor press it forward.

7:35 O Children of Adam!
If Messengers from among you approach

• to relate My Signs to you,
then whoever is Godfearing,
and makes things right,
then *there is* neither fear in them
nor *shall* they feel remorse.

7:36 But those who deny Our Signs,
and grow arrogant against them,
those *are* the Companions of the Fire;°
they *are* ones who shall dwell in it forever.

7:37 Then who *is* he who does greater wrong

than he who devises a lie against God,
or denies His Signs?
They, those shall attain
their share *as stated in* the Book;°
when Our Messengers draw near to gather them,
they shall say:
Where are those you used to call on
other than God?°
They would say: They have gone astray from us;
and they have borne witness against themselves
that, truly they were the ones who were ungrateful.
He would say: Enter among the communities   7:38
of jinn and human kind that passed away before you
into the fire;°
every time a community would enter,
it would curse its sister *community;*°
until when they shall all come successively in it,
the last of them would say to the first of them:
Our Lord! These caused us to go astray
so give them a double punishment of the fire;°
He would say: For everyone *it is* double,
but you know not.
The first of them would say   7:39
to the last of them:
You had no superiority over us
so experience the punishment
for what you were earning.
                              *   Sec. 5

Indeed those who denied Our Signs   7:40
and grew arrogant among them,
the doors of heaven shall not be opened to them
nor shall they enter the Garden
until a he-camel penetrates
through the eye of a needle;°
thus shall We give recompense to ones who are unjust.
For them, hell shall be their cradling   7:41
and above them coverings;°
thus shall We give recompense to ones who are unjust.
But for those who have believed,   7:42

176

the ones who have acted in accord with morality,
We place no burden on any soul
beyond its capacity;
those *shall be* the Companions of the Garden;°
they *are* ones who shall dwell in it forever.

7:43 We drew out grudges
that were in their breasts;
rivers shall run beneath them,°
and they shall say: The Praise *belongs* to God
Who has truly guided us to this!
We would never have been guided
if God had not guided us;°
indeed the Messengers of our Lord drew near us
with The Truth;°
and it shall be proclaimed to them:
That *is* the Garden to be given you as inheritance
for what you were doing.

7:44 The Companions of the Garden would cry out
to the Companions of the Fire:
Indeed we have found
what our Lord had promised us to be true;
have you found what
your Lord promised to be true?°
They would say: Yes;°
then it shall be announced
by one who announces among them:
May the curse of God
be on the ones who are unjust—

7:45 those who bar from the way of God,
who desire it to be crooked,
and in the world to come
they are ones who are ungrateful.

7:46 Between both of them is a partition;°
and on the elevated places *shall be* individuals
who recognize everyone by their marks;°
and they cry out
to the Companions of the Garden:
Peace be on you°
yet they enter it not,

even though they were desirous of it.
When their sight shall be turned away
of their own accord
towards the Companions of the Fire,
they shall say: Our Lord assign us not
with the unjust folk!
*   Sec. 6

The Companions of the Elevated Places would cry out   7:48
to individuals whom they would recognize
by their marks;
they would say: Your amassing has not availed you,
nor that you used to grow arrogant.
Are those, they *about* whom you swore an oath   7:49
that they would never attain mercy from God?°
Enter the Garden;
there is neither fear in you,
nor *shall* you feel remorse.
The Companions of the Fire would cry out   7:50
to the Companions of the Garden:
Pour some water on us
or some of what God has provided you;°
they would say:
Truly God has forbidden them both
to the ones who are ungrateful
who took their way of life to themselves   7:51
as a diversion and as a pastime,
this present life deluded them;°
so today We shall forget them
as they forgot the meeting of this their Day,
and because they used to negate Our Signs.
Indeed We have brought to them   7:52
the Book
in which We have explained distinctly
with knowledge,
a guidance and a mercy
for a folk who believe.
Are they looking for   7:53
nothing but its interpretation?°
The Day its interpretation approaches,

those who had forgotten it before shall say:
Indeed Messengers of our Lord had drawn near us
with The Truth;
have we any intercessors
who shall intercede for us?
Or shall we be returned
so that we do other than what we did before?°
Indeed they have lost themselves;
what they were devising has gone astray from them

*

7:54
Truly your Lord *is* God
Who created the heavens and the earth
in six days,
then turned His attention to the Throne;
He covers the nighttime with the daytime
which seeks it out urgently,
and the sun and the moon
and the stars
are ones that are caused to be subservient
to His command;°
surely, His *is* the creation and the command;°
Blessed be God, Lord of the worlds.

7:55
Call to your Lord humbly and inwardly;°
truly He loves not the ones who are aggressors.

7:56
Make not corruption in the earth
after things have been made right,
and call to Him with fear and hope;°
truly the mercy of God is Near
to the ones who are doers of good.

7:57
It is He Who sends the winds,
ones that are bearers of good tidings
of His mercy;°
when they are charged with a heavy cloud,
We shall drive it to a dead land,
and then send forth water,
and with it We bring out by it fruit of every kind;°
thus We shall bring out the dead
so that perhaps you would recollect.

7:58
As for the good land,

its plants go forth
with permission of its Lord;°
while, as for what is bad,
it goes forth not but scantily;°
thus We diversify the Signs
for a folk who give thanks.

*

Indeed We had sent Noah to his folk,
and he said: O my folk! Worship God!
You *have* no god but He;
truly I fear for you the punishment
of a tremendous Day.
The Council of his folk said:
Truly we see you clearly wandering astray.
He said: O my folk! There is no fallacy in me
but I am a Messenger
from the Lord of the worlds.
I state the messages of my Lord to you,
and advise you,
and I know from God what you know not.
What! Marvel you
that there has drawn near to you
a reminder from your Lord
through a man among you
that he warn you
and that you be Godfearing
so that perhaps you would find mercy?
But they denied him,
and We rescued him
and those who *were* with him on the ship,
and We drowned those who denied Our Signs;°
they, truly they were an unseeing folk.

*

To the Ad *God sent* their brother Hud;°
he said: O my folk! Worship God;
you *have* no god but He;°
shall you not be Godfearing?
The Council of those who were ungrateful said
among his folk:

Truly we see foolishness in **you**,
and truly we think that
you are of the ones who lie.

7:67 He said: O my folk!
There is no foolishness in me;
I am not but a Messenger
from the Lord of the worlds.

7:68 I state the messages of my Lord to you,
and I am one who gives advice to you,
trustworthy.

7:69 What? Marvel you
that there has drawn near to you
a reminder from your Lord
to a man from among you
that he shall warn you?°
Remember when He made you viceregents
after a folk of Noah
and increased you an increase in constitution?°
Then remember the benefits of God
so that perhaps you would prosper.

7:70 They said: Have **you** brought about to us
that we should worship God alone
and forsake what our fathers worshiped?°
So approach us with what **you** promised us
if **you** are of the ones who are sincere.

7:71 He said: Indeed disgrace and anger
have fallen on you from your Lord.°
What? Dispute you with me over names
which you have named, you and your fathers,
for which God has not sent down
any authority?°
Then watch and wait;
I shall be with you
among the ones who are watching and waiting.

7:72 Then We rescued him,
and those with him
by a mercy from Us,
and We severed the last remnant
of those who denied Our Signs;°

and they were not ones who believe.

*

To Thamud *God sent*   7:73
their brother Salih;°
he said: O my folk! Worship God!
There is not for you any god but He;°
indeed have drawn near to you
clear portents from your Lord;°
this *is* the she-camel of God as a Sign;°
so allow her to eat on the earth of God;°
and afflict her not with evil
so that a painful punishment not take you.
Remember when He made you viceregents   7:74
after Ad and placed you on the earth;
you took to yourselves palaces on the plains
and carved out the mounts as houses;°
so remember the benefits of God
and do no mischief as
ones who make corruption in and on the earth.
The Council among his folk   7:75
who had grown arrogant said to those who were
taken advantage of because of their weakness,
to those among them who had believed:
Know you that Salih *is* one who has been sent
by his Lord?°
They said: In what he has been sent,
we are ones who believe.
Those who had grown arrogant said: 7:76
Truly we are in what you have believed,
ones who disbelieve.
Then they crippled the she-camel   7:77
and defied the command of their Lord and said:
O Salih! Approach us
with what **you** have promised
if **you** are one of those who are sent.
So the quaking of the earth took them;   7:78
and it came to be in the morning
they were in their abodes
ones who were fallen prostrate.

7:79 Then he turned away from them and said:
O my folk!
Indeed I have expressed to you the message
of my Lord and advised you,
but you love not the ones who gives advice.

7:80 And Lot, when he said to his folk:
What? You approach indecency
such as not anyone who preceded you
ever in the world has?

7:81 Truly you, you approach
men with lust instead of women?°
Rather you are an excessive folk.

7:82 The answer of his folk was not but that
they said: Bring them out from your town;°
truly they are a clan to be purified.

7:83 Then We rescued him and his people
• except his wife,
she was of the ones who stayed behind.

7:84 We rained down a rain on them;°
so look on how was the Ultimate End
of the ones who sin.

Sec. 11 *

7:85 To Midian *God sent* their brother Shuayb;°
he said: O my folk! Worship God!
You *have* no god but He;°
indeed a clear portent has drawn near to you
from your Lord;°
so live up to the full measure and the Balance,
and diminish not the things of humanity,
nor make corruption in and on the earth
after things have been made right;°
that shall be better for you
if you are the ones who believe.

7:86 Sit not by every path
intimating and barring
those who believe in Him from the way of God;°
you desire it *to be* crooked;°
remember when you were few,
and how He augmented you;°

and look on what was the Ultimate End
of the ones who made corruption.
If there is a section of you who believe
in what I have been sent with,
and a section believe not;
have patience until God gives judgment between us;°
He *is* the Best of one who judges.
***   Part 9

The Council of those who had grown arrogant   7:88
from among his folk said: O Shuayb
We shall certainly drive **you** out from our town,
and those who have believed with **you**,
unless you revert to our creed;°
he said: What? Even if we are ones who dislike it?
Indeed we would have devised a lie against God   7:89
if we were to revert to your creed
after God has delivered us from it.°
It is not for us that we revert to it
unless God, our Lord, will.°
Our Lord encompasses everything
in knowledge;°
in God we put our trust;°
our Lord!
Give victory between us and between our folk;
in Truth **You** *are*
the Best of one who delivers.
But the Council of those who were ungrateful   7:90
among his folk said:
If you follow Shuayb,
then truly you shall be ones who are losers.
Then the quaking of the earth took them,   7:91
and they came to be in the morning,
ones fallen prostrate in their abodes.
Those who denied Shuayb   7:92
were as if they had not dwelt in them;°
those who denied Shuayb
they, they *were* ones who were losers.
So he turned away from them   7:93
and said: O my folk!

Indeed I have expressed to you
the messages of my Lord,
and I have advised you;°
then how should I grieve for an ungrateful folk?

*

7:94   We have not sent any Prophet to a town
but We took its people
with tribulation and desolation,
so that perhaps they would lower themselves.

7:95   Then We substituted in place of evil deeds,
benevolence,
until they exceeded in number and they said:
Indeed our fathers have been touched
by tribulation and happiness;
then We suddenly took them
while they were not aware.

7:96   Had the people of the towns believed
and been Godfearing,
We would have opened blessings for them
from the heaven and the earth,
but they denied,
so We took them for what they were earning.

7:97   Are then the people of the towns to be safe
from Our might's approaching them by night
while they *are* ones who sleep?

7:98   Or *are* the people of the towns to be safe
from Our might's approaching them
in the forenoon while they are playing?

7:99   *Are* they safe from the planning of God?°
No one *deems himself* safe from the planning of God
except the losing folk!

*

7:100   Is it not a guidance
for those who inherit the earth
after its *previous* people
that if We will, We would light on them
for their impieties;°
and set a seal on their hearts
so they hear not?

These *are* the towns;   7:101
their tidings We relate to **you**;°
their Messengers had drawn near to them
with clear portents,
but they would not believe
in what they had denied before;°
thus God set a seal on the hearts
of the ones who were ungrateful.
We found not in many of them any compact;°   7:102
indeed We found many of them *were*
ones who disobey.
Then We raised up Moses after them   7:103
with Our Signs to Pharaoh and his Council,
but they did wrong with them;°
so look on how was
the Ultimate End of the ones who make corruption.
Moses said: 7:104
O Pharaoh! Truly I am a Messenger
from the Lord of the worlds.
I am approved on condition that   7:105
I say nothing but The Truth about God;°
indeed I have drawn near to you
with a clear portent from your Lord,
so send the Children of Israel with me.
He said: If **you** have drawn near with a Sign,   7:106
then approach with it
if **you** *are* among the ones who are sincere.
Then he cast his scepter,   7:107
and lo! It clearly *became* a serpent.
He drew out his hand;   7:108
lo! It *was* white to the ones who looked.
                              *   Sec. 14

The Council of a folk of Pharaoh said: 7:109
Truly this is a knowing sorcerer,
he wants to drive you out from your region;°   7:110
so what *is* your command?
They said: Put him and his brother off,   7:111
and send to the cities *where*
the ones who assemble *are*.

7:112	Let them approach **you** with
	every knowing sorcerer.
7:113	The ones who were sorcerers drew near
	to Pharaoh;
	they said: Truly would we have compensation
	if we were the ones who are victors?
7:114	He said: Yes! Truly you *shall be*
	of the ones brought nearest to me.
7:115	They said: O Moses! Either cast
	or shall we be the ones who cast?
7:116	He said: You cast!°
	So when they cast,
	they cast a spell on the eyes of the personages
	and terrified them,
	and a tremendous sorcery drew near.
7:117	We revealed to Moses:
	Cast **your** scepter!°
	Then behold! It swallowed their lying deceit.
7:118	Thus The Truth came to pass
	and proved false what they were doing.
7:119	So they were vanquished there
	and turned about as the ones who were resigned.
7:120	The ones who were sorcerers fell down
	as ones who prostrate themselves.
7:121	They said: We have believed
	in the Lord of the worlds,
7:122	the Lord of Moses and Aaron.
7:123	Pharaoh said:
	You have believed in Him before
	I gave permission to you!°
	Truly this is a plan you have planned
	in the city that you drive out the people from it;°
	but soon you shall know.
7:124	Truly I shall cut off your hands and your feet
	alternately;
	then I shall crucify you one and all.
7:125	They said: Truly we *are*
	ones who are turning to our Lord.
7:126	**You** take revenge on us

because we have believed in the Signs of our Lord
when they drew near to us;°
our Lord! Pour out patience on us
and call us to **Yourself** as ones who submit.

*

The Council of a folk of Pharaoh said:
Shall **you** forsake Moses and his folk
to make corruption in and on the earth
while they forsake **you** and **your** gods?°
He said: We shall slay their sons
and we shall save alive their women;
and truly we *are*
ones who are ascendant over them.
Moses said to his folk:
Pray for help from God and have patience;°
the earth *belongs* to God;
He gives it as inheritance to whom He will
of His servants;°
and *that is* the Ultimate End
for the ones who are Godfearing.
They said:
We were afflicted with torment
before **you** had come to us
and after **you** drew near to us;°
he said: Perhaps your Lord
shall cause your enemy to perish
and make you successors to him on the earth
so that He shall look on how you do.

*

Indeed We took the people of Pharaoh
with years of diminution of fruit
so that perhaps they would recollect.
When benevolence drew near to them,
they would say: This *belongs* to us;°
but if an evil deed lit on them,
they augured ill of Moses
and those who were with him;°
Certainly their omens
are with God,

but most of them know not.

7:132 They said:
Whatever Sign **you** have advanced to us
to cast a spell on us with it,
we shall not be ones who believe in **you**.

7:133 Then We sent on them the deluge
and the locusts, the lice, the frogs,
and blood as distinct Signs,
but they grew arrogant,
and they were a sinning folk.

7:134 When the wrath fell on them, they would say:
O Moses! Call to **your** Lord for us
because of the compact made with **you**;°
if **you** were to remove the wrath from us,
we shall certainly believe in **you**,
and we shall send
the Children of Israel with **you**.

7:135 But when We removed the wrath from them,
and it reached its term,
then they broke their oath.

7:136 So We requited them
and drowned them in the water of the sea
because they denied Our Signs
and they were ones who were heedless of them.

7:137 We gave as inheritance
to the folk who were
taken advantage of because of their weakness,
the east of the region and its west
We had blessed;°
and the fair words of **your** Lord were completed
for the Children of Israel
because they patiently endured;°
and We destroyed
what Pharaoh and his folk were crafting
and what they were constructing.

7:138 We brought the Children of Israel
over the sea.
Then they approached on a folk
who had given themselves up to their idols;°

they said: O Moses! Make for us a god
like the gods they *have*;°
he said: Truly you are an ignorant folk!
Truly these are the ones who are ruined

for what they *are engaged* in,
and what they were doing *is* falsehood.
He said:

Should I look for any other god than God
for you while He has given you an advantage
over the worlds?
When We rescued you

from the people of Pharaoh
who caused an affliction to befall you
of a terrible punishment;°
they were slaying your sons
and saving alive your women.°
In that was a tremendous trial from your Lord.

*

We appointed thirty nights for Moses;

and We completed them with ten;
and thus the time appointed by his Lord
was fulfilled with forty nights;°
and Moses said to his brother, Aaron:
Be my successor among my folk,
and make things right and follow not the way
of the ones who make corruption.
When Moses drew near Our time appointed,

and his Lord spoke to him,
he said: O my Lord! Cause me to see
that I may look on **You**;°
He said: **You** shall never see Me
but look on the mountain;
then if it stays fast in its place,
you shall see Me;°
when his Lord Self-disclosed to the mountain,
He made it as ground powder,
and Moses fell down swooning;°
and when he recovered he said:
Glory be to **You**! I repent to **You**

and I am the first one who believes.

He said: O Moses!
Truly I have favored **you** above humanity
by My messages and with My assertion,
so take what I have given **you**
and be among the ones who are thankful.

7:145
We wrote down for him on the Tablets
everything and an admonishment
and a decisive explanation of all things;°
so take these firmly and command **your** folk
to take what is fair;°
I shall cause **you** to see the abodes
of the ones who disobey.

7:146
I shall turn away My Signs
from those who unduly increase in pride
on the earth;
and even though they see every Sign,
they believe not in it;
and if they see the way of right judgment,
yet they shall not take that way to themselves,
but if they see the way of error,
they shall take themselves to that way.°
That is because they have denied Our Signs
and *are* ones who were heedless.

7:147
But as for those who deny Our Signs
and the meeting in the world to come,
their actions are fruitless;°
shall they be given recompense
except for what they were doing?

Sec. 18
*

7:148
After *he had gone,* a folk of Moses
took to themselves
from out of their glitter
a saffron-colored calf, a lifeless body
like one that has the lowing sound of flocks;°
see they not that it neither speaks to them
nor guides them *to the* Way?•
Yet they took it to themselves
and they were the ones who were unjust.

When they became remorseful,   7:149
and saw that they indeed had gone astray,   •
they said: If our Lord not have mercy on us,
and forgive us,
we shall certainly be
among the ones who are losers.
When Moses returned to his folk   7:150
angry and grieved he said:
Miserable is what you succeeded in *doing* after me.°
Would you hasten the command of your Lord?°
He cast *down* the Tablets.
He took his brother by his head,
pulling him to himself;°
he said: O son of my mother,
truly a folk took advantage of my weakness
and were about to kill me,
so let not my enemies gloat over me
and assign me not to the unjust folk.
He said: O my Lord! Forgive me and my brother   7:151
and cause us to enter into **Your** mercy,
for **You** *are* One Who is The Most Merciful
of the ones who are merciful.

                        *   Sec. 19

Those who took the calf to themselves   7:152
attained anger from their Lord
and abasement in this present life;°
and thus We give recompense
to the ones who devise.
But those who do evil deeds,   7:153
but repent and after that, believe,   •
truly **your** Lord, after that,
shall be Forgiving, Compassionate.
When the anger subsided in Moses,   7:154
he took the Tablets;°
and in their inscription was guidance and mercy
for those, they who have reverence
for their Lord.
Moses chose of his folk seventy men   7:155
for Our time appointed;°

and when the quaking of the earth took them,
he said: O my Lord! If **You** will,
You would have caused them to perish
and me before;°
would **You** cause us to perish
for what the foolish among us have accomplished?°
It is not but **Your** test;
with it **You** shall cause to go astray
whom **You** will,
and **You** shall guide whom **You** will;°
You are our protector, so forgive us
and have mercy on us;°
for **You** *are* the Best of the ones who forgive.

7:156 Prescribe for us benevolence in the present
and in the world to come;
truly we express our regret to **You**.°
He said: I light My punishment on whom I will;°
and My mercy encompasses everything.°
I shall prescribe it
for those who are Godfearing
and give the purifying alms,
and those who believe in Our Signs.°

7:157 Those who follow the Messenger
—the unlettered Prophet—
whom they shall find with them
in the Torah and the Gospel,
he commands them to what is moral,
and prohibits them from what is immoral;
He permits to them what is good,
and forbids them from deeds of corruption;
He lays down for them severe tests,
and the yokes that were on them;°
so those who have believed in him
and have supported him and have helped him
and have followed the light
which has been sent forth with him,
they, those *are* the ones who prosper.

Sec. 20
7:158 *

Say: O humanity!

Truly I am the Messenger of God to you all
of Him to Whom *is* the dominion
of the the heavens and the earth;°
there is no god but He;
He gives life and He causes to die;°
so believe in God and His Messenger,
the unlettered Prophet, who believes in God,
and in His word and follow him
so that perhaps you would be truly guided.
Among a folk of Moses there is a community   7:159
who guides with The Truth and by it is just.
We sundered them   7:160
into twelve tribes as communities.°
We revealed to Moses
when his folk asked him for water:
Strike the rock with **your** scepter;°
and twelve springs burst forth out of it:°
Each clan knew its drinking place;
and We shaded them with cloud shadows,
We sent forth the manna and the quails for them:°
Eat of what is good
which We have provided you;°
and they did not wrong Us,
but they did wrong themselves.
Recall when it was said to them: 7:161
Inhabit this town
and eat from it wherever you shall and say:
Unburden us *of sin*! Enter the door
as the ones who prostrate themselves,
We shall forgive you your transgressions;°
We shall increase the ones who are doers of good.
But among those who did wrong   7:162
they substituted a saying
other than what was said to them;
then We sent wrath from heaven
because they used to do wrong.
                        *   Sec. 21
                                                     7:163
Ask them about the town,
one that borders the sea;

when they disregarded the Sabbath,
when their fish would approach them
on the day of the Sabbath,
ones that were visible on the shore,

• and that day they kept not the Sabbath,
they approached them not;
thus We tried them
because they were disobedient.

7:164 *Recall* when a community of them said:

• Why admonish a folk
whom God is about to cause to perish
or one who shall be punished
with a severe punishment?°
They said: To be free from guilt
before your Lord,
and so that perhaps they would be Godfearing.

7:165 So when they forgot
about what they had been reminded,
We rescued those who prohibited evil,
but We took those who did wrong
with a terrifying punishment
because they were disobedient.

7:166 When they defied
what they were prohibited
We said to them: Be you apes to be driven away!

7:167 *Recall* when **your** Lord caused to be proclaimed
that He would indeed raise up against them
until the Day of Resurrection
those who cause to befall them
an affliction of a terrible punishment;°
for truly **your** Lord is Swift
in repayment;°
and truly He *is* Forgiving, Compassionate.

7:168 We sundered them in the region
into communities;°
some of them *were*
the ones who were in accord with morality
and others *were* other than that;°
and We tried them with benevolence

and evil deeds
so that perhaps they would return.
But they were succeeded by successors   7:169
who inherited the Book;
they took advantage of the nearer *world*,
and they said: We shall be forgiven;
and if an advantage were to approach them like it,
they would take it;°
was not a solemn promise taken from them
with the Book
that they would say about God nothing but The Truth?
They have studied what *is* in it;°
and *know that* the Last Abode *is* better
for those who are Godfearing;°
shall you not, then be reasonable?
Those who keep fast to the Book   7:170
and perform formal prayer,°
We shall not waste the compensation
of the ones who make things right.
When We shook up the mountain over them,   7:171
as if it were an over shadowing,
and they thought it was about to fall on them:
Take firmly what We have given you
and remember what *is* in it
so that perhaps you would be Godfearing.
                    *   Sec. 22

When **your** Lord   7:172
took from the Children of Adam
their offspring from their generative organs
and called to them to witness to themselves:°
Am I not your Lord?°
They said: Yea!° ^We bear witness°^
so that you say not on the Day of Resurrection:
Truly we were ones who were heedless of this.
Or you should not say: 7:173
Our fathers before us
associated partners with God;
we were offspring after them;°
shall **You** cause us to perish for what

the ones who dealt in falsehood accomplished?

Thus We explain Our Signs distinctly
so that perhaps they would return.

Recount to them
the tiding of him to whom We gave Our Signs,
but he cast them off from them
so Satan pursued him,
and he became as one who was in error.

Had We willed,
We would have exalted him with these,
but he inclined towards the earth,
and followed his desires;°
and his parable is like the parable of a dog;°
if you attack it, it pants,
or if you leave it, it pants;°
that *is* parable of the folk
who deny Our Signs;°
so relate these narratives
so that perhaps they would reflect.

How evil *is* the parable of the folk who deny
Our Signs!
They used to do wrong to themselves.

Whomever God guides,
he *is* one who is truly guided;°
and whoever He causes to go astray,
then they, those *are* the ones who are losers.

Indeed We have made numerous for hell
many of the jinn and human kind;°
they *have* hearts by which they understand not,
they *have* eyes by which they perceive not,
they *have* ears by which they hear not;°
they are like flocks.
Rather they are the ones who have gone astray;°
they, those *are* the ones who are heedless.

To God *belongs* the Beautiful Names,
so call to Him by Them;°
and forsake those who blaspheme His Names;°
they shall be given recompense
for what they were doing.

Of those whom We have created
there is a community
who guides with The Truth,
and in it they are just.

*

Those who have denied Our Signs,
We shall draw them on gradually
from where they shall not know.
While I shall grant them indulgence,°
truly My strategizing is sure.
Have they not reflected?°
There is no madness in their companion;°
he is nothing but a clear warner.
Have they not expected in the kingship
of the heavens and the earth
and things which God has created •
that perhaps their term is near?°
Then in what discourse after this
shall they believe?
Whomever God causes to go astray
then *there is* no one who guides him;°
and He forsakes them
in their defiance
wandering, *unwilling* to see.
They ask **you** about the Hour,
when *shall* it berth?°
Say: The knowledge of that *is*
with my Lord alone;°
none shall display its time but He;
it *is* heavy in the heavens and the earth;°
it shall approach you not but suddenly;°
they shall ask **you** as if **you** were
one who is well-informed about it;°
say: Truly the knowledge of that *is*
with God,
but most of humanity knows not.
Say: I rule over neither hurt nor profit for myself,
but what God has willed;°
if the unseen were known to me,

I should have acquired much good,
and evil would not have afflicted me;°
I am but a warner and
a bearer of good tidings to a folk who believe.

*

7:189 *It is* He Who has created you from a single soul,
and out of it made its spouse
that he may rest in her;°
and when he had laid over her,
she carried a light burden,
and moved about with it;°
but when she *was* weighed down,
they both called to God, their Lord, *saying*:
If **You** give us
one who were to act in accord with morality,
we shall, indeed be
of the ones who are thankful.

7:190 But when He gave them both
one who acted in accord with morality,
they made partners to Him
in what He had given them both;°
but God is Exalted
above the partners they make *with Him*!

7:191 Shall they ascribe partners *unto Him*
who create nothing but *are* themselves created?

7:192 They are not able to help them
nor help themselves?

7:193 If you call them to guidance,
they shall not follow you;°
it is equal whether you call to them,
or you are one who remains quiet.

7:194 Truly those whom you call to other than God
are servants like you;
so call to them and let them respond to you
if you are ones who are sincere.

7:195 Have they feet with which they walk?°
Have they hands with which they take hold?°
Have they eyes with which they perceive?°
Have they ears with which they hear?°

Say: Call you to those who associate *with God*
then try to outwit me and give me no respite.
Truly God *is* my protector,   7:196
He Who sent down the Book,°
and He takes into His protection
the ones who are in accord with morality.
But those whom you call to other than Him,   7:197
they are not able to help you,
nor *are* they *able to* help themselves.
If you call them to guidance,   7:198
they hear not;°
you see them looking on **you**,
but they perceive not.
Take, pardoning,   7:199
and command what is honorable,
and turn aside from the ones who are ignorant.
If a provocation from Satan   7:200
should provoke **you**, then seek refuge in God.°
Surely He *is* Hearing, Knowing.
Truly when those who are Godfearing   7:201
are touched by a visitation from Satan,
they remember and behold,
they *are* ones who perceive.
Their brothers   7:202
cause them to increase in error;
then they never stop short.
When **you** have approached them with a Sign,   7:203
they say: Why have **you** not improvised one?°
Say: I follow not but what is revealed to me
from my Lord;°
this is clear evidence from your Lord
and guidance and mercy
for a folk who believe.
When the Quran is recited,   7:204
listen to it and pay heed
so that perhaps you would find mercy.
Remember **your** Lord in **yourself**   7:205
humbly and with awe,
instead of openly publishing the sayings

at the first part of the day and the eventide;
and be **you** not one who is heedless.

7:206 Truly those who are with **your** Lord
grow not arrogant from their worshiping,
but they glorify Him,
and they prostrate themselves to Him.°‡

*

CHAPTER 8
THE SPOILS OF WAR (*al-Anfāl*)

In the Name of God,

Sec. 1 The Merciful, The Compassionate

8:1 They ask **you** about the spoils of war;°
say: The spoils of war *belong* to God
and the Messenger;°
so be Godfearing of God and make things right
among you;°
and obey God and his Messenger
if you are the ones who believe.

8:2 The ones who believe *are* not but those
whose hearts quake when God is remembered;
when His Signs *are* recounted to them
their belief increases,
and they put their trust in the Lord.

8:3 *They are* those who perform the formal prayer and
spend out of what We have provided them.

8:4 They, those *are* the ones who truly believe;°
there are for them degrees
with their Lord
and forgiveness and generous resources.

8:5 As **your** Lord brought **you** out from **your** house
with The Truth,
truly a group of people among
the ones who believed *were* the ones who disliked it.

8:6 They disputed with **you** about The Truth
—after it had become clear—
as if they were being driven to death
and they are looking at *it*.

8:7 When God promised you

201

one of the two sections:
It shall truly be for you;
and you wish
that the one that *is* unarmed should be yours,
but God wants that He verify The Truth
by His words and to sever
the last remnant of the ones who are ungrateful
so that He verify The Truth   8:8
and prove falsehood untrue
even though the ones who sin dislike it.
When you cried for help from your Lord,   8:9
He responded to you:
Truly I *am* One Who Reinforces you
with a thousand angels,
ones who come one after another.
God made this as good tidings for you   8:10
so that your hearts shall be at rest.°
There is no help
but from God *alone*.°
Truly God *is* Almighty, Wise.
                    *   Sec. 2

When a sleepiness enwrapped you   8:11
as a safety from Him,
He sent down water from heaven for you,
and He purified you from it,
and caused to be put away from you
the defilement of Satan,
He invigorated your hearts,
and made your feet firm by it.
When **your** Lord revealed to the angels: 8:12
I *am*, indeed with you,
so make those who have believed firm;°
I shall cast alarm
into the hearts of those who are ungrateful;
so strike above their necks,
and strike each of their fingers from them.
That *is* because they made a breach between   8:13
God and His Messenger.
To whomever makes a breach between

God and His Messenger,
then truly God *is* Severe in repayment.

8:14 That *is it,* so experience it,
and for the ones who are ungrateful,
there is the punishment of the fire.

8:15 O those who have believed!
When you meet those who are ungrateful
marching to battle,
turn not your backs to them.

8:16 Whoever turns that day, turning his back,
except one who withdraws
from fighting *for a purpose,*
or one who moves aside to *another* faction,
he, indeed shall draw the burden of God's anger
and his place of shelter is hell;°
and how miserable *is that* Homecoming!

8:17 You killed them not,
but God killed them;°
You have not thrown when **you** have thrown
but God threw°
that He might confer on the ones who believe
a fair trial from Him;°
truly God *is* Hearing, Knowing.

8:18 Truly God *is* One Who Makes Frail
the cunning of the ones who are ungrateful.

8:19 If you had sought a judgment
then indeed has drawn near to you the victory;°
and if you refrain
that *would be* better for you;°
and if you revert, We shall revert;°
and your factions shall not avail you at all
• even though they be many,
and God *is* with the ones who believe.

Sec. 3 *

8:20 O those who have believed!
Obey God and His Messenger,
and turn not away from him
when you hear *his command.*°

8:21 Be not like those who said:

We have heard, when they hear not.
Truly the worst of moving creatures
with God

8:22

are those who *are unwilling* to hear and speak
because they are not reasonable.
If God had known any good in them

8:23

He would have caused them *to be willing* to hear;°
and even if He had caused them to hear,
they would have truly turned away
as the ones who turn aside.
O those who have believed!

8:24

Respond to God and to the Messenger
when He calls you to what gives you life;°
and know truly that God comes between
a man and his heart,
and that to Him you shall be assembled.
Be Godfearing of a test

8:25

which truly shall not light particularly
on those of you who did wrong.°
Know that God
is Severe in repayment.
Remember when you *were* few,

8:26

taken advantage of because of your weakness
on the earth;
you feared humanity would snatch you away,
so He gave you refuge,
and confirmed you with His help,
and provided you with what is good
so that perhaps you would give thanks.
O those who have believed!

8:27

Betray not God and the Messenger,
nor knowingly betray your trusts.
Know that your wealth and your children

8:28

are a test and that God,
with Him *is* a sublime compensation.

*

Sec. 4

O those who have believed!

8:29

If you are Godfearing of God,
He shall assign you

a Criterion between right and wrong,
and shall absolve you of your evil deeds,
and shall forgive you;°
and God *is* Possessor of Sublime Grace.

8:30 When those who planned against you,
those who are ungrateful,
to confine **you** or to kill **you**
or to drive **you** out,°
and they were planning
and God planned;°
but God *is* the Best of the ones who plan.

8:31 When Our Signs are recounted to them,
they said: We have heard *this*;
if we would, we would say the like of this;
truly this *is* not but fables of ancient ones.

8:32 When they said: O God!
If this be The Truth from **You**,
rain down rocks on us
from heaven,
or bring us a painful punishment.

8:33 But God would not punish them
while **you** are among them.°
Nor shall God be One Who Punishes them
while they ask for forgiveness.

8:34 What *is* with them
that God should not punish them
while they bar *worshippers*
from the Masjid al-Haram
and they were not its protectors?°
None are its protectors,
but those who are Godfearing,
but most of them know not.

8:35 Their formal prayer at the House was
nothing but whistling and clapping of hands.°
So experience the punishment
for your ingratitude.

8:36 Truly those who are ungrateful
spend their wealth
so that they bar the way of God;°

soon they shall have spent it
and then it shall become a regret for them,
then they shall be vanquished;°
and those who are ungrateful
shall be assembled in hell.
God shall differentiate

the bad from what is good,
and He shall lay the bad, one on another,
and heap them up altogether,
and lay them into hell;°
they, those are the ones who are losers.

*

Say to those who are ungrateful:

If they refrain,
what is past shall be forgiven;°
but if they repeat,
then the customs have passed
of the ancient ones *as a warning*.
Fight them

until there is no persecution,
and the way of life—all of it—be for God;°
but if they refrain,
then truly God *is* Seeing of what they do.
If they turn away,

then know that God *is* One Who Protects you;°
how excellent a One Who Protects,
and how excellent a Helper!

***

Part 10

Know that whatever you gain of booty,

then truly one-fifth of it *belongs* to God,
to the Messenger, to the kin,
the orphans, the needy,
and the traveler of the way;
if you have believed in God,
and in what We sent forth to Our servant
on the Day
of Criterion between right and wrong,
the day when the two multitudes met;°
and God *is* Powerful over everything.

When you *were* on
the nearer bank of the valley,
and they *were* on the farther bank of the valley,
and the cavalcade *was* below you,°
even if you had made a promise together,
you would have certainly been at variance

•   as to the solemn declaration,
because God has decreed a command
that would be accomplished,
so that those who *were* to perish
by a clear portent would perish,
and those who *were* to live
by a clear portent would live;°

•   and truly God *is* Hearing, Knowing.

8:43   *Recall w*hen God caused **you** to see them
as few in **your** slumbering;°
if He had caused **you** to see them *as* many,
you would have lost heart
and contended with one another
about the command,
but God handed it over;°
truly He *is* Knowing of what is in the breasts.

8:44   When He caused you to see them
as few in your eyes
when you met one another,
and He made you few in their eyes
so that God might decree
a command that would be accomplished;°
and commands shall be returned to God.

Sec. 6

*

8:45   O those who have believed!
When you meet a faction,
then stand firm and remember God frequently
so that perhaps you would prosper.°

8:46   Obey God and His Messenger,
and contend not with one another
so that you not lose heart and your competence go
and have patience.°
Truly God *is* with the ones who remain steadfast.°

Be not
like those who went forth
from their abodes
recklessly to show off to personages,
and those who bar those from the way of God;°
for God *is* One Who Encloses what they do.
When Satan made to appear pleasing
their actions to them
and said: No one *shall be*
the ones who are victors *against* you *this* day
from among all personages,
and truly I shall be your neighbor;°
but when the two factions sighted each other,
he receded on his two heels and said:
Truly I am free of you;
truly I see what you see not;
truly I fear God;°
and God *is* Severe in repayment.
*

When the ones who were hypocrites said,
and those in whose hearts there *was* a sickness:
Their way of life has deluded them;°
but whoever puts his trust in God,
truly God *is* Almighty, Wise.
Were **you** to see
when those who are ungrateful are called
by the angels to themselves,   •
striking their faces and their backs:
Experience the punishment of the burning.
That *is* because of what your hands have put forward,
and truly God is not unjust to His servants.
Their custom is similar to the custom
of the people of Pharaoh   •
and of those before them;°
they were ungrateful for the Signs of God,
so God took them for their impieties;°
truly God *is* Strong, Severe in repayment.
That *is* because God shall never alter
a divine blessing

when He has been gracious to a folk

•   unless they alter what is within themselves;

and truly God *is* Hearing, Knowing.

8:54   *Their custom is* similar to the custom

•   of the people of Pharaoh

and those before them;°

they denied the Signs of their Lord,

so We caused them to perish for their impieties,

and We drowned the people of Pharaoh;°

and they were all ones who were unjust.

8:55   Truly the worst of moving creatures

with God

are those who are ungrateful;

so they shall not believe.

8:56   They *are* those with whom you made a contract,

then they break their compact every time,

not being Godfearing.

8:57   So if **you** come upon them in war,

they, those who are behind them

are to be dispersed,

so that perhaps they would recollect.

8:58   If **you** fear treachery from a folk,

then dissolve the relationship

with them equally;°

truly God loves not ones who are traitors.

*

Sec. 8

8:59   Assume **you** not that those who are ungrateful

shall outdo Me;°

truly they *shall* never weaken *the Will of God*.

8:60   Prepare against them

all the strength **you** are able,

including a string of horses,

to put fear in the enemy of God

and your enemy and others besides them;

you know them not,

but God knows them;°

and whatever you shall spend

in the way of God,

the account shall be paid in full to you

and wrong shall not be done to you.
If they tend toward peace, 8:61
you should tend toward it,
and be one who puts his trust in God;°
truly He *is* The Hearing, The Knowing.
But if they want to deceive **you**, 8:62
then truly God is Enough for **you**.°
It is He Who has confirmed you with His help,
and with the ones who believe. •
He has brought their hearts together.° 8:63
If **you** had spent all that *is* in the earth,
you would not have brought together
their hearts,
but God brought them together;°
truly He *is* Almighty, Wise.
O Prophet! 8:64
God *is* Enough for **you**
and for whoever follows **you**
of the ones who believe.

* Sec. 9

O Prophet! 8:65
Encourage fighting to the ones who believe;°
if there are twenty who remain steadfast among you,
they shall vanquish two hundred;°
and if there are a hundred of you,
they shall vanquish a thousand
of those who are ungrateful
because they *are* a folk who understand not.
Now God has lightened *your burden* from you 8:66
for He knows that there *is* a weakness in you;°
so if there are a hundred of you,
ones who remain steadfast,
they shall vanquish two hundred;°
and if there be a thousand of you,
they shall vanquish two thousand
with the permission of God;°
and God is with the ones who remain steadfast.
It is not for a Prophet 8:67
that he should have prisoners of war,

unless he gives a sound thrashing
to the enemy in the region;°
you want the advantages of the present,
but God wants the world to come;°
and God *is* Almighty, Wise.

Were it not *for* a preceding prescription from God,
you would surely, have been afflicted
with a tremendous punishment for what you took.

Eat of what you have gained as booty
what *is* lawful and what is good,°
and be Godfearing of God;°
truly God *is* Forgiving, Compassionate.

*

Sec. 10

8:70 O Prophet!
Say to those who *are* in your hands
of the prisoners of war:
If God knows *any* good in your hearts,
He shall give you better
than what has been taken from you;
and He shall forgive you;°
and God is Forgiving, Compassionate.

8:71 But if they want treachery *against* **you**,
they have betrayed God before,
so He gave you power over them;°
and God *is* Knowing, Wise.

8:72 Truly those who had believed and had migrated,
and have struggled with their wealth and their lives
in the way of God,
and those who have given refuge and have helped,
those *are* protectors, some of one another;°
and those who have believed, but migrated not,
you have no duty of friendship to them at all
until they migrate;°
but if they ask you for help in their way of life,
it *would be* upon you to help them
except against a folk whom
between you and between them
there is a solemn promise;°
and God *is* Seeing of what you do.

Those who are ungrateful,   8:73
some *are* protectors of one another;°
if you accomplish not
there shall be persecution
on the earth and the hateful sin of corruption.
Those who have believed and have migrated,   8:74
and have struggled in the way of God,
and those who have given refuge and help,
those *are* they, the ones who truly believe;°
for them *is* forgiveness and generous resources.
Those who have believed afterwards,   8:75
and have migrated and have struggled beside you,
then these *are* of you;°
and blood relations,
some *are* more deserving than others
in what is prescribed *by* God;°
truly God *is* Knowing of everything.

Chapter 9
Repentance (*al-Tawbah*)

Sec. 1

Immunity from God and His Messenger   9:1
to those with whom you made a contract
among the ones who were polytheists:
Roam about on the earth for four months,   9:2
but know that you *shall* not *be*
ones who frustrate *the Will of* God,
and that God shall cover with shame
the ones who are ungrateful.
The announcement from God,   9:3
and His Messenger to humanity,
on the day of the greater pilgrimage to Mecca:
God and His Messenger *are* free *from any duty*
to the ones who are polytheists;   •
so repentance *shall be* better for you,°
but if you turn away, then know
that you *are* not ones who frustrate *the Will of* God;°
and give good tidings to those who are ungrateful
of a painful punishment,

but those with whom you made a contract
—among the ones who are polytheists—
and who then reduced you nothing,
nor *have* they backed anyone against you
so fulfill their compact with them
until their *term* expires;°
truly God loves the ones who are Godfearing.

9:5 When the months of pilgrim sanctity
have drawn away,
then kill the ones who are polytheists
wherever you find them,
and take them and besiege them,
and sit in each and every place of ambush;°
but if they repent,
and perform the formal prayer,
and give the purifying alms,
then let them go their way;°
God *is* Forgiving, Compassionate.

9:6 If anyone of the ones who are polytheists
seek asylum with **you**, then grant him protection
so that he may hear the assertions of God;
and then convey him to a place of safety;°
that is because they *are* a folk who know not.

*

Sec. 2

9:7 How shall *there be with*
the ones who are polytheists
a compact with God and with His Messenger
except those with whom you made a contract
near the Masjid al-Haram?°
So long as they go straight with you,
you go straight with them;°
truly God loves the ones who are Godfearing.

9:8 How? If they get the better of you,
they regard not ties of relationship with you,
nor a pact.°
They please you with their mouths,
but their hearts refuse;°
and many of them are ones who disobey.

9:9 They sold the Signs of God

for a little price and barred *others* from His way;°
how evil is what they were doing.

They regard towards you 9:10
neither ties of relationship nor a pact;°
it is they, those who are the ones who are aggressors.

But if they repent, 9:11
and perform the formal prayer,
and give the purifying alms,
then they *are* your brothers in *your* way of life;°
We explain the Signs distinctly
for a folk who know.

But if they break their sworn oaths 9:12
after their compact,
and discredit your way of life,
then fight the leaders of ingratitude, •
for truly their sworn oaths are nothing to them,
so that perhaps they would refrain.

Shall you not fight a folk 9:13
who have broken their sworn oaths,
and were about to expel the Messenger,
beginning the first time against you?°
Shall you dread them?°
God has a better right that you should dread Him
if you are ones who believe.

Fight them! 9:14
God shall punish them by your hands,
cover them with shame,
help you against them;
He shall heal the breasts of a believing folk,
and put away the rage in their hearts;° 9:15
and God turns to whom He shall in forgiveness;°
and God *is* Knowing, Wise.

Or assume you that you shall be left 9:16
before God has known
those among you who have struggled
and have not taken *anyone* to yourselves
other than God
and His Messenger and the ones who believe
as intimate friends?°

God *is* Aware of what you do.

*

9:17 It would not be for ones who are polytheists
to cultivate the places of prostration to God,
while they *are* the ones who bear witness
against themselves for their ingratitude;°
the actions of those are fruitless,
ones who shall dwell in the fire forever!

9:18 Only he cultivates places of prostration to God
who believes in God and the Last Day,
performs the formal prayer,
gives the purifying alms,
and dreads none but God;°
perhaps those are to be
among the ones who are truly guided.

9:19 Have you made the giving of water to drink
to the ones who are pilgrims,
and frequenting the Masjid al-Haram
the same as one who believes
in God and the Last Day,
and struggles in the way of God?°
They *are* not on the same level
in the view of God;°
and God guides not the unjust folk.

9:20 Those who have believed and have migrated
and have struggled in the way of God
• with their wealth and their lives
are sublime in their degree *in the view of* God;°
and those *are* the ones who are victorious.

9:21 Their Lord gives them good tidings of a mercy
from Him and His contentment
• and of Gardens for them wherein *is* abiding bliss.

9:22 They are ones who shall dwell in them forever,
eternally.°
Truly with God
is a sublime compensation.

9:23 O those who have believed!
Take not to yourselves
your fathers and brothers as protectors

if they embrace ingratitude instead of belief;°
and whoever of you turns away to them,
then they, those *are* the ones who are unjust.
Say: If your fathers and your sons,

your brothers and your spouses,
your kinspeople,
the wealth you have gained,
the transactions you dread may slacken
and the dwellings
with which you are well-pleased,
are more beloved to you than God,
and His Messenger and struggling in His Way,
then await until God brings His command;°
and God guides not the disobeying folk.

*

God has indeed helped you

in many battlefields,

•

and on the day of Hunayn

•

when you were impressed
with your great numbers,
but it availed you not anything;
and the earth was narrow for you
for all its breadth;
then you turned as ones who draw back.
Then God sent forth His tranquility

on His Messenger and on the ones who believed,
and sent forth armies you saw not,
and punished those who were ungrateful;°
and this *is* the recompense
of the ones who were ungrateful.
Then God shall turn

to whom He will in forgiveness after that;°
and God *is* Forgiving, Compassionate.
O those who have believed!

Truly the ones who are polytheists are unclean
so let them not come near
the Masjid al-Haram after this year;°
and if you fear being poverty-stricken,
God shall enrich you out of His grace had He willed;°

truly God *is* Knowing, Wise.

9:29 Fight those who believe not in God
nor the Last Day nor forbid what
God and His Messenger have forbidden,
nor practice the way of life of The Truth
among those who were given the Book
until they give the tribute out of hand,
and they are of the ones who comply.

*

9:30 The Jews said: Uzayr *is* the son of God
and the Christians say:
The Messiah *is* the son of God;°
that *is* the saying with their mouths;°
they conform to the sayings
of those who were ungrateful before;°
may God take the offensive;°
how they are mislead!

9:31 They have taken to themselves
their learned Jewish scholars
and their monks as lords other than God,
and the Messiah son of Mary;°
and they were not commanded but to worship
The One God;°
there is no god but He!°
Glory be to Him from the partners they make!

9:32 They want to extinguish the light of God
with their mouths,
but God refuses so that He may fulfill His light
even though the ones who are ungrateful dislike it.

9:33 *It is* He Who has sent His Messenger
with the guidance and the way of life of The Truth
so that He shall uplift it over all ways of life,
even though the ones who are polytheists dislike it.

9:34 O those who have believed!
Truly *there are* many
of the learned Jewish scholars and monks
who consume the wealth of humanity
in falsehood
and bar from the way of God;°

CHAPTER 9 REPENTANCE (*al-Tawbah*) STAGE 2 PART 10 SECTION 5   9:29-9:34

and those who treasure up gold and silver,
and spend it not in the way of God;
give good tidings of a painful punishment
on a Day when it shall be hot   9:35
in the fire of hell
and by it are branded their foreheads
and their sides and their backs;°
this is what you treasured up for yourselves
so experience what you used to treasure up.
Truly the period of months   9:36
with God
is twelve months in the Book of God,
on the day when He created the heavens
and the earth;
of them four *are* sanctified;°
that *is* the truth-loving way of life;°
so do not wrong yourselves in it;°
and fight the ones who are polytheists collectively,
even as they fight you collectively;°
but know that God *is* with
the ones who are Godfearing.
Truly the postponing   9:37
is an increase in ingratitude;°
by it are caused to go astray
those who are ungrateful,
for they permit it a year,
and forbid it a year,
so that they agree with the period
that God has forbidden,
and they permit what God has forbidden;°
the evil of their actions
is made to appear pleasing to them;°
but God guides not the ungrateful folk.
*   Sec. 6

O those who have believed!   9:38
What *is it* with you
when it is said to you:
Move forward in the way of God,
you incline heavily downwards to the earth?°

Are you so well-pleased with this present life
instead of the world to come?°
But the enjoyment of this present life
compared to the world to come *is* little.

9:39   Unless you move forward,
He shall punish you with a painful punishment,
and shall have in exchange for you
a folk other than you,
and you shall not injure Him at all;°
God *is* Powerful over everything.

9:40   If you help him not,
then indeed God has helped him
when those who were ungrateful drove him out.
When the second of two,
they *were* both in the cavern,
he said to his companion:
Feel no remorse truly God *is* with us;°
then God sent forth His tranquility on him,
and confirmed him with armies
that you saw not,
and made the word of those who were ungrateful
the lowest;°
and the word of God *is* Loftiest;°
God *is* Almighty, Wise.

9:41   Move forward light and heavy,
and struggle with your wealth and your lives
in the way of God;°
that is best for you if you but knew.

9:42   Had it been a near advantage
and an easy journey,
they would have truly followed **you**,
but the destination of the journey
was distant for them;°
and yet they shall swear by God:
If we had been able,
we would have certainly gone forth with you;
they shall cause themselves to perish
for God knows that they are the ones who lie.

Sec. 7   *

May God pardon **you**!   9:43
Why gave you permission to them
before it became clear to **you**
those who were sincere,
and **you** knew who were the ones who lie?
They ask not of **you** permission,   9:44
—those who believe in God and the Last Day—
to struggle with their wealth
and their lives.°
God *is* Knowing
of the ones who are Godfearing.
Only those ask of **you** permission   9:45
who believe not in God and the Last Day
and whose hearts are in doubt,
as they go this way and that in their doubts.
If they had wanted to go forth,   9:46
certainly they would have prepared for it
some preparation,
but God disliked that they be aroused,
so He caused them to pause and it was said:
Sit along with the ones who sit at home.
If they had gone forth with you,   9:47
they would have increased nothing for you,
but ruination;
they would have rushed to and fro
in your midst with insolent dissension;
there are some among you
of ones who would have harkened to them;°
and God *is* Knowing of the ones who are unjust.
Indeed they were looking for dissension before,   9:48
and turned around and around
the commands for **you** until The Truth drew near,
and the command of God became manifest.
Although they *were* the ones who disliked *it*,
there is among them he who says: 9:49
Give me permission and tempt me not;°
surely they have descended into dissension;°
and truly hell is what encloses
the ones who are ungrateful.

220

9:50
If benevolence lights on **you**,
they are raised to anger;°
but if an affliction lights on **you**,
they say: Indeed We took our commands before.
They turn away and they *are* glad.

9:51
Say: Nothing shall light on us,
but what God has prescribed for us;°
He is the One Who Protects us.°
In God let the ones who believe put their trust.

9:52
Say: Are you watching for something,
but one of the two fair things for us°
while we watch for you,
whether God shall light on you
a punishment from Him
•
or by our hands;°
so watch!
We *are* the ones who wait with you.

9:53
Say: Whether you spend willingly or unwillingly,
it shall not be accepted from you.°
Truly you, you were a disobeying folk.

9:54
Nothing prevents being accepted
their contributions from them,
but that they were ungrateful to God
and His Messenger,
and that they not approach formal prayer,
but lazily,
and they spend *as* the ones who dislike *to spend*.

9:55
So let not their wealth impress **you**
or their children.°
God wants only to punish them
with these things in this present life;
and so that their souls may depart
while they *are* the ones who are ungrateful.

9:56
They swear by God
that they are truly of you
while they *are* not of you,
but they *are* a folk who are in fear.

9:57
If they find a shelter or a place to creep into
or a place of retreat,

they would turn to it
as they rush away.
Among them there are some   9:58
who find fault with **you** about charities;
if they have been given a part of it,
they are well-pleased,
but if they have not been given of it,
lo! They are displeased.
Would that they were well-pleased   9:59
with what God gave them and His Messenger
and that they had said: God *is* Enough for us!
God shall give to us of His grace
and so shall His Messenger;
truly to God we *are* the ones who quest.
                          *
                                              Sec. 8
Charities are not but for the poor and the needy,   9:60
for the ones who work to collect it,
for those whose hearts are brought together,
and to *free* the bond person,
for the ones who are in debt,
and in the way of God,
and for the traveler of the way;°
this is a duty to God;°
and God *is* Knowing, Wise.
Among them are   9:61
those who afflict torment on the Prophet
and say:
He is unquestioning;°
say: He is unquestioning
of what is good for you;
he believes in God,
and believes in the ones who believe,
and he is a mercy
to those of you who have believed;°
and those of you who afflict torment
on the Messenger of God,
for them is a painful punishment.
They swear to you by God   9:62
to please you,

but God and His Messenger have better right
that they should please Him
if they are the ones who believe.

9:63   Know they not that whoever opposes God
and His Messenger,
truly *shall be* the fire of hell—
one who shall dwell in it forever?°
That is a tremendous degradation.

9:64   The ones who are hypocrites are fearful
that a chapter of the Quran
should be sent down against them
to tell you what is in their hearts;°
say: You ridicule us°
but God is truly One Who Drives Out
that of which you are fearful.

9:65   If **you** ask them, they shall say:
Truly we were not but engaging in idle talk
and playing;°
say: Was it God and His Signs
and His Messenger
that you were ridiculing?

9:66   Make no excuses!
You have disbelieved after your belief;°
if We pardon a section of you,
We shall punish another section
because truly they were ones who sin.

Sec. 9

*

9:67   The ones who are male hypocrites
and the ones who are female hypocrites,
some are of the other;°
they command what is immoral
and prohibit what is moral
and close their hands;°
they have forgotten God
so He has forgotten them;°
truly the ones who are hypocrites
they *are* the ones who disobey.

9:68   God has promised
the ones who are male hypocrites

and the ones who are female hypocrites
and the ones who are ungrateful, the fire of hell,
the ones who shall dwell in it forever!°
It *shall be* enough for them;°
God has cursed them;
and for them is an abiding punishment.
Like those before you,   9:69
who had more strength than you,
and more wealth and children;
and they enjoyed their apportionment,
so you enjoyed your apportionment
as those before you
enjoyed their apportionment,
and you engaged in idle talk
as they engaged in idle talk;°
as to those, their actions were fruitless
in the present
and *are such* in the world to come;°
and those *are* the ones who are losers.
Have not the tidings of those before them   9:70
approached them—
a folk of Noah, of the Ad, of Thamud,
of a folk of Abraham,
of the Companions of Midian,
and of the cities overthrown?
Their Messengers approached them
with clear portents;°
it was not God who did wrong to them,
but they used to do wrong to themselves.
The ones who are male believers   9:71
and the ones who are female believers,
some are protectors of the other;
they command to what is moral,
and they prohibit what is immoral,
and they perform the formal prayer,
and give the purifying alms and obey God
and His Messenger;°
those, God shall have mercy on them;°
truly God *is* Almighty, Wise.

God has promised the ones who are male believers
and the ones who are female believers
Gardens beneath which rivers run,
ones who shall dwell in them forever;
and dwellings, those which are good,
in the Gardens of Eden;°
and the greatest contentment *is* with God;°
that *is* the winning the sublime triumph.

Sec. 10

*

9:73
O Prophet!
Struggle with the ones who are ungrateful,
and the ones who are hypocrites,
and be **you** harsh against them;°
their place of shelter is hell.°
How miserable *is* the Homecoming!

9:74
They swear by God that they said not;
but indeed they said the word of ingratitude,
and they were ungrateful after their submission *to God*
and they purposed
what they never attained;°
they took not revenge
except that God had enriched them
and His Messenger with His grace;°
and if they repent, it shall be better for them;°
and if they turn away, God shall punish them

. with a painful punishment
in the present and in the world to come;°
and *there is* for them on earth
neither protector nor helper.

9:75
Of them *are* some who made a contract with God:
If He gives us of His grace,
we shall be charitable,
and certainly we shall be
among the ones who are in accord with morality.

9:76
Then when He gave them of His grace,
they became misers with it and turned away,
and they *were* the ones who turn aside.

9:77
He *made* the consequence *to be* hypocrisy
in their hearts

until the day they shall meet Him,
because they broke
what they had promised God,
because they used to lie against *Him*.
Know they not that God   9:78
knows their conspiring secretly
and their secret,
that God *is* The Knower of the unseen?°
Those who find fault with voluntary donors   9:79
to charities
from among the ones who believe,
and *find fault with* those who find not the means
but their striving,
they deride them;   .
God shall deride them,
and they shall have a painful punishment.
Whether **you** ask for forgiveness for them,   9:80
nor ask not for forgiveness for them;
if **you** ask for forgiveness for them
seventy times,
God shall never forgive them;°
that *is* because they were ungrateful for God,
and His Messenger;°
and God guides not the disobeying folk.

*

Sec. 11

The ones who were left behind were glad   9:81
of their position
behind the Messenger of God,
and they disliked
struggling with their wealth and themselves
in the way of God.
They said: Move not forward in the heat;°
say: The fire of hell has more severe heat;°
would that they understood!
So let them laugh a little and weep much°   9:82
as a recompense for what they were earning.
If God returned **you**   9:83
to a confederate of them,
and they asked **your** permission to go forth;

then say: You shall never ever go forth with me,
nor fight an enemy with me;°
you were well-pleased to sit the first time;
then sit and await with those who lagged behind.

9:84   Pray **you** not formally
for anyone of them who dies, ever,
nor stand up at his grave;°
they were ungrateful to God and His Messenger
and died as ones who disobey.

9:85   Let not their wealth impress you,
nor their children;°
for God wants not but to punish them
with these in the present,
and so that their souls shall depart
while they are ones who are ungrateful.

9:86   When a chapter of the Quran was sent forth:
Believe in God
and struggle along with His Messenger,
the affluent asked permission of **you**
and said: Forsake us;
we would be with the ones who sit at home.

9:87   They were well-pleased
to be with those who stay behind,
and a seal was set on their hearts
so they understood not.

9:88   But the Messenger and those who have believed,
who *are* with him,
have struggled with their wealth and their lives;°
those, for them *are* good deeds;°
and *it is* those who *are* the ones who shall prosper.

9:89   God has prepared for them
Gardens beneath which rivers run,
ones who shall dwell in them forever.°
That *is* the winning the sublime triumph.

*

Sec. 12

9:90   The ones who had excuses drew near
from among the nomads
that permission might be given them,

and they sat back, those who had lied against God,
and His Messenger;°
but soon shall light
a painful punishment
among those who were ungrateful.
But there is no *blame* on the weak,   9:91
nor on the sick,
nor on those who find nothing to spend
if they are true to God and His Messenger;°
there is no way
against the ones who are doers of good°
for God *is* Forgiving, Compassionate.
Nor on those,   9:92
when they approached **you**,
that **you** might find them mounts;
you have said: I find not
to carry you on;°
so they turned away
while their eyes overflowed with tears of grief
when they found there *was* nothing for them to spend.
                    ***   Part 11
The way *is* not but against   9:93
those who ask permission of **you** *to remain behind*
although they *are* rich;°
they are well-pleased to be
with those who stay behind,
and God has set a seal on their hearts
so that they know not.
They shall make excuses to you   9:94
when you return to them.
Say: Make no excuses;
We shall never believe you;
indeed God has told us news about you,
and God and His Messenger
shall consider your actions,
then you shall be returned
to One Who Has Knowledge
of the unseen and the visible;
then He shall tell you

what you were doing.

9:95   They shall swear to you by God
when you turn about to them,
so that you shall renounce them;
so renounce them,
surely they *are* a disgrace
and their place of shelter *is* hell,
a recompense
for what they were earning.

9:96   They swear to you
so that you shall be well-pleased with them,
but while you may be well-pleased with them,
God is not well-pleased
with the disobedient folk.

9:97   The nomads *are* stauncher in ingratitude
and hypocrisy,
and more apt not to know the ordinances
that God has sent forth to His Messenger;°
and God *is* Knowing, Wise.

9:98   Among the nomads *are some who* take
what they spend to themselves
as something owed *them*,
and await for some turn of your fortune;
theirs *shall be* a morally evil turn of fortune,
and God *is* Hearing, Knowing.

9:99   Among the nomads *are* some
who believe in God and the Last Day,
and take what they spend
as an offering to God,
and send blessings on the Messenger;°
truly these are an offering for them;°
God shall cause them to enter into His mercy;°
for God *is* Forgiving, Compassionate.

Sec. 13   *

9:100   As for the foremost Ones Who Outstrip,
among the ones who emigrated
and the helpers,
and those who followed them in kindness,
God is well-pleased with them,

and they too are well-pleased with Him;
He has prepared for them Gardens
beneath which rivers run,
ones who shall dwell in them forever, eternally;°
that *is* the winning the sublime triumph.
Among the nomads around you,   9:101
there are the ones who are hypocrites;°
and from among the people of the city,°
there are some who have grown bold
in hypocrisy;
you know them not;°
but We know them;°
We shall truly punish them twice,
then they shall be returned
to a tremendous punishment.
Others have acknowledged their impieties;   9:102
they have mixed moral acts
with others that are bad deeds;
perhaps God shall turn to them in forgiveness;°
truly God *is* Forgiving, Compassionate.
Take charity from their wealth   9:103
so that **you** would purify them,
and make them pure with it;°
and invoke blessings on them;°
truly **your** supplication
shall bring a sense of rest to them,
and God *is* Hearing, Knowing.
Know they not that God,   9:104
He accepts remorse from His servants,
and takes charities;
and that God,
He *is* The Compassioned
Accepter of Repentance?
Say: Act!   9:105
God shall consider your actions,
and *so shall* His Messenger,
and the ones who believe;°
and you shall be returned *to Him,*
One Who has Knowledge

230

of the unseen and the visible,
and He shall tell you, then what you were doing.

9:106 *There are* others who are waiting in suspense
for the command of God;
either He shall punish them
or He shall turn to them in forgiveness;°
and God *is* Knowing, Wise.

9:107 As for those who took places of prostration
by injuring,
and in ingratitude,
to separate and divide
between the ones who believe,
and as a stalking place
by those who warred against God
and His Messenger before,
they shall indeed swear:
We wanted nothing but fairness;°
and God bears witness
that they *are* indeed ones who lie.

9:108 Never stand up in it!
A place of prostration that was founded
from the first day on Godfearingness
is more rightful that **you** stand up in it;
in it are individuals who love to be purified;°
and God loves ones who keep themselves clean.

9:109 Is one who founds his structure
on the Godfearingness of God,
and His contentment,
better off
than he who founds his structure
on the brink of
a crumbling, tottering bank of a river
so that it tumbles with him
into the fire of hell?°
God guides not the unjust folk!

9:110 The structure they have built shall continue
the skepticism in their hearts
until their hearts are cut asunder;°
and God *is* Knowing, Wise.

Truly God has bought
from the ones who believe,
their selves and their properties,
for the Garden is theirs!
They fight in the way of God
so they kill and are slain;
it is a promise justifiably on Him
in the Torah, the Gospel
and the Quran;°
who fulfills his compact more faithfully
than God?°
Then rejoice in the good tidings
of the bargain that you made
in the trade with Him;°
that, that *is* the winning the sublime triumph

for the repentant worshippers,
the ones who praise,
the ones who are inclined to fast,
the ones who bow down,
the ones who prostrate themselves,
the ones who command what is moral
the ones who prohibit what is immoral,
and the ones who guard the ordinances of God;°
give good tidings to the ones who believe!

It is not for the Prophet
and those who have believed
to ask for forgiveness
for the ones who are polytheists,
even though they be kin,
after it has become clear to them
that they truly are the Companions of Hellfire.

Was not
Abraham asking for forgiveness for his father
only because of the promise he had promised him?
But when it became clear to him
that truly he was an enemy to God,
he cleared himself from him;°
truly Abraham *was* sympathetic

and forbearing.

God would never cause a folk to go astray after
He has guided them
until He had made manifest to them
of what they should be Godfearing;°
truly God *is* Knower of everything.

9:116 Truly to God *belongs* the dominion
of the heavens and the earth;
He gives life and He causes death;°
and other than God,
you *have* neither protector nor helper.

9:117 Indeed God turned towards the Prophet,
and the ones who were emigrants,
and the helpers who followed him
in the hour of adversity
after the hearts of a group of people
were about to swerve among them.
Then He turned towards them;°
truly He *is* Gentle, Compassionate.

9:118 Upon the three who were left behind
when the earth became narrow for them
for all its breadth,
and their souls became narrow for them,
they thought that *there was* no shelter
from God but in Him;
then He turned toward them
so that they would repent;°
truly God, He *is* The Compassioned
Accepter of Repentance.

Sec. 15 *

9:119 O those who have believed!
Be Godfearing of God
and be among the ones who are sincere.

9:120 *It is* not for the people of the city,
and those of the nomads around them,
to stay behind from the Messenger of God,
nor prefer themselves more than him;°
that *is* because they *were* neither lit on by thirst,
nor fatigue, nor famine

in the way of God,
nor treaded they any treading,
enraging the ones who are ungrateful,
nor gleaned any gleaning
against the enemy
but as an act in accord with morality
to be written down for them;°
truly God wastes not the compensation
of the ones who are doers of good.
Nor spend they contributions   9:121
be they small or great;
they cross not over a valley,
but it is written down for them
that God shall give recompense to them
for the fairest of what they were doing.
It was not for the ones who believe   9:122
to move forward collectively;°
but why should not a section move forward
of every section of people among them
to become learned in the way of life,
and to warn their folk
when they return to them
so that perhaps they would beware?
                    *   Sec. 16

O those who have believed!   9:123
Fight the ones who are near you
of the ones who are ungrateful,
and let them find harshness in you;°
and know that God *is* with
the ones who are Godfearing.
Whenever there is sent forth   9:124
a chapter of the Quran,
some of them say:
Which of you has it increased in belief?°
As for those who have believed,
it increases them in belief
and they rejoice at the good tidings.
But as for those whose hearts *are* sick,   9:125
it increases disgrace to their disgrace,

and they die
while they are the ones who are ungrateful.

9:126 Have they not considered that
they are be tried one time or two times in every year?
Yet they neither repent,
nor they recollect.

9:127 Whenever there is sent forth
a chapter of the Quran,
they look upon each other:
Is anyone seeing you?
Then they take flight;°
God has turned from their hearts
because they *are* a folk who understand not.

9:128 Indeed *there has* drawn near you a Messenger
from among yourselves;
it is grievous to him
that you fall into misfortune;
He is anxious for you
and to the ones who believe, Gentle, Compassionate.

9:129 But if they turn away,
say: God is enough for me;
there is no god but He;°
in Him I put my trust;°
and He *is* the Lord of the Sublime Throne.

CHAPTER 10
JONAH (*Yūnus*)

Stage 3 In the Name of God,
Sec. 1 The Merciful, The Compassionate
10:1 *Alif, Lām, Rā;*°
these *are* the Signs of the wise Book.
10:2 It was for humanity to wonder
that We have revealed to a man
from among themselves
who warns humanity,
and gives good tidings to those who have believed
so that they shall have sure footing
with their Lord?°

The ones who were ungrateful said:
Truly this *is* one who is a clear sorcerer.
Truly your Lord *is* God
Who created
the heavens and the earth in six days,
then turned Himself to the Throne;°
managing the command;°
there is no intercessor but with His permission;°
that *is* God, your Lord, so worship Him alone;°
then shall you not recollect?
To Him is the return of all;°
the promise of God *is* The Truth;°
truly He, He begins the creation;
then He shall cause it to return
so that He may give recompense
to those who have believed,
the ones who have acted in accord with morality,
with equity;°
and those who are ungrateful,
for them *is* a drink of boiling water,
and a painful punishment
because they were ungrateful.
It is He Who made the sun an illumination,
and the moon as a light,
and ordained its phases
so that you would know the number of the years
and the reckoning;°
God created this not but in Truth;°
He explains distinctly the Signs
for a folk who know.
Truly in the alternation
of the nighttime and the daytime,
and all that God has created
in the heavens and the earth
are Signs for a folk who are Godfearing.
Truly those who hope not
for their meeting with Us,
but are well-pleased with this present life
and are secure in it,

those who are
ones who are heedless of Our Signs,

10:8 those, their place of shelter *shall be* the fire
because of what they were earning.

10:9 Truly those who have believed,
and the ones who have acted in accord with morality,
their Lord shall guide them in their belief;°
rivers shall run beneath them
in Gardens of Bliss.

10:10 From it they shall call out:
Glory be to You, O God!
Their greetings in it *shall be*: Peace!
The last of their calling out *shall be*:
The Praise *belongs* to God
the Lord of the worlds!

Sec. 2   *

10:11 If God were to quicken chastisement
for humanity,
as they would desire to hasten for the good,
their term would be decided;°
but We leave those who forsake
the meeting with Us
wandering, *unwilling* to see in their defiance.

10:12 When injury afflicts the human being,
he calls to Us
on his side or *as* one who sits at home,
or *as* one who is standing up;
but when We have removed his injury from him,
he passes by as if he had never called to Us
for an injury that afflicted him;°
thus it is made to appear pleasing
to the ones who are excessive
what they were doing.

10:13 Indeed We caused generations to perish
before you

• when they did wrong
while their Messengers drew near
with clear portents,
but they were not such as to believe;°

thus we give recompense to the sinful folk.
Then We made you viceregents on the earth 10:14
after them
that We might look upon how you would do.
When Our Signs are recounted to them, 10:15
clear portents, ·
those who hope not for their meeting with Us said:
Bring us a Quran other than this,
or substitute it;°
say: It is not possible for me to substitute it
of my own accord;°
I follow nothing but what is revealed to me;°
truly I fear, if I *were* to rebel against my Lord,
a punishment on the tremendous Day.
Say: Had God willed 10:16
I would not have recounted to you,
nor would He have caused you to recognize it;°
truly I have lingered in expectation
a lifetime among you before this;°
then shall you not be reasonable?
So who is one who does greater wrong 10:17
than he who devises a lie against God
or denies His Signs?
Truly the ones who sin shall not prosper.
They worship other than God 10:18
things that injure them not,
nor profit them;
and they say:
These are our intercessors with God;°
say: Are you telling God
something which He knows not
in the heavens or in and on the earth?°
Glory be to Him and exalted *is He*
above all partners they make *with Him*.
Humanity was not but one community; 10:19
then they became at variance;°
and had it not been for a word
that preceded from **your** Lord,
it would have been decided between them

about what they were at variance.

They say:
Why has no Sign been sent forth
from his Lord?°
Say: Truly the unseen *belongs* to God alone
so watch and wait;
truly I am with you
of the ones who are watching and waiting.

*

When We caused humanity
to experience mercy
after tribulation had afflicted them,
lo! They conspired against Our Signs;°
say: God is Swifter in planning;°
truly Our messengers write down
what you plan.

It is He Who sets you in motion
through dry land and the sea,°
when you are in boats,
and they run them with the good wind,
and they are glad in it;
a storm wind draws near to them,
waves draw near from every place,
and they think
that they are enclosed by it,
they call to God
sincerely and devotedly
in their way of life for Him:
If **You** were to rescue us from this,
we should be the ones who are thankful.

But when He rescues them,
lo! They are insolent in and on the earth
without right!
O humanity,
your insolence *is* not but against yourselves;°
an enjoyment of this present life;°
to Us *is* your return
when We shall tell you what you were doing.

Truly the parable of this present life *is* like water

that We send forth from heaven;
it mingles with the plants of the earth
from which you eat—humanity and flocks;
until when the earth takes its ornaments
and is decorated,
its people thought that truly
they *were* the ones who had the power over it,
yet Our command approaches it
by nighttime or by daytime;
then We make it stubble
as if yesterday it had not flourished;°
thus We explain distinctly the Signs
for a folk who reflect.

God calls to the Abode of Peace,   10:25
and He guides whom He will
to a straight path.

For those who have done good   10:26
is the fairest and increase;°
neither shall gloom come over their faces
nor abasement;°
those are the Companions of the Garden;°
those, ones who shall dwell in it forever.

For those who have earned evil deeds,   10:27
the recompense of an evil deed shall be its like,
and abasement shall come over them;°
they shall *have* none but God
as one who saves them from harm;°
it is as if their faces had been covered
with a strip of the growing shadowy night;°
they are the Companions of the Fire;
they *are* ones who shall dwell in it forever.

On a Day   10:28
when We shall assemble them altogether,
then We shall say
to those who ascribe partners unto *God*:
Stay where you are,
you and your associates;°
then We shall set a space between them;°
and their associates would say:

It *was* not us that you used to worship

10:29 and God suffices as a witness
between you and us;
indeed we *were* ones who were heedless
of your worship.

10:30 There every soul shall be tried
for what it has done in the past,
and they would be returned to God,
One who is their Real Protector;°
and what they were devising
would go astray from them.

Sec. 4 *

10:31 Say: Who provides for you
from heaven and earth?
Or Who controls
having the ability to hear and sight?
Who brings out the living from the dead,
and brings out the dead from the living?
Who manages the command?°
They shall then say: God!°
Say: Shall you not be Godfearing *of Him*?

10:32 Such is God, your real Lord!°
What else *is there* after The Truth
but wandering astray?°
How then are you turned away?

10:33 Thus has the word of **your** Lord been realized
against those who disobeyed
that they shall not believe.

10:34 Say: Is there among whom
you associate *with God*
one who begins creation
and then causes it to return again?°
Say: God begins creation
and then causes it to return.°
How you are misled!

10:35 Say: Is there among whom
you associate *with God*
that guides to The Truth?°
Say: God guides to The Truth;°

has not He who guides to The Truth
a better right to be followed,
than he who guides not
unless he be guided?°
What is the matter with you?
How you give judgment!
Most of them follow nothing but opinion; °   10:36
truly opinion avails them not
against The Truth at all;°
truly God *is* Knowing
of what they accomplish.
This Quran would not have been devised   10:37
by other than God;
instead, it establishes as true what was
before it
and as a decisive explanation of the Book;
there is no doubt in it;
it is from the Lord of all the worlds.
Or shall they say: He devised it?°   10:38
Say: Bring a chapter of the Quran like it
and call on whomever you are able
other than God,
if you *are* ones who are sincere.
Rather they deny   10:39
the knowledge that they comprehend not,
while the interpretation
has not yet approached them;°
thus those before them denied!°
Look upon what was the Ultimate End
of the ones who were unjust!
Of them *there are* some who believe in it,   10:40
and of them *there are* some who believe not in it;°
and **your** Lord has greater knowledge
of the ones who make corruption.
*   Sec. 5
If they deny **you**,   10:41
you say: For me are my actions,
and for you are your actions;°
you are free of what I do,

and I am free of what you do.

10:42 Among them *are* some who listen to **you**;°
but cause **you** someone *unwilling* to hear, to hear
when they are not reasonable?

10:43 Among them *are* some who look upon **you**;°
but guide **you** the *unwilling* to see
when they perceive not?

10:44 Truly God wrongs not humanity at all,
but humanity does wrong itself.

10:45 On a Day He shall assemble them
as if they had not lingered in expectation
except an hour of the daytime;
they shall recognize one another among themselves;°
indeed those who denied have lost
the meeting with God,
and they were not ones who were truly guided.

10:46 Whether We cause **you** to see
some of what We promise them
or We call **you** to Us,
to Us *is* their return;
then God *shall be* witness
to what they accomplish.

10:47 Every community has its Messenger;°
then when their Messenger draws near,
it shall be decided between them with equity,
and wrong shall not be done to them.

10:48 They say: When *is* this promise
if you are ones who are sincere?

10:49 Say: I control
neither hurt nor profit for myself,
but what God willed;°
to every community *there is* a term;°
when their term draws near,
neither shall they delay it an hour,
nor shall they press it forward.

10:50 Say: Have you yourselves considered?
If His punishment should approach you
at nighttime or at daytime,
for which *portion*

would the ones who sin be impatient?
Is it then when it falls on you   **10:51**
that you shall believe in it?°
Now while you are impatient *for it,*
then the saying *shall be*   **10:52**
to those who did wrong to themselves:
Experience the everlasting punishment!
Shall you be given recompense
but for what you have been earning?
They ask **you** to be told: Is it true?°   **10:53**
Say: O my Lord! Truly it is The Truth;°
and you *are* not one who frustrates *Him.*

*

                                                    Sec. 6

If there would be for every person   **10:54**
who has done wrong
whatever is in or on the earth,
he would indeed offer it for *his* ransom;°
and they would keep secret their self-reproach
when they consider the punishment;°
but it shall be decided with equity,
and wrong shall not be done to them.
Lo! To God *belongs*   **10:55**
all that is in the heavens and the earth;°
lo! The promise of God is true,
but most of them know not.
It is He Who gives life and causes to die,   **10:56**
and to Him you shall return.
O humanity!   **10:57**
Truly an admonishment has drawn near to you
from your Lord
a healing for what is in the breasts,
a guidance and a mercy
for the ones who believe.
Say: In the grace of God and in His mercy   **10:58**
let them be glad;
that *is* better than what they gather.
Say: Have you yourselves considered?   **10:59**
From what God has sent forth to you
of provisions,

you have made some of it unlawful
and *some* lawful?
Say: Has God given *this* permission to you°
or devise you against God?

10:60 What is the opinion
of those who devise a lie against God
on the Day of Resurrection?°
Truly God *is* full of grace to humanity
but most of them *are* not thankful.

Sec. 7
*

10:61 **You** are not on any matter,
nor are **you** recounting from the Quran,
nor are you doing any action
except We *are* ones who bear witness over you
when you press on it;°
nothing escapes from your Lord
of the weight of an atom
in or on the earth nor in heaven,
nor what is smaller than that,
nor what is greater than that,
but it is in a clear Book.

10:62 Lo! With the faithful friends of God
there is neither fear in them,
nor shall they feel remorse.

10:63 Those who have believed
and are Godfearing,

10:64 for them *are* good tidings in this present life
and in the world to come;°
there is no substitution for the words of God;°
this *is* the winning the sublime triumph.

10:65 Let not their saying grieve **you.**•
Truly all renown *belongs* to God;°
He *is* The Hearer, The Knower.

10:66 Lo! To God *belongs*
whoever *is* in the heavens,
and whoever *is* in and on the earth;°
and follow not those who call to the associates—
they follow nothing but opinion;
they do nothing but guess.

It is He Who has made the nighttime for you   **10:67**
so that you may rest in it
and the daytime for one who perceives;°
truly in this *are* Signs
for a folk who hear.
They say God has taken to Himself a son;°   **10:68**
glory be to Him!,
He *is* sufficient!°
To Him *is* whatever
is in the heavens and in and on the earth;°
·   you *have* no authority for this;°
say you against God what you know not?
Say: Truly those who devise   **10:69**
lies against God,
they shall not prosper;
an enjoyment in the present   **10:70**
and then to Us *shall be* their return;
then We shall cause them to experience
the severe punishment
because they were ungrateful.
*   **Sec. 8**

Recount to them   **10:71**
the tidings of Noah,
when he said to his folk:
O my folk!
If my station is troublesome to you,
and my reminding you of the Signs of God,
I have put my trust in God;
so agree upon your affair
along with your associates;
have no doubt in your affair;
decide and give me not respite.
Then if you turn away,   **10:72**
I have not asked you for any compensation;°
my compensation *is* with God,
and I have been commanded
to be of the ones who submit.
They denied him,   **10:73**
so We delivered him and those with him

on the ship
and we made them the viceregents
while We drowned those who denied Our Signs;°
then look upon
what was the Ultimate End
of the ones who had been warned.

10:74 Then We raised up Messengers after him
to their folk;
they drew near them with clear portents,
but they would not believe
what they had denied before;°
thus We set a seal on the hearts
of the ones who are aggressors.

10:75 Then We raised up Moses and Aaron after them
to Pharaoh and his Council
with Our Signs;
they grew arrogant
and they were a sinful folk.

10:76 So when The Truth drew near to them from Us,
they said: Truly this is clear sorcery!

10:77 Moses said: Say you *this* about The Truth
when it has drawn near to you:°
Is this sorcery?
The ones who are sorcerers *shall not* prosper.

10:78 They said: Have **you** drawn near to us
to turn us
from what we found our fathers on
so that you two *may have* dominion on the earth?
We *are* not ones who believe in the two of you.

10:79 Pharaoh said:
Bring to me every knowing sorcerer.

10:80 When the ones who were sorcerers drew near,
Moses said to them:
Cast down with the ones who cast.

10:81 Then when they had cast
Moses said: What you have produced *is* sorcery;°
truly God shall prove it untrue;
truly God makes not right the actions
of the ones who make corruption.

God shall verify The Truth by His words, 10:82
though the ones who sin dislike it much!

But none had believed in Moses 10:83
except the offspring of his folk
because of the fear of Pharaoh and his Council
that he would persecute them;°
and truly Pharaoh
was one who exalted himself on the earth,
and he *was* truly one who was excessive.
Moses said: O my folk! 10:84
If you have believed in God,
then put your trust in Him
if you are the ones who submit.
They said: We put our trust in God. 10:85
Our Lord!
Make us not a temptation
for the unjust folk.
Deliver us by **Your** Mercy 10:86
from the ungrateful folk.
We revealed to Moses and his brother: 10:87
Take houses as dwellings for your folk;
make your houses sanctuaries for formal prayer;
perform the formal prayer;°
give good tidings to the ones who believe.
Moses said: 10:88
Our Lord!
You have given to Pharaoh and his Council
adornment and wealth in this present life.
Our Lord!
Cause them to go astray from **Your** way;°
our Lord!
Obliterate their wealth
and harden their hearts
so that they believe not
until they consider the painful punishment.
He said: Indeed you both have been answered, 10:89
so you both go straight,
and follow not the way of those who know not.

| 10:90 | We brought the Children of Israel |
| | over the sea; |

10:90 We brought the Children of Israel
over the sea;
and Pharaoh and his army pursued them
in insolence and acting impulsively;°
until, when overtaken by drowning, he said:
I believe that *there is* no god but He
in whom the Children of Israel believe,
and I *am* one who submits.

10:91 Now? Indeed **you** have rebelled before
and **you** were one who made corruption.

10:92 So on this day We shall deliver **your** physical form
that **you** may be a Sign
to those who are after **you**; °
and truly many among humanity
are the ones who are heedless of Our Signs.

Sec. 10   *

10:93 Indeed We placed the Children of Israel
in a sound settlement
and provided them with what is good.
They were not at variance
until knowledge drew near to them;°
truly **your** Lord shall decree between them
on the Day of Resurrection
about what they were at variance.

10:94 So if **you** are in uncertainty
about what We have sent forth to **you**,
then ask those who recited the Book
before **you**;°
truly The Truth has drawn near to **you**
from **your** Lord
so be you not of the ones who contest.

10:95 Be **you** not one of those who deny
the Signs of God,
for then **you** shall be of the ones who are losers.

10:96 Truly those for whom are suitable
the words of **your** Lord
shall not believe—

10:97 even if every Sign should draw near to them
until they consider the painful punishment.

Has there been a town that believed
and profited from its faith
other than *the* folk of Jonah?
When they believed,
We removed degradation from them
in this present life
and gave them enjoyment for a while.

10:98

Had **your** Lord willed,
all of those on earth would have believed.°
So would **you** compel humanity against their will
until they become ones who believe?

10:99

It would not be for any person to believe
except by the permission of God;°
and He shall disgrace
those who are not reasonable.

10:100

Say: Look upon what *is*
in the heavens and the earth;°
but neither Signs nor warnings avail
a folk who believe not.

10:101

Watch they and wait like in the days
of those who passed away before them?
Say: Truly I *am* with you so watch and wait;
I shall be with the ones who watch and wait!

10:102

Then We shall rescue Our Messengers
and those who have believed;°
thus *it is* an obligation upon Us to deliver
the ones who believe.

10:103

*

Sec. 11

Say: O humanity!
If you were in uncertainty as to my way of life,
then I shall not worship those whom
you worship other than God,
but I worship God
Who shall call you to Himself;°
and I am commanded to be one who believes.

10:104

Set **your** face to the way of life
of monotheism,
and **you** never be one who is a polytheist.

10:105

Call not to other than God

10:106

what can neither harm nor profit **you**—
and if **you** were to accomplish that
truly **you** *would be* of the ones who are unjust.

10:107 If God afflicts **you** with an injury,
there is no one who removes it but He;°
and if He wants good for **you**,
there is no one who repels His Grace;°
it lights on whomever He will of His servants,
and He *is* The Forgiving, The Compassionate.

10:108 Say: O humanity!
Indeed The Truth has drawn near to you
from your Lord;°
so whoever is truly guided,
then he is not but truly guided for his own self;°
and whoever goes astray,
then he not but strays to his own loss;°
and I *am* not a trustee over you.

10:109 Follow what is revealed to **you**
and have patience until God gives judgment;°
and He *is* the Best of the ones who judge.

CHAPTER 11
HUD *(Hūd)*

In the Name of God,
Sec. 1 The Merciful, The Compassionate
11:1 *Alif Lām Rā;*°
a Book,
the Signs in it have been set clear
then they were explained distinctly
from that which proceeds from the Presence
of One *Who is* Wise, Aware
11:2 that you worship none but God;°
truly I *am* a warner to you from Him
and a bearer of good tidings
11:3 that you ask for forgiveness from your Lord
and then repent to Him
that He may give fair enjoyment
for a determined term;

He gives His grace to every possessor of grace;°
and if you turn away,
I fear for you the punishment of the Great Day.
To God *is* your return;°   11:4
and He *is* Powerful over everything.
Surely they fold up their breasts   11:5
that they may conceal *themselves* from Him;
certainly when they cover themselves
with their garments,
He knows what they keep secret
and what they speak openly;°
truly He *is* the Knowing
of what *is* in their breasts.

*** Part 12

There is no moving creature on earth   11:6
but its provisions *are* due from God;
and He knows its appointed time
and its repository;
all *is* in a clear Book.
It is He Who has created   11:7
the heavens and the earth in six days,
and His Throne was upon the waters
that He might try you,
which of you *is* fairer in actions;°
but if you were to say to them:
Truly you *are* the ones who are to be raised up
after death,
they, those who are ungrateful, would be sure to say:
This is nothing but clear sorcery.
If We postpone the punishment for them   11:8
until a term that is numbered,
they shall surely say: What detains it?°
Surely the day it approaches them,
nothing of that shall be turned away from them
but what they used to ridicule
shall surround them.

* Sec. 2

If We cause mankind to experience   11:9
mercy from Us

and then tear it out from him,
truly he, he becomes hopeless, ungrateful.

11:10 But if We cause him to experience prosperity
after tribulation has afflicted him,
he is certain to say:
Evil deeds have gone from me!°
Truly he becomes glad and boastful.

11:11 But those who have endured patiently,
the ones who have acted in accord with morality,
those—theirs shall be forgiveness
and a great compensation.

11:12 So perhaps **you** would *be* one who leaves
some of what has been revealed to **you**,
and **your** breast *be* one that is narrowed
because they say:
Why has a treasure not been sent forth to him
or an angel drawn near to him?°
You *are* not but a warner,
and God *is* a Trustee over everything.

11:13 Or they say: He has devised it;°
say: Approach you then
with ten chapters of the Quran like it,
forged,
and call to whomever you are able
other than God
if you are the ones who are sincere.

11:14 If they respond not to you,
then know that it has not but been sent forth
by the knowledge of God
and that *there is* no god but He;°
shall you then *be* ones who submit?

11:15 Whoever wants this present life
and its adornment,
We shall pay their account in full to them
for their actions in it,
and they shall not be diminished in it.

11:16 Those *are* they who *have* nothing for them
in the world to come but fire;°
and what they have crafted there has been fruitless,

what they used to do is useless.

What of him who was with a clear portent
from his Lord,
and one who bore witness from Him recounts it?
Before it *was* the Book of Moses,
a leader and a mercy.
It is those believe in it;°
whoever is ungrateful for it among the confederates,
he is promised the fire!
So be **you** not hesitant about it.°
Truly it *is* The Truth from **your** Lord,
but most of humanity believes not.

Who *is* one who does greater wrong than he
who devises a lie against God?°
Those shall be presented before their Lord.
The ones who bear witness shall say:
These *are* they who lied against their Lord;°
truly the curse of God *is* upon
the ones who are unjust,

they who bar from the way of God
and desire in it crookedness;
and they, they *are*
ones who are ungrateful for the world to come.

Those shall not be ones who frustrate *the Will of God*
on the earth,
nor *have* they other than God
any protector. •
For them the punishment shall be multiplied°
for they were neither able to hear
nor they used to perceive.

Those *are* they who have lost their own selves;
what they used to devise has gone astray.

Surely they *are* those who
in the world to come *shall be* ones who are losers.

Truly those who have believed,
the ones who have acted in accord with morality
and humble themselves before their Lord,
those *shall be* the Companions of the Garden;
ones who shall dwell in it forever.

The parable of the two groups of people:
The one *unwilling* to see
unwilling to hear;
and the other, *willing* to see and hear;°
they are not on the same level in likeness;°
shall you not recollect?

Sec. 3   *

11:25   Indeed We sent Noah to his folk:
Truly I *am* a clear warner to you,
11:26   that you worship none but God;°
truly I fear for you the punishment
of a painful Day.
11:27   Then the Council of those who were ungrateful
among his folk said:
We see **you** not except as a mortal like ourselves;
we see that none follow **you** except those who
are, in our view, the vile among us, simple minded;
nor we see you as having any merit above us;
on the contrary, we think
that you are ones who lie.
11:28   He said: O my folk!
Have you yourselves considered?
I am a clear portent from my Lord
and He has given me mercy from Him,
but that has been invisible to you;
shall we fasten you to it
when you are ones who dislike it?
11:29   O my folk!
I ask not of you wealth for it;°
my compensation *is* with my Lord;°
and I shall not drive away
those who have believed;
truly they *are* the ones who shall encounter
their Lord,
but I see you a folk who are ignorant.
11:30   O my folk!
Who would help me against God
if I drive them away?°
Shall you not recollect?

I say not to you:
The treasures of God *are* with me,
nor that I know the unseen,
nor say I: Truly I *am* an angel;
nor I say of those who are despicable in your eyes:
God shall never give them good;°
God has greater knowledge
of what *is* within themselves;°
for indeed I *would* then *be* one who is unjust.

They said: O Noah!
Indeed **you** have disputed with us
and made much of the dispute with us;
now approach us with what **you** have promised us
if **you** *are* one who is sincere.

He said: God shall not but bring it on you
had He willed;
you *shall* not *be* one who frustrates *the Will of God*.

My advice shall not profit you
even if I wanted to advise you,
if God wants to lead you into error;°
He *is* your Lord and to Him you shall return.

Or they say: He has devised it;°
say: If I have devised it,
my sin *is* upon me
and I *am* free of your sins.

*

It was revealed to Noah:
Truly none of your folk shall believe
but those who have already believed;
so be not despondent
because of what they were accomplishing.

Craft the ship under Our Eyes
and by Our Revelation
and address Me not
for those who do wrong;°
they *are* truly ones who are to be drowned.

He crafted the ship.
Whenever the Council of his folk passed by him,
they derided him;°

he said: If you deride us,
so we deride you
as you deride us.

11:39 You shall know
to whom a punishment shall approach
that shall cover him with shame,
and on whom an abiding punishment shall alight.

11:40 When Our Command drew near,
and the oven boiled,
We said: Carry in it
of every *living thing*, a mate, two,
and your people,
except him against whom the saying preceded,
and those who have believed;°
and none except a few had believed with him.

11:41 He said: Embark in it;
in the Name of God
shall be the course of the ship and its berthing;°
truly my Lord *is* Forgiving, Compassionate.

11:42 So it ran with them amidst waves
like mountains,
and Noah cried out to his son,
standing apart:
O my son! Embark with us;
you be not with the ones who are ungrateful!

11:43 He said: I shall take shelter for myself
on a mountain:
It shall save me from the harm of the water.°
He said: *There is* none who saves from harm this day
from the command of God
except him on whom He has mercy;°
and a wave came between them
so he was of the ones who were drowned.

11:44 It was said:
O earth! Take in your water!
O heaven: Desist!
And the water shrank.
The command *of God* was satisfied,
and it was on the same level as El-Judi.°

It was said:
Away with the unjust folk!
Noah cried out to his Lord   **11:45**
and said: O my Lord!
Truly my son *is* of my people;
truly **Your** promise *is* The Truth;
You *are* the Most Just
of the ones who are judges.
He said: O Noah!   **11:46**
Truly he *is* not of **your** people;°
truly he acts not in accord with morality,
so ask not of Me what **you** *have* no knowledge;°
I admonish **you**
so that **you** not be of the ones who are ignorant.
He said: O my Lord!   **11:47**
Truly I take refuge with **You**
so that I not ask **You**
of what I *have* no knowledge;°
unless **You** were to forgive me
and *have* mercy on me,
I would indeed be of the ones who are losers.
It was said: O Noah!   **11:48**
Get down with peace from Us and blessings
upon **you** and upon some communities
of those with **you**;°
and communities
to whom We shall give enjoyment,
then they shall be afflicted by Us
with a painful punishment.
These *are* of the tidings of the unseen   **11:49**
that We reveal to **you**;°
neither **you** nor **your** folk used to know them
before this;°
^so have patience^;
truly the Ultimate End *is* for
the ones who are Godfearing.
                    *   **Sec. 5**

To Ad *We sent* their brother Hud;°   **11:50**
he said: O my folk! Worship God!

258

You *have* not any other god but He;°
you *are* nothing but ones who devise.

O my folk!
I ask not of you any compensation;
my compensation *is* not but with Him
Who originated me;°
shall you not then be reasonable?

O my folk!
Ask your Lord for forgiveness;
then repent to Him;
He shall send abundant rain to you
and increase you
adding strength to your strength,
so turn not away as ones who sin.

They said: O Hud!
Have **you** produced any clear portent for us?
We *shall* not *be* ones to leave our gods
for **your** saying;
we *are* not ones who believe in **you**.

Truly we say nothing but
that some of our gods have chastised **you**
with evil;
he said: Truly I call God to witness
and bear you witness
that I am free from
what you make as partners

with Him;°
so try to outwit me all of you,
give me no respite.

Truly I have put my trust in God,
my Lord and your Lord;°
there is not a moving creature
but He *is the* One Who Takes of its forelock;°
truly my Lord *is* on a straight path.

But if you turn away,
then truly I have expressed to you
what I was sent with to you;°
and my Lord shall make successors
a folk other than you,

and you shall not injure Him at all;°
truly My Lord *is* Guardian over everything.
When Our command drew near,   **11:58**
We delivered Hud
and those who had believed with him
by a mercy from Us,
and We delivered them
from a harsh punishment.
That *was* Ad;°   **11:59**
they negated the Signs of their Lord
and rebelled against His Messengers;
and they followed the command
of every haughty and stubborn *one.*
They were pursued   **11:60**
in this present life by a curse
and on the Day of Resurrection;°
no doubt Ad were ungrateful to their Lord;°
surely at a distance *are* Ad, *the* folk of Hud.

*   **Sec. 6**

To Thamud, *We sent* their brother Salih;   **11:61**
he said: O my folk!
Worship God,
you *have* no god except He;°
He caused you to grow from the earth,
and settled you on it;
so ask forgiveness of Him;
then repent to Him;°
certainly my Lord *is* Near, One Who Answers.
They said: O Salih!   **11:62**
Truly **you** were
one who was the source of hope to us
before this;°
have **you** prohibited us that we worship
what our fathers worship?
Truly we *are* in uncertainty as to
that to which **you** have called us
for *you are* one who arouses suspicion.
He said: O my folk!   **11:63**
Have you yourselves considered?

I am with a clear portent from my Lord.
He has given me a mercy from Himself;
so who then helps me against God
if I were to rebel against Him?°
Then you would increase me not but in decline.

11:64 O my folk!
This *is* the she-camel of God, a Sign for you;
so let her eat on God's earth
and afflict her not with evil,
so that a near punishment take you.

11:65 But they crippled her;
so he said:
Take joy in your abode
for three days;°
that *is* a promise, not one that shall be belied.

11:66 So when Our command drew near,
We delivered Salih
and those who had believed with him
by a mercy from Us
and from the degradation of that Day;°
truly your Lord, He *is* Strong, Almighty.

11:67 The cry took those who did wrong,
happening in the morning in their abodes;
they were the ones who had fallen prostrate

11:68 as if they had not dwelt in them;°
surely Thamud
were ungrateful to their Lord;°
surely away with Thamud!

Sec. 7 *

11:69 Truly Our Messengers drew near
to Abraham with good tidings;
they said: Peace!°
He said: Peace!°
He presently produced a roasted calf.

11:70 But when he saw their hands reach
not out towards it,
he was suspicious and sensed awe of them;°
they said: Fear not;
we have been sent to *the* folk of Lot.

His wife, one who was standing up, laughed
so We gave her good tidings of Isaac
and after Isaac, Jacob.
She said: Woe to me!
Shall I give birth when I *am* an old woman
and this, my husband is an old man?°
Truly this *is* a strange thing!° They said:
What! Marvel **you** at the command of God?°
The mercy of God and His blessings be upon you,
O People of the House.°
Truly He *is* Worthy of Praise, Glorious.
When the panic had gone from Abraham,
and the good tidings had drawn near to him,
he began to dispute for *the* folk of Lot.
Truly Abraham *was* forbearing, sympathetic
and one who turns in repentance.
O Abraham! Turn aside from this;°
truly the command of **your** Lord has drawn near;°
and truly what arrives for them
is a punishment, one that is not to be repelled.
When Our Messengers drew near Lot,
he was troubled for them,
and was concerned for them, distressed,
and he said:
This *is* a distressful day!
Then his folk drew near, running toward him;
and since they used to do evil deeds before,°
he said: O my folk! Here are my daughters!
They *are* purer for you;°
be Godfearing of God
and cover me not with shame
as regards my guests;°
is there not among you a right minded man?
They said: Indeed **you** know
we *have* no interest in **your** daughters,
and truly **you** know well what we want.
He said: Would that I had strength against you
or might take shelter with a stronger column!
They said: O Lot!

11:71

11:72

11:73

11:74

11:75

11:76

11:77

11:78

11:79

11:80

11:81

Truly we *are* the Messengers of **your** Lord;
they shall not reach out to **you**;°
so set forth with **your** people in a part of the night,
and let not any of you look back
except **your** wife;°
truly what shall light on them shall light on her;°
what has been promised to them
is in the morning;°
is not the morning near?

11:82 So when Our command drew near,
We made its high part low,
and We rained down on it rocks of baked clay,
one upon another,

11:83 marked by **your** Lord;°
and they *are* not far from the ones who are unjust.

Sec. 8 *

11:84 To Midian *We sent* their brother Shuayb;
he said: O my folk!
Worship God;
you *have* no god except Him;°
and reduce not the measuring vessel and balance;°
truly I, I consider you as good
and truly I, I fear for you
the punishment of an enclosing Day.

11:85 O my folk!
Live up to the measuring vessel
and Balance in equity;°
and diminish not the things of humanity,
and do no mischief in and on the earth
as ones who make corruption.

11:86 What is left by God is best for you
if you are the ones who believe;°
and *I am* not a Guardian over you.

11:87 They said: O Shuayb! *Is it that* **your** prayer
commands **you**
that we should leave
what our fathers worshiped,
or that we should not accomplish
with our possibilities

whatever we will?
Truly **you** *are* the forbearer, the right minded.
He said: O my folk! 11:88
Have you yourselves considered?
I am a clear portent from my Lord;
He has provided me fair provisions from Himself;°
I want not to go against you
in what I have prohibited you;°
I only want to make things right
so far as I am able;°
and my success *is* but from God;°
in Him I put my trust,
and to Him I am penitent.
O my folk! 11:89
Let not your breach with me drive you
to be lit on
by the like of what lit on *the* folk of Noah,
or *the* folk of Hud,
or *the* folk of Salih;°
and *the* folk of Lot are not far from you.
Ask for forgiveness from your Lord 11:90
and repent to Him;°
my Lord *is* Compassionate, Loving.
They said: O Shuayb! 11:91
We do not understand much of what **you** say
and truly we see **you** weak among us;°
if it had not been for **your** extended family,
we would have stoned **you**;°
and **you** are not mighty against us.
He said: O my folk! 11:92
Is my extended family mightier to you
than God
whom you have taken to yourselves to disregard?°
Truly my Lord *is* One Who Encloses
whatever you do.
O my nation! 11:93
Act according to your ability
and truly I am one who acts;°
soon you shall know

whom the punishment approaches
that shall cover him with shame
and who *is* one who lies.
Be on the watch!
Truly I am watching with you.

11:94   When Our command drew near,
We delivered Shuayb
and those who had believed with him
as a mercy from Us;
and the Cry took those who did wrong;
it happened in the morning in their abodes
they were the ones who had fallen prostrate

11:95   as if they had not dwelled in them;°
surely: Away with Midian
just as: Away with Thamud.

Sec. 9   *

11:96   Indeed *We sent* Moses with Our Signs
and a clear authority

11:97   to Pharaoh and his Council;
but they followed the commands of Pharaoh;°
and the command of Pharaoh
was not right minded.

11:98   He shall go before his folk on the Day of Resurrection
and shall lead them down into the fire;°
how miserable a watering place
to which they are led!

11:99   They were pursued by a curse in this *life*
and on the Day of Resurrection!°
How miserable the offered oblation!

11:100   That *is* from the tidings of the towns
that We relate to **you**;°
of them, *some are* ones that are standing up
and *some* are stubble.

11:101   We did not wrong them,
but they did wrong themselves;°
and of no avail to them were their gods
whom they called to other than God;
when the command of **your** Lord drew near,°
they increased them not in anything

except ruination.

Such *is* the taking of **your** Lord

when He takes the towns

of the ones who *were* unjust;

truly His taking *is* painful, severe.

Truly in that *there is* a Sign

for those who fear the punishment

of the world to come,

that Day humanity *shall be* gathered together for it,

and that *is* a witnessed Day.

We postpone it not but for a numbered term.

On the Day it approaches

no person shall assert *anything*

except with His permission;°

some among them *shall be* disappointed

and others, happy.

As for those who *are* unhappy,

they shall be in the fire;

for them in it *is* sobbing and sighing.

They, ones who shall dwell in it

for as long as the heavens and the earth last,

except what **your** Lord has willed;

truly **your** Lord

is One Who Achieves what He wants.

As for those who are happy,

they shall be in the Garden.

They, ones who shall dwell in it

for as long as the heavens and the earth last,

except what **your** Lord has willed;°

a gift that *is* not to be broken.

So be **you** not hesitant as to what these worship;°

they worship nothing except what

their fathers worshiped before;°

and truly

We *are* the ones who pay their account in full

without reduction.

*

Indeed We gave Moses the Book,

but they were at variance about it;°

and had it not been for a word
preceding from **your** Lord,
it would have been decided between them;°
and truly they *are* uncertain about it,
ones whose suspicions were aroused.

11:111 Truly to each the account shall be paid in full by
your Lord for their actions;°
truly He *is* Aware of what they do.

11:112 So go **you** straight as **you** are commanded,
and those who repent with **you**,
and be not defiant;°
truly He *is* Seeing of what you do.

11:113 Incline not to those who do wrong
so that the fire not afflict you,
and there *shall* not *be* for you
other than God any protectors,
then you shall not be helped.

11:114 Perform the formal prayers
at the two ends of the daytime,
and at nearness of the nighttime;°
truly benevolence
causes evil deeds to be put away;°
that *is* mindfulness for the ones who remember.

11:115 Have patience,
for truly God wastes not
the compensation of the ones who are doers of good.

11:116 Why had there not been among the generations
before you
persons of recollection,
prohibiting corruption in and on the earth,
except a few
of those whom We rescued from among them!°
Those who did wrong followed
that in which they were given ease in it,
and they were the ones who sin.

11:117 **Your** Lord causes not the towns to perish
unjustly
while their people are
ones who make things right.

Had **your** Lord willed, 11:118
He would have made humanity one community;°
but they continue to be at variance—
except him on whom **your** Lord 11:119
has bestowed His mercy,°
—and for that, He created them°—
and the word of **your** Lord has been completed;
certainly I shall fill hell
with genie and humanity altogether.
All that We relate to **you** 11:120
of the tidings of the Messengers
is so that We make **your** mind firm by it;°
and The Truth has drawn near to **you** in this,
and an admonishment for
the ones who believe and are mindful.
Say to those who have not believed: 11:121
Act according to your ability;
truly we *are* ones who act.
Watch and wait; 11:122
we *too* are ones who are watching and waiting.
To God *is* the unseen of the heavens 11:123
and the earth,
and to Him *is* the return of the command,
so worship Him and put **your** trust in Him;°
and **your** Lord *is* not One Who is Heedless
of what you do.

CHAPTER 12
JOSEPH (*Yūsuf*)

In the Name of God,
The Merciful, The Compassionate Sec. 1
Alif Lām Rā;° 12:1
these *are* the Signs of the clear Book.
Truly We have sent forth the Quran in Arabic 12:2
so that you may be reasonable.
We relate to **you** 12:3
the fairest of narratives
through what We have revealed to **you**

of this Quran,
although **you** were before this
of the ones who were heedless.

12:4   When Joseph said to his father:
O my father!
Truly I saw eleven stars
and the sun and the moon;
I saw them *as* ones prostrating themselves to me.

12:5   He said: O my son!
Relate not **your** dream to your brothers
so that they not contrive cunning against **you**;°
truly Satan *is* a clear enemy to mankind.

12:6   Thus **your** Lord shall elect **you**,
and teach you of the interpretation of events,
and He shall fulfill His divine blessing on **you**,
and on the people of Jacob,
just as He fulfilled it on **your** two fathers before,
Abraham and Isaac;°
truly **your** Lord *is* Knowing, Wise.

*

Sec. 2

12:7   Indeed in Joseph and his brothers
are Signs for the ones who ask.

12:8   When they said:
Surely Joseph and his brother
are more beloved to our father than we,
although we are many;
truly our father *is* clearly wandering astray.

12:9   Kill Joseph or fling him to *some other* land
to free the face of your father for you,
you shall be a folk in accord with morality after that!

12:10   One of them said: Kill not Joseph,
but cast him into the bottom of a well.
Some company of travelers shall pick him up,
if you are ones who do *this*.

12:11   They said: O our father!
Why shall **you** not trust us with Joseph
when we are truly
ones who shall look after him?

12:12   Send him with us tomorrow

to frolic and play;
truly we *are* ones who shall guard him.
He said: Truly I am grieved   12:13
that you should go with him,
and I fear that a wolf eat him
while you are ones who are heedless of him.
They said: If a wolf eats him   12:14
while we are many,
truly then we *are* ones who are losers.
So when they went with him,   12:15
and they all agreed
to lay him in the bottom of the well,°
We revealed to him:
Indeed **you** shall tell them of this their affair
when they are not aware.
They drew near their father   12:16
at the time of night, weeping.
They said: O our father!   12:17
Truly we had gone racing
and we left Joseph with our sustenance
and a wolf ate him;°
and **you** shall not be one who believes us,
even when we *would be* ones who are sincere.
They produced his long shirt with false blood.°   12:18
He said: Rather
your mind enticed you with a command;°
having patience is graceful,°
and it *is* God Whose help is sought
against what you allege.
There drew near a company of travelers,   12:19
so they sent their water-drawer
to let down his bucket;
he said: What good tidings, this is a boy!°
So they kept him secret as merchandise;°
and God *is* Knowing of what they did.
They sold him   12:20
for a meager price of numbered coins,
and they were the ones who held him in low esteem.

*

12:21   The man from Egypt who had bought him said
to his wife:
Honor him as a guest with a place of lodging;
perhaps he shall profit us
or we shall take him to ourselves as a son;°
and thus We established Joseph firmly
in the earth
that We might teach him
the interpretation of events;°
God *is* One Who is Victor over His command
but most of humanity knows not.

12:22   When he had grown fully and come of age,
We gave him critical judgment and knowledge
and thus We give recompense to
the ones who are doers of good.

12:23   She in whose house he *was,* solicited him;
she shut the doors
and said: Come!°
He said: I seek refuge with God!°
Truly he is my master
and He has given me a goodly place of lodging;°
truly the ones who are unjust shall not prosper.

12:24   Indeed she would have taken him;°
and he would have taken her,
had he not considered the proof of his Lord;°
thus *it was* that We might turn away
evil from him and depravity;°
and truly he was of Our devoted servants.

12:25   So they raced to the door
and she tore his long shirt from the back;
and they both discovered her chief at the door;°
she said: What is the recompense of him
who wanted evil for **your** household
except that he be imprisoned
or a painful punishment?

12:26   He said: She sought to solicit me.
One who bears witness bore witness
of her people:
If it be his long shirt is torn from the front,

then she is sincere and he is one of those who lies.
But if it be that his long shirt is torn
from behind, then she lies,
and he is among those who are sincere.
When he saw his long shirt was torn from behind,
he said: It is of your (f) cunning;°
truly your (f) cunning is serious.
Joseph! Turn aside from this!°
Woman, **you** ask forgiveness for **your** (f) sin;
truly **you** (f) are
of the ones who are inequitable.

*   Sec. 4

The ladies in the city said: 12:30
The wife of al-Aziz
sought to solicit her young male;
indeed he captivated her longing,
truly we consider her *to be*
clearly wandering astray.
So when she heard of their planning,   12:31
she sent for them (f)
and made ready for them a banquet;
she gave each one of them (f) a knife,
and said *to Joseph*: Go forth before them (f)!
Then when they saw him, they admired him
and cut their hands;
and they (f) said: God save us!
This is not a mortal;
this is nothing but a generous angel!
She said: This is he   12:32
about whom you (f) did blame me;°
and indeed I solicited him,
but he preserved himself from sin;°
and now if he not accomplish what I command
he shall certainly be imprisoned
and shall be one of the ones who are disgraced.
He said: O my Lord!   12:33
Prison is more beloved to me
than what they call me to.°
Unless **You** turn away

their (f) cunning from me,
I shall yearn towards them (f)
and shall be of the ones who are ignorant.

12:34 So his Lord responded to his invocation
and turned away their (f) cunning from him;°
truly He, He *is* The Hearing, The Knowing.

12:35 Then it was shown to them (m),
after they (m) had seen the Signs,
that they (m) should imprison him for a while.

Sec. 5 *

12:36 There entered with him in the prison
two young men;°
one of them said:
Truly I saw myself pressing grapes in season;°
and the other said:
Truly I saw myself carrying bread on my head
from which birds were eating;°
they said: Tell us the interpretation of this;°
truly we think **you** *are*
one of the doers of good.

12:37 He said:
The food you are provided shall not approach you,
but I shall have told you of its interpretation
before it approaches
of what my Lord has taught me;°
truly I have left the creed of a folk
who believe not in God
and in the world to come;
they are the ones who are ungrateful.

12:38 I have followed the creed of my fathers,
Abraham, Isaac and Jacob;°
it was not for us
that we ascribe partners to God at all;°
that *is* from the grace of God to us
and to humanity,
but most of humanity is not thankful.

12:39 O my two prison companions!
Are ones that are separate masters better
or God, The One, The Triumphant?

273

Those whom you worship other than He   12:40
are nothing but names
that you have named—you and your fathers,
for which God has not sent forth any authority;°
the determination *is* from God alone;
He has commanded that you worship
none but Him;°
that *is* the truth-loving way of life,
but most of humanity knows not.
O my two prison companions!   12:41
As for one of you,
he shall pour intoxicants for his master;°
and as for the other,
he shall be crucified
and birds shall eat from his head;
the command
was decided about which you asked advice.
He said to the one of them   12:42
whom he thought
should be *the* one who is saved of the two:
Remember me to **your** master;
but Satan caused him to forget
to remember him to his master;
so he lingered in expectation in prison
for a certain number of years.
                    *   Sec. 6
                                                         12:43
The king said:
Truly I, I saw seven fattened cows
eating seven lean ones,
and seven ears of green wheat
and others dry;°
O Council:
Render an opinion to me concerning my dream
if you are *able* to expound dreams.°
They said: Jumbled nightmares!   12:44
We are not of ones who have knowledge
of the interpretation
of nightmares.
Said the man of the two of them   12:45

who had been delivered
recalling after a period of time:
I shall myself tell you its interpretation so send me.

12:46 Joseph, O **you** just person!
Render an opinion concerning an issue to us:
Seven fattened cows
eaten by seven lean ones,
and seven ears of green wheat
and others dry
that I may return to the personages
so that they may know.

12:47 He said: You shall sow
for seven years similar to present custom;
and of what you reap,
you shall forsake ears of wheat,
except a little of it that you may eat.

12:48 Then seven severe *years* shall approach after that;
you shall devour what you have put forward,
except a little of what you have kept in store.

12:49 Then after that shall approach a year
in which humanity shall be helped
with rain and they shall press in season.

Sec. 7 *

12:50 The king said: Bring him to me!°
But when the messenger was produced,
he said: Return to your master
and ask him what of the ladies
who cut their hands?
Truly my Lord *is* Knowing of their cunning.

12:51 He said: What *was* your (f) business
when you sought to solicit Joseph?
They (f) said: God save us!
We know not any evil against him
The wife of al-Aziz said:
Now The Truth is discovered!
I sought to solicit him;
indeed he *is* one of those who are sincere.

12:52 *Joseph said:* So that he may know
that I betrayed him not in his absence

and that God guides not
the cunning of the ones who are traitors.
***

Part 13

I declare my soul not innocent.°
Truly the soul *is* what incites to evil,
except when my Lord has mercy;°
truly my Lord is Forgiving, Compassionate.
The king said: Bring him to me
so that I may attach him to myself;°
then when he spoke to him he said:
Truly this day
you *are* with us secure, trustworthy.
He said:
Assign me over the storehouses of the region;°
truly I *shall be* a knowing guardian.
Thus We established Joseph firmly in the region
to take his dwelling in it
when or where he wills;°
We light Our mercy on whom We will;°
and We waste not the compensation
of ones who are doers of good.
Truly the compensation
of the world to come *is* better
for those who have believed
and would be Godfearing.
*

Joseph's brothers drew near
and entered before him;
he recognized them,
but they *were* the ones who did not know him.
When he had equipped them
with their food sustenance,
he said: Bring me a brother of yours
from your father;°
see you not that I live up to full measure,
and that I *am* the best of hosts?
But if you bring him not to me,
there *shall be* no full measure for you with me,
nor shall you come near me.

12:53
12:54
12:55
12:56
12:57

Sec. 8
12:58
12:59
12:60

12:61   They said: We shall solicit him from his father
and truly we *are* ones who shall do *it*.

12:62   He said to his male youths:
Lay their merchandise into their saddlebags;
so that perhaps they shall recognize it
when they turn about to their people,
so that perhaps they shall return.

12:63   So when they returned to their father, they said:
O our father! Our measure was refused to us;
so send our brother with us
so that we shall get our full measure;
and truly we *shall be* ones who guard him.

12:64   He said: How shall I entrust him to you
as I entrusted you with
his brother before?°
Yet God *is* the Best one who guards;°
and He is the One Who is the Most Merciful
of the ones who are the most merciful.

12:65   When they opened their supplies,
they found their merchandise
had been returned to them;°
they said: O our father!
This is what we desire;°
our merchandise has been returned to us;°
we shall get provisions for our people;
we shall keep our brother safe
and add a camel's *load* of full measure;°
that *is* an easy full measure.

12:66   He said: I shall not send him with you
until you give me a pledge by God
that you shall bring him *back* to me,
unless it be that you are enclosed;°
and when they gave him their pledge,
he said: God *is* Trustee over what we say.

12:67   He said: O my children!
Enter not by one door,
but enter by separate doors;°
I shall not avail you anything against God;°
truly the determination *is* but with God;°

277

in Him I put my trust;
and in Him put their trust
the ones who put their trust.
When they entered   **12:68**
from where their father had commanded,
it availed them not
against God in the least,
but it was a need of Jacob's inner self
which he satisfied;°
and truly he *was* a possessor of knowledge
because We had taught him;
but most of humanity knows not.

*   **Sec. 9**

When they went in before Joseph,   **12:69**
he himself gave refuge to his brother;°
he said: Truly I *am* **your** brother
so be not despondent for what they were doing.
So when he had equipped them   **12:70**
with their food sustenance,
he put the drinking cup
into their brother's saddlebag;°
then one who announces announced:
O you in the caravan,
truly you *are* ones who are thieves.
They said coming forward: **12:71**
What is it that you are missing?
They said: **12:72**
We are missing the king's drinking cup,
and for him who brings it about
is a camel's load,
and I shall be the guarantor for it.
They said: By God,   **12:73**
indeed you know we have drawn not near
making corruption in the region,
and we were not ones who are thieves.
They said: What then *shall be* the recompense   **12:74**
for him if you were ones who lie?
They said: The recompense for it *shall be*   **12:75**
that he in whose saddlebag it is found

shall be the recompense;°
thus we give recompense
to the ones who are unjust.

12:76 So he began with their sacks,
before the sack of his brother;
then he pulled it out of his brother's sack;°
thus We contrived for Joseph;°
that he would not have taken his brother
into the judgment of the king
unless God will it;°
We exalt in degree whomever We will;°
and above all *are* those endowed with knowledge,
is One Who is Knowing.

12:77 They said: If he had stolen,
truly a brother of his had stolen before.°
But Joseph kept it secret within himself,
not showing it to them;°
he said: You are in a worse station;°
and God has knowledge of what you describe.

12:78 They said: O great one!
Truly he has a very old father
so take one of us in his place;
truly we consider **you**
of the ones who are doers of good.

12:79 He said: God be my refuge that we should take
except him with whom we found our sustenance;
truly we then *would be of* the ones who are unjust.

Sec. 10   *

12:80 So when they became hopeless for him,
they conferred privately;°
the eldest of them said:
Know you not that your father
indeed took a pledge from you by God,
and before that, you had neglected your duty
with Joseph;°
so I shall never quit this region
until my father gives me permission
or God gives judgment in my case;°
and He is the Best of one who judges.

279

Return to your father
and say: O our father!
Truly **your** son has stolen,
and we bear witness not but to what we knew,
so we would not be
ones who guard the unseen.
Ask the town where we have been
and the caravan in which we came forward;
indeed we *are* ones who are sincere.
He said: You have been enticed
by your own selves into an affair;°
so patience is sweet;°
perhaps God shall bring me them altogether;°
truly He, He *is* The Knowing, The Wise.
He turned away from them and said:
O my bitterness for Joseph!
His eyes whitened because of the sorrow
that was choking him.
They said: By God!
You shall never discontinue remembering Joseph
until **you** ruin **your** health
and become one who is perishing.
He said: I make not complaint of my anguish
and sorrow but to God,
and I know from God what you know not.
O my sons! Go off and search for Joseph
and his brother.
Give not up hope of the solace of God;°
truly no one gives up hope
of the solace of God,
but the ungrateful folk.
Then when they entered to him,
they said: O great one!
An injurious *time* has afflicted our family;
We have drawn near merchandise of scant worth,
so live up to the full measure
and be charitable to us;°
truly God gives recompense to
one who gives in charity.

12:81

12:82

12:83

12:84

12:85

12:86

12:87

12:88

| 12:89 | He said: |

Know you what you accomplished with Joseph
and his brother
when you *were* the ones who were ignorant?

| 12:90 | They said: Are **you** truly Joseph? |

He said: I *am* Joseph and this *is* my brother;°
indeed God has shown us grace;°
truly He Who is Godfearing
and endures patiently,
then surely God shall not waste
the compensation of the ones who are doers of good.

| 12:91 | They said: By God! |

Indeed God has held **you** in greater favor
above us,
and truly we have been
ones who were inequitable.

| 12:92 | He said: No blame on you this day!° |

May God forgive you;°
and He *is* One Who is Most Merciful
of the ones who are most merciful.

| 12:93 | Go you with this, my long shirt, |

and cast it over the face of my father;
he shall become seeing,
and bring me your people one and all.

| Sec. 11 | * |

| 12:94 | When they set forth with the caravan, |

their father said:
Truly I find the scent of Joseph;°
if I *am* not of weak mind.

| 12:95 | They said: By God! Truly **you** *are* |

long possessed by **your** wandering astray.

| 12:96 | Then when the bearer of good tidings drew near, |

he cast it over his face
and he went back, seeing;°
he said: I had said to you
truly I know from God what you know not;

| 12:97 | they said: O our father! |

Ask forgiveness for us for our impieties;
truly we have been ones who are inequitable.

I shall ask forgiveness for you with my Lord;°
truly He, He *is*
The Forgiving, The Compassionate.

Then when they entered to Joseph;   12:99
he gave refuge to his parents
and said: Enter Egypt,
had God willed, as ones who are in safety!

He exalted his parents to the throne,   12:100
and they fell down before him
as ones who prostrate themselves;°
and he said: O my father!
This is the interpretation
of my dream from before;
my Lord has made it The Truth;°
indeed He did good to me
when He brought me out of the prison,
and drew you near out of the desert,
after Satan had sown enmity
between me and between my brothers;°
truly my Lord *is* subtle
in bringing about what He will;°
truly He *is* The Knowing, The Wise.

My Lord!   12:101
Indeed **You** have given me of the dominion
and taught me of the interpretation of events;°
the One Who is Originator
of the heavens and the earth,
You are my protector in the present
and in the world to come;°
and **You** shall call me to **Yourself**
as one who submits,
and causes me to join
with the ones who are in accord with morality.

That *is* of the tidings of the unseen   12:102
that We reveal to **you**;°
you were not with them
when they agreed to their affair,
and they were planning.

12:103	Most of humanity *are* not ones who believe, even though **you** be eager.
12:104	**You** ask them not for any compensation.° It *is* not but a reminder to the worlds.
Sec. 12	*
12:105	How many Signs of the heavens and the earth they pass by while they are ones who turn aside from them!
12:106	Most of them believe not in God, but they *be* ones who are polytheists.
12:107	Are they safe from the approach on them of a blanket punishment from God or the approach on them of the Hour suddenly while they are not aware?
12:108	Say: This is my way; with clear evidence I call to God;° I and whoever follows me;° glory be to God! I *am* not of the ones who are polytheists.
12:109	We sent not before **you** except men to whom We revealed— from among the people of the towns;° have they not journeyed on the earth and looked upon what was the Ultimate End of those who *were* before them?° Truly the abode of the world to come is better for those who are Godfearing; *shall* you not, then be reasonable?
12:110	When the Messengers became hopeless and thought that they had been lied against, then Our help drew near, so We delivered whomever We will;° and Our Might shall not be repelled from the sinful folk.
12:111	Indeed there was in their narratives a lesson for those who *have* intuition;° it was not a discourse that was devised, but established as true what *had come* before

and decisively explains everything,
and a guidance and a mercy
for a folk who believe.

CHAPTER 13
THUNDER (*al-Ra^cd*)

In the Name of God,
The Merciful, The Compassionate
Alif Lām Mīm Rā;°
these *are* the Signs of the Book;°
and what has been sent forth
to **you** from **your** Lord *is* The Truth,
but most of humanity believes not.
It *is* He Who exalted the heavens
without any pillars so that you see them;°
then He turned his attention to above the Throne;°
and He caused the sun and the moon
to become subservient
each running for a determined term.
He managed the command;
He explains distinctly the Signs,
so that perhaps you would be certain
of the meeting with your Lord.
It is He Who stretched out the earth
and made in it mountains and rivers;°
and with every kind of fruit
He made in it two mates;°
He covers the night with the day;°
truly in that *are* Signs
for a folk who reflect.
In the earth *there are* neighboring strips,
and gardens of grapevines and plowed lands,
and date palm trees coming from the same root
and not coming from the same root
that are watered with one water,
and We have some preferred some over others
in produce;°
truly in these things there are Signs

for a folk who are reasonable.

13:5
If **you** marvel,
then wonder at their saying:
What! When we are earthy dust,
shall we indeed *be* in a new creation?°
Those who are ungrateful to their Lord,°
those shall have yokes around their necks;°
those *are* the Companions of the Fire;°
they, ones who shall dwell in it forever.

13:6
They bid **you**, being impatient for evil deeds
before the good, although punishments that are
exemplary have passed away before them;°
but truly **your** Lord *is*
The Possessor of Forgiveness for humanity
in spite of their injustice;°
and truly **your** Lord
is Severe in repayment.

13:7
Those who are ungrateful say:
Why has a Sign not been sent forth to him
from his Lord?°
You are not but one who warns,°
and one who is a guide to every folk.

*

13:8
God knows what every female carries
and how much her womb absorbs
and what they add;°
and everything with Him is in proportion.

13:9
He is One Who Has Knowledge of the unseen
and the visible
The Great, One Who is Most High.

13:10
It is the same to you,
the one who keeps secret *his* saying
or the one who publishes them,
or the one, he who conceals himself by nighttime
and goes about carelessly in the daytime.

13:11
For him *there are* the ones who postpone
before him and behind him.
They keep him safe by the command of God;°
truly God alters not a folk

285

unless they alter what is within themselves;
and when God has wanted evil for a folk,
there is no averting it;°
and *there is* none for them
other than He
as a safeguarder.
It is He Who causes you to see the lightning   13:12
in fear and in hope;
and *it is* He Who causes the clouds to grow heavy.
Thunder glorifies His praise,   13:13
and the angels
because of their awe of Him;
He sends thunderbolts,
and He lights on whom He will;
yet they dispute about God,
and He *is* a Severe Force.
For Him *is* the call of The Truth;°   13:14
and those who call to other than Him,
they respond not to them in anything,
like the one who expands the palms of his hands
towards water
so that it should reach his mouth,
but it *is not* that which is carried through;°
and the supplications of the ones who are ungrateful
are nothing but wandering astray.
To God prostrates   13:15
whoever is in the heavens and the earth,
willingly or unwillingly,
and their shade
in the first part of the day and at eventide.‡
Say: Who *is* the Lord   13:16
of the heavens and the earth?
Say: God!
Say: Have you taken other than Him
to yourself as protectors?
They *have* no control over themselves,
neither hurting nor profiting;°
say: Are the *unwilling* to see on the same level
as the *willing to* see?

Are the shadows and the light on the same level?°
Ascribe they associates *with God*
who created as He created
so that creation is alike to them?
Say: God *is* the Creator of everything,
and He *is* The One, The Omniscient.

He sends forth water from heaven,
and it flows into valleys
according to their measure;
but the flood bears away the swelling froth;°
and from what they kindle in a fire
looking for ornaments or sustenance,
a froth the like of it;°
thus God compares truth and falsehood;°
then as for the froth, it goes as swelling scum,°
while what profits humanity
abides in the earth;°
thus God propounds parables.

13:18 For those who respond to their Lord
there is the fairest;°
and for those who respond not to Him,
if they had all that is in and on the earth
and its like with it,
they would offer it as ransom;°
those, for them
shall be a dire reckoning
and their place of shelter *shall be* hell;°
how miserable a cradling!

Sec. 3 *

13:19 What! Is he who knows
what has been sent forth to **you**
from **your** Lord *to be* The Truth
like he who is *unwilling* to see?°
Those who *have* intuition not but recollect:

13:20 Those who live up to their compact with God
and break not their solemn promise;

13:21 those who reach out
to what God has commanded to be joined
and dread their Lord;

287

they fear the dire reckoning;
those who endured patiently, 13:22
looking for the countenance of their Lord,
who performed the formal prayers
and spent out of what We have provided them
in secret and in public,
they drive off the evil deed with benevolence.
Those, for them *is* the Ultimate Abode:
Gardens of Eden 13:23
which they shall enter,
and those who were righteous
from among their fathers,
their spouses and their offspring;°
and angels shall enter to them
from every door:
Peace be to you for what you patiently endured;° 13:24
how excellent is the Ultimate Abode!
But those who break the compact of God 13:25
after its solemn promise
and sever
what God has commanded to be joined,
and make corruption in and on the earth ·
those, for them *is* the curse
and for them *is* the Dire Abode;
God extends the provision 13:26
for whom He will
and measures *it;*°
they are glad in this present life,
and *there is* nothing in this present life
like the world to come,
except *brief* enjoyment.

* Sec. 4

Those who are ungrateful say: 13:27
Why was a Sign not sent forth to him
from his Lord?°
Say: Truly God causes to go astray whom He will
and guides to Himself
those who were penitent,
those who have believed 13:28

and whose hearts are at rest
in the remembrance of God;°
no doubt truly in the remembrance of God
hearts are at rest.

13:29 Those who have believed
and the ones who have acted in accord with morality,
there is joy for them
and a goodness of destination.

13:30 Thus We have sent **you** to a community;
indeed other communities have passed away
before it
so that **you** may recount to them
what We have revealed to **you**;
and they are ungrateful to The Merciful;°
say: He *is* my Lord
there is no god but He;
in Him I have put my trust
and to Him I *am* turning in repentance.

13:31 If only there were a Recitation
that would set mountains in motion with it,
or the earth would be cut off with it,
or the dead would be spoken to—°
actually the command of everything *is* with God!
Have not those who have believed
had knowledge that
if God will
He would have guided all of humanity?°
Those who are ungrateful shall continue *to be* lit
on with disaster because of what they crafted,
or it shall alight close to their abode
until the solemn declaration of God approaches;°
truly God breaks not His word.

Sec. 5 *

13:32 Indeed Messengers were ridiculed
before **you**,
but I granted indulgence
to those who were ungrateful;
then I took them;°
and how was My repayment!

What! *Is* He then One Who Sustains every soul
in spite of what it earns?
Yet they ascribe associates with God!°
Say: Name them!°
Or shall you tell Him of what He knows not
in the earth
or of what is manifest in the saying?
Rather
their planning was made to appear pleasing
to those who were ungrateful
and they have been barred from the way;°
whomever God causes to go astray
has no one to guide him.

For them *is* a punishment in this present life°
and surely the punishment in the world to come
shall be one that presses hard;°
and they *have* not against God
anyone who is a defender.

A parable of the Garden
that has been promised
to the ones who are Godfearing:°
Beneath it rivers run;°
its produce *is* one that is continuous
as *is* its shade.
That *is the* Ultimate *End*
of those who are Godfearing;°
and the Ultimate *End* of the ones who are ungrateful
is the fire.

Those to whom We have given the Book
are glad at what has been sent forth to **you**;°
among the confederates
are those who reject some of it;°
say: I am not but commanded to worship God,
and not to make partners with Him;°
to Him I call,
and to Him is my destination.

Thus We have sent forth
an Arabic determination;°
were **you** to follow their desires

after what has drawn near to **you**
of the knowledge,
you would *have* against God
neither protector, nor one who is a defender.

*

13:38 Indeed We sent Messengers before **you**,
and We assigned for them spouses
and offspring;°
and it was not for a Messenger to bring a Sign,
but with the permission of God;°
there is a Book for each and every term.

13:39 God blots out what He will
and brings to a stand still *what He will;*°
and with Him is the essence of the Book.

13:40 Whether We cause **you** to see some of what
We have promised them
or call **you** to Ourself,
your duty is to deliver the message,
and on Us is the reckoning.

13:41 Have they not considered that We approach the earth,
reducing it from its outlying parts?°
God gives judgment;
there is no one who postpones His determination;°
and He *is* Swift in reckoning.

13:42 Truly those who *were* before them planned,
so to God *is* the plan altogether;°
He knows what every person earns;°
and the ones who are ungrateful shall know
for whom shall be the Ultimate Abode.

13:43 Those who are ungrateful say:
You are not one who is sent;°
say: God suffices as a witness
between me and you,
and whoever has knowledge of the Book.

CHAPTER 14
ABRAHAM (*Ibrāhīm*)

In the Name of God,
The Merciful, The Compassionate   Sec. 1
Alif Lām Rā;°   14:1
a Book We have sent forth to **you**
so that **you** may bring humanity
out from the shadows into the light
with the permission of their Lord
to the path of The Almighty, The Worthy of Praise.
God! To Him *belongs* all that *is* in the heavens   14:2
and all that *is* in and on the earth,°
and woe to the ones who are ungrateful;
for them the severe punishment.
Those who embrace this present life   14:3
instead of the world to come,
and bar from the way of God,
and desire in it crookedness,
those *are* wandering far astray.
We sent not any Messenger   14:4
but with the tongue of his folk
in order that he make *it* manifest for them;°
then God causes to go astray whom He will
and guides whom He will
and He *is* The Almighty, The Wise.
Indeed We had sent Moses   14:5
with Our Signs:
Bring out **your** folk
from the shadows into the light
and remind them of the Days of God;°
truly in them *are* Signs
for every enduring, grateful *one.*
When Moses said to his folk: 14:6
Remember the divine blessing of God for you
when He rescued you from the people of Pharaoh
who were causing an affliction to befall you
—a dire punishment—
and were slaughtering your sons

and saving alive your women;
and in it *was*
a serious trial from your Lord.

*

14:7   When your Lord caused to be proclaimed:
If you are thankful,
I shall increase *blessings,*
but if you *are* not thankful
truly My punishment *shall be* hard indeed.

14:8   Moses said:
Even if you are ungrateful,
you and all that *is* in and on the earth altogether,
yet truly God *is* Sufficient, Worthy of Praise.

14:9   Have not the tidings approached you
of those before you:
The folk of Noah, Ad and Thamud,
^and those after them^
none knows them but God;
their Messengers drew near them
with clear portents
but they ignored them;
they shoved their hands into their mouths
and said: Truly
we are ungrateful for what you have been sent
and we are in uncertainty
as to the suspicious *message* to which you call us.

14:10   Their Messengers said:
Is there any uncertainty about God,
the Originator of the heavens and the earth?°
He calls you so that He may forgive you
of your impieties
and postpone for you a determined term;
they said: You are not but mortal like us;
you want to bar us
from what our fathers used to worship;
then bring us a clear authority.

14:11   Their Messengers said to them:
We are not but mortals like you;
but God shows His grace

on whom He will of His servants;°
and it is not for us that we bring you an authority,
except by the permission of God;
and let the ones who believe put their trust in God.
Why should we not put our trust in God   14:12
while indeed He has guided us to our ways?°
We shall endure patiently
whatever torment you inflict upon us;°
in God let the ones who trust put their trust.

*

Sec. 3

Those who were ungrateful said   14:13
to their Messengers:
Surely we shall drive you out of our region
unless you revert to our creed;°
so their Lord revealed to them:
Surely We shall cause to perish
the ones who are unjust.
Surely We shall cause you to dwell in the region   14:14
after them;°
this *is* for
whoever fears My station
and fears My threat.°
They sought judgment   14:15
and every haughty, stubborn *one was* frustrated;
and with hell beyond him,   14:16
he shall be given watery pus to drink;
he shall gulp it,   14:17
and he shall have scarcely swallowed it
when death shall approach him from every place,
yet he shall not die,
and beyond him, a harsh punishment.
A parable of those who were ungrateful   14:18
for their Lord:°
Their actions *are* as ashes
over which the wind blows strongly
on a stormy day;°
they shall *have* no power
over what they have earned;°
that *is* the far away, wandering astray.

14:19   Have **you** not considered that
God has created the heavens and the earth in Truth?°
If He will, He shall cause you to be put away
and bring a new creation.

14:20   That *is* not a problem for God.

14:21   They shall all depart to God—
then the weak would say
to those who had grown arrogant:
Truly we were followers of yours;
have you ones who avail us
against the punishment of God at all?°
They would say: If God had guided us,
we would have guided you;°
it is equal to us whether we are patientless
or endure patiently;
there is no asylum for us.

*

Sec. 4

14:22   Satan would say
when the command has been decided:
Truly God has promised you a true promise;
I promised you, but I broke it;°
and I had no authority over you,
except that I called to you
and you responded to me;°
so blame me not, but blame yourselves;°
I *am* not one who assists you,
nor *are* you one who assists me;
truly I am ungrateful
for your ascribing me as partner to *God* before,°
truly the ones who are unjust,
for them *is* a painful punishment.

14:23   Those *shall be* caused to enter
who have believed,
and the ones who have acted in accord with morality
into Gardens beneath which rivers run,
They, ones who shall dwell in it forever
with the permission of their Lord;
and their greeting in it shall be: Peace!

14:24   Have **you** not considered

how God has propounded a parable?
A good word *is* like a good tree;
its roots *are* ones that are firm
and its branches *are* in heaven
giving its produce at all times,   **14:25**
with the permission of its Lord,°
and God propounds parables for humanity
so that perhaps they shall recollect.
The parable of a bad word   **14:26**
is that of a bad tree,
to be uprooted from the earth;
it has no stability.
God makes firm those who have believed   **14:27**
with the firm saying
in this present life
and in the world to come;°
and God shall cause to go astray
the ones who are unjust;°
and God accomplishes what He will.
*   **Sec. 5**

Have **you** not considered that   **14:28**
there are those who have substituted
ingratitude for the divine blessing of God,
and caused their folk to live
in abodes of nothingness?
They shall roast in hell;°   **14:29**
how miserable a stopping place!
They made rivals with God,   **14:30**
causing others to go astray from His way,°
say: Take joy,
but truly your homecoming is the fire!
Say to My servants who have believed   **14:31**
that they should perform the formal prayers
and spend
from what We have provided them
secretly and in public
before a Day approaches
when *there is* neither trading nor befriending.
God *is* He Who has created   **14:32**

the heavens and the earth
and sent forth water from heaven
and brought out thereby fruit
as provision for you;°
and causes boats to become subservient to you
that they may run through the sea
by His command;°
and He causes rivers to become subservient to you.

14:33 He caused the sun to be subservient to you
and the moon,
both constant in their work;°
He caused the night to be subservient to you
and the day.

14:34 He gave you all that you asked of Him;
and if you *were* to number
the divine blessing*s* of God,
you would not count them,°
truly the human being *is* wrongdoing and an ingrate.

Sec. 6 *

14:35 When Abraham said:
O my Lord! Make this land one that is safe
and cause me and my children to turn away
from worshipping idols.

14:36 O my Lord! Truly they caused many to go astray
among humanity;°
so whoever heeds me truly he is of me;°
and whoever rebels against me,
then **You** *are* truly
Forgiving, Compassionate.

14:37 O our Lord! Truly I have lodged
some of my offspring
in an unsown valley
by **Your** Sacred House,
O our Lord,
that they may perform the formal prayers;
so make the minds among humanity
yearn for them
and provide **You** them with fruits,
so that perhaps they shall *be* thankful.

Our Lord! Truly **You** know
what we conceal and what we speak openly,°
and nothing is hidden from **You**
in or on the earth or in heaven.

The Praise *belongs* to God
Who has bestowed on me in my old age
Ishmael and Isaac;°
and truly my Lord *is* indeed
hearing of all supplication.

O my Lord!
Make me one who performs the formal prayer
and from my offspring also;°
our Lord! Admit my supplication.

Our Lord!
Forgive me and the ones who are my parents,
and the ones who believe,
on the Day the reckoning arises.

*

Assume not that
God is One Who is Heedless
of what the ones who are unjust do;°
He not but postpones
to a Day when their eyes shall be glazed,

ones who run forward with eyes fixed in horror,
ones whose heads are erect,
not glancing back;°
and their minds void.

Warn humanity of a Day
the punishment shall approach to them;
so those who did wrong shall say:
Our Lord! Postpone for us awhile
so that we may answer **Your** call
and follow the Messengers,°
had you not sworn before
that *there would be* no end for you?

You inhabited the dwellings
of those who did wrong to themselves
and it became clear to you
what We accomplished against them

and We propounded for you parables.

14:46 Indeed they planned their plan
and their plan *was* with God
even if their plan displace mountains.

14:47 So assume not that God
shall be one who breaks His word
to His Messengers;
truly God *is* Almighty, Possessor of Requital.

14:48 On a day
when the earth shall be substituted
for other than this earth,
and the heavens, too;°
they shall depart to The One, The Omniscient God.°

14:49 **You** shall consider that Day the ones who sin,
the ones who are bound in chains.

14:50 Their tunics *are* made of pitch
and fire shall overcome their faces,

14:51 so that God may give recompense
to each soul for what it has earned;°
truly God *is* Swift in reckoning.

14:52 This *is* the delivering of the message to humanity
so that they may be warned thereby
and know that He *is* One God
so that those who *have* intuition may recollect.

CHAPTER 15
THE ROCKY TRACT (*al-Ḥijr*)

In the Name of God,
Sec. 1 The Merciful, The Compassionate
15:1 *Alif Lām Rā;*° these *are* the Signs of the Book
and of a clear Quran.
Part 14 ***

15:2 It may be that those who are ungrateful
would wish that they had been ones who submit.

15:3 Forsake them to eat and let them take joy
and be diverted with hopefulness;°
then they shall know.

15:4 We caused not a town to perish,

but *there was* for it a known prescription.
No community precedes its term,
nor delays it.
They say: O **you**
to whom was sent down the Reminder,
truly **you** *are* one who is possessed.
Why bring **you** not to us angels
if **you** are the ones who are sincere?
We send not angels down
but with The Truth,
and then they shall not be the ones who are respited.
Truly We, We have sent down the Reminder
and truly We are ones who guard it.
Indeed We sent *Messengers* before **you**
to partisans of the ancients.
Approached them not any Messenger
but they used to ridicule him.
Thus We thrust it
to the hearts of the ones who sin.
They believe not in it although
the customs of the ancient ones had passed away.°
Even if We opened a door for them
from heaven
and they were to continue going up thereto,
they would say: Truly our sight is dazzled;
rather we are a bewitched folk.

*   Sec. 2

Indeed We have made
constellations in the heavens,
and We made them appear pleasing
to the ones who look.
We have kept them safe
from every accursed satan,
except him who sought to eavesdrop,
and he was pursued by a clear flame.
We stretched out the earth,
and cast in it firm mountains,
and caused to develop in it
of each well-balanced thing.

15:20	We made for you in it a livelihood,
	and for those for whom you provide not.
15:21	*There is* not a thing
	but its treasuries *are* with Us;
	and We send down not
	but in a known measure.
15:22	We send fertilizing winds,
	then send forth water from heaven,
	satiating you,
	and you *are* not ones who are treasurers.
15:23	Truly it is
	We Who give life and cause to die,
	and We *are* the ones who inherit.
15:24	Indeed We know
	the ones of you who came first
	and indeed We know the ones who come later.
15:25	Truly **your** Lord *is* He Who assembles;°
	truly He *is* Wise, Knowing.
Sec. 3	*
15:26	Indeed We created mankind
	from molded clay.
15:27	We created the spirits before,
	from the fire of a pestilential wind.
15:28	When **your** Lord said to the angels:
	Truly I *am* Creator of mortals
	from molded clay,
15:29	so when I have shaped him
	and have breathed into him of My Spirit,
	fall down before him
	among the ones who prostrate themselves.
15:30	The angels prostrated themselves,
	all of them together,
15:31	except Iblis.
	He refused to be
	of the ones who prostrated themselves.
15:32	He said: O Iblis!
	What *is* with **you** that **you** are not
	one who prostrates himself?
15:33	He said: I shall not prostrate myself before a mortal

whom **You** have created
from molded clay.
God said: Go **you** forth from here, 15:34
for truly **you** *are* accursed!
Truly a curse *shall be* upon **you** 15:35
until the Day of Judgment.
He said: O my Lord! 15:36
Give me respite until the Day they *are* raised up
he said: Then truly **you** *are* 15:37
one who is given respite
until the Day of the known time. 15:38
He said: O my Lord! 15:39
Because **You** have led me into error,
I shall indeed make the earth appear pleasing
to them and I shall lead them all into error,
except **Your** devoted servants among them. 15:40
He said: 15:41
This *is* the straight path to Me.
Truly as for My servants 15:42
you shall *have* no authority over them,
except those who in error follow **you**.
Truly hell has been promised to them all. 15:43
It has seven doors 15:44
and for each door *is* set apart.
* Sec. 4

Truly the ones who are Godfearing 15:45
shall be amidst Gardens and springs.
Enter them in peace as ones who are in security! 15:46
We shall tear out 15:47
any grudges from their breasts
as brothers on couches,
one facing the other.
In it neither fatigue shall afflict them, 15:48
nor *shall* they *be* ones who are driven out.
Tell My servants 15:49
that I *am* The Forgiving, The Compassionate
and that My punishment is a painful punishment. 15:50
Tell them of the guests of Abraham, 15:51
when they entered upon him 15:52

and said: Peace!
He said: Truly we *are* afraid of you.

15:53   They said: Take no notice;
truly we give **you** good tidings of a knowing boy.
He said: You give me good tidings

15:54   even though old age has afflicted me?
So of what, then give you good tidings?

15:55   They said: We give **you** good tidings of Truth,
so be **you** not of the ones who despair.

15:56   He said: Who despairs of the mercy of his Lord
except the ones who go astray?

15:57   He said: Then what is your business,
O ones who have been sent?

15:58   They said: We have been sent to the sinning folk,

15:59   except the family of Lot.
Truly we *are* ones who shall deliver all of them,

15:60   except his wife.

•   We have ordained
that she *is* of the ones who stay behind.

Sec. 5   *

15:61   Then when the ones who were sent
drew near to the people of Lot,

15:62   he said: Truly you are an immoral folk.

15:63   They said: Rather we have drawn near to **you**
with what they were contesting.

15:64   We approach **you** with The Truth,
and truly we are ones who are sincere.

15:65   Then in a part of the night set **you** forth
with **your** family;
follow **you** their backs;
and look not back any of you,
but pass on to where you are commanded.

15:66   We decreed the command to him:
The last remnant of those
would be cut off,
happening in the morning.

15:67   The people of the city drew near
and rejoiced at the good tidings.

15:68   He said: Truly these *are* my guests,

so put me not to shame.

Be Godfearing of God;   15:69

and cover me not with shame.

They said: Prohibited we not **you**   15:70

from some beings?

He said: These are my daughters   15:71

if you *must be* ones who do *something*.

By **your** life truly they *were* dazed,   15:72

wandering *unwilling* to see.

So the Cry took them at sunrise.   15:73

We made its high its low,   15:74

and We rained down on them

rocks of baked clay.

Truly in this *are* Signs for ones who read marks.   15:75

Truly they *were* on an abiding way.   15:76

Truly in it indeed *is* a Sign   15:77

for the ones who believe.

Truly the Companions of the Woods   15:78

were the ones who were unjust.

So We requited them   15:79

and they *were* both on a clear high road.

*   Sec. 6

Truly the Companions of the Rocky Tract denied   15:80

the ones who were sent.

We gave them Our Signs,   15:81

but they were ones who turned aside from them.

They used to carve   15:82

secure houses from mountains,

but the Cry took them,   15:83

happening in the morning,

and what they used to earn availed them not.   15:84

We created not the heavens and the earth,   15:85

and all that is in between them,

except with The Truth,°

and truly the Hour is one that arrives;°

so overlook with a sweet overlooking.

Truly **your** Lord *is* The Knowing Creator.   15:86

Indeed We have given you   15:87

the seven often repeated parts

of the sublime Quran.

15:88 Stretch not **your** eyes
at what We have given of pairs
to them to enjoy, nor feel remorse for them,
and make low **your** wing
to the ones who believe,

15:89 and say: Truly I *am* a clear warner.

15:90 Even as We have sent forth
the ones who are partitioners,

15:91 those who have made the Quran into fragments,

15:92 so by **your** Lord,
We shall certainly ask them one and all

15:93 about what they were doing.

15:94 So call aloud what **you** are commanded;
turn **you** aside from the ones who are polytheists.

15:95 Truly We shall suffice **you** against
the ones who ridicule;

15:96 those who made with God
another god.°
But soon they shall know.

15:97 Indeed We know that
your breast became narrowed
because of what they say.

15:98 So glorify the praises of **your** Lord,
and be of the ones who prostrate themselves,

15:99 and worship **your** Lord,
until the certainty approaches **you**.

CHAPTER 16
THE BEE (*al-Naḥl*)

In the Name of God,
Sec. 1 the Merciful, the Compassionate

16:1 The command of God is approaching;
be not impatient for it.°
Glory be to Him and exalted *is He*
above all the partners they make with Him.

16:2 He sends down the angels
with the Spirit of His command

to whom He will of His servants
to warn that: There is no god but I,
so be Godfearing of Me.
He has created the heavens and the earth   16:3
with The Truth.°
He is to be exalted above
all partners they make with Him.
He created mankind from a seminal fluid;   16:4
behold! He is a clear adversary.
He has created the flocks,°   16:5
in which *there are* warmth and many uses,
and of them you eat;
in them *is* a beauty for you   16:6
when you give them rest;
and when you drive flocks forth to pasture,
they carry your load to a land,   16:7
one you would not reach except
under adverse circumstances to yourselves.°
Truly your Lord *is* indeed Gentle, Compassionate.
Horses, mules and donkeys,   16:8
for you to ride
and as an adornment;°
and He creates what you know not.
With God *is* the showing of the way,   16:9
but some of them *are* ones who swerve.°
If He had willed, He would have guided you all.
                    *   Sec. 2
He *it is* Who sends forth water from heaven;°   16:10
for you to drink;
and from it, trees
wherein you pasture *herds.*
He causes crops to develop for you,   16:11
and the olives, the date palm, the grapevines,
and from them every kind of fruit,°
truly in that *is* a Sign for a folk who reflect.
He causes to become subservient   16:12
the night, the day, the sun and the moon;°
and the stars *are* subservient to His command;°
surely in that *are* Signs for a folk,

ones who are reasonable.

16:13 Whatever He made numerous for you
in and on the earth,
of variant hues,°
in that *is* a Sign for a folk who recollect.

16:14 He *it is* Who
has caused the sea to become subservient to you
so that you eat from it succulent meat
and pull out of it ornaments to wear;
and you see the ships,
ones that plow through the waves
that **you** may be looking for His grace,
and so that perhaps you would be thankful.

16:15 He cast on to the earth mountains
so that it should not vibrate with you,
and rivers and roads,
so that perhaps you would be truly guided

16:16 and landmarks.°
They *are* truly guided by the stars;

16:17 *is* then He Who creates as one who creates not?°
Shall you not then recollect?

16:18 If you *try to* count the divine blessing of God,
you shall not *be able* to count it,°
truly God *is* Forgiving, Compassionate.

16:19 God knows what you keep secret
and what you speak openly.

16:20 Those whom you call to other than
God,
they create not anything
and they are *themselves* created.

16:21 *They are* lifeless, not living;°
and they are not aware of
when you shall be raised up.

Sec. 3 *

16:22 Your God *is* One God.°
But for those who believe not
in the world to come,
their hearts *are* ones that know not
and they *are* ones who grow arrogant.

307

Without a doubt, God knows what they keep secret,   16:23
and what they speak openly.°
Truly He loves not ones who grow in arrogance.
When it is said to them: 16:24
What is that your Lord sent forth?   •
They say: Fables of the ancient ones!
They shall carry their own heavy loads   16:25
completely on the Day of Resurrection,
and of the heavy loads of those
whom they caused to go astray
without knowledge,°
how evil *is* what they shall bear!
*   Sec. 4

Indeed those who were before them planned,   16:26
then God approached their structures
from the foundations,
and the roof fell down upon them from above,
and the punishment approached them
from where they were not aware.
Then on the Day of Resurrection,   16:27
He shall cover them with shame
and say:
Where *are* those you used to associate with Me
for whom you were to make a breach?
Those who have been given knowledge shall say:
Truly degradation *this* day and evil
upon the ones who are ungrateful,
those whom the angels called to themselves   16:28
while they *were* ones unjust to themselves;°
then they shall give a proposal of surrender:
We used not to do any evil.°
Yea truly! God is Knowing
of what you were doing.
So enter the doors of hell—   16:29
ones who shall dwell in it forever!
Indeed how miserable a place of lodging
it is for the ones who increase in pride!
When it is said to those who are Godfearing: 16:30
What *is it that* your Lord has sent forth?

They shall say: Good!°
For those who do good in this present life,
there is good.°
The abode of the world to come *is* better;
and how excellent is the abode
of the ones who are Godfearing!

16:31   Gardens of Eden which they shall enter
beneath which rivers run;°
they shall *have* in them all that they will.°
Thus God gives recompense
to the ones who are Godfearing.

16:32   Those whom the angels call to themselves
while *they are* the ones who are good,
they say *to them*: Peace!
Enter the Garden because of what you were doing.

16:33   Look they not upon *anything*
but that the angels should approach them
or the command of **your** Lord?°
So accomplished those before them;°
and God did not wrong them,
but they used to do wrong to themselves.

16:34   Then their evil deeds lit on them
for what their hands had done
and they were surrounded
by what they used to ridicule.

Sec. 5   *

16:35   Those who made partners with God said:
Had God willed
neither would we have worshiped
anything but He,
neither we nor our fathers;
nor would we have forbidden
anything other than Him;°
thus accomplished those who *were* before them;°
then *what is* with the Messengers
but the clear delivery of the message?

16:36   Indeed We have raised up in every community
a Messenger:
Worship God

and avoid false deities;°
then of them *were* some whom God guided
and of them *were* some upon whom
their misjudgment was realized;°
so journey through the earth
and look upon what was the Ultimate End
of the ones who denied.
If **you** are eager for them to be guided,   16:37
then truly God shall not guide
those who caused *others* to go astray;°
and they shall *have* none who helps.
They swore by God   16:38
their most earnest oaths: ·
God shall not raise up him who dies;
rather *it is* a promised obligation upon Him,
but most of humanity knows not.
In order to make manifest for them   16:39
about what they were at variance,
and so that those who are ungrateful may know
that they were ones who deny.
Our saying to a thing when We wanted it *is*   16:40
not but that We say to it: Be! And it is!
*
                Sec. 6

As for those who emigrated in the way of God   16:41
after they had been wronged,
We shall certainly *have* a place of settlement
with benevolence in the present for them;°
and indeed the compensation
of the world to come would be greater;°
if they had known—
those who endure patiently,   16:42
and they put their trust in their Lord.
We sent not before **you**   16:43
except men to whom We revealed:°
Ask the People of Remembrance
—if you know not—
with the clear portents and the Psalms;°   16:44
and We have sent forth the Reminder to **you**
that **you** might make manifest to humanity

what was sent down to them
and so that perhaps they shall reflect.

16:45 Are those who planned evil deeds safe
that God shall not cause the earth to swallow them,
or that the punishment shall *not* approach them
from where they are not aware?

16:46 Or that He may take them
in their going to and fro where
they *shall* not *be* ones who frustrate *the Will of God?*

16:47 Or that He take them, destroying them little by little?
Truly **your** Lord is Gentle, Compassionate.

16:48 Have they not considered that
whatever thing God has created
casts its shade
to the right and to the left
of the ones who prostrate to God,
and they *are* ones who are in a state of lowliness?

16:49 To God prostrates
all that *is* in the heavens
and all that *is* in and on the earth
of moving creatures and the angels,
and they grow not arrogant.

16:50 They fear their Lord above them
and accomplish what they are commanded.‡

Sec. 7 *

16:51 God said: Take not two gods to yourselves;°
truly He *is* One God;°
then *have* reverence for Me.

16:52 To Him *belongs*
all that *is* in the heavens and the earth
and His *is* the way of life—that is forever.°
Shall you then be Godfearing of other than God?

16:53 Whatever you *have* of divine blessing
is from God;°
then when injury afflicts you,
you make entreaties to Him.

16:54 Then when He has removed the injury from you,
behold! A group of people of you
make partners with their Lord.

They are ungrateful for what We have given them,°   16:55
so let them take joy;°
soon they shall know.
They assign to what they know not   16:56
a share from what We have provided them;°
by God! You shall certainly be asked
about what you used to devise.
They assign daughters to God!   16:57
Glory be to Him!   •
To them *is* that for which they lust!
When given good tidings to any of them   16:58
of a female,
his face stays *as* one that is clouded over
and he chokes.
He secludes himself from the folk   16:59
out of distress at the good tidings
he has been given.°
Shall he hold it back with humiliation
or bury it in earthy dust?
Certainly how evil *is* the judgment they give!
For those who believe not in the world to come   16:60
there is a morally evil description
while the loftiest description *belongs* to God,
and He *is* The Almighty, The Wise.
*   Sec. 8

If God were to take humanity to task   16:61
for their injustice,
He would not leave on it a moving creature,
but He would postpone them for a determined term,
and when their term draws near,
neither shall they delay it an hour,°
nor press it forward.
They assign to God   16:62
what they dislike,
their tongues allege the lie
that the fair things shall be theirs;°
without a doubt, for them *is* the fire,
and they *shall be* made to hasten *to it*.
By God!   16:63

Indeed We have certainly sent *Messengers*
to communities before **you**;
Satan made their actions appear pleasing to them,
so he is their protector on *this* day;
and theirs *shall be* a painful punishment.

16:64 We sent not forth the Book to **you**,
except that **you** may make manifest to them
• those things in which they are at variance
and as a guidance and a mercy
for a folk who believe.

16:65 God sent forth water from heaven,
and gave life thereby to the earth after its death;°
truly in this *is* a Sign for a folk who hear.

Sec. 9 *

16:66 Truly for you in the flocks *is* a lesson;°
We satiate you from what is in their bellies,
—from between waste and blood—
what is exclusively milk,
delicious to the ones who drink.

16:67 From fruits of the date palm trees and grapevines
you take to yourself of it an intoxicant
and fair provisions,°
truly in it *is* indeed a Sign
for a folk who are reasonable.

16:68 **Your** Lord reveals to the bee:
Take to **yourself** houses from the mountains
and on the trees
and in what they construct;

16:69 then eat of all fruits,
and insert yourself
submissively in the ways of **your** Lord;°
drink goes forth from its belly
in a variance of hues
wherein *is* healing for humanity,°
truly in this *is* certainly a Sign
for a folk who reflect.

16:70 God has created you,
then He shall call you *to Himself.*°
Of you *there are* some who are returned

to the vilest of lifetimes,
so that he knows nothing
after having known something;°
truly God *is* Knowing, Powerful.

God has preferred some of you above others
in provisions.°
But those who have been preferred
are not ones who restore wealth
to what their right hands possess
so that they are equal in it.°
Why have they negated the divine blessing of God?
God has assigned to you
mates of your own kind
and has assigned you from your mates,
children and grandchildren,
and has provided you with what is good.°
How then believe they in falsehood
and are ungrateful for the divine blessing of God?
They worship other than God,
what has no power to provide for them
anything from the heavens and the earth;
nor are they able *to do so.*
So propound not parables for God.°
Truly God Knows and you know not.
God propounds a parable
of a chattel servant
who has no power over anything,
and *is* one whom We have provided from Us
a fair provision;
and he spends thereof secretly
and openly;°
are they on the same level?°
The Praise *belongs* to God;°
Yea! But most of them know not!
God propounds a parable
of two men, one of them speaks not,
he has no power over anything
and he *is* a heavy burden

to the one who protects him;
whichever way his face is turned
he brings no good;°
is he on the same level

 •   as the one who commands justice
and *is* on the straight path?

*

To God *is* the unseen
of the heavens and the earth;°
and the command of the Hour
is not but the twinkling of an eye to one's sight
or nearer;
truly God *is* Powerful over everything.

God brought you out
from the wombs of your mothers;
and you knew not anything,
and He assigned to you the ability to hear

 •   and sight and mind
so that perhaps you would be thankful.

Have you not considered the birds,
the ones who are subservient in the firmament
of the heavens?
None holds them back but God,°
truly in this *are* Signs
for a folk who believe;

God has assigned for you
your houses as places of rest
and assigned for you
the hides of flocks for houses
which you find light

 •   on the day of your departing
and the day of your halting;
and of their wool
and fur and hair
furnishings and enjoyment for a while.

God has made for you
shade out of what He created
and has made the mountains
as a refuge in the time of need,

and has made for you tunics
to protect you from the heat,
and tunics to protect you from your violence;°
thus He fulfills His divine blessing to you
so that perhaps you would submit.
Then if they turn away,   16:82
for **you** *is* not but to deliver the clear message.
They recognize the divine blessing of God,   16:83
yet they reject it;
most of them *are* the ones who are ungrateful.
                              *   Sec. 12

On the Day We shall raise up   16:84
from every community a witness,
then no permission shall be given
to those who are ungrateful,
nor shall they ask to be favored.
When those who did wrong consider   16:85
the punishment,
then it shall not be lightened to them,
nor shall they be given respite.
When those who made partners with God   16:86
consider the associates *with God,*
they shall say: Our Lord,
these are our associates whom we used to call to
other than **You**;°
but they shall cast their saying at them:
Truly you *are* the ones who lie!
They shall give a proposal to God on that day   16:87
of surrender;
what they used to devise had led them astray.
Those who were ungrateful   16:88
and barred from the way of God,
We shall increase punishment to their punishment
because they used to make corruption.
On the Day We raise up in every community   16:89
a witness against them from among themselves;°
and We shall bring **you** about as a witness
against these;°
and We have sent down the Book to **you**

as an exposition that makes everything clear,
and as a guidance and mercy
and good tidings for the the ones who submit.

Truly God commands justice and kindness
and giving to *one's* kin,
and He prohibits depravity,
immorality and insolence;°
He admonishes you
so that perhaps you would recollect.

16:91 Live up to the compact of God
when you have made a contract;
and do not break your oaths
after ratification;
indeed you have made God surety over you;°
truly God knows what you accomplish.

16:92 Be not like her who would break
what she has spun after firming its fibers
by taking your oaths in mutual deceit
among yourselves
as you are a community *that is* more numerous
than another community;°
God tries you not but by this;°
and He shall make manifest to you
on the Day of Resurrection
about what you were at variance.

16:93 Had God willed,
He would have made you all one community,
but He causes to go astray whom He will
and guides whom He will;°
and certainly you shall be asked
about what you were doing.

16:94 Take not your oaths to yourself as mutual deceit
among yourselves,
so that a foot should not backslide,
after standing firm and you experience
the evil of having barred
from the way of God;°
and for you *shall be* a serious punishment.

Exchange not the compact for a little price;°   16:95
truly what *is* with God is better for you
if you were to know.
Whatever *is* with you shall come to an end;°   16:96
and what *is* with God *is* what shall endure,°
We shall give recompense
to those who endure patiently
—their fair compensation—
for what they were doing.
One who has acted in accord with morality,   16:97
whether male or female
while *being* one who believes,
We shall give life—a good life;°
and We shall give recompense to them
—their compensation—
of the fairest for what they were doing.
So when **you** recite the Quran,   16:98
seek refuge with God
from the accursed Satan.
Truly he has no authority   16:99
over those who have believed,
and in their Lord they put their trust.
His authority is not but   16:100
over those who turn away to him
and the ones who are polytheists.
*   Sec. 14

When We substitute a Sign   16:101
in place of another Sign,
and God has greater knowledge
of what He sends down,
they say: **You** *are* not but one who devises!
But most of them know not.
Say: The hallowed Spirit has sent it down   16:102
from **your** Lord with The Truth
to make firm those who have believed
and as a guidance and good tidings
for the ones who submit.
Indeed We know that they say: 16:103
It is not but a mortal who teaches him,°

the tongue of him whom they hint at
is non-Arab;
while this *is* a clear Arabic tongue.

16:104 Truly those who believe not in the Signs of God,
God shall not guide them;
and for them *is* a painful punishment.

16:105 *It is* not but those who devise falsity,
who believe not in the Signs of God;°
and those, they *are* the the ones who lie.

16:106 Whoever is ungrateful to God
after belief—except
someone who is compelled to do it against his will
while his heart is one that is at rest in belief—
but whoever expands his breast to ingratitude,
on them *is* the anger of God,
and for them *is* a serious punishment.

16:107 That *is* because they embraced this present life
instead of the world to come
and God guides not the ungrateful folk.

16:108 Those *are* they
upon whose hearts God has set a seal
and upon their hearing and their sight;°
and they, those *are* the ones who are heedless.

16:109 Without a doubt, they shall be
the ones who are losers in the world to come.

16:110 Then truly **your** Lord, for those who emigrated
after they were persecuted
and then struggled and endured patiently,
truly **your** Lord
is Forgiving, Compassionate.

Sec. 15   *

16:111 On a Day when every soul shall approach,
disputing for itself,
and every soul shall *have* its account paid in full
for what it did,
and wrong shall not be done to them.

16:112 God propounds a parable:
A restful and safe town
its provisions approaching it

freely from every place;
then it is ungrateful for the divine blessing of God,
and so God causes it to experience
extreme hunger and fear
because of what they were crafting.
Indeed had drawn near to them   16:113
a Messenger from among themselves,
but they denied him,
so the punishment took them
while they were ones who were unjust.
So eat of what God has provided you   16:114
as lawful and what is good
and be thankful for the divine blessing of God
if it is Him that you worship.
He has not but forbidden to you carrion,   16:115
and the blood and the flesh of swine,
and what *is* hallowed for other than God;°
but if one is to be compelled
without *being* one who desires it,
nor one who is turning away,
then truly God *is* Forgiving, Compassionate.
Say not   16:116
to what your lying tongues allege:
This *is* lawful and this *is* unlawful,
so as to devise lies against God;
truly those who devise lies against God
shall not prosper.
But a little enjoyment,   16:117
and then for them *is* a painful punishment.
We have forbidden those who became Jews   16:118
what We have related to **you** before;°
and We did not wrong them,
but they used to do wrong to themselves.
Then truly **your** Lord   16:119
to those who do evil in ignorance
then repent after that and make things right,
truly **your** Lord thereafter
is Forgiving, Compassionate.
*

16:120   Truly Abraham was a community obedient to God
—a monotheist—
and he was not one of the polytheists.

16:121   He was one thankful for His divine blessings.°
He elected him
and guided him to a straight path.

16:122   We gave him in the present benevolence,
and truly he, in the world to come, *shall be*
among the ones who are in accord with morality.

16:123   Then we revealed to **you**
to follow the creed of Abraham,
—a monotheist—°
and he was not of the ones who are polytheists.

16:124   The Sabbath was made
for those who were at variance about it;°
truly **your** Lord shall give judgment between them
on the Day of Resurrection
about what they were at variance.

16:125   Call **you** to the way of **your** Lord with wisdom
and fair admonishment;°
and dispute with them in a way that *is* fairer;°
truly **your** Lord *is* He Who has greater knowledge
of who has gone astray from His way;°
and He has greater knowledge
of the ones who are truly guided.

16:126   If you chastise,
then chastise with the like
of that with which you were chastised;°
but if you endure patiently
truly it *is* better for
the ones who remain steadfast.

16:127   Have **you** patience
and **your** patience is not but from God;
and feel **you** not remorse over them,
nor take to heart what they plan.

16:128   Truly God *is* with those who are Godfearing
and those who *are* the ones who are doers of good.

Part 15   ***

CHAPTER 17

THE JOURNEY BY NIGHT (*al-Isrā᾿*)

In the Name of God,　　　　　　　　　Stage 4
The Merciful, The Compassionate　　　　Sec. 1
Glory be to Him Who　　　　　　　　　17:1
made His servant journey by night
from the Masjid al-Haram
to the Masjid al-Aqsa
around which We *have* blessed
so that We cause him to see Our Signs;
truly He, He *is* The Hearing, The Seeing.
We gave Moses the Book　　　　　　　　17:2
and made it a guidance for
the Children of Israel:
Take not to yourselves
other than Me as Trustee,
the offspring of those whom We carried　17:3
with Noah;°
truly he was a grateful servant.
We decreed for the Children of Israel　　17:4
in the Book:
Indeed you shall make corruption
in and on the earth twice,
and indeed you shall exalt yourselves
in a great self-exaltation.
So when the promise drew near　　　　　17:5
for the first of the two,
We raised up against you
servants of Ours who had severe might;
they ransacked your abodes;°
and the promise was one that was accomplished.
Then We returned to you a turn of luck over them,　17:6
and We furnished you relief
with children and wealth,
and made you more in soldiery:
If you do good,　　　　　　　　　　　17:7
you would do good for your own souls;°
and if you do evil,

it is for them;°
then when the second drew near,
they raised anger on your faces
and they entered the temple
just as they had entered it the first time
to shatter all that they had ascended to
with a shattering.

17:8 Perhaps your Lord may have mercy on you.°
But if you revert, We shall revert.•
We have made hell
a jail for the ones who are ungrateful.

17:9 Truly this Quran guides
to what is upright
and gives good tidings to the ones who believe,
ones who have acted in accord with morality,
that they *shall have* great compensation.

17:10 As for those who believe not
in the world to come,
We have made ready
a painful punishment for them.

Sec. 2 *

17:11 The human being calls for the worst
as much as he supplicates for the good;°
and the human being is hasty.

17:12 We have made the nighttime and the daytime
as two Signs;°
then We blotted out the Sign of nighttime
and We made the Sign of daytime
for one who perceives
that you may look for grace from your Lord
and that you may know the number of years
and the reckoning;°
and We have explained everything distinctly,
with a decisive explanation.

17:13 For each human being We have fastened his omen
to his neck;°
and We shall bring out for him
on the Day of Resurrection
a book in which he shall meet

what has unfolded.

Recite **your** book! Against **you** 17:14
this day **your** soul suffices as **your** reckoner.

Whoever is truly guided 17:15
is truly guided not but for his own soul;°
and whoever goes astray,
then not but goes astray against it;°
and no one bears the heavy load of another;
and We *are* never the ones who punish
until We have raised up a Messenger.

When We wanted to cause a town to perish, 17:16
then We *send* a command
to those who have been given ease,
but they disobey in it,
so the saying is to be realized against it;
then We cause it to be destroyed
with *utter* destruction.

How many generations have We caused to perish 17:17
after Noah!°

Your Lord suffices as
Knower, Seeing of the impieties of His servants.

Whoever wants what hastens away, 17:18
We quicken in it for him
what We will to whomever We want;
then We assign hell for him;
he shall roast in it,
one who is condemned,
one who is rejected;

and whoever has wanted the world to come, 17:19
and endeavors for it endeavoring
while he *is* a believer,
the endeavor of those shall be appreciated.

To each We furnish relief, these and these, 17:20
with the gift of **your** Lord;°
and this gift of **your** Lord
would not be one that is confined.

Look upon 17:21
how We preferred some of them
over others;°

and indeed the world to come *shall be* greater
in degrees and greater in excellence.

17:22 Assign not another god with God,
for then you shall be put
as one who is to be condemned,
one who is damned.

17:23 **Your** Lord has decreed
that you worship none but Him!
Kindness to the ones who are one's parents;°
if at your side one of them or both of them reach
old age
then say not to them: Fie,
nor scold them;
but say a generous saying to them.

17:24 Make low to them
the wing of the sense of humility
through mercy;
and say: O my Lord! *Have* mercy on them,
just as they reared me when I was small.

17:25 Your Lord has greater knowledge
of what is within yourselves;°
if you are the ones who are in accord with morality,
then truly He is Forgiving
to those who are penitent.

17:26 Give to kin justifiably,
and to the needy and to the traveler of the way;
but spend not extravagantly
an extravagant spending.

17:27 Truly the ones who spent extravagantly
were brothers of the satans;°
and Satan was ungrateful to his Lord.

17:28 If **you** turn aside from them,
looking for mercy from **your** Lord
for which **you** hope,
then say to them a saying softly.

17:29 Make not **your** hand be one that is restricted
to **your** neck,
and extend it not to its utmost expansion

so that you not sit as
one who is blameworthy,
one who is to be denuded.
Truly **your** Lord extends the provision 17:30
for whom He will
and He straitens;
truly He, He was Aware, Seeing of His servants

* Sec. 4

Kill not your children 17:31
in dread of want;°
We shall provide for them and for you;°
truly the killing of them is a great inequity.
Come not near committing adultery;° 17:32
truly it is a great indecency! How evil a way!
Kill not a soul 17:33
which God has forbidden,
except justifiably,°
and whoever is slain
as one who has been treated unjustly,
then indeed We have assigned
for his protector an authority,
but he should not exceed all bounds in killing;°
truly he is one who shall be helped.
Come not near the property of the orphan, 17:34
except with what is fair,
until he reaches the coming of age;°
and live up to the compact;°
truly the compact would be
one that is to be questioned.
Live up to the full measure 17:35
when you measure,
and weigh with a straight scale;°
that is best and fairer interpretation.
Follow up not of what 17:36
you *have* no knowledge;°
truly having the ability to hear
and sight and mind,
each of these shall be
ones that are to be questioned.

17:37   Walk not on the earth exalting;
truly **you** shall never make a hole in the earth;°
and shall never reach the mountains in height.

17:38   All of that—the bad deeds *are*
disliked by **your** Lord.

17:39   That *is* of what
your Lord revealed to **you** of wisdom,°
so set not up with God another god
that **you** should be cast down into hell
as one who is blameworthy,
as one who is condemned.

17:40   Has your Lord selected for you sons
and taken for Himself
females from among the angels?
Truly you, you say a serious saying!

Sec. 5   *

17:41   Surely We have diversified
in this Quran
that they may recollect,
but it increases them not except in aversion.

17:42   Say: If there were gods along with Him
as they say,
then they would have certainly been looking for
a way to the Lord of the Throne.

17:43   Glory be to Him!
Exalted *is He* above what they say,
greatly exalted.

17:44   The seven heavens glorify Him,
and the earth
and all that is in and on them;°
there is not a thing but it glorifies His praise;
but you understand not their glorification,°
truly He has been Forbearing, Forgiving.

17:45   When **you** recite the Quran,
We made between **you**
and between those who believe not
in the world to come
a partition obstructing *their* vision.

17:46   We have laid a sheath over their hearts

so that they should not understand it,
and heaviness in their ears;°
when **you** have remembered **your** Lord alone in
the Quran,
they turn their backs in aversion.
We have greater knowledge of what they listen for   17:47
when they listen to **you**.
When they conspire secretly,
when the ones who are unjust say:
You follow not but a bewitched man.
Look upon how they have propounded   17:48
parables for **you**;
so they have gone astray
and they are not able to be on a way.
They say: Is it when we are bones   17:49
and broken bits
that we *shall be* the ones who are raised up
in a new creation?
Say: Should you be rocks or iron   17:50
or a creature that shall be even more troublesome   17:51
in your breasts?°
Then they shall say: Who shall cause us to return?°
Say: He Who originated you the first time;°
then they shall nod their heads at **you**
and say: When shall it be?
Say: Perhaps it is near.
On a Day when He calls to you   17:52
and you shall respond to Him with His praise;
and you shall think
that you lingered in expectation but a little.
*   Sec. 6

Say to My servants   17:53
that they should say what is fair;°
truly Satan provokes among them;
surely Satan is a clear enemy to mankind.
Your Lord has greater knowledge of you;°   17:54
if He will, He shall *have* mercy on you,
and if He will, He shall punish you;
and We have not sent **you** as a trustee over them.

17:55 **Your** Lord has greater knowledge
of all those who are in the heavens
and in and on the earth,°
and indeed We have preferred
some of the Prophets over others;°
and to David We gave the Psalms.

17:56 Say: Call to those whom you claim
other than Him;
yet they *are* neither in control
to remove injury from you,
nor to change it.

17:57 Those to whom they call,
they are looking for an approach to their Lord,
whoever is nearer;
and they hope for His mercy
and they fear His punishment;°
truly the punishment of **your** Lord
was *something* to beware of.

17:58 *There is* not a town
but We shall cause it to perish
before the Day of Resurrection,
or *be* ones who punish it
with a severe punishment;°
that was inscribed in the Book.

17:59 Nothing prevents Us from sending Signs,
except that the ancient ones denied them.°
We gave to Thamud the she-camel
as one to be perceived,
but they did wrong to her.°
We sent not the Signs,
except as a deterrence.

17:60 When We said to **you**:
Truly **your** Lord comprehends humanity;°
and We made not the dream
which We caused **you** to see,
but *as* a test for humanity;
and the tree—one that was cursed in the Quran;°
and We frighten them,
but it increases them not but in great defiance.

*

When We said to the angels: 17:61
Prostrate to Adam!
So they prostrated *themselves* except Iblis;
he said: Shall I prostrate to one
whom **You** have created from clay?
He said: Have **You Yourself** considered?   17:62
You have held this one in esteem above me?
If **You** were to postpone for me
to the Day of Resurrection,
I shall certainly bring his offspring,
except a few, under control.
He said: Go off with **you**;   17:63
and whoever of them heeds **you**,
then truly hell shall be your recompense,
an ample recompense.
Hound whom **you** are able to of them   17:64
with **your** voice,
and rally against them with **your** horse
and **your** foot soldiers,
and share with them in their wealth
and children,
and promise them;°
but Satan promises them nothing but delusion.
Truly My servants,   17:65
over them **you** have no authority;°
and **your** Lord suffices as a Trustee.
Your Lord *is* He Who propels the boats for you   17:66
on the sea
so that you may look for His grace;°
truly He was ever Compassionate toward you.
When an injury afflicts you upon the sea,   17:67
those that you call to other than Him go astray;°
but when He delivers you to land,
you turn aside;°
and mankind was ungrateful.
Are you *feeling* safe   17:68
that He shall not cause the earth to swallow you up
or send you to the shore of the land

a storm of pebbles against you?
Then you shall find that you *have* no trustee.

17:69 Or are you *feeling* safe
that He shall not cause you to return to it
a second time,
and send against you a hurricane of wind,

• and drown you because you were ungrateful?
Then you shall not find for yourselves
against Us in it an advocator.

17:70 Indeed We held the Children of Adam in esteem,
and We carried them on dry land and on the sea,
and provided them with what is good,
and We have preferred them with excellence
over many of those whom We created.

Sec. 8 *

17:71 On a Day when We shall call to all the clans
with their record,
whoever is given his book in his right hand
those shall recite their book,
and wrong shall not be done to them,
even the extent of a date-thread.

17:72 Whoever is *unwilling* to see here
shall be unseeing in the world to come,
and one who goes astray from the way.

17:73 Truly they were about to persecute **you**
for what We revealed to **you**,
so that **you** would devise against Us
other than it;°
and then they would certainly have taken **you**
to themselves as a friend.

17:74 If We had not made **you** firm,
truly **you** might have inclined
to them a little.

17:75 Then We would have caused **you** to experience
a double of this life
and a double after dying;
then **you** would have found for **yourself**
no helper against Us.

17:76 They were about to hound **you** from the region

that they might drive **you** out of it;°
then they would not have lingered in expectation
after **you**,
but for a little while.
This was Our custom with whomever 17:77
We sent before **you** of Our Messengers,
and **you** shall not find any change
in Our custom.

*

Perform the formal prayer 17:78
from the sinking sun
until the darkening of the night,
and the dawn recital;°
truly the dawn recital
is one that shall be witnessed.
Keep vigil with it in the night 17:79
for an unexpected gift for **you**;
perhaps **your** Lord shall raise **you** up to a station
of one who is to be praised.
Say: My Lord! 17:80
Cause me to enter a gate in sincerity
and bring me out,
one who is caused to leave in sincerity,
and assign me a helping authority,
that which proceeds from **Your** Presence.
Say: The Truth draws near 17:81
and falsehood has vanished!
Truly falsehood would vanish away.
We send down in the Quran 17:82
what *is* a healing and a mercy
for the ones who believe, •
and it increases not the ones who are unjust
but in a loss.
When We are gracious to the human being, 17:83
he turns aside and withdraws aside;°
and when worse afflicts him, he becomes hopeless.
Say: Each does according to his same manner; 17:84
and **your** Lord has greater knowledge of him
who is better guided on the way.

*

17:85   They shall ask **you** about the spirit;°
say: The spirit *is* of the command of my Lord;
and you have not been given knowledge
but a little.

17:86   Had We willed,
We would surely take away
what We have revealed to **you**;
then **you** would not find for **you** in that
against Us any trustee

17:87   except a mercy from **your** Lord;°
truly His grace was ever great upon **you**.

17:88   Say: If human kind were to be gathered together
and jinn to bring
the like of this Quran,
they approach not the like of it,
even if some of them were supporters of others.

17:89   Indeed We have diversified for humanity
in this Quran every kind of parable,
but most of humanity refused in ingratitude.

17:90   They say:
We shall not believe in **you** until
you *have* a fountain gush out of the earth for us;

17:91   or there be a garden for **you**
of date palms and grapevines,
and you cause rivers to gush forth
with a gushing forth;

17:92   or **you** cause heaven to drop
upon us in pieces as **you** have claimed,
or bring God and the angels
as a warranty;

17:93   or *there* be for **you** a house of ornament;
or **you** ascend up into heaven,
and we shall not believe in **your** ascension
until **you** send down for us a Book
that we would read;°
say: Glory be to my Lord,
am I anything but a mortal Messenger?

Sec. 11   *

Nothing prevented humanity from believing
when the guidance drew near to them,
but that they said:
Has God raised up a mortal as a Messenger?
Say: If *there* were angels on earth
walking around and ones who were at rest,
then We would certainly have sent down
to them from heaven
an angel as a Messenger.
Say: God suffices as a witness
between me and between you;°
truly He was of His servants Aware, Seeing.
He whom God guides
is one who is truly guided;°
and whomever He causes to go astray—
never shall **you** find for them protectors
other than Him;°
and We shall assemble them
on the Day of Resurrection
on their faces;
unwilling to see, *unwilling* to speak,
unwilling to hear;°
their place of shelter shall be hell;°
whenever it declines
We shall increase the blaze for them.
That *is* their recompense
because they were ungrateful for Our Signs
and said: When we are bones and straw,
would we be ones who are to be raised up
as a new creation?
Have they not considered that
God Who created the heavens and the earth
is One Who Has the Power
to create the like of them?
He has assigned a term for them
whereof *there is* no doubt in it;
but the ones who are unjust refuse
nothing but ingratitude.
Say: If you possessed

17:94

17:95

17:96

17:97

17:98

17:99

17:100

the treasures of the mercy of my Lord,
then you would certainly hold back
for dread of spending;°
for mankind shall be ever stingy.

*

17:101   Indeed We gave
Moses nine Signs, clear portents;°
then ask the Children of Israel
how he drew near to them;
then Pharaoh said to him:
Truly O Moses, I think that **you** are indeed
one who is bewitched.

17:102   He said:
Truly **you** knew no one has sent forth these
except the Lord of the heavens and the earth
as clear evidences;
and truly, O Pharaoh, I think that **you** are
one who is damned.

17:103 So he wanted to hound them in the region,
but We drowned him
and *those* who *were* with him altogether.

17:104 We said to the Children of Israel after him:
Inhabit the region.
But when draws near
the promise of the world to come,
We shall bring you about a mixed group.

17:105   We sent it forth with The Truth
and it has come down with The Truth,°
and We sent it not to **you**
except as one who gives good tidings
and as a warner.

17:106 *It is* a Recitation; We have separated it
in order that **you** may recite it to humanity
at intervals;
and We have sent it down
a sending successively down.

17:107   Say: Believe in it
or believe not.°
Truly those who were given knowledge

335

before it,
when it is recounted to them,
they fall down in prostration on their faces.
They say: Glory be to our Lord!   17:108
Truly the promise of our Lord
is one that shall be accomplished.
They fall down on their faces weeping,   17:109
and it increases them in humility.‡
Say: Call to God or call to the Merciful;°   17:110
by whatever you call *Him*,
to Him *are* the Fairest Names;°
and **you** be not loud in **you**r formal prayer,
nor speak in a low tone;
look for a way between.
Say: The Praise *belongs* to God,   17:111
Who has taken neither a son to Himself;
nor has He any associate
in the dominion,
nor has He any protector
out of a sense of humility;°
and magnify Him a magnification!

CHAPTER 18
THE CAVE (*al-Kahf*)

In the Name of God,
the Merciful, the Compassionate   Sec. 1
The Praise *belongs* to God   18:1
Who has sent forth to His servant the Book,
and has not made for it any crookedness.°
A truth-loving *Book* to warn of severe violence   18:2
from that which proceeds from His Presence
and to give good tidings to the ones who believe,
the ones who have acted in accord with morality,
that they shall *have* a fair compensation.
Ones who abide in it eternally   18:3
and to warn those who say: 18:4
God has taken to Himself a son.
They *have* no knowledge about it,   18:5

nor had their fathers;°
troublesome is the word
that goes forth from their mouths;°
and they say nothing but a lie.

18:6 So perhaps **you** *would be*
one who consumes himself with grief
for their sake
if they should not believe
in this discourse out of bitterness.

18:7 Truly We have assigned whatever
is on the earth as adornment for it
so that We may try them with it
as to which of them *are* fairest in actions.

18:8 Truly We *are* ones who make
whatever *is* on the barren dry earth.

18:9 Have **you** assumed that
the Companions of the Cave
and the Bearers of Inscription
were a wonder among Our Signs?

18:10 When the male youths took shelter in the Cave,
and they said: Our Lord! Give us a mercy
from that which proceeds from **You**
and finish us right minded with our affair.

18:11 So We sealed their ears in the Cave
for a multiple of years.

18:12 Then We raised them up so that We might know
which of the two confederates
was better in calculating
the space of time they had lingered in expectation.

Sec. 2   *

18:13 We relate this tiding to **you** with The Truth;°
truly they *were* male youths
who believed in their Lord,
and We increased them in guidance.

18:14 We invigorated their hearts
when they stood up and said:
Our Lord *is* the Lord
of the heavens and the earth;
we shall never call to any god other than He;°

for then we would have said an outrageous thing.
These, our folk have taken to themselves gods   18:15
other than He°
even though they bring not to them
a clear portent of authority.°
Who *is* one who does greater wrong
than one who devises a lie against God?
When you have withdrawn from them   18:16
and from what they worship other than God,
then take shelter in the cave;
your Lord shall unfold for you from His mercy
and shall furnish you
with a gentle issue in your affair.
You might have seen the sun when it came up,   18:17
it inclines from their cave towards the right;
and when it begins to set,
it passed them on the left
while they *were* in one of its fissures;°
that *is* of the Signs of God,°
he whom God guides,
he *is* one who is truly guided,
and he whom He causes to go astray,
you shall never find for him a protector,
or one who shall show him the way.

                              *   Sec. 3

You would have assumed them to be awake   18:18
while they *were* ones who were sleeping;°
and We turned them around to the right
and to the left;°
and their dog,
one expanding its paws at the threshold,
and if **you** were to peruse them,
you would certainly
have turned from them, fleeing,
and you would certainly have been filled with
alarm at them.
Thus it was that We raised them up   18:19
that they might question one another;°
one among them said:

How long have you lingered in expectation?°
They said: We have
lingered in expectation a day or a part of a day;°
they said: Your Lord has greater knowledge
of how long you have lingered in expectation;
so raise up one of you
and with this, your money, *send* to the city
and let him look upon which is the purest food,
and let him bring you provisions from there;
and let him be courteous,
and apprise not anyone.

18:20   Truly if it becomes manifest,
they shall stone you;
or they shall cause you to return to their creed;
and in that case you shall never ever prosper.

18:21   Thus We made the case known
that they might know
that the promise of God *is* true,
and that, as for the Hour,
there is no doubt about it;
when they contend among themselves
about their affair;°
they said: Build over them a structure;°
their Lord has greater knowledge about them;°
those who prevailed over their affair said:
We truly shall take to ourselves over them
a place of prostration.

18:22   They say: *They were* three,
the fourth of them *being* their dog,
and they shall say: *There were* five,
the sixth of them *being* their dog,
guessing at the unseen;°
and they shall say: *There were* seven,
the eighth of them *being* their dog;
say: My Lord has greater knowledge
of their amount;
no one knows them but a few,°
so altercate not about them
except *with* a manifest argumentation,

and ask not for advice about them
of anyone of them.

*

Say not of anything:

Truly I shall be one who does that tomorrow,
without adding: If God will;°

and remember **your** Lord
when **you** have forgotten;
and say: Perhaps my Lord shall guide me
nearer to right mindedness than this.
They lingered in expectation in their cave

three hundred years,
and they added nine.
Say: God has greater knowledge

of how long they lingered in expectation;°
and to Him belongs the unseen
of the heavens and the earth.°
How well He perceives
and how well He hears!
They *have* not other than Him any protector,
and He has no partner in His determination—none.
Recount

what has been revealed to **you**
from the Book of **Your** Lord;°
there is no one who changes His words;
and **you** shall never find other than Him,
a haven.
Have patience **yourself** with those

who call to their Lord
after the formal morning prayer,
and in the afternoon,
wanting His countenance;°
and let not **your** eyes pass over them
wanting the adornment of this present life;°
and obey not
him whose heart We have made neglectful
of Our Remembrance
and who follows his own desires,
and whose command has been all excess.

Say: The Truth *is* from your Lord;°
and let whoever has willed believe,
and let whoever has willed be ungrateful;
truly We have made ready
for ones who are unjust a fire;
its large tent shall surround them;°
and if they cry for help,
their cry for help shall be answered;
they shall be helped with rain like molten copper
that shall scald their faces;°
how miserable is the drink,
and how evil a place of repose!

18:30   Truly those who have believed,
the ones who have acted in accord with morality,
truly We shall not waste the compensation
of him who does good.

18:31   Those, for them *are* Gardens of Eden,
beneath which rivers run;
they shall be adorned in them
with bracelets of gold,
and they shall wear green garments
of silk and brocade;
they *shall be* ones who are reclining in it
on raised benches.°
How excellent is the reward,
and how excellent a place of rest!

Sec. 5   *

18:32   Propound for them the parable of two men:
We had assigned to one of them
two gardens of grapevines
and We had encircled them with date palm trees,
and We made crops between them.

18:33   Both gardens gave their produce
and failed nothing in the least;°
and *We* caused a river to gush forth through them.

18:34   There was fruit for him,
and he said to his companion
while he was conversing with him:
I *am* more than **you** in wealth

and mightier in a group of men.
He entered his garden   18:35
while he was one who was unjust to himself.
He said:
I think that this shall never be destroyed.
I think that the Hour shall never be   18:36
one that looms near;
and if I am returned to my Lord,
I shall surely find better than this
as an overturning.
His companion said to him   18:37
while he was conversing with him:
Are **you** ungrateful to Him Who created **you**
out of earthy dust,
then out of seminal fluids,
then shaped **you** into a man?
But He *is* God, my Lord,   18:38
and I shall not make a partner
of anyone with my Lord.
Would that when **you** enter **your** garden   18:39
you had said: Had God willed!
There is no strength but with God!°
If **you** see I *am* less than **you** in wealth
and children,
perhaps my Lord shall give me   18:40
better than **your** garden,
and shall send on it a thunderclap
from heaven;
then it shall come to be in the morning
slippery earth.
Or it shall come to be in the morning   18:41
that its water *shall be* sinking into the ground
so that **you** shall never be able to seek it out.
Its fruit was enclosed,   18:42
and it came to be in the morning
he began turning his palms around and around
for what he had spent on it,
while it had fallen down in ruins;
and he was saying: Would that I had not

made anyone partners with my Lord!

18:43
There was no faction to help him
other than God;
and he was one who was helpless.

18:44
There, all protection belongs to God,
The Truth;°
He *is* Best in rewarding for good deeds
and Best in consequence.

*

18:45
Propound for them
the parable of this present life:
It is like water that We send forth from heaven,
and plants of the earth mingle with it
and it becomes straw in the morning
that winnow in the winds,°
and God *is* over everything
One Who is Omnipotent.

18:46
Wealth and children
are the adornment of this present life;°
but those things which endure *are*
the ones who have acted in accord with morality;
that is better with **your** Lord,
as a reward for good deeds
and better for hopefulness.

18:47
On a Day We shall set in motion
the mountains,
and you shall see the earth
as what has departed;
and We shall assemble them,
and leave out none of them.

18:48
They shall be presented
before **your** Lord ranged in rows;
now indeed you have drawn near to Us
as We created you the first time.°
Rather you claimed
that We had never assigned for you a promise.

18:49
The Book shall be set in place,
and **you** shall see the ones who sin
apprehensive as to what *is* in it;

and they shall say: Woe to us!
What *is* this Book?
It neither leaves out *anything* small or great,
but has counted *everything;*°
they shall find present what their hands had done,
and **your** Lord does not wrong anyone.

*

When We said to the angels:
Prostrate to Adam!
So they prostrated except Iblis;
he was one of the jinn
and he disobeyed the command of His Lord.°
What? Shall you then take him to yourselves
and his offspring to be protectors
rather than Me,
while they *are* enemies to you?°
How miserable a substitute for
ones who are unjust!
I called them not to witness the creation
of the heavens and the earth,
nor to their own creation of themselves,
nor was I to take to the ones who are led astray
as assistants.
On a Day when He shall say:
Call on My associates, those whom you claimed,
then they shall cry out to them,
but they shall not respond to them,
and We shall make a gulf of doom between them.
You shall see the ones who sin in the fire,
who think that they *are*
ones who are about to fall in it,
and they shall not find from it a way to escape.

*

Indeed We have diversified in this Quran
every kind of parable for humanity;°
but mankind *is* more than anything
argumentative.
Nothing prevented humanity from believing
when guidance drew near to them,

18:50

18:51

18:52

18:53

18:54

18:55

or from asking forgiveness of their Lord
except what approaches them
by the way of the ancient ones
or being approached by the punishment.

18:56   We send not the messengers
except as ones who give good tidings
and as ones who warn;°
and those who are ungrateful dispute
falsely
in order to rebut The Truth by it;°
and they take My Signs to themselves
and what they are warned of
in mockery.

18:57   Who *is* one who does greater wrong
than he who is reminded
of the Signs of his Lord,
but turns aside from them,
and forgets what his hands have put forward?°
Truly We have laid sheaths over their hearts
so that they should not understand it,
and heaviness in their ears;°
and if **you** call them to guidance,
they shall not be truly guided then never.

18:58   **Your** Lord *is* Forgiving, Possessor of Mercy;°
if He takes them to task
for what they have earned,
He would have quickened their punishment;°
but they *have* what has been promised,
they shall never find other than Him,
a way to elude it.

18:59   Those towns, We caused them to perish
when they did wrong
and We assigned for their destruction
what was promised.

*

Sec. 9

18:60   When Moses said to his male youth:
I shall not quit
until I reach the place of meeting of the two seas,
although I shall go on for many years.

But when they reached the place of the meeting   18:61
between them,
they forgot their fish
and it took to itself a way through the sea
burrowing.
Then when they had crossed,   18:62
he said to his male youth:
Give us our breakfast;
indeed we have met fatigue from our journey.
He said: Have **you yourself** considered?   18:63
When we took shelter at the rock,
truly I forgot the fish,
and none but Satan caused me to forget
to remember it.°
It took its way into the sea
in a wondrous way.
He said: That *is* what we have been looking for!°   18:64
So they went back, following their footsteps.
Then they found a servant of Our servants   18:65
to whom We had given mercy from Us
and We had taught him knowledge,
that which proceeds from Our Presence.
Moses said to him: May I follow **you**   18:66
so that **you** may teach me something
of what **you** have been taught
of right judgment?
He said: Truly **you** shall never be able to have   18:67
patience with me.
How shall **you** endure a thing patiently   18:68
that **you** have not comprehended
with awareness?
He said: **You** shall find me,   18:69
if God has willed, one who remains steadfast,
and I shall not rebel against **your** command.
He said: Then if **you** follow me   18:70
ask me not about anything
until I cause a remembrance of it to be evoked in **you**.

*   Sec. 10

So they both set out   18:71

until when they embarked in a vessel;
he made a hole in it;°
he said: Have **you** made a hole in it
in order to drown the people?
Indeed **you** have brought about a dreadful thing!

18:72 He said: Said I not to **you**
that **you** would not be able
to have patience with me?

18:73 He said: Take me not to task for what I forgot,
and constrain me not
with hardship for my affair.

18:74 Then they both set out
until when they met a boy; then he killed him;
he said: Have **you** killed a pure soul
without *his having slain* anyone?
Indeed **you** have brought about a horrible thing!

Part 16
***

18:75 He said:
Said I not that **you** would not be able
to have patience with me?

18:76 He said: If I ask **you** about anything after this,
then keep not company with me;
indeed **you** have reached *enough*
of excusing from my presence!

18:77 Then they both set out
until when they approached a people of a town;
they asked for food;
its people refused to receive them as guests;
then they found in it a wall
that was meant to tumble down,
so he fixed it;
he said: If **you** had willed
you would have taken
compensation to yourself for it.

18:78 He said:
This is the parting between me and **you**!
I shall tell **you** the interpretation
about which **you** have not been able
to have patience.

347

As for the vessel, it was of some needy *people*   18:79
who toiled on the sea,
so I wanted to mar it
as there was a king after them
who was taking every vessel forcefully.
As for the boy,   18:80
both his parents were ones who believed,
and we dreaded that he should constrain them
with defiance and ingratitude;
so we wanted   18:81
their Lord to give to them in exchange
one better than he in purity,
and nearer in sympathy.
As for the wall,   18:82
lo! It was *that* of two orphan boys
in the town;
and beneath it was a treasure of theirs;
their father had been
one who acted in accord with morality,
so **your** Lord wanted that
they be fully grown, *having* come of age,
and then pull out their treasure
as a mercy from **your** Lord.°
I accomplished that not of my own command.°
This is the interpretation
of that for which **you** were not able to have patience.
                          *   Sec. 11

They shall ask **you** about Dhu-l Qarnayn;°   18:83
say: I shall recount to you
a remembrance of him.
Truly We established him firmly on the earth,   18:84
and gave him a route to everything.
So he pursued a route,   18:85
until when he reached the setting of the sun;   18:86
he found it beginning to set
in a spring of muddy water,
and he found near it a folk,°
We said: O Dhu-l Qarnayn!
Either punish them

18:87 or take them to yourself with goodness.
He said: As for him who does wrong,
him we shall punish;
then he shall be returned to his Lord
Who shall punish him
with a horrible punishment.
18:88 But as for him who has believed,
one who has acted in accord with morality,
he *shall have* the fairest recompense;°
and We shall speak to him our command with ease.
18:89 Then he pursued a route
18:90 until he reached the rising place of the sun;
he found it coming up on a folk
for whom We had not made any obstruction against it.
18:91 Thus We had comprehended,
in awareness of whatever was near him.
18:92 Then he pursued a route
18:93 until when he reached between two embankments;
he found behind them a folk
who would almost not understand any saying.
18:94 They said: O Dhu-l Qarnayn!
Truly Gog and Magog
are ones who make corruption in and on the earth;
shall we assign to **you** payment
if **you** make an embankment
between us and them?
18:95 He said:
What my Lord has established firmly for me
is better,
so assist me with strength;
I shall make a fortification between you and them.
18:96 Give me ingots of iron;°
until when he made level between the two cliffs,
he said: Blow!°
Until when he had made it a fire,
he said: Give me molten copper to pour out over it.
18:97 So they were not able to scale it,
nor were they able to dig through it.
18:98 He said: This *is* a mercy from my Lord;°

but when the promise of my Lord draws near,
He shall make it powder;°
and the promise of my Lord is true.
That Day We shall leave some of them
to surge against others;°
and the trumpet shall be blown;
then We shall gather them altogether.
On that Day We shall present the depths of hell
to ones who are ungrateful,
to those whose eyes had been screened
from My Remembrance
and who were not able to hear.

*

Assume those who are ungrateful
that they may take My servants
to themselves as protectors instead of Me?°
Truly We have made hell ready
as a welcome for ones who are ungrateful.
Say: Shall We tell you who shall be
the ones who are losers by their actions?
Those whose endeavoring goes astray
in this present life
while they assume
that they are doing good by their handiwork.
They *are* those who are ungrateful
for the Signs of their Lord
and the meeting with Him,
so their actions are fruitless;
and so on the Day of Resurrection,
We shall not perform any weighing for them.
That *shall be* their recompense—hell—
because they were ungrateful
and took to themselves
My Signs and My Messengers
in mockery.
Truly those who have believed,
ones who have acted in accord with morality,
shall have a welcome in the Gardens of Paradise,
ones who shall dwell in them forever;

18:99

18:100

18:101

Sec. 12
18:102

18:103

18:104

18:105

18:106

18:107

18:108

they *shall have* no desire for dislocation from there.

Say: If the sea were ink
for the words of my Lord,
the sea would come to an end
before the words of my Lord would come to an end
even if We brought about replenishment the like of it.

18:110 Say: I *am* not but a mortal like you.
It has been revealed to me
that your God *is* One;°
so whoever hopes for
the meeting with his Lord,
let him be one who has acted in accord with morality,
and makes not a partner
in the worship of his Lord.

CHAPTER 19
MARY (*Maryam*)

In the Name of God,
Sec. 1   the Merciful, the Compassionate
19:1   *Kāf Hā Yā ʿAīn Ṣād;*
19:2   a reminder of the mercy of **your** Lord
to His servant Zechariah,
19:3   when he cried out to his Lord, secretly crying out.
19:4   He said: O my Lord!
Truly I—my bones have grown feeble
and my head is aglow with greyness of hair,
yet I have never been
disappointed in my supplication to **You**, O my Lord.
19:5   Truly I, I fear the ones whom I protect
after me and my wife is a barren women
so bestow on me an heir,
from that which proceeds from **Your** Presence,
19:6   who shall inherit from me
and inherit from the family of Jacob;°
and make him, Lord, pleasing.
19:7   O Zechariah!
Truly We give **you** the good tidings of a boy;
his name *shall be* John,

and We have not assigned
this namesake for anyone before.
He said: My Lord! 19:8
How shall I have a boy
while my wife is a barren woman;
and indeed I have reached an advanced old age?
He said: Thus *it shall be*! 19:9
Your Lord said: It *is* insignificant for Me,
certainly I have created **you** before
when **you** were nothing.
He said: My Lord! 19:10
Assign for me a Sign.°
He said: **Your** Sign is that
you shall not speak to humanity,
although being without fault, for three nights.
So he went forth to his folk 19:11
from the sanctuary,
then he revealed to them:
Glorify in the early morning dawn
and in the evening.
O John! 19:12
Take the Book with strength!°
We gave him critical judgment while a lad,
and tender feelings 19:13
from that which proceeds from Our Presence
and purity and he was devout,°
and pious to ones who were his parents; 19:14
and neither was he haughty, nor rebellious.
Peace be to him 19:15
the day on which he was given birth
and the day he dies,
and the day he shall be raised up, living.
* Sec. 2

Remember Mary in the Book 19:16
when she went apart from her people
to an eastern place.
Then she took a partition to herself *against* them, 19:17
so We sent Our Spirit to her,
and he presented himself before her

as a mortal without fault.

19:18 She said: Truly I take refuge in The Merciful
from **you** if **you** are devout.

19:19 He said: I am not but a messenger from **your** Lord
that I may bestow on **you** (f) a pure boy.

19:20 She said: How shall I have a boy
when no mortal has touched me,
nor am I an unchaste woman?

19:21 He said: Thus *it shall be;*
your Lord said: It *is* insignificant for Me;°
and: We shall assign him as a Sign
to humanity,
and as a mercy from Us.°
It was a decreed command.

19:22 So she conceived him,
and she went apart with him to a farther place.

19:23 The birthpangs surprised her
at the trunk of a date palm tree.
She said: O would that I had died before this,
and I had been one who is forgotten,
—a thing forgotten!

19:24 So he cried out to her from beneath her:
Feel not remorse!
Indeed **your** Lord has made under **you** (f) a brook.

19:25 Shake towards **you** (f) the trunk
of the date palm tree;
it shall cause ripe, fresh dates to tumble on **you**.

19:26 So eat and drink and be refreshed;°
if **you** see any mortal,
say: I have vowed a formal fast to The Merciful
so I shall not speak to any man this day.

19:27 Then she approached her folk with him,
carrying him;°
they said: O Mary!
Indeed **you** have drawn near a monstrous thing!

19:28 O sister of Aaron!
Your father was not a morally evil man,
nor was **your** mother an unchaste woman.

19:29 Then she pointed to him;°

they said: How speak we
to one who was in the cradle, a lad?
He said: Truly I am a servant of God;   19:30
He gave me the Book,
and made me a Prophet.
He has made me one who is blessed   19:31
wherever I may be,
and bequeathed to me the formal prayer,
and the purifying alms so long as I am living,
pious toward one who was my mother,   19:32
and made me not haughty nor disappointed;
and peace be on me   19:33
the day on which I was given birth,
and the day I die,
and the day I shall be raised up, living.
That *is* Jesus son of Mary.°   19:34
A saying of The Truth,
yet they contest about it.
It was not for God that He should take to Himself   19:35
a son;°
glory be to Him!°
When He has decreed a command
He not but says to it: Be! And it is!
Truly God *is* my Lord and your Lord,   19:36
so worship Him.°
This *is* a straight path.
The confederates were at variance among themselves;°   19:37
woe to those who are ungrateful
at a scene of a tremendous Day!
How well they shall hear,   19:38
and they shall perceive
on the Day they shall approach Us:°
But the ones who are unjust *are*
today, clearly, wandering astray!
Warn them of the Day of Regret   19:39
when the command has been decided
while they *are* careless
and they believe not.
Truly We shall inherit the earth   19:40

and whatever *is* in and on it
and to Us they shall be returned.

*

19:41   Remember Abraham in the Book;°
truly he was a just person, a Prophet,

19:42   when he said to his father: O my father!
Why worship **you**
what hears not, perceives not
and avails **you** not anything?

19:43   O my father!
Truly knowledge has drawn near to me
of what approached **you** not,
so follow me and I shall guide **you**
to a faultless path.

19:44   O my father!
Worship not Satan!
Truly Satan
is rebellious towards The Merciful!

19:45   O my father!
Truly I fear
that a punishment should afflict **you**
from The Merciful,
so that **you** become a protector of Satan.

19:46   He said: *Are* **you** one who shrinks from my gods,
O Abraham?
If **you** shall not refrain **yourself**,
certainly I shall stone **you**;°
so abandon me for some while.

19:47   He said: Peace be to **you**!°
I shall ask for forgiveness from my Lord for **you**;°
truly He *is* One Who is Gracious to me.

19:48   I shall withdraw from you,
and what you call to other than God,
and I shall call to my Lord;
perhaps I shall not be
disappointed in my supplication to my Lord.

19:49   So when he had withdrawn from them,
and what they worshiped other than God,
We bestowed on him Isaac and Jacob;°

and each of them We made a Prophet.
We bestowed on them from Our mercy,   19:50
and We assigned them the tongue of lofty sincerity.
*

Remember Moses in the Book.°   19:51
Truly he was one who was devoted,
and he was a Messenger, a Prophet.
We proclaimed to him   19:52
from the right edge of the mountain,
and We brought him near privately.
We bestowed on him out of Our mercy,   19:53
his brother Aaron, a Prophet.
Remember Ishmael in the Book.°   19:54
Truly he was one who was sincere in his promise,
and he was a Messenger, a Prophet.
He would command his people to the formal prayer,   19:55
and the purifying alms, and he was
one with whom His Lord was well-pleased.
Remember Enoch in the Book.°   19:56
Truly he was a just person, a Prophet.
We exalted him to a lofty place.   19:57
Those *are* they to whom God has been gracious   19:58
from among the Prophets of the offspring of Adam,
and those whom We carried with Noah,
and of the offspring of Abraham and Israel;
from among those whom We guided and elected.°
When the Signs of the Merciful
were recounted to them
they fell down,
crying in prostration.‡
Then after them succeeded a succession   19:59
who wasted the formal prayer
and followed their appetites;°
so they shall meet error,
except those who have repented and have believed,   19:60
ones who have acted in accord with morality;
such shall enter the Garden
and wrong shall not be done to them in anything,
Gardens of Eden which The Merciful has promised   19:61

His servants in the unseen.
Truly He, His promise is what is kept.

19:62 They shall not hear in them idle talk;
nothing but: Peace!°
They shall have their provision in them
in the early morning at dawn and evening.

19:63 This is the Garden
which We shall give as inheritance
to those of Our servants who have been devout.

19:64 We come forth not
except by the command of **your** Lord;°
to Him *belongs* whatever *is* in advance of us
and whatever *is* behind us,
and whatever *is* in between those two.°
Your Lord is not forgetful,

19:65 the Lord of the heavens and the earth,
and what *is* between them!
So **you** worship Him
and maintain patience in His worship.°
Know **you** any namesake for Him?

Sec. 5 *

19:66 The human being says: When I am dead,
shall I be brought out living?

19:67 Shall the human being not remember
that We created him before
while he was nothing?

19:68 So by **your** Lord,
indeed We shall assemble them
and the satans;
then indeed We shall parade them around hell,
ones who are crawling on their knees.

19:69 Then indeed We shall tear out every partisan,
whoever of them
was more severe in stubborn rebellion to The Merciful.

19:70 Then truly We have greater knowledge
of those, they who *are* most deserving
of roasting in it.

19:71 *There is* none of you but ones who go down to it.°
This is a thing decreed, determined by **your** Lord.

Then We shall deliver those who were Godfearing,
and We shall forsake the ones who are unjust
in it, ones crawling on their knees.
When Our Signs are recounted, clear portents,   19:73
those who disbelieved would say
to those who believed:
Which of the two groups of people *is* best
in station and fairer in association?
How many before them have We caused to perish,   19:74
whose generation *was* fairer in furnishings
and outward show?
Say: Whoever misjudges,   19:75
The Merciful shall prolong his prolonging°
until they see what they were promised,
either the punishment, or the Hour;
then they shall know whose place is worse,
and whose army *is* weak.
God increases in guidance,°   19:76
those who are truly guided,°
enduring in accord with morality;
they *are* better with **your** Lord
in reward for good deeds
and better for turning back *to God.*
Have **you** seen him who was ungrateful for Our Signs   19:77
who said: Indeed I shall be given wealth and children?
Has he perused the unseen,   19:78
or has he taken to himself
a compact from The Merciful?
Nay!°   19:79
We shall write down what he says;
We shall cause the punishment to increase for him,
prolonging it.
We shall inherit from him all that he says,   19:80
and he shall approach Us individually.
They have taken to themselves   19:81
gods other than God
that they might be a triumph for them.
Nay!°   19:82
Soon they shall be ungrateful

for *what* they worship,
and they shall be taking a stand against them.

*

19:83　　　Have **you** not considered
that We have sent satans
against the ones who are ungrateful
to confound them with confusion?

19:84　　　So hasten not against them;°
We number for them not but a sum

19:85　　　on the Day We shall assemble
the Godfearing
to The Merciful like an entourage.

19:86　　　We shall drive the ones who sin
to hell, herding them.

19:87　　　They shall not possess intercession,
except those who have taken to themselves
a compact with The Merciful.

19:88　　　They said: The Merciful has taken to Himself
a son!

19:89　　　Indeed you have brought about
a disastrous thing

19:90　　　whereby the heavens are almost split asunder
and the earth is split,
and the mountains fall crashing down

19:91　　　that they attribute a son to The Merciful

19:92　　　when it is not fit and proper for The Merciful
that He should take a son to Himself!

19:93　　　There is none in the heavens and the earth
except *he* be one who arrives to The Merciful
as a servant.

19:94　　　Indeed He has counted
and numbered a sum for them!

19:95　　　Everyone of them
shall be ones who arrive to Him
individually on the Day of Resurrection.

19:96　　　Truly those who have believed,
ones who have acted in accord with morality,
The Merciful shall assign ardor for them.

19:97　　　Indeed We have made this easy on **your** tongue

so that **you** may give good tidings with it
to one who is Godfearing,
and warn a most stubborn folk with it.
How many
a generation have We caused to perish before them?
Are **you** conscious of anyone of them
or hear *so much as* a whisper from them?

CHAPTER 20
TA HA *(Ṭā Hā)*

In the Name of God,
The Merciful, The Compassionate
Ṭā Hā;   20:1
We have not sent forth the Quran to **you**   20:2
that **you** should be unhappy,
but as an admonition   20:3
to him who dreads;
a sending down successively from Him   20:4
Who has created the earth
and the lofty heavens.
The Merciful turned His attention to the Throne.   20:5
To Him *belongs* whatever *is* in the heavens,   20:6
whatever *is* on the earth,
whatever *is* between them,
and whatever *is* under the soil.
If **you** were to publish a saying,   20:7
then truly He knows the secret
and what is more hidden.
God, *there is* no god but He;°   20:8
to Him *are* the Fairest Names.
Has the conversation of Moses approached **you**?   20:9
When he saw a fire,   20:10
he said to his people: Abide!
Truly I observed a fire
so that perhaps I would bring you
some firebrand from there,
or I may find guidance at the fire.
When he approached it,   20:11

it was proclaimed: O Moses!

20:12 Truly I, I *am* **your** Lord!

So take off **your** shoes;°

truly **you** are in the sanctified valley of Tuwa.

20:13 I have chosen **you**,

so listen to what is revealed:

20:14 Truly I, I *am* God;

there is no god but Me,

so worship Me and perform the formal prayer

in My Remembrance.

20:15 Truly the Hour is one that shall arrive;

I am about to conceal it

so that every soul may be given recompense

for what it endeavors.

20:16 So let none bar **you** from it

who believes not in it

and who follows his own desires

so that **you** not survive.

20:17 What is that in **your** right hand O Moses?

20:18 He said: This *is* my scepter;

I lean on it,

and beat down leaves from a tree with it

for my herd of sheep,

and for me in it *are* other uses.

20:19 He said: Cast it, O Moses!

20:20 So he cast it,

lo! It was a viper sliding.

20:21 He said: Take it and fear not;°

We shall cause it to return to its first state.

20:22 Clasp **your** hand under **your** armpit;

it shall emerge white without any evil

as another Sign

20:23 that We cause **you** to see of Our greater Signs.

20:24 Go **you** to Pharaoh!

Truly he *is* defiant.

Sec. 2 *

20:25 He said: O my Lord!

Expand my breast for me

20:26 and make my affair easy for me;

361

and untie the knot from my tongue   20:27

that they may understand my saying;   20:28

and assign to me a minister from my people: 20:29

Aaron, my brother.   20:30

Strengthen my vigor with him.   20:31

Make him a partner in my affair,   20:32

that we may glorify **You** much,   20:33

and we may remember **You** frequently.   20:34

Truly **You**, **You** have been Seeing of us.   20:35

He said: 20:36

Indeed **you** are given **your** petition, O Moses!

Indeed We showed grace on **you** another time   20:37

when We revealed to **your** mother   20:38

what was revealed:

Cast him adrift in the ark,   20:39

and cast it adrift into the water of the river;

then the water of the river shall cast it up

on the bank,

and he shall be taken by an enemy of Mine

and enemy of his.°

I cast on **you** fondness from Me

that **you** may be trained under My Eye.

When **your** sister walked and she said: 20:40

Shall I point you to one who shall take control of him?°

So We returned **you** to **your** mother

that her eyes might settle down,

and she not feel remorse.°

You killed a soul,

but We delivered **you** from lament,

and We tried **you** with an ordeal.°

Then **you** have lingered in expectation years

among the people of Midian;

then **you** drew near,

according to a measure, O Moses!

I have chosen **you** for service for Myself.   20:41

Go **you** and **your** brother with My Signs   20:42

and neither of you two be inattentive

to My Remembrance.

Go both of you to Pharaoh;   20:43

truly he has become defiant.

20:44 Both say to him a saying gently,
so that perhaps he would recollect or dread.

20:45 They both said: Our Lord!
Truly we fear that he should exceed against us
or that he be defiant.

20:46 He said: Fear not!°
Truly I *am* with both of you;
I hear. I see.

20:47 So approach you both to him and say:
Truly we *are* Messengers of **your** Lord;
so send the Children of Israel with us,
and punish them not;°
indeed we have drawn near to **you** with a Sign
from **your** Lord;°
and peace *be* to him who follows the guidance.

20:48 Truly indeed it has been revealed to us
that the punishment *is* on him who denied
and turned away.

20:49 He said: Then who *is* the Lord of you two,
O Moses?

20:50 He said: Our Lord *is* He
Who gave each thing its creation;
then He guided it.

20:51 He said: Then what of the first generations?

20:52 He said: That knowledge *is* with my Lord
in a Book;°
my Lord neither goes astray nor forgets,

20:53 He Who assigned for you the earth as a cradle,
and threaded ways for you in it,
and sent forth water from heaven;
We brought out from it diverse pairs of plants:

20:54 Eat and pasture your flocks,°
truly in this *are* indeed Signs
for the people who have sense.

*

Sec. 3

20:55 We created you from it,
and into it We shall cause you to return,
and from it We shall bring you out a time again.

Indeed We caused him to see Our Signs 20:56
—all of them—
but he denied and refused them.
He said: Have **you** drawn near to us 20:57
to drive us out of our region with your sorcery,
O Moses?
Then truly we shall bring for **you** sorcery like it. 20:58
So make a promise between us and between you
—neither we nor **you** shall break it—
at a mutually agreeable place.
He said: The promise *shall be for* the feast day, 20:59
and let humanity be assembled
in the forenoon.
So Pharaoh turned away; 20:60
then he gathered his cunning and he approached.
Moses said to them: Woe to you! 20:61
Devise not a lie against God
so that He put an end to you with a punishment;°
and indeed he who devises is frustrated.
Then they contended 20:62
with one another about their affair,
and they kept secret, conspiring secretly.
They said: Truly these two 20:63
are the ones who are sorcerers
who want to drive you out
from your region with their sorcery,
and abolish your most ideal behavior.
So summon up your cunning, 20:64
then approach ranged in rows;
and indeed he who gains the upper hand
shall prosper *this* day.
They said: O Moses! 20:65
Either you cast
or let us be the first to cast.
He said: On the contrary, you cast!° 20:66
Then their ropes and their scepters
seemed to him, by their sorcery,
to be as though they were sliding.
So Moses sensed awe in himself. 20:67

We said: Fear not!
Truly **you, you** *are* the lofty!

20:69 Cast what *is* in **your** right hand;
it shall swallow what they have crafted;°
what they have crafted *is* not but the cunning
of one who is a sorcerer;°
and one who is a sorcerer shall never prosper
in whatever he may approach.

20:70 Then the ones who were sorcerers were cast down
as the ones who prostrate themselves.
They said: We believe
in the Lord of Aaron and Moses.

20:71 *Pharaoh* said: Have you believed in Him
before I give you permission?
Truly he *is* the teacher who taught you sorcery;°
so indeed I shall cut off your hands and your feet
alternately,
and indeed I shall crucify you
on the trunks of date palm trees,
and indeed you shall know
which of us *is* more severe in punishment,
and one who endures.

20:72 They said: We shall never hold **you** in greater favor
above the clear portents that have drawn near to us
nor above Him Who originated us;°
so decide whatever **you** shall *as* one who decides;°
you shall decide not but about this present life.

20:73 Truly We have believed in our Lord
that He may forgive us our transgressions
and what we were compelled *to do*
of sorcery,°
and God is *the* Best of ones who endure.

20:74 Truly whoever approaches his Lord
as one who sins, then surely, for him *is* hell;
neither shall he die in it nor shall he live.

20:75 Whoever approaches Him
as one who believes,
one who has acted in accord with morality;
for them *are* lofty degrees,

Gardens of Eden,
beneath which rivers run,
ones who shall dwell in them forever.°
That *is* the recompense of
one who purifies oneself.

Indeed We revealed to Moses: 20:77
Set forth by night with My servants;
then strike for them a dry road in the sea,
neither fearing nor dreading to be overtaken.
Then Pharaoh and his army pursued them, 20:78
but the water of the sea overcame them
by what overcomes.
Pharaoh caused his folk to go astray, 20:79
and he guided *them* not.
O Children of Israel! 20:80
Indeed We rescued you from your enemy,
and We appointed someone with you
on the right edge of the mountain,
and We sent down to you the manna and the quails.
Eat from those which are good that We provided you, 20:81
and be not defiant
so that My anger not alight on you;°
and he on whom My anger alights
indeed shall be hurled to ruin.
Truly I *am* a Forgiver 20:82
of him who has repented and has believed,
one who has acted in accord with morality;
then he *is* truly guided.
What caused **you** to hasten from **your** folk, 20:83
O Moses?
He said: They *are* close on my footsteps 20:84
and I hastened to **You**, My Lord,
that **You** might be pleased.
He said: Then truly We have tried **your** folk 20:85
after **you**,
and the Samaritan has caused them to go astray.
Then Moses returned to his folk 20:86
angry, grieved.°

He said: O my folk!
Has not your Lord promised you a fair promise?°
Was what was promised too long *a wait* for you?
Or wanted you
that the anger of your Lord alight on you
so you broke my compact?

20:87 They said: We broke not
what was promised to **you**
from what is within our power,
but we were charged with a heavy load
of the adornments of the folk.
Then we hurled them as the Samaritan had cast.

20:88 Then he brought out for them a calf;
a lifeless body that had the lowing sound of flocks;
then they said: This *is* your god,
and the God of Moses, but he has forgotten.

20:89 What? See they not that it could not return to them
a saying,
nor possess for them either hurt nor profit?

Sec. 5
*

20:90 Indeed Aaron said to them before:
O my folk!
You are not but being tempted by it;°
and truly your Lord *is* The Merciful
so follow me and obey my command.

20:91 They had said:
We shall never quit
being ones who give ourselves up to it
until Moses returns to us.

20:92 He said: O Aaron!
What prevented **you**
when **you** saw them going astray

20:93 that **you** follow me not?
Have **you** then rebelled against my command?

20:94 He said: O son of my mother!
Take me not by my beard, nor by my head!
Truly I dreaded that **you** should say:
You have separated and divided
between the Children of Israel,

and **you** have not regarded my saying.

He said: Then what *is* **your** business 20:95
O Samaritan?

He said: I kept watch over what they kept not watch, 20:96
so I seized a handful
from the footprints of the Messenger
and cast it forth.
Thus my soul enticed me.

He said: Then go off! 20:97
Truly for **you** in this life *is* that **you** shall say:
Untouchable!
There is for **you** something promised
you shall never break!
Look on **your** god
that **you** have stayed with and given **yourself** up to!
Certainly we shall burn it,
then certainly we shall scatter it
in the water of the sea in a scattering.

Your God *is* not but God; 20:98
there is no god but He;
He encompasses everything in His knowledge.

Thus We relate to **you** 20:99
some tiding of what preceded.°

Indeed We have given **you** a Reminder
from that which proceeds from Our Presence.

Whoever turned aside from it, 20:100
then truly he shall carry
a heavy load on the Day of Resurrection,
ones who shall dwell in it forever; 20:101
how evil on the Day of Resurrection
shall be the load for them!

On the Day the trumpet shall be blown,° 20:102
We shall assemble
the ones who sin, white-eyed on that Day.

They shall whisper among themselves: 20:103
You have lingered in expectation but ten *days.*

We have greater knowledge of what they shall say 20:104
when the most ideal of them in conduct says:
You have lingered in expectation not but a day!

*

20:105   They ask shall **you** about the mountains;
say: My Lord shall scatter them a scattering.

20:106   Then He shall forsake it
as a leveled spacious plain.

20:107   **You** shall see not in it
any crookedness nor unevenness.

20:108   On that Day they shall follow
one who calls;
there shall be no crookedness in him;°
and voices shall be hushed for The Merciful,
so **you** shall hear nothing but a murmuring.

20:109   On that Day intercession shall not profit *anyone*
except him to whom permission has been given
by The Merciful,
and with whose saying He is well-pleased.

20:110   He knows what *is* in advance of them,
and what *is* behind them
and they shall not comprehend Him
in their knowledge.

20:111   Faces shall be humbled
before The Living, The Eternal;°
while indeed he who is burdened by injustice
shall be frustrated.

20:112   But the one who had acted in accord with morality,
should he be one who believes,
then he shall fear neither injustice nor unfairness.

20:113   Thus We have sent it forth
as an Arabic Recitation,
and We have paraphrased the threats in it
so that perhaps they would be Godfearing
or cause the Reminder to be evoked by them.

20:114   Then exalted be God, The True King!°
Hasten not the Recitation
before its revelation has been decreed to **you**;°
and say: My Lord! Increase me in knowledge!

20:115   Indeed We made a compact with Adam before,
then he forgot;
and We found no constancy in him.

*

When We said to the angels:
Prostrate yourselves to Adam!
They prostrated except Iblis;
he refused.
Then We said: O Adam!
Truly this *is* an enemy to **you** and to **your** spouse
so let him not drive you both out from the Garden
so that **you** not be unhappy.
Truly *it is* not for **you** that **you** be hungry in it,
nor shall **you** be naked;
Truly **you, you** shalt not thirst in it
nor suffer the heat of the sun.
Then Satan whispered evil to him.
He said: O Adam!
Shall I point **you** to the Tree of Everlastingness
and a dominion that shall not decay?
Then they both ate from that
so their intimate parts were shown to them,
and they took to stitching together for themselves
tree leaves from the Garden.°
Adam rebelled against his Lord
and he erred.
Then his Lord elected him,
so He turned in forgiveness to him
and guided him.
He said:
Get you both down from here altogether;°
some of you an enemy to some *others;*°
then if guidance approaches you from Me,
whoever follows My Guidance,
neither shall he go astray,
nor shall he be unhappy.
Whoever turns aside from My Reminder,
then truly for him *is* a livelihood of narrowness.
We shall assemble him on the Day of Resurrection
unwilling to see.
He said: O my Lord!
Why have **You** assembled me with the *unwilling* to see

20:116
20:117
20:118
20:119
20:120
20:121
20:122
20:123
20:124
20:125

when indeed I was seeing?

20:126 He would say: *It is* thus:
Our Signs approached **you**, but **you** forgot them;
thus this Day **you** shall be forgotten.

20:127 Thus We give recompense to him
who exceeds all bounds
and believes not in the Signs of his Lord.°
Surely punishment in the world to come
is more severe and one that endures.

20:128 Has He not guided them?
How many
generations have We caused to perish before them
amidst whose dwellings they walk?°
Truly in this *are* Signs
for the people who *have* sense.

*

20:129 If a word had not preceded
from **your** Lord for a determined term,
it would be close at hand.

20:130 So have patience with what they say,
and glorify the praises of **your** Lord
before the coming up of the sun
and before sunset;°
and during the watches of the nighttime,
and glorify at the end of the daytime,
so that perhaps **you** would be well-pleasing.

20:131 Stretch not out **your** eyes
for what We have given of enjoyment
to spouses among them
as the flower of this present life
so that We may try them by it.°
The provision of **your** Lord *is* best,
and one that endures.

20:132 Command **your** people to the formal prayer,
and to maintain patience in it;°
We ask not of **you** *for any* provision;°
We provide for **you**,°
and the Ultimate End *shall be* for the Godfearing.

20:133 They say: Why brings he not to us

a Sign from his Lord!°
Has *there* not approached them clear portents
that *were* in the first scriptures?
If We had caused them to perish   20:134
with a punishment before it,
indeed they would have said: Our Lord!
Why had **You** not sent to us a Messenger
so that we might have followed **Your** Signs
before we were degraded and humiliated!
Say: Each one is waiting   20:135
so watch;°
then you shall know
who *are* the Companions of the Path without fault
and who are truly guided.
***
                                                    Part 17

CHAPTER 21
THE PROPHETS (*al-Anbiyāʾ*)

In the Name of God,
the Merciful, the Compassionate   Sec. 1
The reckoning for humanity is near   21:1
while they *are* ones who turn aside
in heedlessness.
A renewed reminder from their Lord   21:2
never approaches them
but they listen to it while they play—
ones whose hearts are diverted,°   21:3
and they, those who did wrong
kept secret, conspiring secretly.
Is this other than a mortal like you?°
Shall you then approach sorcery
while you perceive?
He said: My Lord knows   21:4
the saying in the heavens and the earth;°
and He *is* The Hearing, The Knowing.
They said: Rather,   21:5
jumbled nightmares!
Rather, he has but devised it!

Rather, He *is* but a poet!
Let him bring us a Sign
as the ancient ones were sent!

21:6   No town has believed before them
of those We have caused to perish;°
shall they then believe?

21:7   We sent not before you
except as men to whom We revealed;°
so ask the People of the Reminder
if you know not.

21:8   We made them not bodies
that ate not food,
nor were they ones who shall dwell forever.

21:9   Then We were sincere in the promise,
so We rescued them and those whom We will;
We caused the ones who were excessive to perish.

21:10   Indeed We have sent forth to you a Book
which is your Reminder;°
shall you not then be reasonable?

Sec. 2   *

21:11   How many a town have We damaged
in which were ones that were unjust
and caused to grow after them another folk?

21:12   Then when they were conscious of Our Might,
lo! They made haste from it!

21:13   Make not haste
but return to
what you have been given ease in it
and to your dwellings,
so that perhaps you would be asked.

21:14   They said: Woe to us!
Truly we have been ones who were unjust!

21:15   Then they continued calling out
until We made them as stubble,
ones silent and stilled.

21:16   We created not the heavens and the earth,
and what is between them, *as* ones in play.

21:17   Had We wanted that
We would have taken some diversion,

indeed We would have taken it to Ourselves
from that which proceeds from Our Presence
if We *were* ones who were to do so.
Rather We hurl The Truth against falsehood   **21:18**
so it prevails over it;
then lo! *Falsehood* vanishes.°
Then woe to you for what you allege.
To Him *is*   **21:19**
whatever *is* in the heavens
and the earth.°
Those who *are* near Him,
they grow not too arrogant to worship Him,
nor they become weary.
They glorify *Him* nighttime and daytime;   **21:20**
they never decrease.
Or have they taken gods to themselves   **21:21**
from the earth,
ones who revive *the dead*?
Had there been gods in it, other than God,   **21:22**
indeed both would have gone to ruin.°
Then glory be to God!
Lord of the Throne! *High above* what they allege.
He shall not be asked   **21:23**
as to what He accomplished,
but they shall be asked.
Or have they taken gods to themselves other than He?   **21:24**
Say: Prepare your proof;°
this Reminder *is* for those with me
and a Reminder for those who *were* before me,°
but most of them know not The Truth;°
so they *are* ones who turn aside.
We sent not before **you** any Messenger,   **21:25**
but We revealed to him:
There is no god but I, so worship Me.
They say: The Merciful has taken to Himself   **21:26**
a son!°
Glory be to Him!°
They are but honored servants!
They precede Him not in saying,   **21:27**

and they act by His command.
He knows what *is* in advance of them
and what *is* behind them;
and they intercede not
except for him with whom He is content.
They—from apprehension of Him—
are ones in dread.

21:29
Whoever says of them:
Truly I *am* a god other than He,
then We shall give recompense to him *with* hell.°
Thus We give recompense
to the ones who are unjust.

Sec. 3
*

21:30
Are those who are ungrateful, not considering
that the heavens and the earth were interwoven
and We unstitched them°
and that We have made every living thing of water?
Would they then not believe?

21:31
We have made firm mountains on the earth
so that it should not vibrate with them,
and We made in it ravines as ways
so that perhaps they would be truly guided.

21:32
We have made heaven as a guarded roof,
yet they *are* the ones who turn aside from its Signs.

21:33
It is He Who has created the nighttime
and the daytime, the sun and the moon;°
each swimming in orbit.

21:34
We assigned not to any mortal before **you**
immortality;°
If **you** were to die,
shall they be ones who dwell forever?

21:35
Every soul shall experience death,°
and We shall try you with a chastisement
and good as a test;°
and to Us you shall be returned.

21:36
When those who are ungrateful see **you**,
they take **you** not to themselves
except in mockery:
Is this the one who mentions your gods?

As for the Reminder of The Merciful,
they *are* ones who are ungrateful.
The human being is created of haste.°   21:37
Soon I shall cause you to see My Signs,
so be not impatient!
They say: When shall this promise *be*   21:38
if you *are* the ones who are sincere?
If those who are ungrateful but knew the time when   21:39
they shall not ward off the fire from their faces,
nor from their backs
and they shall not be helped.
Rather it shall approach them suddenly!   21:40
Then they shall be dumfounded,
so they shall not be able to repel it,
nor shall they be given respite.
Indeed Messengers were ridiculed before **you**;   21:41
then those who derided them were surrounded
by what they used to ridicule.

*   Sec. 4

Say: Who shall guard you   21:42
in the nighttime and the daytime
for The Merciful?°
Rather they *are* the ones who turn aside
from the Reminder of their Lord.
Or *have* they gods who can secure them from Us?°   21:43
They are neither able to help themselves,
nor shall they be rendered safe from Us.
Rather We gave enjoyment *to* their fathers   21:44
until their lifetime was long for them; what?
Considered they not how We approach the earth;
We reduce it of its outlying parts.°
Is it then they *shall be* the ones who are the victors?
Say: I warn you not but by the revelation.°   21:45
But those *unwilling* to hear
shall not hear the supplication
when *they are* warned.
If a breath were to afflict them   21:46
of **your** Lord's punishment,
they would indeed say: Woe to us!

Truly we have been ones who were unjust.

21:47 We shall lay down the balances of equity
on the Day of Resurrection;
then wrong shall not be done to any soul at all;°
even if *be* the weight of a grain of a mustard seed,
We shall bring it,
and We suffice as ones who reckon.

21:48 Indeed We gave Moses and Aaron
the Criterion between right and wrong,
and as an illumination and as a Reminder
for the ones who are Godfearing,

21:49 those who dread their Lord in the unseen
and who are apprehensive of the Hour.

21:50 This *is* a blessed Reminder
that We have sent forth.°
Are you then ones who know not of it?

Sec. 5   *

21:51 Indeed We gave Abraham his right judgment
before,
and We had knowledge of him.

21:52 When he said to his father and his folk:
What *are* these statues
to which you *be* ones who give yourselves up?

21:53 They said:
We found our fathers
as ones who were worshippers of them.

21:54 He said: Indeed you and your fathers
were clearly wandering astray.

21:55 They said: Have **you** drawn near The Truth
or *are* **you** of the ones who play?

21:56 He said: Rather your Lord *is* Lord
of the heavens and the earth,
He Who originated them;
and I *am* of the ones who bear witness to this:

21:57 By God indeed I shall contrive
against your idols
after you have turned as ones who draw back.

21:58 So he made them broken pieces,
except the greatest of them,

377

so that perhaps they would return to it.

They said: Who has accomplished this 21:59
with our gods?

Truly he *is* of the ones who are unjust!

They said: We heard a male youth 21:60
mention them;
he is called Abraham.

They said: Then approach with him 21:61
before the eyes of personages
so that perhaps they would bear witness.

They said: Have **you** accomplished this with our gods 21:62
O Abraham?

He said: Rather it was accomplished 21:63
by the greatest of them;
ask them if they would speak for themselves.

So they returned to one another; 21:64
then they said:
Truly you, you *are* the ones who are unjust.

They were put into confusion: 21:65
Indeed you know
that these speak not for themselves.

He said: Worship you, then other than God 21:66
what neither profits you nor hurts you at all?

Fie on you on what you worship other than God!° 21:67
You are not reasonable.

They said: Burn him and help your gods 21:68
if you shall be the ones who do *so*!

We said: O fire! 21:69
Be coolness and peace for Abraham!

They wanted *to be* cunning, 21:70
but We made them the ones who are losers.

We delivered him and Lot to the region 21:71
which We have blessed for the worlds.

We bestowed Isaac on him, 21:72
and Jacob as an unexpected gift;°
and We made both of them
ones who are in accord with morality.

We made them leaders 21:73
guiding by Our command;

and We revealed to them
the accomplishing of good works,
and the performing the formal prayer,
and the giving of the purifying alms;
and they were the ones who were worshippers of Us.

21:74   To Lot, We gave him
critical judgment and knowledge,
and We delivered him from the town
which had been doing deeds of corruption;°
truly they were a morally evil folk,
ones who disobey.

21:75   We caused him to enter into Our Mercy;°
he *is* of ones who are in accord with morality.

Sec. 6
*

21:76   And Noah when he cried out before,
and We responded to him;
We delivered him and his people
from the tremendous distress.

21:77   We helped him against the folk
who denied Our Signs.°
Truly they were a morally evil folk
so We drowned them one and all.

21:78   And David and Solomon,
when they gave judgment about cultivation,
when a herd of the sheep of his folk had strayed,
and We were ones who bear witness
to their critical judgment.

21:79   So We caused Solomon to understand it.°
We gave each of them
critical judgment and knowledge.°
With David We caused to become subservient
the mountains and birds to glorify *God*;°
and We are the ones who have been the doers.

21:80   We taught him
the art of *making* garments of chain mail
to fortify you from your violence;°
shall you then be ones who are thankful?

21:81   To Solomon, the stormy wind
running by His command

toward the earth which We have blessed.°
We are ones who have knowledge of everything.
Among the satans *were* some who dived for him,   21:82
and did acts other than that;°
and We were ones who guard over them.
And Job when he cried out to his Lord: 21:83
Truly distress has afflicted me,
and **You** *are* one the Most Merciful
of the ones who are merciful.
So We responded to him;   21:84
then We removed his distress;°
and We gave him *back* his people
and others like them,
as a mercy from Us;
and be mindful of ones who are worshippers.
And Ishmael, Idris and Dhul-Kifl;°   21:85
all *were* of the ones who remained steadfast.
We caused them to enter into Our mercy;°   21:86
they *were* the ones who were in accord with morality.
And Jonah, when he went   21:87
as one who was enraged,
and thought that We would never have power
over him,
and then he cried out through the darkness:
There is no god but **You**!
Glory be to **You**!
Truly I have been of the ones who are unjust.
So We responded to him,   21:88
and We delivered him from the lament.°
Thus We rescue the ones who believe.
And Zechariah, when he cried out to his Lord: 21:89
O my Lord!
Forsake me not without an heir,
and **You** *are* the Best of the ones who inherit.
So We responded to him,   21:90
and We bestowed John on him,
and We made things right for his wife and for him.°
Truly they used to compete with one another
in good works,

and they used to call to Us
with yearning and reverence;°
and they were ones who were humble before Us.

21:91 She guarded her private parts,
then We breathed into her Our Spirit,
and We made her and her son
a Sign for the worlds.

21:92 Truly this *is* your community, one community,
and I *am* your Lord,
so worship Me.

21:93 But they have cut asunder their command;°
yet all of them *are* ones who return to Us.

Sec. 7 *

21:94 Whoever has acted in accord with morality,
and *is* one who believes,
then his endeavors shall not *be* rejected,
and truly We shall inscribe it for him.

21:95 There is a ban on the town
that We have caused to perish;
they shall not return

21:96 until Gog and Magog are let loose,
and they slide down from every slope.

21:97 The true promise is near,
then lo!
Glazed over shall be the sight
of those who are ungrateful!
Woe to us;
indeed we were in heedlessness of this;
on the contrary, we were ones who were unjust.

21:98 Truly you and what you worship,
other than God,
are fuel material for hell;
you *are* the ones who go down to it.°

21:99 If those had been gods,
they would never have gone down to it;°
all *are* ones who shall dwell in it forever.

21:100 There shall be sobbing in it for them,
and they shall not hear in it.

21:101 Truly those to whom there has preceded

fairness from Us,
those *are* ones who are to be far removed from it.
They shall not hear the low sound of it;° 21:102
and they, in that for which their souls lust,
shall be ones who shall dwell in it forever.
The great terror shall not grieve them, 21:103
and the angels shall have received them:
This *is* your day that you were promised!
On a Day when We roll up the heavens 21:104
like the rolled up written scrolls of manuscripts.°
As We began the first creation,
We shall cause it to return.°
It is a promise from Us.°
Truly We are ones who are doers.
Indeed We have written down in the Psalms 21:105
after the Reminder: My servants
who are in accord with morality shall inherit the earth.
Truly the delivering of this message *is* 21:106
for the worshipping folk.
We have not sent **you** 21:107
but as a mercy to the worlds.
Say: It is not but revealed to me 21:108
that your god *is* One God;°
shall then you *be* ones who submit?
But if they turn away, 21:109
then say: I have proclaimed to you all equally;°
and I was not informed
whether what you were promised is near or far.
Truly He knows the openly published saying 21:110
and He knows what you keep back.
I was not informed 21:111
so that perhaps it would be a test for you,
and an enjoyment for a while.
He said: 21:112
My Lord! Give judgment with The Truth;°
and our Lord *is* The Merciful,
He Whose help is sought
against what you allege.

CHAPTER 22
THE PILGRIMAGE TO MECCA (al-Ḥajj)

In the Name of God,

Sec. 1 the Merciful the Compassionate

22:1 O humanity! Be Godfearing of your Lord.°
Truly the earthquake of the Hour
is a tremendous thing.

22:2 On a Day you shall see it,
every one who is suckling (f)
shall be negligent of what she suckled,
and every pregnant woman shall bring forth a foetus;
and **you** shall see humanity as intoxicated,
yet they shall not be intoxicated;
but the punishment of God *shall be* severe.

22:3 Among humanity *is he* who disputes
about God
without knowledge,
and follows every rebel satan.

22:4 against whom it has been written down
that whoever turns away,
truly he shall cause him to go astray,
and shall guide him
to the punishment of the Blaze.

22:5 O humanity!
If you are in doubt about the Uprising,
truly We created you from earthy dust,
then from seminal fluids,
then from a clot,
then from tissue that is formed
and that is not formed
so that we may make *it* manifest to you.°
We establish in the wombs whom We will
for a determined term;
then We bring you out as infant children;
then you may reach the coming of age;°
among you *there is* he whom death calls to itself,
and among you *there is* he who is to be returned
to the vilest lifetime

so that he knows not anything
after *some* knowledge.°
You see the earth lifeless;
yet when We send forth water on it,
it quivers and it swells
and puts forth every lovely pair.
That *is* because God, He *is* The Truth, 22:6
and *it is* He Who gives life to the dead,
and He *is* Powerful over everything.
Truly the Hour *is* one that arrives; 22:7
there is no doubt about it,
and that God shall raise up
those who *are* in the graves.
Among humanity *is* he who disputes 22:8
about God
without knowledge nor guidance,
nor an illuminating Book,
turning to his side *as* one who turns away 22:9
to cause to go astray from the way of God;°
for him in this world *is* degradation;°
and We shall cause him to experience
on the Day of Resurrection
the punishment of the burning.
That *is* because of 22:10
what **your** two hands have put forward!
Truly God is not unjust to His servants.

*

Among humanity *is* he who worships God 22:11
on the fringes;°
if good lights on him, he is at rest with it;°
and if a test lights on him,
he turns completely over;
he loses the present and the world to come.°
That *it is* the clear loss.
He calls to other than God 22:12
what neither hurts him nor profits him.°
That *is* a far wandering astray.
He calls to him whose hurting 22:13
is nearer than his profiting.

Indeed miserable is the one who protects
and indeed miserable is the acquaintance.

22:14 Truly God shall cause to enter
those who have believed,
ones who have acted in accord with morality,
Gardens beneath which rivers run.
Truly God accomplishes what He wants.

22:15 Whoever thinks that God shall never help him
in the present and in the world to come,
let him stretch out a cord to heaven,
then let him sever it,
then let him look on
whether his cunning has caused to be put away
what enrages him.

22:16 Thus We sent forth as Signs, clear portents;
and that God guides whom He wants.

22:17 Truly those who have believed,
and those who became Jews, the Sabaeans
and the Christians and the Zoroastrians
and those who make partners—
truly God shall distinguish between them
on the Day of Resurrection;
truly God over everything *is* a Witness.

22:18 Have **you** not considered that
whatever *is* in the heavens prostrates to God
and whatever *is* in and on the earth,
and the sun, the moon and the stars,
the mountains, the trees and the moving creatures,
and many of humanity?°
The punishment shall be realized for many;°
and whom God despises,
then *there is* none who honors him.°
Truly God accomplishes whatever He will.‡

22:19 These two disputants strive against one another
about their Lord;°
then for those who are ungrateful,
garments of fire shall be cut out for them;
over their heads, scalding water shall be unloosed;

22:20 what *is* in their bellies shall melt by it,

into their skins.
For them *are* maces of iron.
Whenever they want
to go forth from there because of lament,
they shall be caused to return to it
and experience the punishment of burning.
*   Sec. 3

Truly God shall cause to enter   22:23
those who have believed,
ones who have acted in accord with morality,
Gardens beneath which rivers run.
They shall be adorned in them with bracelets
of gold and pearls;°
and their garments in it *shall be* of silk.
They are guided to what is good of the saying,   22:24
and they are guided to the Path
of Him Who is Worthy of Praise.
Truly those who are ungrateful,   22:25
and bar from the way of God
and the Masjid al-Haram,
which We have made for humanity
for the ones who inhabit it equally
with the ones who are desert dwellers.°
Whoever wants to violate it
or *intends* injustice,
We shall cause him to experience
a painful punishment.
*   Sec. 4

When We placed Abraham   22:26
in the place of the House:
Make nothing partners with Me
and purify My House
for the ones who circumambulate it,
and *for* the ones who *are* standing up,
the ones who bow down,
and the ones who prostrate themselves.
Announce to humanity the pilgrimage to Mecca;   22:27
they shall approach **you** on foot
and on every thin *camel*;

they shall approach from every deep ravine

22:28
that they may bear witness
to what is profitable to them
and remember the Name of God
on known days
over whatever He has provided them
from flocks of animals;°
then eat of it
and feed the ones who are in misery and the poor.

22:29
Then let them finish their ritual uncleanliness,
and live up to their vows,
and circumambulate the Ancient House.

22:30
That!
Whoever holds the sacred things of God in honor,
then that *is* better for him with his Lord,°
and permitted to you are the flocks,
except what shall be recounted to you;°
so avoid the disgrace of graven images,
and avoid saying the untruth,

22:31
turn to God as monotheists
not as ones who are polytheists.°
Whoever ascribes partners to God,
it is as if he had fallen down from heaven;
the birds snatch him
or the wind hurls him to ruin
in a place far away.

22:32
That!
Whoever holds the waymarks of God in honor,
then it is, truly from the Godfearingness of hearts.

22:33
You *have* in them what is profitable
for a determined term;
their place of sacrifice is by the Ancient House.

Sec. 5

22:34

*

For every community
We have assigned devotional acts
that they may remember the Name of God
over what We have provided them
of flocks of animals;°
and your God *is* One God;

submit to Him,°
and give good tidings
to the ones who humble themselves.
Those—   22:35
when God is remembered,
the hearts of the ones who remain steadfast quake
against whatever may light on them,
the ones who perform the formal prayer,
and who spend out of what We have provided them.
We have made for you the beasts of sacrifice   22:36
among the waymarks of God.
You *have* in them much good;°
so remember the Name of God
over them standing in ranks;°
then when they collapse on their sides,
eat from them,
and feed the ones who are paupers
and the ones who are poor persons who do not beg.°
Thus We have caused them to be subservient to you
so that perhaps you would be thankful.
Neither their flesh nor their blood attains God,   22:37
but your Godfearingness attains Him.°
Thus He caused them to be subservient to you
that you might magnify God
in that He has guided you,
and give good tidings
to the ones who are doers of good.
Truly God defends those who have believed,°   22:38
truly God loves not
anyone who is an ungrateful betrayer.
*   Sec. 6

Permission has been given   22:39
to those who have been fought against
because they, they have been wronged.°
Truly God has the power to help them,
those who   22:40
have been driven out from their abodes
without right
because they said: Our Lord *is* God!°

Had it not been that God drove back humanity,
some by some other,
cloisters would have been demolished,
and churches and synagogues,
and places of prostration
in which is remembered much
the Name of God;°
truly God shall help those who help Him,°
truly God *is* Strong, Almighty,

22:41 those who,
if We establish them firmly on the earth,
they perform the formal prayer,
and give the purifying alms,
they command to morality,
and they prohibit immorality—°
and with God *is* the Ultimate End of the command.

22:42 If they deny **you**,
indeed the folk of Noah had denied before **you**,
and those of Ad and Thamud,

22:43 and the folk of Abraham,
and the folk of Lot,

22:44 and the Companions of Midian;°
and Moses was denied,
but I granted indulgence
to the ones who are ungrateful,
then I took them;°
and how was My disapproval!

22:45 How many a town have We caused to perish
while they *were* ones who were unjust,
so that it *is* fallen down in ruins,
and well water ignored, and a tall palace.

22:46 What? Have they not journeyed through the earth,
and *have* they not hearts
to be reasonable or ears to hear?°
Truly *it is* not their sight that is in darkness,
but their hearts that are in darkness
within their breasts!

22:47 Impatient for the punishment, they *ask* **you** *for it;*
God never breaks His Promise.°

389

Truly a day with your Lord
is as a thousand years of what you number.
How many a town I have granted indulgence
while it *was* one that was unjust;
then I took it,
and to Me *was* the Homecoming.

*

Say: O humanity!
Truly I *am* a clear warner to you;
so those who have believed,
ones who have acted in accord with morality,
for them *is* forgiveness
and a generous provision.
Those who endeavor against Our Signs,
the ones who strive to thwart,
those *are* the Companions of Hellfire.
We sent not before you
any Messenger or Prophet
but that Satan cast into him fantasies
to fantasize,
but God annuls what Satan casts;
then God sets clear His Signs,°
and God *is* Knowing, Wise,
for He makes what Satan casts
a test for those whose hearts are sick
and their hearts hardened,
and truly the ones who are unjust
are in a wide breach.
Those who have been given knowledge know
that it *is* The Truth from **your** Lord
so that they may believe in it,
and humble their hearts to Him,°
and truly God *is* The One Who Guides
those who have believed
to a straight path.
Those who are ungrateful continue
to be hesitant about it,
until the Hour suddenly approaches them,
or the punishment of a withering Day?

22:56   On that Day the dominion shall *belong* to God;
He shall give judgment between them.°
So those who have believed,
the ones who have acted in accord with morality,
shall be in Gardens of Bliss.

22:57   Those who were ungrateful
and denied Our Signs,
for them *shall be* a despised punishment.

Sec. 8   *

22:58   Those who emigrated in the way of God,
then they were slain or died,
indeed God shall provide them a fair provision.°
Truly God, *it is* He who indeed
is the Best one who provides.

22:59   Indeed He shall cause them to enter a gate
with which they shall be well-pleased,°
and truly God *is* indeed Knowing, Forbearing.

22:60   That! Whoever has chastised
with the like of what he was chastised,
and then again is wronged,
God shall certainly help him,°
truly God *is* Pardoning, Forgiving.

22:61   That *is* because God causes the nighttime
to be inserted into the daytime
and He causes the daytime
to be inserted into the nighttime.
Truly God *is* Hearing, Seeing.

22:62   That *is* because God, He *is* The Truth,
and what they call to other than Him
is falsehood,
and that God, He *is* The Lofty, The Great.

22:63   Have **you** not considered that
God sends forth water from heaven,
and the earth becomes green,°
truly God *is* Subtle, Aware.

22:64   To Him *is* whatever *is* in the heavens
and whatever is in and on the earth,°
and truly God, He *is* The Sufficient,
The Worthy of Praise.

391

*

Have **you** not considered that · 22:65
God has caused to be subservient to you
what *is* in and on the earth;
the boats run through the sea by His command
and He holds back the heaven
so that it not fall on the earth,
except by His permission;°
truly to humanity God
is Gentle, Compassionate.
It is He Who gave you life, · 22:66
then He shall cause you to die,
then He shall give you life again,°
truly the human being *is* ungrateful.
For every community · 22:67
We have assigned devotional acts
so that they *be* ones who perform rites;°
so let them not bicker with **you** in the command,°
and call **you** to **your** Lord;°
truly **You** *are* indeed on a straight guidance.
If they dispute with **you**, · 22:68
then say:
God has greater knowledge of what you do.
God shall give judgment among you · 22:69
on the Day of Resurrection
about what you were at variance.
Know **you** not that God knows · 22:70
what *is* in the heaven and the earth?°
Truly that *is* in a Book.°
Truly that *is* easy for God.
They worship other than God, · 22:71
that for which He has sent down no authority,
and of what they *have* no knowledge!°
There is no helper for the ones who are unjust.
When · 22:72
Our Signs are recounted to them
clear portents,
you shall recognize
rejection on the faces of those who are ungrateful;

they are about to rush upon
those who recount Our Signs to them;°
say: Shall I tell you
of worse than that?
God has promised the fire
to those who are ungrateful.
How miserable shall be the Homecoming!

Sec. 10

22:73   O humanity!
Listen to a parable that is propounded.°
Truly those whom you call to other than God,
shall never create a fly,
even though they be gathered together for it;°
and if the fly were to rob them of something,
they would never seek to deliver it from *the fly*,
so weak are the ones who are seekers
and the ones who are sought.

22:74 They have not duly measured the measure of God;°
truly God *is* Strong, Almighty.

22:75 God favors Messengers from the angels
and from humanity.°
Truly God *is* Hearing, Seeing.

22:76 He knows what *is* in advance of them,
and what *is* behind them,°
and to God all commands return.

22:77 O those who have believed!
Bow down and prostrate *yourselves;*
worship your Lord,
and accomplish good
so that perhaps you would prosper.‡

22:78 Struggle for the sake of God
in a true struggling°
for He has elected you,
and has not made any impediment for you
in your way of life.°
It is the creed of your father Abraham.°
It is He Who named you the ones who submit
before and in this
so that perhaps the Messenger

would be a witness over you;
and you would be witnesses over humanity.°
So perform the formal prayer
and give the purifying alms and cleave firmly to God.
He *is* your Lord!°
How excellent a one who protects
and how excellent a helper!

***

CHAPTER 23
THE BELIEVERS (*al-Muʾminūn*)

In the Name of God,
The Merciful, The Compassionate   Sec. 1
Indeed the ones who believe have prospered,   23:1
they, those who in their formal prayers,   23:2
are ones who are humble;
and they, those who from idle talk   23:3
are ones who turn aside;
and they, those who for the purifying alms   23:4
are ones who do,
and they, those who of their private parts   23:5
are ones who guard,
except from their spouses   23:6
or what their right hands possess;
truly they *are* ones who are unreproachable.
Whoever looks for *something* beyond that,   23:7
then they, those are the ones who are turning away;
and they, those who   23:8
in their trusts and to their compacts
are ones who are as shepherds,
and they, those who over their formal prayers   23:9
are watchful;
they, those *are* ones who shall be inheritors,   23:10
those who shall inherit Paradise;   23:11
they *are* ones who shall dwell in it forever.
Indeed We have created the human being   23:12
from an extraction of clay;
then We made him into seminal fluid   23:13
in a stopping place, secure,

23:14	then We created a clot from seminal fluids,
	then We created tissue from the clot,
	then We created bones from tissue,
	then We clothed the bones with flesh,
	then We caused another creation to grow.°
	So blessed be God, fairest of creators!
23:15	Then truly after that, you *shall be* dead.
23:16	Then truly you shall be
	raised up on the Day of Resurrection.
23:17	Indeed We have created above you seven tiers.
	We *are* not ones who are heedless of the creation.
23:18	We sent forth water from heaven
	in measure,
	and We lodged it in the earth;°
	and We *are* ones who have the power to take away.
23:19	We caused to grow for you
	gardens of date palm trees and grapevines
	where *there is* much sweet fruit for you,
	and you eat of it,
23:20	and a tree that goes forth from the mountain of Sinai
	that bears oil and *it is* a seasoning
	for the ones who eat *it*.
23:21	Truly for you in the flocks *there is* indeed
	a lesson;°
	We satiate you with what is in their bellies;
	in them *are* many uses and of them you eat,
23:22	and you are carried on them
	and on boats.

*

Sec. 2	
23:23	Indeed We sent Noah to his folk
	and he said: O my folk! Worship God!
	You *have* no other god but Him;°
	shall you not, then be Godfearing?
23:24	But said the Council who were ungrateful
	among his folk:
	This *is* nothing but a mortal like you.
	He wants to gain superiority over you.
	Had God willed, He could have sent forth angels;
	we have not heard such a thing

from our ancient ones.
He *is* nothing but a man in whom *there is* madness, 23:25
so watch him for a while.
He said: O my Lord! 23:26
Help me because they deny *me*.
So We revealed to him: 23:27
Craft **you** the ship under Our eyes
and by Our revelation.
Then when Our command draws near,
and the oven boils,
insert two pairs of each kind
and **your** people, except
those against whom the saying has preceded;°
and address Me not
for those who have done wrong;°
truly they *are* to be drowned.
When **you** and whoever *is* with **you** are seated 23:28
in the ship,
then say: All Praise *belongs* to God
Who has delivered us
from the unjust folk.
Say: My Lord! 23:29
Harbor **you** me with a blessed harbor
for **You** *are* The Best of ones who harbor.
Truly in this *there are* indeed Signs, 23:30
and truly We are the ones who test.
Then after them, 23:31
We caused another generation to grow.
We sent a Messenger to them from among them: 23:32
Worship God!
You *have* no other god except Him;°
shall you then not be Godfearing?
*
The Council of his folk 23:33
who were ungrateful
and denied the meeting in the world to come,
and to whom We had given ease
in this present life, said:
This *is* nothing but a mortal like you;

Sec. 3

he eats of what you eat,
and he drinks of what you drink.
23:34 If you obey a mortal like yourselves,
truly then you *are* ones who are losers.
23:35 What? Has He promised that when you have died
and have become earthy dust and bones,
that you *shall be* ones who are to be brought out?
23:36 Absurd, absurd is what you are promised!
23:37 *There is* nothing but this present life;
we die and we live,
and we are not ones who shall be raised up.
23:38 He *is* nothing but a man
who has devised a lie against God,
and we *are* not ones who shall believe in him.
23:39 He said: O my Lord!
Help me because they deny me.
23:40 He said: In a little while
they shall become ones who are remorseful.
23:41 So a Cry duly took them,
and We made them into refuse;
so away with the unjust folk!
23:42 Then after them, We caused to grow
other generations.
23:43 No community can precede its term,
nor delay it.
23:44 Then We sent Our Messengers one after another;°
whenever a community drew near
to their Messenger,
they denied him;
so We caused some of them to follow others,
and We made them tales.°
So away with the folk who believe not!
23:45 Then We sent Moses and his brother Aaron
with Our Signs and clear authority
23:46 to Pharaoh and his Council,
but they grew arrogant
and they were a folk who exalted themselves.
23:47 Then they said:
Shall we believe in two mortals like ourselves

397

while their folk *are* ones who are worshippers of us?
So they denied both of them   23:48
and became the ones who were caused to perish.
Indeed We gave Moses the Book   23:49
so that perhaps they would be truly guided.
We made the son of Mary   23:50
and his mother
as a Sign,
and We gave them refuge on a hillside,
a stopping place and a spring of water.

O you Messengers!   23:51
Eat of what is good
and *be* one who acts in accord with morality;°
truly I *am* Knowing of what you do.
Truly this community *is* one community   23:52
and I *am* your Lord,
so be Godfearing.
But they cut their affair asunder   23:53
among themselves into sects;°
each party glad with what *was* with them,
so forsake them for a while in their obstinacy.   23:54
Assume they that what relief We furnish them   23:55
of wealth and children,
is because We compete with them in good works?   23:56
Rather they are not aware.
Truly they, those who dread their Lord   23:57
and who are apprehensive,
and they, those who,   23:58
believe in the Signs of their Lord
and they, those who   23:59
make not partners with their Lord,
and they, those who give what they give   23:60
with their hearts quaking because
they *are* ones who shall return to their Lord—
those compete with one another in good works;   23:61
they *are* Ones Who Outstrip them.
We place not a burden on any soul,   23:62
but to its capacity;

and with Us *is* a Book that speaks The Truth itself.°
They shall not be done wrong.

23:63 Rather their hearts
are in overwhelming heedlessness of this,
and they *have* actions other than that;
they *are* the ones who labor

23:64 until when We take those of them
who have been given ease
with the punishment,
lo! They make entreaties.

23:65 Make not entreaties this Day;°
truly you shall not be helped by Us.

23:66 Indeed My Signs
were recounted to you,
but you used to recede on your heels

23:67 as ones who grow in arrogance,
and ones who nightly talk nonsense,
talking foolishly.

23:68 Have they not meditated on the saying
or has anything drawn near to them
that approached not their fathers,
the ancient ones?

23:69 Or recognize they not their Messenger
so that they *are* ones who disavow him?

23:70 Or say they: *There is* madness in him?
Rather he drew near them with The Truth,
but most of them *are* ones who dislike The Truth.

23:71 If The Truth had followed their desires,
the heavens and the earth would have gone to ruin
and whoever *is* in it.°
Rather we have brought them their Reminder,
but they *are* ones who turn aside
from their Reminder.

23:72 Or *is it* that **you** ask them for payment?
But the revenue from **your** Lord *is* better;°
and He *is* the Best of ones who provide.

23:73 Truly **you** have called them to
a straight path.

23:74 Truly those who believe not

399

in the world to come
are ones who have moved away from the path.
Even if We had mercy on them,

and had removed the distress which *is* on them,
they would still be resolute in their defiance,
wandering *unwilling* to see.
Indeed We took them with punishment,

but they gave in not to their Lord,
nor did they lower themselves,
until when we opened a door for them

of a severe punishment;
they *shall be*
ones seized with despair!

*

He *it is* Who has caused you to grow,

have the ability to hear
and sight and mind.°
But few are thankful!
It is He Who has made you numerous on the earth,

and to Him you shall be assembled.
It is He Who gives life and causes to die,

and from Him *is*
the alteration of nighttime and daytime.°
Shall you not then be reasonable?
Rather they said the like of what

the ancient ones had said:
They said: When we are dead

and have become earthy dust and bones,
shall we indeed *be* the ones who are raised up?
Truly we have been promised this,

we and our fathers before;
this *is* nothing but the fables of the ancient ones.
Say: For whom *is* the earth

and whoever *is* in it
if you were to know?
They shall say: To God!°

Say: Shall you not, then recollect?
Say: Who *is* the Lord of the seven heavens

and Lord of the Sublime Throne?

23:87	They shall say: It *belongs* to God!°
	Say: Then *shall* you not be Godfearing?
23:88	Say: In whose hand is the kingship
	of everything
	and who grants protection?
	There is no one to grant protection
	against Him
	if you *were* to know.
23:89	They shall say: It *belongs* to God!°
	Say: Then how you are under a spell!
23:90	Rather We have brought them The Truth,
	and truly they *are* ones who lie.
23:91	God has not taken to Himself a son,
	nor is any god there along with Him.°
	For then, each god would have taken away
	what he had created,
	and some of them would have ascended
	over others.°
	Glory be to God! Above all that they allege!
23:92	*He is* the One Who Has Knowledge
	of the unseen and the visible.
	Exalted be He
	over the partners they make *with Him.*

Sec. 6

*

23:93	Say: My Lord!
	If **You** should cause me to see
	what they are promised,
23:94	then assign me not, my Lord,
	among the unjust folk.
23:95	Indeed We are able
	to cause **you** to see
	what We have promised them.
23:96	Drive back evil deeds with what *is* better.°
	We have greater knowledge of what they allege.
23:97	Say: My Lord!
	I take refuge with **You**
	from the evil suggestions of the satans.
23:98	I take refuge with **You**, my Lord,
	so that they not attend me.

When death draws near to one of them,   23:99
he says: My Lord!
Return me
so that perhaps I would   23:100
be one who acts in accord with morality
in what I have left behind.°
But nay!°
Indeed it *is* a word that one who converses *says;*°
and behind them *is* a barrier
until the Day they *are* raised up.
Then when the trumpet is blown,   23:101
there shall be no kinship among them that Day,
nor shall they inquire of one another.
Then those whose balance is heavy   23:102
they *are* the ones who prosper.
Those whose balance has been made light,   23:103
they have lost themselves;
they *shall be* ones who shall dwell in hell forever.
Their faces shall fry in the fire,   23:104
and they *shall be* the ones who are morose in it.
Were not My Signs   23:105
recounted to you,
but then you denied them?
They shall say: Our Lord!   23:106
Our agony prevailed over us;
we were a folk who have gone astray.
Our Lord! Bring us out of this;   23:107
then if ever we revert,
indeed we *shall be* the ones who are unjust.
He would say: Be driven away in it   23:108
and speak not to Me.
Truly there was a group of people   23:109
of My servants
who were to say: Our Lord!
We have believed,
so forgive us and have mercy on us,
for **You** *are* the Best of ones who are most merciful.
But you took them to yourselves   23:110
as a laughing stock,

until they caused you to forget
My Reminder,
and you were to laugh at them.

23:111 Truly I have given recompense this Day
for what they patiently endured;
indeed they, they *are* the ones who are victorious!

23:112 He would say:
You lingered in expectation on the earth
for what number of years?

23:113 They would say: We lingered in expectation a day
or a part of a day;
so ask one who counts.

23:114 He would say:
You lingered in expectation not but a little;
if you had but known. What?

23:115 Assumed you that We created you in amusement,
and that to Us you would not be returned?

23:116 So exalted be God! The true King!°
There is no god but He,
the Lord of the Generous Throne!

23:117 Whoever calls with God another god,
he *has* no proof of it,
then truly his reckoning *is* with his Lord.°
Truly the ones who are ungrateful shall not prosper.

23:118 Say: My Lord!
Forgive and have mercy,
and **You** *are* the Best
of the ones who are the most merciful.

CHAPTER 24
THE LIGHT (*al-Nūr*)

In the Name of God,
Sec. 1 The Merciful, The Compassionate
24:1 *This is* a chapter of the Quran
that We have sent forth
and We have imposed in it
Signs, clear portents
so that perhaps you would recollect.

403

Scourge the one who is an adulterer 24:2
and the one who is an adulteress;
each one of them one hundred strokes;
and let not tenderness for them take you
from the judgment of God,
if you believe in God and the Last Day;°
and let witness be borne to their punishment
by a section of the ones who believe.
One who is an adulterer 24:3
shall not marry
except one who is an adulteress
or the one who is a female polytheist;
and none shall marry the adulteress
except an adulterer or a male polytheist.°
All that is forbidden to the ones who believe.
Those who accuse 24:4
the ones who are free, chaste females,
but bring not four witnesses,
then scourge them eighty strokes,
and never accept their testimony,
and they, those are ones who disobey,
except those who repent after that, 24:5
and make things right.
So truly God is Forgiving, Compassionate.
Those who accuse their wives, 24:6
and there are no witnesses but themselves,
let the testimony of one of them
be four testimonies *sworn* by God, •
that he *is* one who is sincere;
and a fifth that the curse of God *be* on him 24:7
if he is one who lies.
It shall drive off the punishment from her 24:8
if she bears witness
with four testimonies *sworn* by God
that he is one who lies;
and the fifth, that the anger of God be on her 24:9
if he were one who is sincere.
Had it not been for the grace of God on you 24:10
and His mercy,

and that God *is* Accepter of Repentance, Wise.

*

24:11   Truly those who draw near with calumny
are many among you;
assume *it* not *to be* worse for you;
on the contrary it *is* good for you.°
To every man of them
is what he has deserved of sin.°
As for him who had the greater part
from among them,
there *shall be* a tremendous punishment.

24:12   Why when you heard about it
have not the ones who are male believers
and the ones who are female believers thought
the best of themselves
and say: This *is* a clear calumny?

24:13   Why have they not produced four witnesses for it?
Since they brought not witnesses,
then with God, they, those *are* the ones who lie.

24:14   Had it not been for the grace of God to you
and His mercy
in the present and in the world to come,
a tremendous punishment would afflict you
for what you had spoken.

24:15   When you had received it on your tongues
and said with your mouths,
that of which you had no knowledge,
you assumed it insignificant,
but with God it *was* serious.

24:16   Why, when you heard it, said you not:
It is not for us to assert this;
glory be to **You**!
This *is* a
serious false charge to harm the reputation of another.

24:17   God admonishes you
that you never revert to the like of it,
if you be ones who believe.

24:18   He makes manifest to you
the Signs.°

God *is* Knowing, Wise.

Truly those who love that indecency be spread 24:19
among those who have believed,
there is a painful punishment for them
in the present and in the world to come;
and God knows and you know not.

Had it not been for the grace of God on you and 24:20
His mercy—
and that God *is* Gentle, Compassionate.

*

O those who have believed! 24:21
Follow not in the steps of Satan.°
Whoever follows in the steps of Satan,
then truly he commands depravity,
and what is immoral,
and had it not been for the grace of God on you
and His mercy,
none of you would ever have been pure in heart,
but God makes pure whom He will,°
and God *is* Hearing, Knowing.

Let not those with grace 24:22
and plenty among you forswear
to give to kin and the needy
and the ones who are emigrants in the way of God,
and let them pardon and overlook;°
love you not that God should forgive you?°
God *is* Forgiving, Compassionate.

Truly those who accuse 24:23
the ones who are chaste, heedless, believing females
are cursed in the present
and the world to come;
and for them *shall be* a serious punishment.

On a Day 24:24
when witness shall be borne against them
by their tongues and their hands and their feet
as to what they were doing.

On a Day God shall pay them their account in full, 24:25
what *is* justifiably due,
and they shall know that God,

He *is* The clear Truth.

Bad women *are* for bad men
and bad men *are* for bad women;°
and good women *are* for good men
and good men *are* for good women.°
Those *are* ones declared innocent of what they say;°
for them *is* forgiveness and generous provision.

*

O those who have believed!
Enter not houses other than your houses
until you have announced your presence
and greeted the people.° That *is* better for you
so that perhaps you would recollect.

If you find not in it anyone,
then enter them not
until permission has been given to you;°
and if it is said for you to return;°
then return; it is purer for you.°
God *is* Knowing of what you do.

There is no blame on you
in entering
uninhabited houses
wherein you have enjoyment;
and God knows what you show
and what you keep back.

Tell the ones who believe to lower their sight
and keep their private parts safe.°
That *is* purer for them,°
truly God *is* Aware of what they craft.

Say to ones who are female believers
to lower their (f) sight,
and keep their (f) private parts safe,
and not show their (f) adornment,
except what is manifest of it;°
and let them (f) draw their head covering
over their (f) bosoms,
and not show their (f) adornments
except to their (f) husbands,
or their (f) fathers,

or the fathers of their (f) husbands,
or their sons or the sons of their (f) husbands,
or their (f) brothers,
or the sons of their (f) brothers,
or the sons of their (f) sisters,
or their (f) women that their (f) right hands possess,
or males, the ones who have no sexual desire,
or children to whom nakedness of women
has not been manifest;
and let them (f) not stomp their feet so as
to make known
what they (f) conceal of their adornment.°
Turn to God altogether for forgiveness,
O ones who believe,
so that perhaps you would prosper.
Wed unmarried women among you   24:32
to the ones who are in accord with morality
of your male bond servants
and your female bond servants.°
If they be poor,
God shall enrich them of His grace,°
and God *is* One Who Embraces, Knowing.
Let those who find not   24:33
the means for marriage have restraint
until God enriches them of His grace,
as for those who are looking for emancipation
from among what your right hand possesses,
contract with them
if you know good in them;°
and give them of God's wealth,
which He has given you.°
Your female youth, compel them not against their will
to prostitution if they (f) have wanted chastity
because you are
looking for the advantage of this present life.°
He who compels them to it against their will,
yet after their (f) compulsion,
God *shall be* Forgiving, Compassionate.
Indeed We have sent forth to you   24:34

manifest Signs,
and a parable of those who passed away before you,
and an admonishment for ones who are Godfearing.

Sec. 5   *

24:35   God *is* the Light of the heavens and the earth.°
The parable of His Light
is as a niche in which there *is* a lamp;°
the lamp *is* in a glass;°
the glass *is* as if it were a glittering star,
lit from a blessed tree, an olive,
neither eastern nor western,
whose oil would almost illuminate
although no fire touched it.°
Light on light,°
God guides to His Light whom He will!°
God propounds parables for humanity,°
and God *is* Knowing of everything.

24:36   The Light is in houses God gave permission
to be lifted up,
and that His Name be remembered in it,
He is glorified in the first part of the day
and the eventide

24:37   by men
whom neither trade nor trading diverts
from the remembrance of God,
and performing the formal prayer,
and the giving of purifying alms;
they fear a Day when heart and sight
shall go to and fro in it,

24:38   that God may give recompense to them
according to the fairest of what they have done,
and increase even more for them from His grace,°
and God provides to whom He will
without reckoning.

24:39   As for those who are ungrateful,
their actions *are* like a mirage in a spacious plain.
The thirsty one assumes it *to be* water,
until when he draws near it.
He finds it *to be* nothing

but he finds God with him
Who shall pay his account in full,°
and God *is* Swift at reckoning.
Or like the darknesses in an obscure sea;

24:40

overcome by a wave, above which is a wave,
above which is a cloud.°
Darkness, one above another;
when he brings out his hand
he almost sees it not,
and he for whom God has not assigned light,
there is no light for him.

*

Have **you** not considered that   24:41
God is glorified by everything
in the heavens and the earth;
and the birds spreading their wings,
each knows his prayer and his glorification,°
and God *is* Knowing of what they accomplish.
To God *is* the dominion   24:42
of the heavens and the earth;°
and to God *is* the Homecoming.
Have **you** not considered how God propels clouds,   24:43
then brings them together,
then lays them into a heap,
and **you** see the rain drops that go forth in the midst;
and He sends down from the heaven
mountains in which *there is* hail.
He lights it on whom He will,
and turns away from it whom He will;°
the gleams of His lightning
almost take away the sight.
God turns round and round   24:44
the nighttime and the daytime.°
Truly in this *is* a lesson for those who have insight.
God created every moving creature from water;°   24:45
of them, *there is* what walks on its belly,
and of them, *there is* what walks on two feet,
and of them, *there is* what walks on four.°
God creates what He will.°

Truly God *is* Powerful over everything .

24:46 Indeed We have sent forth manifest Signs.°
God guides whom He will to a straight path.

24:47 They say: We have believed in God
and the Messenger,
and we obey;
then a group of people among them turn away
after that.°
Those *are* not the ones who believe.

24:48 When they are called to God
and His Messenger
to give judgment among them,
then a group of people among them
are ones who turn aside.

24:49 But if they are in the right,
they would approach him
as ones who are yielding.

24:50 Are their hearts sick?
Or be they in doubt
or fear
that God and His Messenger shall be unjust to them?°
Rather they, those *are* the ones who are unjust.

Sec. 7
*

24:51 The saying of the ones who believe
when they are called to God and His Messenger
that He give judgment between them
is to say: We hear and obey.°
Such are the ones who prosper.

24:52 Whoever obeys God and His Messenger
and dreads God and is Godfearing,
they, those are the ones who are victorious.

24:53 They swear by God their most earnest oaths
that if **you** would command them,
they would go forth.
Say: Swear not;°
moral obedience *is better.*°
Truly God *is* Aware of what you do.

24:54 Say: Obey God and obey the Messenger;
but if you turn away,

then on him *is* not but what he loaded on himself,
and on you *is* what you loaded on yourselves;°
and if you obey him, you shall be truly guided.°
There is not *a duty* on the Messenger
except delivering the clear message.
God has promised
those who have believed among you,
the ones who have acted in accord with morality,
that He shall make them successors in the earth,
even as He made successors among those before them,
that He shall establish their way of life firmly for them
by which He is content with them;
and He shall substitute a place of sanctuary
for their fear.°
They worship Me,
not making any partner with Me.°
Whoever after that is ungrateful,
they, those *are* the ones who disobey.
Perform the formal prayers
and give the purifying alms,
and obey the Messenger
so that perhaps you would find mercy.
Assume not those who are ungrateful
that they *are*
ones who shall frustrate *the will of God* in the region.°
Their place of shelter *is* the fire;°
and how miserable *is* the Homecoming!

*

O those who have believed!
Let your permission be asked for by
those whom your right hands possess
and those who have not reached puberty,
three times:°
Before the dawn formal prayer,
when you lay down your garments at noon
and after the time of night formal prayer.°
These are the three times of privacy for you.°
There is not on you nor on them blame after these.°
Other than these, go about

some of you with some others.°
Thus God makes manifest to you the Signs,°
and God *is* Knowing, Wise.°

24:59 When infant children reach puberty among you,
then let them ask permission
as permission was asked
by those who *were* before them.°
Thus God makes manifest for you His Signs,°
and God *is* Knowing, Wise.

24:60 Women who are past child-bearing,
who hope not for marriage,
there is no blame on them (f)
if they lay down their (f) garments,
but not as the ones who flaunt themselves
and *their* adornment;°
that they have restraint *is* better for them (f),°
and God *is* Hearing, Knowing.

24:61 There is no fault on the blind,
nor on the lame,
nor on the sick,
nor on yourselves,
that you eat from your houses,
or the houses of your fathers,
or the houses of your mothers,
or the houses of your brothers,
or the houses of your sisters,
or the houses of your paternal uncles,
or the houses of your paternal aunts,
or the houses of your maternal uncles,
or the houses of your maternal aunts,
or of that for which you possess its keys,
or your ardent friend.°
There is no blame on you
that you eat together or separately.°
But when you enter houses,
then greet each other
with a greeting from God,
one that is blessed and what is good.°
Thus God makes manifest for you the Signs

413

so that perhaps you would be reasonable.

*

The ones who are true believers *are* not but
those who believe in God
and His Messenger.
When they are with him on a collective matter,
they go not
until they have asked his permission.°
Truly those who ask **your** permission
those *are* they who have believed in God
and His Messenger.°
So if they ask for **your** permission
for some of their affairs,
give permission to whom **you** willed of them,
and ask God for forgiveness for them.°
Truly God *is* Forgiving, Compassionate.

The supplication of the Messenger among you
is not as your supplication of one another.°
Indeed God knows you
who slip away under cover.°
Let those who go against his command beware
so that a test should not light on them,
or a painful punishment not light on them.

Surely to God
belongs whatever *is* in the heavens and the earth;°
indeed He knows what your hands have done,
and on the Day when they are returned to Him,
then He shall tell them what their hands have done,°
and God *is* Knowing of everything.

CHAPTER 25
THE CRITERION (*al-Furqān*)

In the Name of God,
The Merciful, The Compassionate
Blessed was He Who sent down
the Criterion between right and wrong
to His servant
so that

414

he may be a warner to the worlds;

He to Whom *belongs* the dominion
of the heavens and the earth,
and Who took not *to Himself* a son.
There is no associate for Him in the dominion,
and He created everything
and has ordained it a foreordaining.

25:3 Yet they have taken gods other than Him
who create nothing
and are *themselves* created,
and they neither possess for themselves
hurt nor profit
nor *have* they dominion
over death, nor this life, nor rising.

25:4 Those who were ungrateful said:
Maybe this *is* nothing but a calumny he devised
and other folk have assisted him;°
so they have produced injustice and an untruth.

25:5 They said: Fables of the ancient ones
which he has caused to be written down!
They are recounted to him
at early morning at dawn and at eventide.

25:6 Say: It has been sent forth by Him
who knows the secret
in the heavens and the earth.°
Truly He *is* Forgiving, Compassionate.

25:7 They say: What Messenger is this
that he eats food

• and walks in the markets?
Why has an angel not been sent forth to him
to be a warner with him?

25:8 Or a treasure not cast down to him,
or a garden not for him
so he may eat from it?°
The ones who are unjust said:
You follow nothing but a bewitched man.

25:9 Look on how they propound parables for **you**
for they *are* all gone astray
and are not able *to find* a way.

*

Blessed was He Who,
had God willed, assigned for you better than that,
Gardens beneath which rivers run,
and He shall assign for **you** palaces.
Rather they deny the Hour;°   25:11
and We have made ready a blaze
for him who denied the Hour.
When it sees them from a far place,   25:12
they would hear it raging furiously and roaring.
When they are cast down from it   25:13
into a narrow place,
ones who are chained,
they would call to be damned:
It shall be said to them: Call not today   25:14
for a single damnation,
but call for many damnations.
Say: *Is* that better   25:15
or the Garden of Eternity which *is* promised
the Godfearing?°
It would be a recompense for them
and a Homecoming.
For them in it *shall be* whatever they will,   25:16
ones who shall dwell in it forever.°
That was a promise besought from your Lord.
On the Day He shall assemble them   25:17
and what they worship other than God.
This He shall say:
Was it you who caused My servants to go astray?
Or have they caused *themselves* to go astray
from the way?
They shall say: Glory be to **You**!   25:18
It was not fit and proper for us
to take to ourselves other than **You** any protectors,
but **You** gave to them enjoyment
and to their fathers
until they forgot the Reminder
and became a lost folk.
Truly they have denied you in what you say;   25:19

you shall neither be able to turn away from it,
nor have help.°
Whoever does wrong among you,
We shall cause him to experience
the great punishment.

We sent not before **you** any one who is sent
except that truly they ate food
and walked in the markets,°
and We have made
some of you as a test for some others;
shall you patiently endure?°
Your Lord *is* Seeing.

***

*

25:21 Those who hope not for a meeting with Us say:
Why were angels not sent forth to us
and why see we not our Lord?°
Indeed they grew arrogant in themselves,
and defiant, turning in great disdain.

25:22 On a Day they shall see the angels,
there shall be no good tidings for ones who sin,
and they shall say: Unapproachable! Banned!

25:23 We shall advance on whatever actions they did;
We shall make them as scattered dust.

25:24 The Companions of the Garden on that Day
shall have the best resting place
and the fairest place of noonday rest.

25:25 On a Day when heaven shall be split open
with the cloud shadows
and the angels shall be sent down
as a sending down successively.

25:26 On that Day the true dominion
shall belong to The Merciful.°
It would be a Day
difficult for the ones who are ungrateful.

25:27 On a Day when one who is unjust
shall bite his hands,
he shall say: Would that
I had taken myself to a way with the Messenger!

Woe is me! 25:28
Would that I had not taken so-and-so to myself
as a friend!
Indeed he has caused me to go astray 25:29
from the Reminder
after it had drawn near to me,°
and Satan *is* a betrayer of the human being.
The Messenger said: O my Lord! 25:30
Truly my folk took the Quran
as something to be abandoned!
Thus We assigned for every Prophet 25:31
an enemy of the ones who sin,°
and your Lord suffices
as one who guides and as a helper.
Those who were ungrateful said: 25:32
Why is the Quran not sent down to him all at once?
^Thus^ We shall make firm your mind by it;°
and We have chanted a chanting.
They bring **you** no parable, 25:33
but We bring about The Truth to **you**;°
and the fairer exposition.
Those who shall be assembled on their faces 25:34
in hell,
those *are* worse situated,
ones who have gone astray from the way.

Sec. 4

Indeed We gave Moses the Book, 25:35
and assigned his brother Aaron to him
as a minister.
We said: You both go to the folk 25:36
who have denied Our Signs,
then We destroyed them,
causing them to be destroyed.
The folk of Noah, 25:37
when they denied the Messengers,
We drowned them,
and We made them as a Sign for humanity;°
and We have made ready a painful punishment
for the ones who are unjust,

418

CHAPTER 25 THE CRITERION (*al-Furqān*) STAGE 4 PART 19 SECTION 4 25:28-25:37

| 25:38 | and Ad and Thamud |

and the Companions of Rass,
and many generations in between those.

25:39   We propounded parables for each of them;°
and We shattered each a shattering.

25:40   Surely they have approached the town
where an evil rain rained down on them;
have they not considered it?°
Rather they were not hoping for any rising.

25:41   When they see **you**,
they take **you** not but in mockery:
Is this the one whom God has raised up
as a Messenger?

25:42   He was about to cause us to go astray
from our gods
had it not been that we patiently endured in them!°
Soon they shall know,
at the time when they see the punishment,
who *it is* who has gone astray from the way.

25:43   Have **you** considered him who has taken to himself
his own desires as his god?
Would **you** then be over him a trustee?

25:44   Or assume **you**
that most of them hear or are reasonable?°
They *are* not but as flocks;°
rather they *are* ones who have gone astray
from the way.

*

Sec. 5

25:45   Have **you** not considered
how **your** Lord stretched out the shade,
and had He willed, He would have made it still;
then We made the sun an indicator over it.

25:46   Then We seize it to Us an easy seizing.

25:47   *It is* He Who makes the nighttime
a garment for you and sleep a rest,
and makes the daytime for a rising.

25:48   *It is* He Who sends the winds
as that which bears the good tidings
in advance of His Mercy.°

We sent forth undefiled water from heaven
that We may give life by it to a lifeless land   25:49
and with it We satiate
the many flocks and men that We have created.
Indeed We diversify among them   25:50
so that they may recollect,
but most of humanity refuses *everything*
except ingratitude.°
Had We willed,   25:51
We would have raised up a warner in every town.
So obey not the ones who are ungrateful,   25:52
but struggle against them
with a great struggling.
It is He Who has let forth the two seas;   25:53
this, agreeable and water of the sweetest kind,
and this, salty, bitter;
between the two
is an unapproachable, banned barrier.
It is He Who created a mortal from water   25:54
and has made blood kindred for him
and kin by marriage,°
and **your** Lord *is* ever Powerful.
Yet they worship other than God,   25:55
what neither profits them,
nor hurts them,°
and the one who is ungrateful
is ever an abettor against his Lord.
We have not sent **you**   25:56
except as one who gives good tidings
and as a warner.
Say: I ask of you no compensation   25:57
except that whoever willed, should take himself
on a way to his Lord.
Put your trust in the Living   25:58
Who *is* Undying,
and glorify His praise.°
He Suffices,
Aware of the impieties of His servants,
He Who created the heavens and the earth   25:59

and all that *is* between the two
in six days
then He turned His attention to the Throne.°
The Merciful!
So ask the aware about Him.

25:60 When it was said to them:
Prostrate yourselves to The Merciful,
they said: What is The Merciful?
Shall we prostrate ourselves
to what **you** have commanded us?
It increased aversion in them.‡

*

25:61 Blessed was He Who
made constellations in the heaven,
and has made in it a light-giving lamp
and an illuminating moon.

25:62 He *it is* Who made
the nighttime and the daytime to follow in succession
for whom He had wanted to recollect,
or He had wanted thankfulness.

25:63 The servants of The Merciful
are those who walk on the earth in meekness;
and when the ones who are ignorant address them,
they say: Peace!

25:64 Those who spend the night with their Lord
as ones who prostrate and upright *in worship*,

25:65 and those who say: Our Lord!
Turn us away from the punishment of hell;
truly its punishment shall be continuous;

25:66 truly it is evil an habitation and resting place.

25:67 Those who, when they spend,
neither exceed all bounds nor *are they* tightfisted,
but *they take* a just stand between those *two*.

25:68 Those who call not to another god
other than God,
nor kill a soul
which God has forbidden
except justifiably,
nor commit adultery.°

Whoever accomplishes this
shall meet sinfulness;
the punishment shall be multiplied for him   25:69
on the Day of Resurrection,
and he shall dwell in it forever,
as one who is despised.
But whoever has repented and has believed,   25:70
one who has acted in accord with morality,
for those God shall substitute benevolence
for their evil deeds
and God *is* Forgiving, Compassionate.
Whoever repents,   25:71
one who has acted in accord with morality,
he truly repents to God,
turning in repentance.
Those who bear not witness untruthfully,   25:72
when they pass by idle talk,
they pass by nobly.
Those who fall not down   25:73
when they are reminded
of the Signs of their Lord,
unwilling to hear, *unwilling* to see.
Those who say: Our Lord!   25:74
Bestow on us
the comfort of our eyes
from our wives and our offspring
and make us leaders
of ones who are Godfearing;
those shall be given recompense   25:75
in the highest chambers,
because they patiently endured.
They shall be in receipt of greetings and peace,
ones who shall dwell in it forever,°
an excellent habitation and resting place!   25:76
Say: My Lord would not concern Himself with you   25:77
had it not been for your supplication;°
but indeed you have denied
so it shall be close at hand.

CHAPTER 26
THE POETS (*al-Shuᶜarāʾ*)

In the Name of God,

the Merciful, the Compassionate

26:1 *Ṭā Sīn Mīm;*

26:2 these *are* the Signs of the clear Book.

26:3 It may be that
you are one who consumes **yourself** in grief
because they become not ones who believe.

26:4 If We will, We could send down to them
from heaven a Sign
so that perhaps their necks would stay
ones that are bent in humility

26:5 and there would not approach them
any renewed Reminder from The Merciful
except that they are the ones who turn aside from it.

26:6 But they have denied it;
so soon the tiding shall approach them
about which they were ridiculing.

26:7 Have they not considered the earth
how much We caused to develop in it,
every generous pair?

26:8 Truly in that *is* a Sign;°
yet most of them were not ones who believe.

26:9 Truly **your** Lord, He *is*, indeed
The Almighty, The Compassionate.

Sec. 2

*

26:10 When **your** Lord proclaimed to Moses:
Approach the unjust folk,

26:11 *the* folk of Pharaoh.°
Shall they not be Godfearing?

26:12 He said: My Lord!
Truly I fear that they shall deny me,

26:13 and my breast be narrowed,
and my tongue shall not be loosened.
So send to Aaron.

26:14 They have a charge against me,
so I fear that they shall kill me.

He said: Nay!° 26:15
Both of you go with Our Signs;°
truly We shall be with you,
ones who are listening.
So both of you go to Pharaoh and say: 26:16
We are the Messengers of the Lord of the worlds,
so send the Children of Israel with us. 26:17
Pharaoh said: 26:18
Had we not raised **you** up among us as a child?
Lingered **you** not in expectation with us
for many years of **your** lifetime?
You have accomplished 26:19
your accomplishment what **you** have accomplished
and **you** *are* of the ones who are ungrateful.
Moses said: I accomplished it 26:20
while I *was*
of the ones who had gone astray.
So I ran away from you when I feared you, 26:21
but my Lord bestowed on me critical judgment,
and made me of the ones who are sent.
Beyond this past favor 26:22
with which **you** reproach me,
you have enslaved the Children of Israel.
Pharaoh said: What *is* the Lord of the Worlds? 26:23
Moses said: The Lord of the heavens and the earth 26:24
and all that *is* between the two of them;°
if you are one who is certain.
Pharaoh said to those around him: 26:25
Listen you not?
Moses said: Your Lord 26:26
and the Lord of your fathers, the ancient ones.
Pharaoh said: 26:27
Truly your Messenger who has been sent to you
is one who is possessed!
Moses said: The Lord of the East and the West 26:28
and all that *is* between the two of them;°
if you would be reasonable!
Pharaoh said: If **you** take to **yourself** a god 26:29
other than me,

I shall indeed assign **you** to be imprisoned!

26:30 *Moses* said: What if I draw something near to **you**
that makes it clear?

26:31 *Pharaoh* said: Bring it
if **you** are one who is sincere.

26:32 So he cast his scepter and lo!
It was clearly a serpent.

26:33 He drew out his hand and lo!
It was white to the ones who looked.

Sec 3 *

26:34 He said to the Council around him:
Truly this *is* one who is a knowing sorcerer!

26:35 He wants to drive you out from your region
by his sorcery.
What *is it,* then that you suggest?

26:36 They said: Put him and his brother off,
and raise up the ones who summon in the cities;

26:37 they shall bring every knowing witch to **you**.

26:38 So the ones who were sorcerers were gathered
at a time appointed on a known day,

26:39 and it was said to humanity:
Are you ones who shall be gathered together?

26:40 *They said:* Perhaps we would follow
the ones who are sorcerers
if they be the ones who are victors.

26:41 So when the ones who were sorcerers drew near,
they said to Pharaoh:
Is there a compensation for us
if we should be the ones who are victors?

26:42 *Pharaoh* said: Yes!
Truly you *shall be* ones brought near *to me.*

26:43 Moses said to them:
Cast as the ones who cast.

26:44 So they cast their ropes and their scepters,
and said: By the great glory of Pharaoh,
we, we *shall* surely *be* the ones who are victors!

26:45 Then Moses cast his scepter
and lo!
It swallowed their lying deceit.

The ones who were sorcerers were cast down 　　26:46
as ones who prostrate.
They said: 　　26:47
We believe in the Lord of the worlds,
the Lord of Moses and Aaron. 　　26:48
Pharaoh said: 　　26:49
You have believed in him
before I gave permission to you?
He *is* indeed your foremost;
he is the one who has taught you sorcery,
soon truly you shall know.°
I shall cut off your hands and your feet
alternately,
and I shall crucify you all.
They said: No harm! 　　26:50
Truly to our Lord we *are the* ones who are turning;
truly we are desirous 　　26:51
that Our Lord forgive us our transgressions,
as we are the first of the ones who believed.
* 　　Sec. 4

We revealed to Moses: 　　26:52
Set forth by night with My servants;
truly you *are* ones who shall be followed.
Then Pharaoh sent to the cities 　　26:53
ones who summon.
They said: Truly these are a small crowd 　　26:54
and truly they have enraged us; 　　26:55
truly we *are* altogether ones who are cautious, 　　26:56
so We drove them out from gardens and springs, 　　26:57
and treasures and a generous station. 　　26:58
We thus gave them as inheritance 　　26:59
to the Children of Israel.
So they pursued them at sunrise 　　26:60
and when the two multitudes sighted each other, 　　26:61
the Companions of Moses said:
Truly we *are* ones who are overtaken.
Moses said: Nay!° 　　26:62
Truly my Lord *is* with me
and He shall guide me.

26:63	Then We revealed to Moses:
	Strike the sea with **your** scepter!°
	It divided,
	and each became a separate part
	like a high, tremendous mountain.
26:64	We brought the others close there,
26:65	and We rescued Moses
	and those with him one and all;
26:66	then We drowned the others.
26:67	Truly in this *is* a Sign;°
	yet most of them *were* not ones who believe.
26:68	Truly **your** Lord, He *is*
	The Almighty, The Compassionate.
Sec. 5	*
26:69	Recount to them
	the tidings of Abraham,
26:70	when he said to his father and his folk:
	What is it you are worshipping?
26:71	They said: We worship idols,
	and we shall stay
	ones who give themselves up to them.
26:72	He said: Are they to hear you
	when you call them?
26:73	Are they profiting you or hurting you?
26:74	They said:
	Rather we found our fathers acting likewise.
26:75	He said:
	See now what you worship,
26:76	you and your fathers, the elders?
26:77	Truly they *are* an enemy to me
	except the Lord of the worlds
26:78	Who has created me,
	and *it is* He Who guides me
26:79	and *it is* He, He Who feeds me
	and gives me drink;
26:80	and when I am sick, *it is* He Who heals me,
26:81	and Who causes me to die, then shall give me life,
26:82	and from Whom I am desirous
	that He shall forgive me my transgressions

on the Day of Judgment.

My Lord! Bestow on me critical judgment, 26:83
and cause me to join
the ones who are in accord with morality;

and assign me a good repute 26:84
in the later generations;

and make me one who is an inheritor 26:85
of the Garden of Bliss;

and forgive my father, 26:86
truly he was of the ones who have gone astray.

Cover me not with shame 26:87
on a Day they shall be raised up,

on a Day neither wealth nor children 26:88
shall profit,

except him who approaches God 26:89
with a pure-hearted heart.

The Garden would be brought close 26:90
for the ones who are Godfearing,

and hellfire would be advanced 26:91
to the ones who are in error.

It would be said to them: 26:92
Where *is* what you used to worship
other than God? 26:93

Are you helped by them
or help they themselves?

Then they shall be thrown down into it, 26:94
they and the ones who were in error,

and the army of Iblis, one and all. 26:95

They shall say while they are in it 26:96
striving against one another:

By God! Truly we were clearly wandering astray 26:97
when we made you equal 26:98
with the Lord of the worlds;

and no one caused us to go astray 26:99
but the ones who sin;

now we have none who are intercessors, 26:100
nor an ardent friend, a loyal friend. 26:101

Would that *there were* for us a return again, 26:102
then we would be of the ones who believe!

428

26:103	Truly in this *is* a Sign;°
	yet most of them *were* not ones who believe.
26:104	Truly **your** Lord, He *is*
	The Almighty, The Compassionate.
Sec. 6	*
26:105	*The* folk of Noah denied the ones who were sent
26:106	when their brother, Noah, said to them:
	Shall you not be Godfearing?
26:107	Truly I *am* a trustworthy Messenger to you
26:108	so be Godfearing of God and obey me.
26:109	I ask not of you for any compensation for it;°
	my compensation *is* not but
	from the Lord of the worlds
26:110	so be Godfearing of God and obey me.
26:111	They said: Shall we believe in **you**
	when *it is* the vilest that follow **you**?
26:112	He said: What knowledge have I
	of what they were doing?
26:113	Truly their reckoning *is* but with my Lord,°
	if you be aware.
26:114	I *am* not to drive away the ones who believe;
26:115	I *am* not but a clear warner.
26:116	They said: If **you** refrain not **yourself**, O Noah
	you shall indeed be
	of the ones who are stoned!
26:117	He said: My Lord!
	My folk have denied me,
26:118	so give **You** deliverance between me and them
	and victory and deliver me and those
	who *are* among the ones who believe with me.
26:119	We rescued him
	and those with him in the laden boat;
26:120	after that We drowned the ones who remained.
26:121	Truly in this *is* a Sign;
	yet most of them were not ones who believe.
26:122	Truly, **your** Lord, He *is*
	The Almighty, The Compassionate.
Sec. 7	*
26:123	*The* Ad denied the ones who were sent,

when their brother Hud said to them: 26:124
Shall you not be Godfearing?
Truly I *am* a trustworthy Messenger to you 26:125
so be Godfearing of God and obey me; 26:126
I ask not of you for any compensation for it;° 26:127
my compensation *is* not but
from the Lord of the worlds.
Build you a Sign on every high hill to amuse? 26:128
Take you for yourselves castles, 26:129
so that perhaps you would dwell in them forever?
When you seize by force, 26:130
seize you by force haughtily?
So be Godfearing of God and obey me. 26:131
Be Godfearing of Him Who 26:132
has furnished relief to you with all that you know.
He has furnished relief for you 26:133
with flocks and children,
and gardens and springs. 26:134
Truly I fear for you 26:135
the punishment of a tremendous Day.
They said: *It is* equal to us 26:136
whether **you** have admonished,
or **you** were not the ones who admonish.
Truly this is nothing but morals of the ancient ones, 26:137
and we are not ones to be punished. 26:138
So they denied him, 26:139
and We caused them to perish.°
Truly in this *is* a Sign;°
yet most of them were not ones who believe.
Truly **your** Lord, He *is* 26:140
The Almighty, The Compassionate.

*

Sec. 8

Thamud denied the ones who were sent, 26:141
when their brother Salih said to them: 26:142
Shall you not be Godfearing?
Truly I *am* a trustworthy Messenger to you 26:143
so be Godfearing of God and obey me. 26:144
I ask not of you for any compensation for it;° 26:145
my compensation *is* not but

430

from the Lord of the worlds.

26:146 Shall you be left ones who are in safety
in what you *have* here

26:147 in gardens and springs

26:148 and crops of slender spathes of date palm trees?

26:149 Shall you carve houses out of the mountains
as ones who are skillful?

26:150 So be Godfearing of God and obey me.

26:151 Obey not the command
of the ones who are excessive,

26:152 who make corruption in and on the earth
and make not things right.

26:153 They said: Truly **you** are not but
of the ones against whom a spell has been cast;

26:154 **you** *are* nothing but a mortal like us.
So bring us a Sign
if **you** were among the ones who are sincere.

26:155 He said: This *is* a she camel;
she has *a right* to drink,
and you have *a right* to drink on a known day,

26:156 and afflict her not with evil
so that you should not take the punishment
of a tremendous Day.

26:157 But they crippled her,
and then it came to be in the morning
that they were ones who were remorseful.

26:158 So the punishment took them.°
Truly in this *is* a Sign;°
yet most of them were not ones who believe.

26:159 Truly **your** Lord, He *is*
The Almighty, The Compassionate.

Sec. 9 *

26:160 *The* folk of Lot denied the ones who were sent

26:161 when their brother, Lot, said to them:
Shall you not be Godfearing?

26:162 Truly I *am* a trustworthy Messenger to you

26:163 so be Godfearing of God and obey me.

26:164 I ask not of you for any compensation for it;°
my compensation *is* not but

431

from the Lord of the worlds.

What? You approach the male creatures, 26:165
forsaking 26:166
wives whom your Lord has created for you?°
Rather you are a folk who are turning away.
They said: If **you** refrain not yourself, O Lot, truly 26:167
you shall be of ones who shall be driven out.
He said: Indeed I *am* 26:168
of the ones with hatred for your actions.
My Lord! 26:169
Deliver me and my people from what they do!
So We delivered him and his people one and all 26:170
except an old woman among 26:171
the ones who stayed behind.
Then afterwards We destroyed the others, 26:172
and We rained down on them a rain; 26:173
and how evil was the rain
of the ones who had been warned!
Truly in this *is* a Sign, 26:174
yet most of them were not ones who believe.
Truly **your** Lord, He *is* 26:175
The Almighty, The Compassionate.

*

The Companions of the Woods denied 26:176
the ones who were sent.
When Shuayb said to them: 26:177
Shall you not be Godfearing?
Truly I *am* a trustworthy Messenger to you 26:178
so be Godfearing of God and obey me; 26:179
I ask not of you for any compensation for it;° 26:180
my compensation *is* not but
from the Lord of the worlds.
Live up to the full measure, 26:181
and be not of the ones who cause loss by fraud,
and weigh with a straight scale, 26:182
and diminish not to humanity their things, 26:183
nor do mischief in or on the earth
as ones who make corruption.
Be Godfearing of Him Who created you 26:184

and the array of the ancient ones.

26:185 They said: Truly **you** *are*
of the ones against whom a spell has been cast.

26:186 **You** *are* nothing but a mortal like us;
truly we think **you** *are* of the ones who lie.

26:187 So drop on us pieces of heaven,
if you should be among the ones who are sincere.

26:188 He said: My Lord has greater knowledge
of what you do.

26:189 But they denied him,
so they were taken by
the punishment on the overshadowing day.°
Truly that was the punishment
of a tremendous Day!

26:190 Truly in this *is* a Sign;°
yet most of them were not ones who believe.

26:191 Truly **your** Lord, He *is*
The Almighty, The Compassionate.

Sec. 11   *

26:192 This truly *is* the sending down successively
by the Lord of the worlds

26:193 that the Trustworthy Spirit has brought down

26:194 on **your** heart
that **you** may be one who warns

26:195 in a clear Arabic tongue.

26:196 Truly *it is*
in the ancient scrolls of the ancient ones.

26:197 Was it not a Sign for them
that *it was* known to the Children of Israel?

26:198 If We had sent it down
to some of the non-Arabs,

26:199 and he had recited it to them,
they would not be ones who believe in it.

26:200 Thus We have thrust it
into the hearts of the ones who sin;

26:201 they shall not believe in it
until they see the painful punishment,

26:202 so it shall approach them suddenly,
while they are not aware.

Then they shall say: 26:203
Are we ones respited?
Are they impatient for Our punishment? 26:204
Have **you yourselves** considered? 26:205
If We give them enjoyment for years,
and afterwards there draws near to them 26:206
what they were promised,
of what avail shall be to them 26:207
what they used to be given of enjoyment?
We caused no town to perish 26:208
but that it had the ones who warn
to be mindful; 26:209
and We have not been ones who are unjust.
It came not forth by the satans 26:210
and neither is it fit and proper 26:211
for them, nor are they able.
Truly they, from having the ability to hear, 26:212
are the ones who are set aside.
So call not to any god other than God, 26:213
so that **you** should not be
among the ones who are punished.
Warn your nearest kin, kinspeople. 26:214
Make low **your** wing 26:215
to him who would follow **you**
of the ones who believe;
then if they rebel against **you**, 26:216
say: Truly I *am* free of what they do.
Put **your** trust in 26:217
The Almighty, The Compassionate,
Who sees **you** at the time **you** have stood up, 26:218
and **your** going to and fro 26:219
among the ones who prostrate themselves.
Truly He *is* The Hearing, The Knowing. 26:220
Shall I tell you in whom come forth the satans? 26:221
They come forth in every sinful false one, 26:222
who give listen, having the ability to hear, 26:223
but most of them *are* the ones who lie.
As for the poets, 26:224
ones who are in error follow them.

26:225 Have **you** not considered that
truly they, they wander about in every valley,

26:226 and how they say what they accomplish not?

26:227 But those who have believed,
the ones who have acted in accord with morality,
remember God frequently,
and help themselves
after wrong has been done to them;°
and those who do wrong shall soon know
by what overturning they shall be turned about!

CHAPTER 27
THE ANTS (*al-Naml*)

In the Name of God,

Sec. 1 the Merciful, the Compassionate

27:1 *Ṭā Sīn;*
these *are* the Signs of the Quran
and a clear Book,

27:2 a guidance and good tidings
for the ones who believe,

27:3 truly those who perform the formal prayer
and give the purifying alms
so that they, they are certain of the world to come.

27:4 Truly as for those who believe not
in the world to come,
We have made their actions appear pleasing to them
so that they wander *unwilling* to see;

27:5 those *are* they for whom *is*
the tragic punishment and they, they *shall be*
the ones who are losers in the world to come.

27:6 Truly as for **you, you** are in receipt of the Quran,
that which proceeds from the Presence
of *One who is* Wise, Knowing.

27:7 When Moses said to his people:
Truly I have observed a fire!
I shall bring you news from it
or I shall approach you with a flaming firebrand
so that perhaps you would warm yourselves.

But when he drew near to it,   **27:8**
it was proclaimed:
Blessed *is* He Who is in the fire
and He Who *is* around it,
and glorify God, the Lord of the Worlds
O Moses! Truly I am God   **27:9**
the Almighty, The Wise.
Cast down **your** scepter.°   **27:10**
But when he saw it quivering
as if it *were* a snake,
he turned as one who draws back
to retrace his steps:°
O Moses! Fear not!
The ones who are sent fear not My nearness.
except he who has done wrong;   **27:11**
then for evil he has substituted goodness,
and truly I *am* Forgiving, Compassionate.
Cause **your** hand to enter into **your** bosom;   **27:12**
it shall go forth white without evil;°
one among nine Signs to Pharaoh and his folk.°
Truly they are a disobedient folk.
But when Our Signs drew near to them,   **27:13**
ones who perceive,
they said: This *is* a clear sorcery.
They negated them,   **27:14**
although their souls confessed to them;
out of injustice and self-exaltation.°
So look on
the ultimate end of the ones who make corruption.

*   **Sec. 2**

Indeed We gave David and Solomon knowledge;°   **27:15**
and they said: All Praise *belongs* to God
Who has given us advantage
over many of His believing servants.
Solomon inherited from David,   **27:16**
and he said: O humanity!
We have been taught the language of the birds,
and everything has been given to us;
truly this indeed *is* clearly grace.

27:17   *There* assembled before Solomon
his armies of jinn and human kind and birds,
and they were marching in ranks,

27:18   until when they approached the Valley of the Ants,
one ant said: O ants!
Enter your dwellings
so that Solomon and his armies not crush you
while they are not aware.

27:19   So he smiled *as* one who laughs at its saying
and he said: My Lord!
Arouse me that I may be thankful
for **Your** divine blessings
which **You** have been gracious
to me and my parents that I may be
one who is in accord with morality;
may **You** be well-pleased,
and cause me to enter by **Your** Mercy
among **Your** servants who act in accord with morality.

27:20   He reviewed the birds
and said:
Why see I not the hoopoe bird?
Is he among the absent?

27:21   I shall surely punish him
with a severe punishment
or deal a death blow to him
unless he brings me a clear authority!

27:22   But it was not long in coming,
and it said: I have comprehended
what **you** have not comprehended,
and I have drawn near to **you** from Sheba
with certain tidings.

27:23   Truly I found a woman controlling them,
and she has been given everything,
and for her *is* a sublime throne.

27:24   I found her and her folk prostrating to the sun
instead of God,
and Satan has made to appear pleasing to them
their actions,
and has barred them from the way,

so they have not been truly guided.
So they prostrate themselves not to God   27:25
Who brings out what is hidden
in the heavens and the earth;
and He knows what you conceal
and what you speak openly.
God, *there is* no god except He,   27:26
the Lord of the Sublime Throne.‡
Solomon said: We shall look on   27:27
whether **you** be sincere or **you** be one who lies.
Take away my letter and cast it to them,   27:28
then turn away from them
and look on what they return.
The Queen of Sheba said: O Council!   27:29
Truly a generous letter has been cast down to me
truly it *is* from Solomon,   27:30
and truly it *is* in the Name of God,
The Merciful, The Compassionate.
Rise not up against me,   27:31
but approach me as ones who submit.
                    *   Sec. 3

She said: O Council!   27:32
Render me an opinion in my affair;
I am not one who decides
until you bear witness.
They said: 27:33
We *are* of strength and of vigorous might,
but the command *is* for **you**;
so look for what **you** shall command.
She said: Truly when kings enter a town,   27:34
they make corruption in it,
and make the most mighty
of its people humiliated in spirit;°
thus they accomplish *it*.
But truly I (f) *am* one who shall send   27:35
to them a present
and *shall be* one who looks
at what the ones who were sent return with.
So when they drew near Solomon,   27:36

he said: What?
Are you furnishing me with wealth by way of relief?
What God has given me
is better than what He has given you.
Rather it is you who are glad
with your present!

27:37 Return to them,
and We truly shall approach them with armies
against which they shall be incapable,
and we shall drive them out from there
as ones who are disgraced,
and they *shall become* humble-spirited.

27:38 He said: O Council!
Which of you shall bring me her throne
before they approach me as ones who submit?

27:39 A demon from among the jinn said:
I shall bring it to **you**
before **you** shall stand up from **your** station;°
and truly I *am* strong and trustworthy.

27:40 One who had knowledge of the Book said:
I shall bring it to **you**
before **your** glance goes back to **you**.°
Then when he saw it settled before him,
he said: This *is* from the grace of my Lord
to try me whether I am thankful or ungrateful.
Whoever is thankful,
indeed he is thankful for himself;°
and certainly whoever is ungrateful,
my Lord *is* Rich, Generous.

27:41 He said: Disguise her throne for her
that we may look on
whether she shall be truly guided
or she shall be of those who are not truly guided.

27:42 So when she drew near, it was said:
Is **your** throne like this?°
She said: *It is* as though it *were* it.°
Solomon said: Knowledge was given us before her,
and we were ones who had submitted.

27:43 She had been barred

from what she used to worship
other than God;°
for indeed she was of an ungrateful folk.
It was said to her: Enter the pavilion!   27:44
When she saw it,
she assumed it to be a pool,
and she bared her legs.
He said: Truly
it *is* a smooth, crystal pavilion.°
She said: My Lord!
Truly I have done wrong to myself,
and I submit with Solomon to God,
the Lord of the worlds.

*   Sec. 4

Indeed We sent to Thamud   27:45
their brother, Salih:
Worship God!
Rather they *became* two groups of people
striving against one another.
He said: O my folk!   27:46
Why are you impatient
for the evil deed rather than benevolence?
Why ask you not for forgiveness of God,
so that perhaps you shall find mercy?
They said: We auger ill of **you**   27:47
and those with **you**.°
He said: Your omen *is* with God;°
rather you *are* a folk who are being tried.
There were nine groups of people in the city   27:48
who made corruption in the earth
and had not made things right.
They said: Swear by God   27:49
that we shall indeed attack him by night
and his people
and then we shall indeed say to his protector:
We bore not witness to the destruction of his people
and truly we *are* ones who are sincere.
So they planned a plan   27:50
and We planned a plan

while they were not aware.

27:51 So look on how was the ultimate end
of their planning!
Truly We destroyed them and their folk one and all.

27:52 These *are* their houses fallen down in ruin
for what they did wrong,°
truly in this *is* indeed a Sign
for the folk who know.

27:53 We rescued those who have believed
and were Godfearing.

27:54 And Lot when he said to his folk:
You perceive yet you approach indecency?

27:55 Why approach you men with lust
instead of women?°
Rather you *are* a folk who are ignorant.

27:56 So *there* was no answer by his folk,
except that they said:
Drive the people of Lot out from your town;°
truly they are a clan that would be purified.

27:57 So We rescued him and his people,
except his wife.
We ordained her *to be*
of the ones who stayed behind.

27:58 We rained down on them a rain;°
how evil was the rain
to the ones who had been warned!

Sec. 5 *

27:59 Say: The Praise *belongs* to God
and peace *be* on His servants
those whom He has favored,°
is God better
or what they make as a partner *with Him*?

Part 20 ***

27:60 Or Who created
the heavens and the earth,
and sent forth water for you from the heavens?
We caused a joyous plantation to develop;
it was not for you to cause their trees to develop.°
What? Is there a god besides God?

Rather
they are the folk who equate *others with God*!
Who made the earth a stopping place,

and made rivers in its midst
and has made firm mountains for it
and has made between the two seas
what hinders?°
Is there a god besides God?°
Rather most of them know not!
Who answers

the one who is compelled
when he calls to Him
and He removes the evil
and assigns you viceregents on the earth?°
Is there a god besides God?
Little is what you recollect!
Who guides you

in the darkness of the dry land and the sea
and Who sends the winds in advance of
ones who bear good tidings of His mercy?°
Is there a god besides God?°
Exalted is God above all the partners
that they make with Him!
Who begins creation,

then shall cause it to return
and Who provides you
from the heavens and the earth?
Is there a god besides God?°
Say: Bring forth your proof
if you are ones who are sincere!
Say: None in the heavens and the earth

know the unseen except God.°
Nor *are* they aware
when they shall be raised up.
Rather their knowledge

of the world to come fails.°
Rather they *are* in uncertainty about it;°
Rather they *are* in the dark about it.

*

27:67	Those who were ungrateful said: When we become earthy dust *like* our fathers shall we really *be* the ones who are brought out?
27:68	Indeed we were promised this, and our fathers before; truly this is nothing but fables of the ancient ones.
27:69	Say: Journey in the earth, and look on how has been the Ultimate End of the ones who sin.
27:70	Feel **you** not remorse for them, nor take to heart what they plan.
27:71	They say: At what time *is* the promise if you are ones who are sincere?
27:72	Say: Perhaps that for which you are impatient is close behind you.
27:73	Truly **your** Lord *is* Possessor of Grace for humanity; yet most of them thank *Him* not.
27:74	Truly **your** Lord indeed knows what their breasts hide and what they speak openly.
27:75	*There is* nothing of the unseen in the heaven and the earth, but that it *is* in the clear Book.
27:76	Truly this Quran relates about the Children of Israel and most of what about which they were at variance.
27:77	Truly it is a guidance and a mercy for the ones who believe.
27:78	Truly **your** Lord shall decree between them with His determination.° He *is* The Almighty, The Knowing.
27:79	So put **your** trust in God;° truly **you** *are* on The clear Truth.
27:80	Truly **you** cause not the dead to hear nor cause **you** the *unwilling* to hear to hear the supplication when they have turned to *being* ones who draw back.
27:81	Nor *are* **you** one who guides the *unwilling* to see

out of their misjudgment;°
you cause to hear,
only those who believe in Our Signs,
and they *are* ones who have submitted.
When the saying falls on them, 27:82
We shall bring out a moving creature for them
from the earth
that shall speak to them
because humanity was not certain of Our Signs.
*

On a Day when We shall assemble 27:83
a unit out of every community
of those who denied Our Signs
and they shall be marching in rank.
When they draw near, 27:84
He shall say: Have you denied My Signs
without comprehending them in knowledge
or what was it that you were doing?
The saying shall fall on them 27:85
because they have done wrong,
and they shall speak nothing for themselves.
Have they not considered that 27:86
We made the nighttime for them to rest in it
and the daytime for ones who perceive?°
Truly in that *are* Signs for the folk who believe.
On a Day on which the trumpet shall be blown, 27:87
and they who *are* in the heavens shall be terrified,
and who *are* on the earth
except him whom God willed.°
All shall approach Him
as ones who are in a state of lowliness.
You shall see the mountains 27:88
you have assumed *to be* fixed,
but they shall pass by as the passing of the clouds—°
the handiwork of God
Who creates everything very well.°
Truly He *is* Aware of what you accomplish.
Whoever draws near with benevolence, 27:89
there shall be better for him from it,

Sec. 7

and they *would* from the terror *be*
ones who are safe on that Day.

27:90 Whoever draws near with evil deeds,
they would be slung on their faces in the fire:
Are you given recompense
except with what you were doing?

27:91 Indeed I have been commanded
to worship the Lord of this land
which He has made sacred,
and to Whom all things *belong;*°
and I have been commanded
to be of the ones who submit,

27:92 and to recount the Recitation;
so whoever is truly guided,
then he is truly guided not but for himself;°
and to whoever goes astray
say: Truly I *am* not but one who warns.

27:93 Say: The Praise *belongs* to God;
He shall cause you to see His Signs,
and you shall recognize them;
your Lord *is* not one who is heedless of what you do.

CHAPTER 28
THE STORY (*al-Qaṣaṣ*)

In the Name of God,
Sec. 1 The Merciful, The Compassionate
28:1 *Ṭā Sīn Mīm;*
28:2 these *are* the Signs of the clear Book.
28:3 We narrate to **you**
the tiding of Moses and Pharaoh with The Truth
for the folk who believe.
28:4 Truly Pharaoh exalted himself on the earth
and made his people castes
—taken advantage of because of their weakness—
a section among them,
slaughtering their sons,
and saving alive their women.°
Truly he was of the ones who make corruption.

445

We want to show grace 28:5
to those who were
taken advantage of because of their weakness
on the earth,
and We make them leaders,
and We make them the ones who are inheritors,
and establish them firmly on the earth. 28:6
We cause Pharaoh and Haman to see
their armies
as that of which they were fearful.
We revealed to the mother of Moses: 28:7
Suckle him;°
but if **you** fear for him,
then cast him into the water of the river,
and neither fear nor feel remorse;°
truly We shall be ones who restore him to **you**,
ones who make him
among the ones who were sent.
Then the people of Pharaoh picked him out 28:8
to be an enemy to them
and *a cause of* grief;
truly Pharaoh and Haman
and their armies
were ones who were inequitable.
The wife of Pharaoh said: 28:9
He shall be a comfort to our eyes for me
and for **you**;°
kill him not,
perhaps he may profit us,
or we may take him to ourselves as a son.
They were not aware.
It came to be in the morning 28:10
that the mind of the mother of Moses
became empty;°
truly she was about to show him
had We not invigorated her heart
so that she became among the ones who believe.
She said to his sister: Track him;° 28:11
so she kept watching him from afar,

CHAPTER 28 THE STORY (*al-Qaṣaṣ*) STAGE 5 PART 20 SECTION 1 28:5-28:11

while they were not aware.

28:12 We had forbidden
any suckling woman for him.
Then she said:
Shall I point you to the people of a house
who shall take control of him for you
and they *shall be* ones who shall look after him?

28:13 Then We returned him to his mother,
that her eyes might settle down,
and she not feel remorse,
and that she might know
that the Promise of God *is* true;
but most of them know not.

Sec. 2 *

28:14 When he was fully grown, come of age,
and he straightened himself up
We gave him critical judgment and knowledge.°
Thus We give recompense
to the ones who are doers of good.

28:15 He entered the city
at a time of heedlessness of its people
and he found in it two men fighting one another,
this one from among his partisans
and this one from his enemies.°
The one who *was* among his partisans cried for help
against him who *was* among his enemies
so *Moses* struck him
and Moses made an end of him.°
He said: This *is* the action of Satan;°
truly he *is* a clear enemy who leads astray.

28:16 He said: My Lord!
Truly I have done wrong to myself so forgive me
and He forgave him;°
truly He *is* The Forgiving, The Compassionate.

28:17 He said: My Lord!
For that with which **You** have been gracious to me
I shall never be a sustainer of ones who sin.

28:18 So it came to be in the morning in the city
one who is fearful and vigilant,

when lo! The one who had asked for help
shouted aloud.°
Moses said to him:
Truly **you** are indeed clearly a hothead.
Then when he wanted to seize by force, 28:19
an enemy of both of them, he said:
O Moses! Would **you** want to kill me
as **you** have killed a soul yesterday?°
You want nothing but *to be* haughty
on the earth,
and **you** want not to be
among the ones who makes things right.
A man drew near from the farther *part* of the city, 28:20
coming eagerly, he said: O Moses!
Truly the Council
is conspiring against **you** to kill **you**,
so go forth;
truly I am one who gives advice to **you**.
So he went forth from there 28:21
as one who is fearful, being vigilant;°
he said: My Lord!
Deliver me from the unjust folk.

* Sec. 3

When he turned his face towards Midian 28:22
he said: It may be my Lord
guides me to the right way.
When he went down to the well of Midian, 28:23
he found a community there of personages
drawing water,
and he found other than them,
two women who were keeping away;°
he said: What *is* your business?°
They said: We draw not water
until the ones who are shepherds move on;°
and our father is an aged, old man.
So he drew water for them, 28:24
then he turned away to the shade
and said: My Lord!
Truly I am indeed in need

of whatever **You** sent forth to me of good.

28:25 Then drew near to him one of the two *women,*
walking bashfully.
She said: Truly my father calls to **you**
that he may give **you** recompense of compensation
because **you** have drawn water for us.°
So when he drew near to him
and related to him the narrative,
he said: Fear not;°
you have been delivered from the unjust folk.

28:26 One of the two *women* said:
O my father! Employ him;°
truly the best that **you** would employ
is the strong, the trustworthy;

28:27 he said:
Truly I want to wed **you**
to one of my two daughters,
on the condition that **you** were to hire **yourself** to me
for eight years;°
but if **you** fulfill ten years,
then it shall be from **you,**
for I want not to press **you** hard.°
For **you** shall find me, had God willed,
one who is in accord with morality.

28:28 He said:
That *is* between **you** and me;°
whichever of the two terms I satisfy,
there shall be no deep seated dislike from me;°
and God *is* Trustee over what we say.

Sec.4 *

28:29 Then when Moses had satisfied the term
and was journeying with his people,
he observed at the edge of the mountain a fire.
He said to his people: Abide!
Truly I have observed a fire;
so that perhaps I would
bring you some news from it
or burning wood of fire
so that perhaps you may warm yourselves.

So when he approached it, 28:30
it was proclaimed
from the right bank of the valley,
in a corner of the blessed ground
from the tree:
O Moses!
Truly I *am* God, the Lord of the worlds.
Cast **your** scepter;° 28:31
but when he saw it quivering
as if it were a snake,
he turned as one who draws back,
but he retraced not his steps:°
O Moses! Come forward and fear not;°
truly **you** *are* of the ones who are in safety.
Insert **your** hand into **your** bosom; 28:32
it shall go forth white, without evil.
Clasp **your** arms to **your** side *to guard against* fright;°
these are two proofs from **your** Lord
to Pharaoh and his Council.°
Truly they are a disobedient folk.
He said: My Lord! 28:33
Truly I have killed a soul among them,
and I fear that they shall kill me.
My brother Aaron, 28:34
he *is* more eloquent than I in oratory,
so send him with me as a helpmate
to establish me as true;°
truly I fear that they shall deny me.
He said: We shall strengthen **your** arm 28:35
through **your** brother
and assign to you both authority,
so that they reach not out to you both.°
With Our Signs, you two
and those who follow you two *shall be*
the ones who are victors.
Then when Moses drew near to them 28:36
with Our Signs, clear portents,
they said: This *is* nothing but forged sorcery;
we never heard of this

from our fathers, the ancient ones.

28:37   Moses said: My Lord has greater knowledge
of who drew near with guidance from Him
and what shall be
the Ultimate End in the Abode;°
truly the ones who are unjust shall not prosper.

28:38   Pharaoh said: O Council!
I know not of any god for you
other than me
so kindle for me, O Haman, a fire on the clay
and make a pavilion for me.
so that perhaps I would peruse the God of Moses.
Truly I think
that he *is* of the ones who lie.

28:39   He grew arrogant, he and his armies,
on the earth without right,
and they thought that
they would not return to Us.

28:40   So We took him and his armies,
and We cast them forth in the water of the sea;°
so look on how was the Ultimate End
of the ones who are unjust.

28:41   We have made them leaders who call to the fire;°
and on the Day of Resurrection,
they shall not be helped.

28:42   We made a curse pursue them in the present;°
and on the Day of Resurrection,
they *shall be* of the ones who are spurned.

Sec. 5

*

28:43   Indeed We gave Moses the Book
after We caused previous generations to perish,
as clear evidence for humanity
and a guidance and a mercy
so that they may recollect.

28:44   **You** were on the western edge
when We decreed the command to Moses,
and **you** were not
of the ones who bear witness;

28:45   but We caused generations to grow

451

and their lifetimes continued to be long.
You were not one who was a dweller
with the people of Midian,
recounting Our Signs to them,
but it is We Who are the ones who are sent.
You were not at the edge of the mountain
when We proclaimed,
but as a mercy from **your** Lord
that **you** may warn a folk
to whom no warner had approached them
before **you**
so that perhaps they would take admonition.
So that if
affliction should light on them
for what their hands have put forward,
they say: Our Lord!
Why have **You** not sent a Messenger to us
that we would have followed **Your** Signs,
and we would have been of the ones who believe?
But when The Truth drew near to them from Us,
they said: Why is he not given
the like of what was given to Moses?°
They were ones who were ungrateful
for what had been given to Moses before;°
they said:
Two kinds of sorcery, each helping the other.
They said: Truly we *are*
ones who disbelieve in both.
Say: Then bring a Book from God
which *is* better guided than these two
that I may follow it
if you are ones who are sincere.
But if they respond not to **you**,
then know that they not but follow their own desires.°
Who *is* one who goes further astray
than one who follows his own desires
without guidance from God?°
Truly God guides not the unjust folk.

*

28:46

28:47

28:48

28:49

28:50

Sec. 6

28:51	Indeed We have caused the saying to reach them so that perhaps they would take admonition.
28:52	Those to whom We gave the Book before it, they believe in it.
28:53	When it is recounted to them, they say: We have believed in it; truly it *is* The Truth from our Lord; indeed even before it, we have been ones who submit.
28:54	To those shall be given their compensation twice because they patiently endured and drove off evil deeds with benevolence, and they spend out of what We have provided them.
28:55	When they heard idle talk, they turned aside from it and said: To us *are* our actions, and to you *are* your actions; peace be to you! We are not looking for the ones who are ignorant.
28:56	Truly **you** guide not whom **you** have loved, but God guides whomever He will.° He has greater knowledge of the ones who are truly guided.
28:57	They said: If we were to follow the guidance with **you**, we would be snatched away from our region.° Have We not established firmly for them a holy, safe place where all kinds of fruit are collected as a provision from that which proceeds from Our Presence? But most of them know not.
28:58	How many a town that We have caused to perish boasted about its livelihood?° Those are their dwellings, uninhabited after them except a little;° and truly We, We are the ones who are the inheritors.

Yet **your** Lord never caused the towns to perish   28:59
until He had raised forth a Messenger
to their mother-*town*
who recounted Our Signs to them.°
We have never caused the towns to perish
unless their people *were* ones who were unjust.
Whatever things you have been given   28:60
are enjoyment for this present life,
and its adornment,
and what *is* with God *is* better
for one who endures.°
Shall you not be reasonable?

*

Sec. 7

Is he to whom We promised a fair promise,   28:61
and he is one that reaches fulfillment
like him to whom
We have given the enjoyment of enjoyment
for this present life?
Then on the Day of Resurrection
who shall be of the ones who are charged?
On that Day He shall proclaim to them   28:62
and say: Where *are* My associates
whom you used to claim?
Those about whom the saying shall be realized   28:63
would say: Our Lord!
These are they whom we led into error;
we led them into error
even as we erred;°
we clear ourselves with **You**—°
they never worshiped us.
It would be said: Call to your associates.   28:64
They shall call to them,
but they shall not respond to them,
They shall see the punishment.°
If only they had been truly guided!
On a Day when He would proclaim to them   28:65
and He would say:
What have you answered
to the ones who were sent?

28:66	Then the tidings on that day shall be in darkness,
	and they shall not inquire of one another.
28:67	As for him who has repented and has believed,
	one who has acted in accord with morality,
	then perhaps he shall be
	of the ones who prosper.
28:68	**Your** Lord creates whatever He will
	and chooses.°
	They *have* no choice.°
	Glory be to God and exalted is He
	above all the partners they make with Him!
28:69	**Your** Lord knows what their breasts hide,
	and what they speak openly.
28:70	He, God, *there is* no god but He;°
	The Praise *belongs* to Him
	in the First and in the Last;°
	and His *is* the determination,
	and to Him you shall be returned.
28:71	Say: Have you yourself not considered?
	If God had made the nighttime endless for you
	until the Day of Resurrection,
	what god other than God could bring you
	illumination?°
	Shall you then not hear?
28:72	Say: What would you see
	if God had made the daytime endless
	until the Day of Resurrection?
	What god other than God brings you nighttime
	wherein you may rest?°
	Then perceive you not?
28:73	*It is* out of His mercy
	that He has assigned for you
	the nighttime and the daytime
	that you may rest in it;°
	and that you may be looking for His grace
	and so that perhaps you shall be thankful.
28:74	When He shall proclaim to them
	and say: Where *are* My associates
	whom you used to claim?

We shall tear out
from a witness every community,
and We shall say: Prepare your proof.
Then they shall know
that The Truth *is* with God,
and what they used to devise
has gone astray from them

*

Truly Korah was of the folk of Moses,   28:76
but he was insolent towards them;°
and We gave him of the treasures
that indeed the keys of it
would have been a heavy ordeal
to many of strength.
His folk said to him: Exult not;°
truly God loves not those who *are* exultant.
But be looking for the Last Abode   28:77
through what God has given **you**;°
and forget not **your** share of the present;°
and do good
even as God has been a good-doer to **you**;°
and be not insolent corrupting in and on the earth;°
truly God loves not the ones who make corruption.
Korah said: I have been given it   28:78
because of the knowledge with me.°
What? Knew he not that God
has caused generations to perish
before him
who *were* more vigorous in strength than he
and more numerous in multitude?°
The ones who sin shall not be asked
about their impieties.
So he went forth before his folk in his adornment;°   28:79
and those who want this present life said:
Would that we had
the like of what has been given to Korah!
Truly he *is* the possessor of a sublime allotment.
Those who were given knowledge said: 28:80
Woe to you!

The reward for good deeds from God
is better for those who have believed,
ones who have acted in accord with morality,
and none shall be in receipt of it
except the ones who remain steadfast.

28:81 So We caused the earth to swallow him
and his abode.
Then there was not any faction
to help him against God,
and he was of the ones who are helpless.

28:82 It came to be in the morning
that they who had coveted his place
yesterday were saying:
God extends the provision
to whomever He will of His servants
and confines it;°
had it not been that God showed grace to us,
He would have caused the earth to swallow us;°
know you that
the ones who are ungrateful shall not prosper.

Sec. 9 *

28:83 This is the Last Abode
that We shall assign to those
who want not self-exaltation in the earth
nor corruption.°
The Ultimate End
is for the ones who are Godfearing.

28:84 Whoever brings about benevolence,
for him *there shall be* better than it;°
and whoever brings about an evil deed,
and those who do evil deeds,
shall not be given recompense
other than for what they were doing.

28:85 Truly He Who imposed the Quran on **you**
shall indeed be the one who restores **you**
to the place of return.°
Say: My Lord has greater knowledge
of him who draws near guidance
and of him who *is* clearly wandering astray.

457

You *have* no hope 28:86
that the Book would be cast down to **you**
except as a mercy from **your** Lord;°
be not a sustainer of ones who are ungrateful.
Let them not bar **you** from the Signs of God 28:87
after they have been sent forth to **you**;°
and call to **your** Lord;°
and be not of the ones who are polytheists.
Call not to any god other than God. • 28:88
There is no god but He!°
Everything perishes except His Face.°
To Him *is* the determination
and to Him you shall be returned.

CHAPTER 29
THE SPIDER (*al-ʿAnkabūt*)

In the Name of God,
The Merciful, The Compassionate Sec. 1
Alif, Lām, Mīm; 29:1
has humanity assumed that they shall be left 29:2
because they say: We have believed,
and they shall not be tried?
Indeed We tried those who *were* before them;° 29:3
and indeed God knows those who are sincere
and knows the ones who lie.
Or assume **you** that those who do evil deeds 29:4
shall outstrip Us?°
How evil is that about which they give judgment!
Whoever is hoping for the meeting with God, 29:5
then truly the term of God *is* one that arrives.°
He *is* The Hearing, The Knowing.
Whoever struggles, he struggles not but for himself.° 29:6
Truly God *is* Sufficient for the worlds.
Those who have believed, 29:7
ones who have acted in accord with morality,
indeed We shall absolve them of their evil deeds
and We shall give recompense for the fairest
of what they were doing.

29:8
We have charged the human being
with goodness to ones who are his parents;°
and if they struggle against you
for **you** to make someone a partner with Me,
that of which **you** have no knowledge,
then obey them not.°
To Me *is* your return,
and I shall tell you what you were doing.

29:9
Those who have believed,
the ones who act in accord with morality,
We indeed shall cause them to enter
among the ones who are in accord with morality.

29:10
Of humanity *is* he who says:
We have believed in God,
but if he is afflicted with torment for the sake of God,
he mistakes the persecution by humanity
for a punishment by God;
and if victory draws near from **your** Lord,
they shall surely say: We were with you.°
Has not God greater knowledge
of what *is* in the breasts of the creatures?

29:11
Truly God knows those who have believed,
and truly He knows the ones who are hypocrites.

29:12
Those who are ungrateful
say to those who have believed:
Follow our way
and we shall indeed carry your transgressions,
while they are not ones who carry
any of their *own* transgressions;°
truly they are the ones who lie.

29:13
Indeed they shall carry their own lading;°
and other ladings with their own ladings
and truly they shall be asked
on the Day of Resurrection
about what they were devising.

Sec. 2
*

29:14
Indeed We had sent Noah to his folk,
and he lingered in expectation among them
a thousand years less fifty years.

The Deluge took them
while they *were* the ones who were unjust.
Then We rescued him,
and the Companions of the Vessel,
and made it a Sign for the worlds.
When Abraham said to his folk:
Worship God and be Godfearing of Him;°
that *would be* better for you if you were to know.
You worship graven images other than God,
and you create calumny.°
Truly those whom you worship
other than God
possess not for you any power to provide for you.
So look for the provision of God,
and worship Him and be thankful to Him;°
to Him you shall return.
If you deny,
then indeed communities have denied
before you;°
it is not but for the Messenger
to deliver the clear message.
Have they not considered
how God causes the creation to begin
then He causes it to return?°
Truly that for God is easy.
Say: Move throughout the earth,
and look on how He began the creation;
then God shall cause the last growth to grow.°
Truly God *is* Powerful over everything.
He punishes whom He will,
and has mercy on whom He will;°
and to Him you shall come back.
You shall not *be* ones who frustrate *the Will of God,*
on the earth, nor in the heaven.°
Other than God
there is for you neither protector nor helper.
*
Those who are ungrateful for the Signs of God
and the meeting with Him,

they, those give up hope for My mercy,
and those, for them there *shall be*
a painful punishment.

29:24 So the answer of his folk was nothing
but that they said: Kill him or burn him!
Then God rescued him from the fire.°
Truly in this *are* indeed Signs
for a folk who believe.

29:25 He said:
You have taken graven images to yourselves
instead of God
because of affection among yourselves
for the present life;°
then on the Day of Resurrection,
you shall disbelieve in each other
and curse each other,
and your place of shelter *shall be* the fire.
For you *there is* not anyone of those who help.

29:26 So Lot believed in him
and he said:
Truly I am one who emigrates for my Lord;°
truly He *is* The Almighty, The Wise.

29:27 We bestowed Isaac and Jacob on him,
and We assigned to his offspring
prophethood and the Book.
We gave him his compensation in the present life;°
truly in the world to come he *shall be*
of the ones who are in accord with morality.

29:28 And Lot when he said to his folk:
Truly you approach indecency
which none in the world who preceded you *committed.*

29:29 What? You approach men
and sever the way,
and approach immorality in your conclave?°
But the answer of his folk
was that they said:
Bring on us the punishment of God,
if you are of the ones who are sincere.

29:30 He said: My Lord!

Help me against the corrupt folk.

*

When Our messengers drew near to Abraham
with the good tidings,
they said: Truly We shall cause to perish
the people of this town;°
truly its people have been ones who are unjust.
He said: Truly in it *is* Lot.°
They said: We have greater knowledge
of who *is* in it;°
we shall truly deliver him and his family,
except his wife,
she would be of the ones who stay behind.
When Our messengers drew near to Lot,
he was troubled because of them,
and he was concerned for them, distressed,
and they said: Neither fear nor feel remorse;°
truly we *are* the ones who shall deliver **you**
and **your** family except **your** wife;
she would be of the ones who stay behind.
Truly we are about to send forth
on the people of this town
a defilement from heaven
because they disobey.
Indeed We have left in it
a Sign, clear portents for the folk who are reasonable.
To Midian, their brother Shuayb;
he said: O my folk! Worship God
and hope for the Last Day,
and do not mischief in and on the earth
as the ones who make corruption.
They denied him;
so the quaking took them,
and it came to be in the morning,
so they *were* in their abodes
as ones who had fallen prostrate.
And Ad and Thamud:
Indeed it became clear to you from their dwellings;°
Satan made their actions appear pleasing to them

and barred them from the way,
and they were ones who saw clearly.

29:39 And Korah, Pharaoh and Haman;
and indeed Moses had drawn near to them
with clear portents,
but they grew arrogant on the earth,
and they were not ones who outstripped Us.

29:40 So We took each of them in his impiety;°
and of them were some
on whom We sent a storm of pebbles,
and of them *were* some
who were taken by a Cry,
and of them *were* some
whom We caused the earth to swallow,
and of them *were* some
whom We drowned.°
God had not done wrong to them,
but it was they who had done wrong to themselves.

29:41 The parable of those who
take other than God to themselves as protectors
is that of the spider who takes a house to itself,
but truly the frailest of houses
is the house of the spider°
if they but knew.

29:42 Truly God knows
what they call to instead of Him.°
He *is* The Almighty, The Wise.

29:43 We propound these parables for humanity;°
but no one is reasonable among them
except the ones who have knowledge.

29:44 God created the heavens and the earth
with The Truth.°
Truly in that indeed *is* a Sign
for the ones who believe.

Sec. 5 *

29:45 Recount
what has been revealed to **you** of the Book,
and perform the formal prayer;°
truly the formal prayer prohibits

greater depravity
in ones who are immoral,°
and truly the remembrance of God is greater,°
and God knows what you craft.

***

Part 21

Dispute not with the People of the Book
except in a way that *is* fairer,
except for those who do wrong.
Say: We have believed
in what has been sent forth to us
and what has been sent forth to you
and our God and your God *is* One
and we *are* the ones who submit to Him.
Thus We have sent forth the Book to **you**;
those to whom We have given the Book before
believe in it,
and these, *there are* some who believe in it
and none negate Our Signs
except the ones who are ungrateful.
Neither were **you** to recount from any book
before it,
nor have **you** written it with **your** right hand;°
for then indeed ones who deal in falsehood,
they would have been in doubt.
Rather it is clear Signs
in the breasts
of those who have been given knowledge.°
None negates Our Signs
except ones who are unjust.
They say:
Why *are* Signs not sent forth to him from his Lord?
Say: The Signs *are only* with God,
and truly I *am* nothing but a clear warner.
Suffices it not for them
that We have sent forth to **you** the Book
which is recounted to them?
Truly in that *is* a mercy and mindfulness
for a folk who believe.

*

29:46

29:47

29:48

29:49

29:50

29:51

Sec. 6

29:52 Say: God suffices
as a witness between me and between you;
He knows whatever
is in the heavens and the earth.
Those who have believed in falsehood,
and are ungrateful to God,
they, those are the ones who are losers.

29:53 They are impatient for the punishment!°
Had it not been for a determined term,
the punishment would have drawn near them,
and truly it shall approach them suddenly,
while they are not aware.

29:54 They are impatient for the punishment,
and truly hell *shall be* what encloses
the ones who are ungrateful.

29:55 On a Day when the punishment overcomes them
from above them,
and from beneath their feet,
He shall say: Experience what you were doing!

29:56 O my servants who have believed,
truly My earth *is* one that is extensive,
so worship Me!

29:57 Every soul *shall be* one who experiences death;°
then to Us you shall be returned.

29:58 Those who have believed,
the ones who have acted in accord with morality,
to them We shall indeed place a settlement
in the highest chambers in the Garden,
beneath which rivers run,
ones who shall dwell in it forever.°
How excellent is the compensation
for the ones who work,

29:59 those who endure patiently
they put their trust in their Lord.

29:60 How many a moving creature
carries not its own provision,
but God provides for it and for you.°
He *is* The Hearing, The Knowing.

29:61 If **you** were to ask them:

Who created the heavens and the earth
and caused the sun and the moon to be subservient?
They shall surely say: God!°
How then are they mislead?
God extends the provision 29:62
for whom He will of His servants
and confines it *for whom He will.*°
Truly God *is* Knowing of everything.
If **you** were to ask them: 29:63
Who sends down water from heaven
and gives life by it to the earth after its death,
truly they would say: God!°
Say: The Praise *belongs* to God.°
But most of them are not reasonable.

This present life *is* 29:64
nothing but a diversion and a pastime.°
Truly the Last Abode *is* the eternal life,°
if they but knew!
When they embark on the boats, 29:65
they call to God
sincerely and devotedly
in the way of life for Him;
but when He delivers them to dry land,
lo! They make partners *with God,*
being ungrateful for what We have given them, 29:66
so let them take joy°
for soon they shall know!
Have they not considered that We have made 29:67
a safe, holy place
while humanity is being snatched away
all around them?°
Then believe they in falsehood?
Are they ungrateful for the divine blessing?
Who *is* one who does greater wrong 29:68
than he who devises a lie against God,
or denies The Truth when it draws near to him?°
Is there not in hell a place of lodging
for the ones who are ungrateful?

As for those who struggle for Us,
We shall truly guide them to Our ways.°
Truly God *is* with ones who are doers of good.

CHAPTER 30
THE ROMANS (*al-Rūm*)

In the Name of God,
The Merciful, The Compassionate

Alif Lām Mīm;

30:2 the Romans have been vanquished

30:3 in the closer region,
and they, after being vanquished,
shall be the vanquishers

30:4 within a certain number of years.°
To God *belongs* the command before and after,°
and that Day ones who believe shall be glad

30:5 with the help of God.
He helps whom He will;°
and He *is* The Almighty, The Compassionate.

30:6 *It is* the promise of God;°
God breaks not His Promise,
but most of humanity knows not.

30:7 They know only what is manifest
in this present life;
of the world to come
they are ones who are heedless.

30:8 Or have they not reflected on themselves?°
God created not the heavens and the earth
and all that *is* between the two
except with The Truth and for a determined term.°
Indeed most of humanity
are ones who are ungrateful
for the meeting with their Lord.

30:9 Or have they not journeyed on the earth,
and looked on
how was the Ultimate End
of those before them?°
They were superior to them in strength;

467

they plowed the earth,
and cultivated it more
than what these have cultivated it;
and drew near to them their Messengers
with clear portents;°
then God did not wrong them,
but they were doing wrong to themselves.
Then the Ultimate End   30:10
of those who did misdeeds was to do evil,
because they denied the Signs of God
and ridiculed them.

*

God begins the creation,   30:11
then He causes it to return;
then to Him you shall be returned.
On a Day   30:12
when the Hour shall be secured for you,
the ones who sin shall be seized with despair.
None of those whom they associated with God   30:13
shall be intercessors for them,
and their associates themselves shall be
ones who are ungrateful.
On a Day   30:14
when the Hour shall be secured for them,
that Day they shall be split up.
Then as for those who have believed,   30:15
ones who have acted in accord with morality,
they shall be walking with joy
in a well watered-meadow.
As for those who were ungrateful   30:16
and denied Our Signs
and the meeting of the world to come,
those are ones who are charged with the punishment.
So glory be to God   30:17
at the time of the evening hour
and at the time when it comes to be in morning!
To Him be The Praise   30:18
in the heavens and the earth
and in the evening and at the time of noon.

He brings out the living from the dead,
and He brings out the dead from the living,
and He gives life to the earth after death.°
Thus you shall be brought out.

*

Among His Signs *is* that He created you
from earthy dust;
then lo! You *were* mortals diffused.

Among His Signs *is* that He created for you
wives from among yourselves,
that you may rest in them;
He has made affection and mercy between you.°
Truly in that *are* indeed Signs
for a folk who reflect.

Among His Signs *is* the creation
of the heavens and the earth
and the alteration of your languages and hues.°
Truly in that *are* indeed Signs
for all beings who have knowledge.

Among His Signs *is* your slumbering
by nighttime and by daytime,
and your looking for His grace.°
Truly in that *are* indeed Signs
for a folk who hear.

Among His Signs *is* that
He causes you to see the lightning
in fear and in hope;
He sends water down from heaven,
and gives life by it to the earth
after its death.°
Truly in that *are* indeed Signs
for a folk who are reasonable.

Among His Signs *is* that
the heaven and the earth are secured for you
by His command;°
then when He has called you by a call
from the earth,
lo! You shall go forth!

To Him *belongs*

whatever *is* in the heavens and the earth;°
all *are* ones who are morally obligated to Him.
He *it is* Who begins the creation,

and then causes it to return;
and this *is* insignificant for Him.°
His *is* the Lofty Parable
in the heavens and the earth;°
He *is* The Almighty, The Wise.

*

He propounds a parable for you

from yourselves:°
Have you
among those whom your right hands possess
associates
in what We have provided you,
so that you are equal in *its respect*
and you fear them
as you have awe for each other?°
Thus We explain distinctly the Signs
to a folk who are reasonable.
Rather those who did wrong

followed their own desires without knowledge;°
then who shall guide him
whom God has caused to go astray?°
They shall have none who helps.
So set **your** face towards a way of life

as a monotheist.°
It is the nature originated by God
in which He originated humanity.°
There is no substituting the creation of God.°
That *is* the truth-loving way of life,
but most of humanity knows not:

*

Ones who turn in repentance to Him

and are Godfearing
and perform the formal prayer
and are not among the ones who are polytheists
or of those who separate and divide their way of life

and become partisans:°

Each party glad in what they have.

30:33 When distress afflicts humanity,
they call to their Lord
as ones who are repentant to Him;
then when He causes them to experience
His mercy,
lo! A group of people among them
make partners with their Lord,

30:34 ungrateful for what We have given them.
Take joy, then you shall know.

30:35 Or have We sent forth to them an authority
which might assert
what they were making as partners with Him?

30:36 When We cause humanity to experience mercy,
they are glad of it;°
but when an evil deed lights on them
because of what their hands have put forward,
lo! They are in despair.

30:37 Have they not considered that
God extends the provision for whom He will
and confines it *for whom He will*?°
Truly in that *are* indeed Signs
for a folk who believe.

30:38 So give to kin justifiably,
to the needy and to the traveler of the way.°
That *is* better
for those who want the countenance of God;°
and *it is* those who are the ones who prosper.

30:39 What you give in usury
in order that it may swell the wealth of humanity
has not swelled with God;°
and what you give in purifying alms,
wanting the countenance of God,
then they, those *are* the ones given manifold.

30:40 God *is* He Who created you;
He provided for you;
He causes you to die;
then He gives you life;°
has anyone that you made partners *with Him*

accomplished anything of that?°
Glory be to Him! Exalted is He
above what that they associate *with Him*!
Corruption has become manifest   30:41
on dry land and the sea
because of what the hands of humanity have earned,
that He causes them to experience
a part of what they have done
so that perhaps they would return.
Say: Journey on the earth   30:42
and look on
how was the Ultimate End
of those before.°
Most of them were ones who were polytheists.
So set your face to the truth-loving way of life   30:43
before the Day approaches;
there *is* no turning back from God;°
on that Day they shall be split up.
Whoever *is* one who is ungrateful,   30:44
his ingratitude *is* on him;°
and whoever has acted in accord with morality,
and makes provisions for themselves that
He may give recompense to those who have believed, 30:45
the ones who have acted in accord with morality,
out of His grace.°
Truly He loves not ones who are ungrateful.
Among His Signs *are* that He sends the winds   30:46
as ones that give good tidings
and cause one to experience His mercy,
and so that the boats may run at His command
and that you be looking for His grace
so that perhaps you would be thankful.
Indeed We have sent Messengers before **you**   30:47
to their own folk;
they drew near to them with clear portents
then We requited those who sinned;
and it was an obligation on Us
to help ones who believe.
God *is He* Who sends the winds   30:48

so they stir up clouds;
He extends them in the heaven how He will,
and He makes them into pieces
until **you** see rain drops go forth from its midst;°
then when He has made them
light on whomever He will of His servants,
lo! They rejoice at the good tidings.

30:49 Truly they had been
ones seized with despair
even before it was sent down on them.

30:50 Look on the effects of the mercy of God,
how He gives life to the earth after its death!°
Truly He *is* One Who Gives Life to the dead;°
and He *is* Powerful over everything.

30:51 If We send a wind,
and they see it yellowing,
they would stay ungrateful after that.

30:52 Truly **you** cause not the dead to hear,
nor **you** cause the *unwilling* to hear
the supplication when they turn
as ones who draw back.

30:53 **You** are not one who guides the *unwilling* to see
from their misjudgment;°
you cause none to hear,
but those who believe in Our Signs,
and they *are* ones who submit.

Sec. 6 *

30:54 God *is He* Who created you in *your* weakness,
then assigned strength after weakness,
then after strength assigned
weakness and grey hair.
He creates what He will;°
and He *is* The Knowing, The Powerful.

30:55 On a Day when the Hour is secured,
the ones who sin shall swear
that they lingered in expectation but an hour.°
Thus they were misled.

30:56 Those who had been given
knowledge and belief

said:
Indeed you have lingered in expectation
by the prescription of God,
until the Day of the Uprising;°
this is the Day of Uprising,
but you were not knowing.
So on that Day, 30:57
the excuses of those who did wrong
shall not profit them,
nor shall they ask to be favored.
Indeed We have propounded for humanity 30:58
in this Quran every *kind of* parable.°
But if **you** bring about any Sign to them
they, those who are ungrateful, shall say:
Truly you are nothing
but ones who deal in falsehood.
Thus God sets a seal on the hearts 30:59
of those who know not.
So have **you** patience; 30:60
truly the promise of God *is* True;°
and let not **yourself** become irritated
by those who are not certain.

CHAPTER 31
LUQMAN (*Luqmān*)

In the Name of God,
The Merciful, The Compassionate Sec. 1
Alif Lām Mīm; 31:1
these *are* the Signs of the wise Book, 31:2
a guidance and a mercy 31:3
to the ones who are doers of good,
those who perform the formal prayer 31:4
and give the purifying alms,
and they are certain of the world to come.
Those *are* on a guidance from their Lord;° 31:5
and they, those *are* the ones who prosper.
Of humanity *is he* 31:6
who exchanges the diversion of conversation

to cause *others* to go astray from the way of God
without any knowledge,
and he takes it to himself in mockery.°
Those—for them *shall be* a despised punishment.

31:7　　When Our Signs are recounted to him,
he turns as one who grows arrogant,
as if he heard them not,
as if *there is* heaviness in his ears;°
so give him the good tidings of a painful punishment.

31:8　　Truly those who have believed,
the ones who have acted in accord with morality,
for them *are* Gardens of Bliss,

31:9　　ones who shall dwell in them forever;°
it is a true promise of God.°
He *is* The Almighty, The Wise,

31:10　　He has created the heavens
without any pillars so that you see them;°
He has cast firm mountains on the earth
so that it should not vibrate with you;
He disseminated in and on it
every moving creature;
We sent forth water from heaven,
and We caused every generous kind to develop in it.

31:11　　This *is* the creation of God,
so demonstrate to me
what other than He has created?
Rather the ones who are unjust
are clearly wandering astray.

*

Sec. 2

31:12　　Indeed We gave Luqman wisdom;
he said: Be thankful to God.°
Whoever is thankful,
is thankful not but for himself;°
and whoever is ungrateful—
then truly God *is* Sufficient, Worthy of Praise.

31:13　　When Luqman said to his son
as he was admonishing him:
O my son! Ascribe not associates with God;
truly associating *with God*°

is indeed a tremendous injustice.

We have charged the human being
about ones who are his parents;
his mother carried him
in feebleness on feebleness,
and his weaning *is* in two years
be thankful to Me
and to ones who are **your** parents;
to Me *is* the Homecoming.

31:14

But if they both struggle against **you**
that **you** make partners with Me
of what **you** *have* no knowledge,
then obey them not;°
but keep their company in the present
as one who is moral
and follow the way
of him who is penitent to Me.°
Then to Me shall be your return
and I shall tell you of what you were doing.

31:15

O my son!
Indeed even if it be the weight
of a grain of a mustard seed
and though it be in a rock
or in the heavens or in or on the earth,
God will bring it.°
Truly God *is* Subtle, Aware.

31:16

O my son!
Perform the formal prayer;
command to morality;
prohibit immorality
and have patience with whatever lights on **you**;°
truly *that is*
constancy of affairs.

31:17

Turn not **your** cheek away to humanity,
nor walk through the earth exultantly;
truly God loves not a proud boaster.

31:18

Be moderate in **your** walking
and lower **your** voice.°
Truly the most horrible of all voices

31:19

476

is indeed the voice of the donkey.

*

31:20

Have you not considered that
God has caused to become subservient to you
whatever *is* in the heavens
and whatever *is* in and on the earth
and has lavished on you His divine blessing
—what is manifest
and what is inward—°
yet among humanity *is*
he who disputes about God
without knowledge,
without guidance
and without an illuminating Book.

31:21

When it is said to them:
Follow what God has sent forth,
they say: Rather we shall follow
what we found our fathers on.°
What? Even though Satan was calling them
to the punishment of the blaze?

31:22

Whoever submits his face to God
while he is one who is a doer of good,
then indeed he has held fast
to the most firm handhold,°
and to God *is* the Ultimate End of affairs.

31:23

As for whoever is ungrateful,
let not his ingratitude grieve **you**.°
To Us *is* their return,
and We shall tell them what they did.°
Truly God *is* Knowing of what is in the breasts.

31:24

We give them enjoyment for a little while,
and then We shall compel them
to a harsh punishment.

31:25

If you ask them
who has created the heavens and the earth,
they shall indeed say: God!°
Say: The Praise *belongs* to God!°
But most of them know not.

31:26

To God *belongs*

whatever *is* in the heavens and the earth;°
truly God, He *is*
The Sufficient, The Worthy of Praise.
If all the trees on the earth were pens,   31:27
and the sea *that* was caused to increase
with seven more seas *were ink,*
yet the words of God would not come to an end,°
truly God *is* Almighty, Wise.
Your creation and your Uprising   31:28
are *to Us* not but like that of a single soul;°
truly God *is* Hearing, Seeing.
Have **you** not considered   31:29
how God causes the nighttime to be inserted
into the daytime,
and causes the daytime to be inserted
into the nighttime,
and causes the sun to become subservient
and the moon,
each running for a determined term,
and that God *is* Aware of all that you do?
That *is* because God, He *is* The Truth,   31:30
and what they call to other than Him
is falsehood,
and that God, He *is* The Lofty, The Great!
*

Have **you** not considered   31:31
how the boats run through the sea
by the divine blessing of God
that He may cause you to see His Signs?°
Truly in that *are* Signs
for every enduring, grateful one.
When a wave overcomes them   31:32
like an overshadowing,
they call to God
sincerely and devotedly
in the way of life for Him;
when He delivers them to dry land,
some among them *are* ones who are moderate.°
None negates Our Signs

478

but every ungrateful turncoat.

31:33 O humanity! Be Godfearing of your Lord
and dread a Day
when recompense shall not be given
by one to whom a child is born
for his child,
nor by the child
for one to whom the child is born.°
Truly the promise of God *is* True;°
so let not this present life delude you,
nor let the deluder delude you about God.

31:34 Truly the knowledge of the Hour is with God;
He sends plenteous rain water down;
He knows what is in the wombs;°
and no soul is informed
of what it shall earn tomorrow,
and no soul is informed in what region it shall die.°
Truly God *is* Knowing, Aware

CHAPTER 32
THE PROSTRATION (*al-Sajdah*)

In the Name of God,
Sec. 1 The Merciful, The Compassionate
32:1 *Alif Lām Mīm;*
32:2 the sending down successively of the Book,
there is no doubt in it;
it is from the Lord of the worlds.
32:3 Or they say: He has devised it.°
Rather it *is* The Truth from **your** Lord
that **you** may warn a folk
to whom no warner has approached them
before **you**,
so that perhaps they would be truly guided.
32:4 God! *It is* He Who created
the heavens and the earth
and all that *is* between them
in six days;
then He turned His attention to the Throne;°

you *have* none other than Him as protector,
no intercessor;
shall you not recollect?
He manages every command   32:5
from the heaven to the earth;
then it shall go up to Him
in a day when the span
is a thousand years
of what you number.
That *is the* One Who has Knowledge   32:6
of the unseen and the visible,
The Almighty, The Compassionate
Who did everything that He created well;°   32:7
and He began the creation of the human being
from clay;
then He made *mankind's* progeny   32:8
from the extraction of despicable water.
Then He shaped him   32:9
and breathed into him His Spirit;°
He made for you
the ability to hear and sight
and minds;°
little are you thankful!
They said: When we are lost into the earth,   32:10
shall we indeed be in a new creation?°
Rather they *are* ones who disbelieve
in the meeting with their Lord.
Say: The angel of death who is charged over you   32:11
shall call you to itself;
then you shall return to your Lord.
*   **Sec. 2**
If **you** but see   32:12
when the ones who sin
become ones who bend down their heads
before their Lord:
Our Lord! We have perceived and heard,
so return us
as ones who have acted in accord with morality;
truly we *are now* ones who are certain.

32:13   Had We willed it,
We would have surely given every soul its guidance,
but My saying was realized:
I shall fill hell
with genies and humanity altogether.

32:14   Then experience *it*.
As you forgot the meeting of this Day of yours,
truly We have forgotten you;°
experience the punishment for eternity
for what you were doing.

32:15   Only those believe in Our Signs,
who, when they are reminded of them,
fall down as ones who prostrate themselves,
and glorify the praise of their Lord,
and they grow not arrogant,‡

32:16 whose sides deliberately avoid their sleeping places
to call to their Lord in fear and hope,
and they spend of what We have provided them.

32:17   No soul knows
what is concealed for them
of comfort for their eyes
as a recompense
for what they were doing.

32:18   What? Is he who believes
like he who disobeys?°
They are not on the same level.

32:19   As for those who have believed,
ones who have acted in accord with morality,
for them are Gardens as places of shelter,
a welcome to them for what they were doing.

32:20   As for those who disobeyed,
their place of shelter *is* the fire;°
every time they wanted to go forth from there,
they shall be caused to return to it,
and it shall be said to them:
Experience the punishment of the fire
which you used to deny!

32:21   Truly We shall cause them to experience
the closer punishment

before the greater punishment,
so that perhaps they would return.
Who *is* one who does greater wrong
than he who is reminded of the Signs of His Lord,
then he turns aside from them?°
Truly We *are* ones who requite
ones who sin.

*

Indeed We gave Moses the Book
so be **you** not hesitant about meeting Him;°
and We assigned it as a guidance
for the Children of Israel.
We assigned leaders from among them
to guide under Our command
when they had endured patiently°
and were certain of Our Signs.
Truly **your** Lord *is* He Who shall distinguish
among them
on the Day of Resurrection
about what they were at variance.
Have they not been guided
to how many We have caused to perish
of generations before them
amidst whose dwellings they walk?°
Truly in that *are* Signs!°
Shall they not hear?
Have they not considered
that We drive water to the barren dust of earth?
We drive out crops with it
from which their flocks eat, and they themselves also;°
shall they not perceive?
They say:
When *is* this victory
if you were ones who were sincere?
Say: On the Day of Victory
there shall be no profit
for the belief of those who were ungrateful,
nor shall they be given respite.
So turn aside from them and watch and wait;

32:23

32:24

32:25

32:26

32:27

32:28

32:29

32:30

truly they are ones who are watching and waiting.

CHAPTER 33
THE CONFEDERATES (*al-Aḥzāb*)

In the Name of God,

The Merciful, The Compassionate

O Prophet!
Be Godfearing of God,
and obey not the ones who are ungrateful,
and the ones who are hypocrites,°
truly God is Knowing, Wise.

33:2
Follow what has been revealed to **you**
from **your** Lord.°
Truly God *is* Aware of what you do.

33:3
Put **your** trust in God.°
God shall suffice as a Trustee.

33:4
God made not
two hearts for any man in his interior.°
Nor has He made your wives
to whom you would say:
Be as the back of my mother!°
Nor has He made your adopted sons, your sons;
that *is* but a saying of your mouths;°
God says The Truth;
He guides to the way.

33:5
Call to them by their fathers;
that *is* more equitable to God.°
But if you know not their fathers,
they are your brothers in the way of life,
and ones you protect.°
There is no blame on you
in what mistake you make in it
but what your hearts premeditate.°
God *is* Forgiving, Compassionate

33:6
The Prophet *is* closer to ones who believe
than their own souls;°
his wives *are* their mothers;°
and those who are blood relations,

some of them *are* closer to each other
in what is prescribed by God
than the ones who believe and the emigrants
except what you accomplish for your protectors
as ones who are moral.°
This has been inscribed in the Book.
Recall when We took a solemn promise   33:7
from the Prophets and from **you**,
from Noah and Abraham
Moses and Jesus son of Mary;°
We took an earnest solemn promise from them,
so that He may ask the ones who are sincere   33:8
about their sincerity.°
He has prepared for the ones who are ungrateful
a painful punishment.
*
O those who have believed!   33:9
Remember the divine blessing of God to you
when armies drew near to you
and We sent the winds against them;
and armies you saw not.°
God was Seeing of what you do.
When they drew near to you   33:10
from above you and from below you,
when the sight swerved,
and the hearts reached the throats,
you thought thoughts about God,
there the ones who believe were tested   33:11
and convulsed with a severe convulsing.
Recall when the ones who are hypocrites *were* saying, 33:12
as well as those in whose hearts *is* a sickness:
The promise of God and His Messenger
is nothing but delusion.
Recall when a section of them said: 33:13
O people of Yathrib!
There is no habitation for you, so return.°
A group of people among them asked permission
of the Prophet
saying: Truly Our houses *are* exposed;

but they *were* not exposed;°
they want only to flee.

33:14

If the *enemy* had forced entry
from all areas,
and they had been asked
to dissent,
they would have given in to it,
and they would not have but briefly hesitated,

33:15

although they had made a contract
with God before
that they would not turn their backs *to the enemy.*°
They *are* ones who shall be questioned
about their compact with God.

33:16

Say: Fleeing shall never profit you;
should you flee from death or being killed,
then you shall be given enjoyment
but for a little.

33:17

Say:
Who shall save you from harm except God;
if He had wanted evil for you
or had wanted mercy for you?°
They shall not find for themselves
other than God *any* protector or helper.

33:18

Truly God knows the ones of you who hold off,
and the ones who converse with their brothers
saying: Come to us!°
They approach not the battle themselves
except a little,

33:19

being ungenerous towards **you;**°
then when fear draws near
you shall see them looking on you,
their eyes rolling
like one who is about to be overcome by death;°
but when their fear goes,
they abuse you with sharp tongues
in their greed for good things.°
Such believe not
and God causes their actions to fail.°
That was easy for God.

They assume the confederates have not gone;°   33:20
and if the confederates should approach you,
they would wish
they were nomads
among the ones who were desert dwellers,
asking tidings about you;°
and if they were not among you,
they would fight but a little.

*

Indeed you *have* in the Messenger of God   33:21
a good, fair example
for those who hope for God and the Last Day
and remember God frequently.
When the ones who believe saw the confederates,   33:22
they said:
This *is* what God and His Messenger promised us;
and God and His Messenger are sincere.°
It increased them
only in belief and submission.
Among the ones who believe *are* men   33:23
who are sincere in the contracts they have made
with God;°
of them *are* some
who satisfy by fulfilling their vow with death,
and of them *are* some
who watch and wait;°
and they have not substituted any substitution,
so that God gives recompense   33:24
to the ones who are sincere for their sincerity,
and punishes the ones who are hypocrites
had He willed;
or He turns in forgiveness to them.°
Truly God is Forgiving, Compassionate.
God repelled those who were ungrateful in their rage,   33:25
without their attaining any good.°
God spared the ones who believe from fighting.°
God is Strong, Almighty.
He sent forth   33:26
those who were behind

of the People of the Book
from their strongholds,
and He hurled alarm into their hearts
so that you killed a group of people
and made captives of another group of people.

33:27 He gave their region as an inheritance
and their abodes and their wealth
and a region you had not tread.°
God *is* Powerful over everything!

*

33:28 O Prophet!
Say to **your** wives:
If you want this present life and its adornment,
then approach now;
I shall give you enjoyment
and shall release you a setting free graciously.

33:29 If you want God and His Messenger,
and the Last Abode,
then truly God has prepared
for the ones who are doers of good among you
a sublime compensation.

33:30 O wives of the Prophet!
Whoever of you (f) approaches glaring indecency
her punishment shall be multiplied for her twofold.°
That *is* easy for God.

***

Part 22

33:31 Whoever of you (f) is morally obligated
to God and His Messenger,
ones (f) who have acted in accord with morality,
We shall give her her compensation twice *over*.
We have made ready a generous provision for her.

33:32 O wives of the Prophet!
You (f) are not like any other wives.°
If you (f) are Godfearing,
then be not soft in *your* saying
so that he in whose heart is a sickness not be desirous,
but say a saying of one who is moral.

33:33 Settle down (f) in your (f) houses,
and flaunt (f) not your (f) finery

as one who flaunted one's finery
in the Age of Ignorance;°
perform the formal prayer,
and give the purifying alms,
and obey God and His Messenger.°
God wants to cause disgrace to be put away from you,
O People of the House,
and purify you *with* a purification.

*

Remember what is recounted in your (f) houses   33:34
of the Signs of God and wisdom.°
Truly God is Subtle, Aware.
Truly the ones who are males who submit,
the ones who are females who submit,   33:35
the ones who are males who believe,
the ones who are females who believe,
the ones who are morally obligated males,
the ones who are morally obligated females,
the ones who are sincere males,
the ones who are sincere females,
the ones who are males who remain steadfast,
the ones who are females who remain steadfast,
the ones who are humbled males,
the ones who are humbled females,
the ones who are charitable males,
the ones who are charitable females,
the ones who are males who fast,
the ones who are females who fast,
the males who guard their private parts,
the females who guard,
ones who are males who remember God frequently,
and ones who are females who remember,
God has prepared for them forgiveness
and a sublime compensation.
It would not *be* for the one who is a male believer,   33:36
and the one who is a female believer,
when God and His Messenger have decreed an affair
that there should be any choice for them
in their affair,°

and whoever rebels against God,
and His Messenger,
indeed he goes astray, clearly wandering astray.

33:37   When **you** have said to him
to whom God has been gracious and **you** have
been gracious: Hold back **your** wife to **yourself**,
and be Godfearing of God,
but **you** have concealed in **yourself**
what God was to show,
and **you** have dreaded humanity
whereas God has a better right
that **you** should dread Him;°
so when Zayd had satisfied the *necessary formality*,
We gave her to **you** in marriage
so that there be no fault for ones who believe
in respect of the spouses of their adopted sons
when they have satisfied the *necessary formality*.°
The command of God *is*
one that shall be accomplished.

33:38   There is no fault with the Prophet
in what he undertakes as a duty from God;
that was the custom of God
with those who passed away before.°
The commands of God
are a measured measure

33:39   for those who state the messages of God,
and dread Him,
and dread none except God;°
God suffices as a Reckoner.

33:40   Muhammad was not the father
of any men among you,
but *he is* the Messenger of God
and the Seal of the Prophets,°
and God *is* Knowing of everything.

*

Sec. 6

33:41   O those who have believed!
Remember God with a frequent remembrance,

33:42   and glorify Him in the early morning at dawn
and at eventide.

He *it is* Who gives blessings to you 33:43
and His angels
that He may bring you
out of the shadows into the light.°
He was Compassionate to ones who believe.
Their greetings on the Day they shall meet Him 33:44
shall be: Peace!
He has prepared for them
a generous compensation.
O Prophet! 33:45
Truly We have sent **you**
as one who bears witness,
as one who gives good tidings,
as a warner,
as one who calls to God 33:46
by His permission
and a light-giving illuminating lamp.
Give good tidings to the ones who believe 33:47
that for them is a great grace from God.
Obey not the ones who are ungrateful 33:48
and the ones who are hypocrites;
heed not their hurtfulness;
put **your** trust in God.°
God has sufficed as a Trustee.
O those who have believed! 33:49
If you marry the ones who are female believers,
and divorce them before you have touched them (f),
then *there is* no waiting period to reckon;°
so give them (f) enjoyment,
and let them (f) go, releasing them graciously.
O Prophet! 33:50
Truly We have permitted to **you your** wives
to whom **you** have given their compensation,
and those whom **your** right hand possesses
from those that God has given **you** as spoils of war;
and the daughters of **your** paternal uncle,
the daughters of **your** paternal aunts,
the daughters of **your** maternal uncles,
the daughters of **your** maternal aunts,

who emigrated with **you**
and a woman who has believed
if she bestows herself on the Prophet;
if the Prophet wanted to take her in marriage
—that is exclusively for **you**—
not for the *other* ones who believe;°
indeed We know
what We have undertaken as a duty from Us
concerning their wives
and those whom their right hands possess
so that there should be no fault on **you**;°
God has been Forgiving, Compassionate.

33:51 **You** may put off whom **you** will of them (f),
and **you** may give refuge to whom **you** will;
whomever **you** may be looking for
of those whom **you** have set aside,
there is no blame on **you** *to receive her again.*°
That *is* better
that they may be refreshed,
and they not feel remorse,
and may all of them be well-pleased
with what **you** may give them.°
God knows what is in your hearts.°
God *is* Knowing, Forbearing.

33:52 Women are not lawful for **you** *in marriage* after this,
nor that **you** take them (f) in exchange
for other wives
even though their goodness may impress **you**,
except those whom **your** right hand possesses,°
and God is One Who Watches Over all things.

*

Sec. 7

33:53 O those who have believed!
Enter not the houses of the Prophet
for food unless permission be given to you.
But one who looks for the proper time,
and when you are called to enter,
when you have eaten your meal then disperse,
and be not one who lingers for conversation.°
Truly such *is* to cause annoyance

to the Prophet,
and he is ashamed *to ask* you *to leave,*°
but God is not ashamed of The Truth.°
When you ask *his wives* for sustenance,
then ask them from behind a partition.°
That *is* purer for your hearts and their hearts.°
It is not for you to cause annoyance
to the Messenger of God,
nor may you marry his wives after him.°
Truly that would be serious with God.
Whether you show anything or conceal it,   33:54
truly God has been Knowing of everything.
There is no blame on **your** *wives to converse freely*   33:55
with their (f) fathers or their (f) sons,
or their (f) brothers or the sons of their (f) brothers
or the sons of their (f) sisters
or their (f) women
or what their (f) right hands possess,°
and be Godfearing of God.°
Truly God has been Witness over everything.
Truly God and His angels   33:56
give blessings to the Prophet.°
O those who have believed!
Give your blessings to him and blessings of peace
and invoke peace for him.
Truly those who inflict torment on God   33:57
and His Messenger,
God has cursed them in the present
and in the world to come
and has prepared for them a despised punishment.
Those who inflict torment   33:58
on the ones who are male believers,
and the ones who are female believers,
without their deserving *it,*
indeed they lay a burden on themselves
of false charges to harm another's reputation
and a clear sin.
*   Sec. 8

O Prophet!   33:59

492

Say to **your** wives and **your** daughters
and the women who believe
to draw their outer garments closer
over themselves.°
That *is* more fitting so that they be recognized
and not be afflicted with torment;
God *is* Forgiving, Compassionate.

33:60 If the ones who are hypocrites refrain not themselves,
those in whose hearts *is* a sickness
and the ones who make a commotion in the city,
We shall cause **you** to overpower them;
then they shall not be your neighbors
except a little *while;*

33:61 the ones who are cursed,°
they shall be taken
wherever they are come on by someone,
and killed with *a terrible* slaying.

33:62 This *was* the custom of God
with those who passed away before;°
and **you** shall never find in the custom of God
a substitution.

33:63 Humanity asks **you** about the Hour;°
say: The knowledge of it is not but with God.°
What shall cause **you** to recognize
that perhaps the Hour is near?

33:64 Truly God has cursed the ones who are ungrateful
and has prepared a blaze for them,

33:65 ones who shall dwell in it forever, eternally;°
neither shall they find protector nor helper.

33:66 On a Day when their faces
shall be turned upside down in the fire,
they shall say:
O would that we had obeyed God
and obeyed the Messenger!

33:67 They shall say:
Our Lord!
Truly we obeyed our chiefs and our great ones,
and they caused us to go astray from the way.

33:68 Our Lord!

Give them double the punishment
and curse them with a great cursing!

*

O those who have believed! 33:69
Be not like those who inflicted torment on Moses,
those God declared innocent of what they said,°
and he was well-esteemed
with God
O those who have believed! 33:70
Be Godfearing of God
and say an appropriate saying.
He shall make your actions right for you 33:71
and forgive you your impieties,°
and whoever obeys God and His Messenger
has indeed won a triumph, a sublime triumph!
Truly We presented the trust 33:72
to the heavens and the earth
and the mountains, but they refused to carry it
and were apprehensive of it;
but the human being carried it;°
truly he was wrongdoing, very ignorant.
God punishes the ones who are male hypocrites, 33:73
and the ones who are female hypocrites,
and the ones who are male polytheists,
and the ones who are female polytheists,
and God shall turn in forgiveness
toward the ones who are male believers
and the ones who are female believers,°
and God is Forgiving, Compassionate.

CHAPTER 34
SHEBA (*al-Sabā˒*)

In the Name of God,
The Merciful, The Compassionate Sec. 1
The Praise *belongs* to God; 34:1
to Him *belongs* whatever *is* in the heavens
and whatever *is* in and on the earth;
His *is* The Praise in the world to come.°

He *is* The Wise, The Aware.

34:2 He knows whatever penetrates into the earth
and what goes forth out of it
and what goes forth from the heaven
and what comes down from it.°
He *is* The Compassionate, The Forgiving.

34:3 Those who are ungrateful say:
The Hour shall not approach us.
Say: Yea! By my Lord
it shall indeed approach you.
He is One Who has Knowledge of the Unseen;°
not an atom's weight escapes from Him
in the heavens, nor in and on the earth,
be it smaller or greater,
except that *it is* in a clear Book;

34:4 that He may give recompense
to those who have believed,
the ones who have acted in accord with morality.
Those, for them *there is* forgiveness
and a generous provision.

34:5 But those who endeavor against Our Signs
as ones who strive to thwart,
those, for them *there is* a painful punishment
of defilement.

34:6 Those who have been given knowledge
see that what is sent forth to **you** from **your** Lord
is The Truth,
and it guides to the path
of The Almighty, The Worthy of Praise.

34:7 Those who are ungrateful said:
Shall we point you to a man who shall tell you
when what is torn to pieces
is fully torn to pieces;
then you *shall* indeed *be* in a new creation?

34:8 Has he devised a lie against God,
or *is* there a madness in him?°
Rather those who believe not
in the world to come
are in torment and a far going astray.

Have they not considered what *is* in advance of them
and what *is* behind them
of the heaven and the earth?°
If We will, We could cause the earth to swallow them,
or drop on them pieces of heaven.°
Truly in this *is* a Sign for every repentant servant.

*

Indeed We gave David grace from Us:°
O you mountains! Echo psalms of praise with him
and the birds;
and We softened iron for him,
saying: Make **you** coats of mail
and calculate the links,°
act as one who *is* in accord with morality;°
truly I *am* Seeing of what you do.
To Solomon *We subjected* the wind,
the first part of the day was a month's *journey*
and the evening course a month's *journey*;°
We caused a spring of molten brass to flow for him;°
We gave him certain of the jinn
who toiled for him
with the permission of his Lord;°
whoever of them swerved from Our command
We caused to experience
the punishment of the blaze.
They toiled for him whatever he willed:
Sanctuaries, statues and basin like cisterns
as large as water-troughs
and cooking pots—ones firmly fixed.°
O People of David! Act with thankfulness!°
But few of My servants *are* grateful.
Then when We decreed death for him;
nothing pointed out his death to them
except a moving creature of the earth
which consumed his staff;°
so when he fell down,
it became clear to the jinn
that if they had known the unseen,
they would not have lingered in expectation

in the despised punishment.

There was indeed a Sign for Sheba
in their dwelling *place*:°
Two gardens on the right hand and on the left hand:°
Eat of the provision of your Lord
and thank Him *for*:°
A good land
and a forgiving Lord.

34:16 But they turned aside,
so We sent against them the flood of Iram,
and We substituted for their two gardens,
gardens yielding a sour harvest,
and tamarisks,
and lote-trees here and there.

34:17 We recompensed them
because they were ungrateful;°
have We given *this* recompense
except to those who are ungrateful?

34:18 We made between them
and the towns which We had blessed,
manifest towns;
We ordained journeying between them:°
Journey through them
as ones who are in safety night and day.

34:19 But they said: Our Lord!
Cause a distance between our journeys;
they did wrong to themselves
so We made them as tales,
and We tore them to pieces—a total tearing to pieces;
truly in this indeed *are* Signs
for every enduring grateful one.

34:20 Indeed established as true about them
was the opinion of Iblis,
and they all followed him,
except a group of people of the ones who believed.

34:21 Yet he had no authority over them
except that We might know
those who believe in the world to come
from those who *are* in uncertainty of it,°

and **your** Lord *is* Guardian over everything.

*

Say: Call on those whom you claim
other than God!°
They possess not the weight of an atom
in the heavens nor on the earth;
nor have they in either any association;
nor among them *is there* any sustainer for Him.
No intercession profits with Him
except for him to whom He gives permission.°
Yet when their hearts are lifted from terror,
they say: What *is it* that your Lord said?°
They say: The Truth;°
and He *is* the Lofty, the Great.
Say: Who provides for you
from the heavens and the earth?°
Say: God!°
Truly we or you *are either* on the guidance
or clearly going astray.
Say: You shall not be asked about our sins,
nor shall we be asked about what you do.
Say: Our Lord shall gather us,
then He shall explain The Truth among us,
and He *is* The Opener, The Knowing.
Say: Cause me to see those whom
you have caused to join with Him as associates;°
nay!°
Rather He *is* God, The Almighty, The Wise.
We have not sent **you**,
but collectively for humanity,
as a bearer of good tidings and a warner,
but most of humanity knows not.
They say:
Where *is* this promise,
if you are ones who are sincere?
Say: Yours *is* the solemn declaration of a Day
which you may not delay
for an hour nor press forward.

*

34:22
34:23
34:24
34:25
34:26
34:27
34:28
34:29
34:30
Sec. 4

34:31 Those who are ungrateful say:
We shall never believe in this Quran,
nor in what *was* in advance of it,°
but if **you** were to see
when the ones who are unjust
are ones who are stationed
before their Lord,
returning the saying, some of them to others.
Those who were
taken advantage of because of their weakness
say to those who grew arrogant:
Had it not been for you,
we should indeed have been ones who believe.

34:32 Those who had grown arrogant
would say to those who were
taken advantage of because of their weakness:
Have we barred you from guidance
after it had drawn near to you?°
Rather you were ones who sin.

34:33 Those who were
taken advantage of because of their weakness
would say to those who had grown arrogant:
Rather *it was your* planning
by nighttime and daytime
when you commanded us to be ungrateful to God
and to assign rivals to Him.°
They kept *their* self-reproach secret
when they saw the punishment;
We assigned yokes around the necks
of those who were ungrateful.°
Are they given recompense,
except for what they were doing?

34:34 We sent not any warner to a town
but that those given ease said:
Truly in what you have been sent
we are ones who are ungrateful.

34:35 They said:
We *are* more *than you* in wealth and in children,
and we are not ones who shall be punished!

Say: Truly my Lord extends the provision
to whom He will
and confines it *to whom He will*,
but most of humanity knows not.

*   Sec. 5

It is not your wealth nor your children   34:37
that shall bring you near to Us,
except he who has believed,
one who has acted in accord with morality.
As for those, they shall have recompense doubled
for what they did,
and they *shall live* in the high chambers
as ones who are in safety.
Those who endeavor against Our Signs,   34:38
as one who strives to thwart *them*,
those—
ones who are to be charged with the punishment.
Say: Truly my Lord extends the provision   34:39
for whomever He will of His servants,
and confines for him *what He will.*°
Whatever you have spent of anything,
He shall replace it;°
He *is* The Best of the ones who provide.
On a Day He shall assemble them all together;   34:40
then He shall say to the angels:
Was it these who used to worship you?
They would say: Glory be to **You**!   34:41
You are our Lord and not they!°
Rather they used to worship the jinn;°
most of them *were* ones who believed in them.
Today   34:42
some of you shall possess over others
neither profit, nor hurt,
and We shall say to those who did wrong:
Experience the punishment of the fire
which you used to deny.
When are recounted to them   34:43
Our Signs, clear portents, they said:
This *is* not but a man who wants to bar you

from what your fathers used to worship;
they said: This *is* not but a forged calumny.°
Those who were ungrateful for The Truth said
when it had drawn near to them:
This *is* nothing but clear sorcery.

34:44 We have not given them Books
which they study,°
nor sent We to them any warner before **you**.

34:45 Those before them denied
and they have not reached one-tenth
of what We had given them,
yet they denied My Messengers;°
so how was My disapproval *of them*!

*

Sec. 6

34:46 Say: I admonish you in not but one thing:°
That you stand up for God,
by twos and one by one,
and then reflect.°
There is no madness in your companion.°
He *is* nothing but a warner to you
of a severe punishment.

34:47 Say: Whatever compensation I have asked of you
is for you;°
my compensation *is* not but from God;°
and He *is* a Witness over everything.

34:48 Say: Truly my Lord hurls The Truth;
He is The Knower of the unseen.

34:49 Say: The Truth draws near
and falsehood neither causes to begin
nor causes to return.

34:50 Say: If I go astray,
truly I shall go astray not but by myself;°
and if I am truly guided,
it is because of what my Lord reveals to me.°
Truly He *is* Hearing, Ever Near.

34:51 If **you** were to see
when they would be terrified with no escape;
they would be taken from a near place.

34:52 They shall say: We have believed in it.

But how could they reach *it* from a far place?
Indeed they were ungrateful for it before;° 34:53
they hurl at the unseen from a far place.
Between them shall be a barrier 34:54
and between that for which they lust,
as was accomplished for partisans before.°
Truly they were in the uncertainty of suspicion.

CHAPTER 35
THE ORIGINATOR (*al-Fāṭir*)

In the Name of God,
The Merciful, The Compassionate Sec. 1
The Praise *belongs* to God, 35:1
The One Who is the Originator
of the heavens and the earth,
the one who made the angels messengers
with wings by twos and threes and fours.°
He increases in creation what He will.°
Truly God *is* Powerful over everything.
Whatever God may open of mercy to humanity, 35:2
there is not one who holds it back;°
and what He holds back,
there is not one who sends it after that.°
He *is* The Almighty, The Wise.
O humanity! 35:3
Remember the divine blessing of God on you!°
Is there any creator other than God
Who provides for you
from heaven and the earth?°
There is no god but He;°
how then are you misled?
If they deny **you**, 35:4
indeed Messengers before **you** were denied.°
To God all affairs return.
O humanity! 35:5
Truly the promise of God *is* True,°
so let not this present life delude you;°
let not the deluder delude you about God.

35:6 Truly Satan *is* an enemy to you
so take him as an enemy.°
He calls not but his party
that they may become
among the Companions of the Blaze.

35:7 Those who are ungrateful,
for them *shall be* a severe punishment;°
and those who have believed,
ones who have acted in accord with morality,
for them *there is* forgiveness
and a great compensation.

*

Sec. 2

35:8 Is there someone whom,
the direness of his action
was made to appear pleasing,
so that he saw it as fair?°
Truly God causes to go astray
whomever He will
and guides whomever He will;°
so let not **your** soul be wasted in regret for them.°
Truly God *is* Knowing of what they craft!

35:9 *It is* God Who sent the winds
so that they stir up the clouds;
We drove them to a dead land;
We gave life to the earth by them
after its death.°
Thus *shall be* the rising!

35:10 Whoever would want renown,
renown *belongs* to God altogether;°
to Him words of what is good rise;
He exalts an act in accord with morality.°
But those who plan evil deeds,
theirs *shall be* a severe punishment;°
and the planning of those—
it shall come to nothing.

35:11 God created you from earthy dust,
then from seminal fluid,
then He made you pairs.°
No female carries nor brings forth a baby

except with His Knowledge.°
No one *is* given a long life,
nor is *anything* reduced from his lifetime
but it *is* in a book.°
Truly that *is* easy for God.
The two seas are not on the same level.   35:12
This *is* agreeable, water of the sweetest kind
and delicious to drink
and *the other is* salty and bitter;°
but from both you eat succulent flesh
and pull out glitter that you wear;°
and you see the boats
plowing through the waves in it
that you may be looking for His grace
so that perhaps you would be thankful.
He causes the nighttime to be inserted   35:13
into the daytime and He causes the daytime
to be inserted into the nighttime;
He causes the sun to become subservient
and the moon;
each runs *its course* for a determined term;
that *is* God, our Lord,
for Him *is* the dominion!°
Those whom you call other than Him
possess not even the skin of a date stone.
If you called them,   35:14
they would not hear your supplication;
even if they heard, they would not respond to you;°
and on the Day of Resurrection,
they shall disbelieve in your associates.°
None tells you like One Who is Aware.
*   Sec. 3

O humanity!   35:15
It is you who *are* poor in relation to God;°
and God—He *is* Sufficient, Worthy of Praise.
If He will, He would cause you to be put away   35:16
and bring a new creation.
That for God *is* not a hard thing to do.   35:17
No laden soul shall bear another's load.°   35:18

504

If one weighed down calls for *help*
for his heavy load,
nothing of it shall be carried *for him*,
even though he be near of kin.°
Warn **you** not but those who dread their Lord
in the unseen,
and perform formal prayer.°
He who purifies himself
then not but purifies for himself.°
To God *is* the Homecoming.
Not on the same level
35:19   *are* the *unwilling* to see and the seeing;
35:20   nor *are* shadows and light,
35:21   nor *are* the shade and the torrid heat,
35:22   nor *are* the living and the lifeless on the same level.°
Truly God causes to hear whom He will;°
and **you** are not one who causes to hear
those *who are* in graves.
35:23   **You** are not but a warner.
35:24   Truly We have sent **you** with The Truth,
a bearer of good tidings and a warner.°
There *is* not any community,
but a warner had passed away among them.
35:25   If they deny **you**,
so indeed those who *were* before them denied.
Their Messengers drew near to them
with clear portents
and with the scrolls and the illuminating Book.
35:26   Then I took those who were ungrateful;°
how was My disapproval!

Sec. 4   *

35:27   Have **you** not considered that
God sent forth water from the heavens;
then We brought out fruits of varying hues?°
Among the mountains *are* white and red streaks
—ones of varying hues—
and *others* raven black.
35:28   Of humanity, moving creatures and flocks,
there are thus likewise ones of varying hues.°

505

Only those of His servants who dread God
are those who are knowing;°
truly God *is* Almighty, Forgiving.
Truly those who   35:29
recount the Book of God,
perform the formal prayer,
and spend out of what We have provided for them
secretly and in public,
hoping for a trade
that *shall* never come to nothing,
that He may surely pay the account in full   35:30
for compensation
and increase them more out of His grace.°
Truly He *is* Forgiving, Ready to Appreciate.
What We revealed to **you** of the Book   35:31
is The Truth,
establishing as true what *was* in advance of it,°
truly God *is* Aware, Seeing of His servants.
Then We gave the Book as an inheritance   35:32
to those whom We favored of Our servants;°
then of them *are* ones who are unjust,
and then of them *are* ones who are moderate,
and some of them *are* Ones Who Outstrip
with good works by permission of God.°
That is the greater grace.
Gardens of Eden—they shall enter them;   35:33
they shall be adorned in them
with bracelets of gold and pearl;°
and their garments in them *shall be* silk.
They shall say: The Praise *belongs* to God   35:34
Who causes grief to be put away from us;°
truly our Lord *is* indeed
Forgiving, Ready to Appreciate.
He Who has caused us to live in a habitation 35:35
out of His grace,
fatigue *shall* not afflict us there,
nor shall we be afflicted with exhaustion there.
Those who are ungrateful,   35:36
for them *shall be* the fire of hell:

Neither shall it be decided for them
so that they die
nor shall its punishment be lightened for them.°
Thus We give recompense to every ungrateful *one.*

They shall shout aloud in it:
Our Lord! Bring us out
as ones who have acted in accord with morality,
not what we were doing!°
Gave We not you a long enough life
so that whoever recollects should recollect there?
The warner drew near to you.°
So experience *it*
because ones who are unjust have no helper.

*

Sec. 5

35:38 Truly God *is* One Who has Knowledge
of the unseen of the heavens and the earth.°
Truly He *is* Knowing of what *is* in the breasts.

35:39 He *it is* Who has made you viceregents
on the earth.°
So whoever is ungrateful,
then his ingratitude *shall be* against him;°
and the ingratitude increases not
ones who are ungrateful to their Lord
except in repugnance;
their ingratitude increases not
ones who are ungrateful to their Lord
except in loss.

35:40 Say:
Have you considered your associates
to whom you call to other than God?
Cause me to see what they have created of the earth,
or *have* they any association in the heavens?
Or have We given them a Book
so that they *have* a clear portent from there?°
Rather the ones who are unjust
some of them to others
promise nothing but delusion.

35:41 Truly God holds back the heavens and the earth
so that they are not displaced.°

If they are displaced,
there is none who holds them back but He.°
Truly He has been Forbearing, Forgiving.
They swore by God the most earnest oaths,   35:42
that if a warner drew near to them,
they would be better guided
than any of the communities;°
yet when a warner drew near to them,
it increased nothing in them but aversion,
growing arrogant on the earth   35:43
and planning bad deeds.°
The plan of bad deeds surrounds
none but those people *themselves.*°
Then look they on
nothing but the custom of the ancient ones?°
You shall not find in the custom of God
any substitution;°
you shall not find in the custom of God
any revision.
Have they not journeyed on the earth   35:44
and looked on how was the Ultimate End
of those who *were* before them,
and they were stronger than they *are* in strength?°
God is not weakened by anything
in the heavens nor in or on the earth;°
truly He has been Knowing, Powerful.
If God were to take humanity to task   35:45
for what they earned,
He would not leave on the back of *the earth*
any moving creature,
but He postpones to a determined term
and when their term has drawn near,
then truly God has been Seeing of His servants.

CHAPTER 36

YA SIN (*Yā Sīn*)

In the Name of God,

The Merciful, The Compassionate

36:1 *Yā Sīn;*

36:2 by the Wise Quran,

36:3 truly **you** are of the ones who are sent,

36:4 on a straight path.

36:5 This is sent down successively
by The Almighty, The Compassionate,

36:6 that **you** might warn a folk
whose fathers were not warned,
so they *were* ones who were heedless.

36:7 Indeed the saying is to be realized
against most of them,
for they believe not.

36:8 Truly We have laid yokes on their necks
up to the chins,
so that they *are* ones who are stiff-necked.

36:9 We have laid in front of them
an embankment
and behind them an embankment;
We have covered them so they perceive not.

36:10 Equal *it is* to them
whether **you** were to warn them
or **you** were not to warn them;
they shall not believe.

36:11 **You** not but warn him
who follows the Reminder
and dreads The Merciful in the unseen;°
so give him good tidings of forgiveness
and a generous compensation.

36:12 Truly We give life to the dead
and We write down what they put forward
and their effects.°
We have counted everything in a clear record.

*

Propound a parable for them: 36:13
The Companions of the Town,
when ones who were sent drew near them.
When We sent to them two,   36:14
they denied them both,
so We replenished them with a third.
They said:
Truly We *are* ones who have been sent to you.
They said: You *are* nothing but mortals like ourselves   36:15
and The Merciful has not sent forth anything.
You are only lying!
They said: Our Lord knows   36:16
that we *are* ones who have been sent to you;
on us *is* not but the delivery of a clear message.   36:17
They said: Truly we auger ill of you;°   36:18
if you refrain not yourself,
we shall indeed stone you.
Indeed a painful punishment shall afflict you from us.
They said: One who augers ill *be* with you!°   36:19
What? If you were reminded?°
Rather you *are* a folk,
ones who are excessive.
A man drew near   36:20
from the farther part of the city, coming eagerly.
He said: O my folk! Follow the ones sent!
Follow those who ask not of you any compensation,   36:21
and they *are* ones who are truly guided.
                           ***   **Part 23**

What *is it* for me that I worship not Him   36:22
Who has originated me
and to Whom you shall be returned?
What? Shall I take gods to myself other than He   36:23
when, if The Merciful wants any distress for me,
their intercession shall not avail me at all,
nor shall they save me.
Then truly I should be clearly going astray.   36:24
Truly I have believed in your Lord   36:25
so hear me!
It was said: Enter the Garden;°   36:26

he said: Would that my folk had known

36:27 that my Lord has forgiven me
and made me one who is honored!

36:28 We sent not forth against his folk after him
an army from heaven,
nor would We have sent forth.

36:29 It was but one Cry
and lo! They *were* ones who were silent and still.

36:30 O how regrettable of the servants!°
Never a Messenger approached them
but they used to ridicule him.

36:31 What? Have they not considered
how many generations We caused to perish
before them
who indeed return not to them.

36:32 Truly all of them shall be
ones who shall be charged in Our Presence.

Sec. 3 *

36:33 A Sign for them *is* the dead body of the earth;
to it We gave life
and We brought out grain from it
so that they ate from there.

36:34 We have made in them gardens of date palm trees
and grapevines,
and We have caused a spring to gush forth

36:35 so that they may eat of the fruits from there
that their hands have not made;°
shall they then not be thankful?

36:36 Glory be to Him Who created pairs, all of them,
of what the earth causes to develop
as well as of their own kind,
and of what they know not!

36:37 A Sign for them is the nighttime;
We pluck the daytime from it,
and lo! They are in darkness!

36:38 The sun runs
to a resting place for it.°
That *is* foreordained by The Almighty, The Knowing.

36:39 For the moon We have ordained mansions

until it reverts like an ripe aged, dry, date stalk.

It is not permitted   36:40
for the sun to overtake the moon,
nor the nighttime to outstrip the daytime.°
They each swim in an orbit.

A Sign for them *is* that We carry their offspring   36:41
in a laden boat.

We have created for them of its like   36:42
that they ride.

If We will, We shall drown them;   36:43
there shall be none who cries aloud for help for them,
nor shall they be saved,

unless it be a mercy from Us   36:44
and as an enjoyment for a while.

Recall when it was said to them: 36:45
Be Godfearing of what *is* before you
and what *is* behind you
so that perhaps you would find mercy.

There never approached them any Sign   36:46
from the Signs of their Lord,
but they were ones who turned aside from it.

When it was said to them: 36:47
Spend of whatever God has provided you,
those who were ungrateful said
to those who had believed:
Shall we feed
those whom He would have fed, if He will?
You are nothing but in a clear going astray.

They say: When *is* this promise   36:48
if you are one who is sincere?

They expect but one Cry   36:49
which shall take them,
while they strive against one another.

Then they shall not be able to leave a legacy,   36:50
nor shall they return to their people.

                          *   Sec. 4

The trumpet shall be blown!   36:51
Lo! There they shall be
sliding down to their Lord from their tombs.

36:52   They would say: Woe on us!
Who has raised us up from our place of sleep?°
This *is* what The Merciful had promised;
the ones who are sent were sincere.

36:53   The Cry shall be but one,
and truly they *shall be* in Our Presence altogether—
ones who are charged.

36:54   Today wrong shall not be done to any soul,
nor shall you be given recompense
except for what you were doing.

36:55   Truly the Companions of the Garden that Day
are ones who are joyful in *their* engagements,

36:56   they and their spouses,
in shade on raised benches,
ones who are reclining.

36:57   They *shall have* in it sweet fruits,
and they *shall have* whatever they call for:

36:58   Peace! A saying from the Compassionate Lord.

36:59   Be separated on this Day, O ones who sin.

36:60   Made I not a compact with you,
O Children of Adam,
that you not worship Satan;°
truly he is a clear enemy,

36:61   and that you should worship Me?°
This is a straight path.

36:62   Indeed He caused to go astray
a great array of you;°
shall you not be reasonable?

36:63   This *is* hell which you were promised.

36:64   Roast in it this Day
for what you were ungrateful.

36:65   This Day We shall set a seal on their mouths,
their hands shall speak to Us,
their feet shall bear witness
to what they were earning.

36:66   If We will,
We would indeed have obliterated their eyes;
then were they to race towards the path,
how would they have perceived?

If it had been Our will,　　　　　　　　
We would have transformed their ability;
then they would not have been able
to pass on, nor would they have returned.

*

He to whom We give a long life,　　　　36:68
We bend him over in his constitution;°
shall they not then be reasonable?
We have not taught him poetry.°　　　　36:69
It is not fit and proper for him;
this is nothing but a Reminder and a clear Recitation
to warn whomever has lived,　　　　　　36:70
and that the saying may be realized
against the ones who are ungrateful.
Have they not considered how We have created　36:71
for them out of what Our hands have done,
flocks, so that they have become
ones who are possessors of them?
We have subdued them to them　　　　　36:72
so that of them, some *are* riding animals
and some of them, they eat.
They *have* uses from them　　　　　　36:73
and a drinking place;°
shall they not then be thankful?
They have taken to themselves　　　　　36:74
gods other than God
so that perhaps they would be helped.
They are not able to help them　　　　　36:75
while they *are* to them as a charged army.
So let not their saying grieve **you.**•　　36:76
Truly We know what they keep secret
and what they speak openly.
Has the human being not considered　　　36:77
that We have created him from seminal fluid?
So then behold, he becomes a clear adversary.
He propounds parables for Us　　　　　36:78
and forgets his own creation;°
he said: Who shall give life to these bones
when they have decayed?

36:79	Say: He shall give life to them
	Who caused them to grow the first time;°
	and He *is* The Knowing of every creation.
36:80	*It is* He Who makes for you
	fire out of a green tree,
	and behold, you kindle from it.
36:81	Is it not He Who created
	the heavens and the earth
	one who has the power to create the like of them?°
	Yea, indeed! He *is* The Knowing Creator.
36:82	Truly His command when He wanted a thing
	is but to say to it: Be! And it is!
36:83	Glory be to Him
	in Whose hand *is* the kingship of everything!
	To Him you shall be returned.

CHAPTER 37
THE ONES STANDING IN RANKS (*al-Ṣāffāt*)

Stage 6	In the Name of God,
Sec. 1	The Merciful, The Compassionate
37:1	By the ones standing in ranks, ranged in rows,
37:2	those who scare in a scaring,
37:3	those who recount the Reminder.
37:4	Truly your God *is* indeed One;
37:5	the Lord of the heavens and the earth
	and all that *is* between them,
	and the Lord of the sunrise.
37:6	Truly We have made to appear pleasing
	the present heaven
	with the adornment of the stars
37:7	kept safe from every emboldened Satan.
37:8	They pay no attention to the lofty Council
	for they are hurled at from every edge,
37:9	rejected;°
	and theirs is a punishment that lasts forever;
37:10	except for him who snatches a fragment
	so a piercing flame there pursues him.
37:11	So ask them for advice:

515

Are they stronger in constitution
or those *others* whom We have created?°
Truly We have created them of clinging clay.
Rather **you** have marveled   37:12
while they derided.
When they are reminded, they remember not.   37:13
When they see a Sign, they scoff at it.   37:14
They say: 37:15
This *is* nothing but clear sorcery.
What? When we are dead,
and have become earthy dust and bones,
shall we indeed *be* ones who are to be raised up
and also, our fathers, the ancient ones?   37:17
Say: Yes,   37:18
you *shall be* ones who *shall be* in a state of lowliness.
There shall be not but one Scare,   37:19
so when they look on *it,*
they shall say: Woe to us!   37:20
This *is* the Day of Judgment!
This *is* the Day of Decision,   37:21
which you used to deny.
                          *   Sec. 2

Assemble those who did wrong and their spouses,   37:22
and what they used to worship
instead of God   37:23
and guide them to the path to hellfire.
Stop them°   37:24
for they *are* ones who are questioned:
What *is* the matter with you   37:25
that you help not one another?
Rather they are on that Day   37:26
ones who resign themselves to submission.
Some of them come forward to others,   37:27
inquiring of one another.
They shall say: 37:28
Truly you, you were approaching us
from the right.
They shall say: 37:29
Rather you were not ones who believed.

37:30	We had no authority over you;°
	rather you were a defiant folk.
37:31	So the saying has been realized against us
	by our Lord;°
	that truly we shall indeed be
	ones who experience *the punishment.*
37:32	So we led you into error,
	truly we were ourselves ones who were in error.
37:33	Then truly they shall be on that Day
	ones who are partners in the punishment.
37:34	Truly thus We accomplish with ones who sin.
37:35	Truly when it was said to them:
	There is no god but God,
	they grew arrogant.
37:36	They say: *Should* we indeed *be*
	ones who leave our gods for a possessed poet?
37:37	Rather he has drawn near with The Truth
	and he established as true the ones who were sent.
37:38	Truly you are one who shall experience
	the painful punishment,
37:39	and you shall be given recompense,
	nothing but for what you were doing,
37:40	except the devoted servants of God,
37:41	those, for them is a known provision.
37:42	Sweet fruits,°
	and they shall be ones who are honored
37:43	in the Gardens of Bliss,
37:44	on couches—ones who face one another.
37:45	A cup from a spring of water is passed around,
37:46	white, a delight to ones who drink *it.*
37:47	Neither in that *is* headache
	nor intoxication.
37:48	With them *are* ones (f) who are restrained
	of glance, lovely eyed
37:49	as if they *were* well-guarded eggs.
37:50	So some of them shall come forward to others,
	questioning one another.
37:51	One of them who converses would say:
	Truly I had a comrade

who would say:

Are **you** of the ones who establish as true?

When we die

and become earthy dust and bones,

shall we *be* ones who are judged?

He said: *Shall* you *be* the one who peruses?   **37:54**

So he perused and saw him amidst hellfire.   **37:55**

He said: By God, you were   **37:56**

about to deal me destruction.

Had it not been for the divine blessing of my Lord   **37:57**

I would indeed

have been of the ones who are charged.

Then *are* we not in dead bodies?   **37:58**

Other than our first death,   **37:59**

are we not ones who are punished?

Truly this, it *is* indeed   **37:60**

the winning the sublime triumph.

For the like of this, let the ones who work, work.   **37:61**

Is this better as a welcome or the tree of Zaqqum?   **37:62**

Truly We made it a test for ones who are unjust.   **37:63**

Truly it *is* a tree   **37:64**

that goes forth, its roots of hellfire,

its spathes are like the heads of satans.   **37:65**

So truly they, they *are* ones who eat from it,   **37:66**

ones who fill their bellies with it.

Then truly on top of that   **37:67**

for them *is* a brew of scalding water.

Then truly their return is to hellfire.   **37:68**

Truly they discovered their fathers gone astray,   **37:69**

yet they ran in their footsteps.   **37:70**

Indeed most of the ancient ones   **37:71**

went astray before them,

and indeed We had sent among them   **37:72**

ones who warn.

Then look on   **37:73**

how was the Ultimate End

of the ones who were warned,

except the devoted servants of God.   **37:74**

*

Sec. 3

37:75	Indeed Noah had cried out to Us,
	and how excellent *were* the ones who answered!
37:76	We delivered him and his people
	from tremendous distress;
37:77	We have made his offspring
	the ones who remained.
37:78	We left for him *to say* among the later ones:
37:79	Peace be on Noah among the worlds.
37:80	Thus We give recompense
	to *the* ones who are doers of good.
37:81	Truly he *is* one of Our believing servants.
37:82	Then We drowned the others.
37:83	Truly among his partisans *was* Abraham.
37:84	When he drew near to his Lord
	with a pure-hearted heart,
37:85	when he said to his father and to his folk:
	What *is* it that you worship?
37:86	A calumny that you wanted gods other than God!
37:87	What then is your opinion
	about the Lord of the worlds?
37:88	He looked on with a glimpse at the stars,
37:89	and he said: Truly I am ill!
37:90	So they turned away,
	ones who drew back from him,
37:91	and he turned upon their gods and said:
	Shall you not eat?
37:92	What *is* the matter with you
	that you speak not for yourselves?
37:93	Then he turned upon them,
	striking them with his right hand.
37:94	Then they came forward towards him rushing.
37:95	He said: Worship you
	what you yourselves carve
37:96	while God created you and what you do?
37:97	They said: Build for him a structure,
	then cast him into hellfire.
37:98	So they wanted cunning against him,
	but We made them the lowest.
37:99	He said: Truly I *am* one who is going to my Lord;

519

He shall guide me:
My Lord! bestow on me   37:100
of the ones who are in accord with morality.
So We gave him the good tidings of a forbearing boy.   37:101
When he reached maturity   37:102
endeavoring with him,
he said: O my son!
Truly I have seen while slumbering
that I am sacrificing **you**?
Look on! Have **you yourself** considered?°
He said: O my father!
Accomplish whatever **you** have been commanded;
you shall find me, had God willed,
of the ones who remain steadfast.
Then when they had both submitted themselves,   37:103
and he flung him on his brow,
We cried out to him: O Abraham: 37:104
Truly **you** have established the dream as true.   37:105
Thus We give recompense
to the ones who are doers of good.
Truly that *was* indeed the clear trial.   37:106
Then We took ransom for him   37:107
with a sublime slaughter.
We left for him *a good name* with the later ones: 37:108
Peace be on Abraham!   37:109
Thus indeed We give recompense   37:110
to the ones who are doers of good.
Truly he *is* one of Our believing servants.   37:111
We gave him the good tidings of Isaac,   37:112
a prophet,
among the ones who are in accord with morality.
We blessed him and Isaac.°   37:113
Of their offspring *are* ones who are doers of good,
and ones who are clearly unjust to themselves.

*

                                                             Sec. 4

Indeed We showed Our grace   37:114
to Moses and Aaron.
We delivered them and their folk   37:115
from the tremendous distress,

37:116	and helped them,
	so that they, they were the ones who were the victors.
37:117	We gave them the manifest Book
37:118	and guided them to the straight path.
37:119	We left for them *a good name* with the later ones:
37:120	Peace be on Moses and Aaron!
37:121	Truly thus We give recompense
	to *the* ones who are doers of good.
37:122	Truly they were Our believing servants.
37:123	Truly Elias was
	of the ones who were sent.
37:124	When he said to his folk:
	Shall you not be Godfearing?
37:125	Shall you call to Baal
	and forsake the fairest of Creators
37:126	God,
	your Lord and the Lord of your ancient fathers?
37:127	But they denied him,
	so they truly *were* ones who are changed
37:128	except the devoted servants of God
37:129	We left for him *a good name* with the later ones:
37:130	Peace be on Elias!
37:131	Truly thus We give recompense
	to the ones who are doers of good.
37:132	Truly he *was* of Our believing servants.
37:133	Truly Lot
	was of the ones who are sent.
37:134	We delivered him and his people, one and all,
37:135	except an old woman
	among the ones who stayed behind.
37:136	Then We destroyed the others.
37:137	Truly you pass by them,
	when it happened in the morning
37:138	and at night;
	shall you not then be reasonable?
Sec. 5	*
37:139	Truly Jonah was one
	of the ones who are sent.
37:140	When he fled

to the laden boat;

he cast lots with them,   37:141

and he was

of the ones who were refuted.

Then the fish engulfed him   37:142

while he was one who was answerable.

Had it not been   37:143

that he *was* of the ones who glorify,

he would have indeed lingered in expectation   37:144

in its belly until the Day they are raised up.

Then We cast him forth in the wilderness   37:145

while he was ill.

We caused a gourd plant to develop over him.   37:146

We sent him to *a community of* a hundred thousand,   37:147

or they even exceeded *that*.

They have believed,   37:148

and We gave them enjoyment for a while.

Then ask them for advice: *Has* **your** Lord daughters   37:149

and they *have* sons?

Or created We female angels,   37:150

while they *were* ones who bear witness?

Truly *it is* out of their calumny   37:151

that they say:

God has procreated!   37:152

Truly they *are* ones who lie.

Has He favored daughters over sons?   37:153

What is the matter with you?   37:154

How you give judgment!

Shall you not then recollect?   37:155

Or *is there* for you a clear authority?   37:156

Then bring your Book,   37:157

if you would be ones who are sincere.

They have made a kinship   37:158

between him and between the genies.°

But indeed the genies knew well

that they *were* ones who would be charged.

Glory be to God from what they allege,   37:159

except the devoted servants of God.   37:160

37:161	So truly you and those whom you worship
37:162	*shall* not *be* ones who are tempters against Him,
37:163	except he who would roast in hellfire.
37:164	There *is* not any of us but he has a known station.
37:165	Truly we *are* ones standing in ranks.
37:166	Truly we *are* the ones who glorify.
37:167	Indeed they used to say:
37:168	If we had had a Reminder from the ancient ones,
37:169	we would have indeed been servants of God —ones who are devoted—
37:170	but they are ungrateful, and they shall know;°
37:171	and truly Our word has preceded for Our servants, the ones who were sent.
37:172	They truly *are* ones who shall be helped.
37:173	Truly Our armies indeed, they *are* the ones who are victors.
37:174	So turn away from them for a while,
37:175	and perceive them and they shall *soon* perceive.
37:176	Are they impatient for Our punishment?
37:177	Then when it comes down into their courtyard, how evil *shall be* the morning daybreak of the ones who have been warned!
37:178	So turn away from them for a while,
37:179	and perceive and they shall perceive.
37:180	Glory be to **your** Lord, the Lord of Renown, from what they allege about Him.
37:181	Peace be to the ones who were sent.
37:182	The Praise *belongs* to God, the Lord of the worlds!

CHAPTER 38
SAD (*Ṣād*)

In the Name of God,

Sec. 1	The Merciful, The Compassionate
38:1	*Ṣād;*° by the Quran, possessor of the Reminder.
38:2	Rather those who were ungrateful

are in conceit and breach.

How many before them have We caused to perish 38:3
of generations!
They cried out;
there was no time for escape.

They marveled that had drawn near them 38:4
one who warns from among themselves;°
and the ones who were ungrateful said:
This *is* one who is a sorcerer, a liar.

Has he made all gods One God?° 38:5
Truly this *is* an astounding thing!

The Council set out from them, *saying*: 38:6
Begone and have patience with your gods;°
truly this *is* a thing to want.

We have not heard the like of this 38:7
in the later creed;
this *is* nothing but made up tales!

What? Has the Reminder *only* been sent forth to him 38:8
from among us?°
Rather they *are* in uncertainty
about My Reminder;°
Rather they have not experienced
My punishment!

Or *are* they owners of the treasures 38:9
of mercy of **your** Lord
The Almighty, The Giver?

Or *is* theirs the dominion 38:10
of the heavens and the earth
and what is between them?°
Let them climb up with cords!

Some army *was* there from among 38:11
the confederates that were put to flight.

The folk of Noah before them denied, 38:12
and Ad
and Pharaoh, possessor of the stakes,

and Thamud and a folk of Lot, 38:13
and the Companions of the Woods.°
Those *were* the confederates;

all of them denied the Messengers 38:14

so My repayment was to be realized.

*

38:15   These expect not
except one Cry,
there was for it no delay.

38:16   They said: Our Lord!
Quicken the judge's sentence on us
before the Day of Reckoning.

38:17   Be patient with what they say,
and remember Our servant David
the possessor of potency;°
truly he was penitent.

38:18   Truly We
caused the mountains to become subservient
to glorify
at evening and at the rising of the sun.

38:19   The birds *are* ones who are assembled;
all *are* penitent to Him.

38:20   We empowered his dominion
and gave him wisdom
and decisiveness in argument.

38:21   Has the tiding of the disputants
approached **you**
when they climbed over the wall of a sanctuary?

38:22   When they entered in on David,
he was terrified of them.°
They said: Fear not;°
two disputants have been insolent,
one of us to the other.
So give judgment duly between us
and transgress not;
guide us to the right path.

38:23   Truly this *is* my brother,
he has ninety-nine ewe,
while I *have* one ewe.
He said: Place it in my charge,
and he triumphed over me in argument.

38:24   *David* said: Indeed he has done wrong to **you**
in asking for **your** ewe

in addition to his ewe;°
and truly many partners in business
are insolent, one to another,
except those who have believed,
ones who have acted in accord with morality,
and they are few!°
David thought that We had tried him
and he asked for forgiveness of his Lord
and fell down *as* one who bows down penitent.‡
So We forgave him that;°   38:25
and truly for him *is* a nearness to Us
and a goodness of destination.
O David!   38:26
Truly We have made **you** a viceregent on the earth;
so give judgment duly among humanity,
and follow not desire,
for it shall cause **you** to go astray
from the way of God.°
Truly those who go astray from the way of God,
for them, a severe punishment,
because they forgot the Day of Reckoning.
*
                                                          Sec. 3
We created not the heaven and the earth   38:27
and all that is between the two
in falsehood.°
That *is* the opinion of those who are ungrateful.°
Then woe to those who disbelieve in the fire.
Or shall We make those who have believed,   38:28
ones who have acted in accord with morality,
be as those, the ones who make corruption
in and on the earth,
or shall We make the ones who are Godfearing
as the ones who act immorally?
It *is* a blessed Book that We have sent forth to **you**   38:29
so that they may meditate on its Signs,
and those who have intuition may recollect.
We have bestowed Solomon on David;   38:30
how excellent a servant!
Truly he *was* penitent.

38:31   When presented before him in the evening were
steeds standing with one foot slightly raised,

38:32   he said:
Truly I cherished and loved the good,
instead of remembering my Lord
when *the sun* secluded itself
behind the partition *of the night.*

38:33   Return them to me;°
then he took to wiping over their legs
and their necks.

38:34   Indeed We tried Solomon;
We cast a *lifeless* body on his seat;
then he was penitent.

38:35   He said: My Lord! Forgive me,
and bestow on me a dominion, such that
shall not *be* fit and proper to another after me;°
truly **You** *are* The Giver.

38:36   So We caused the wind to become subservient to him;
a gentle wind, it ran at his command
wherever it lighted.

38:37   *We made subservient* the satans
and every builder and diver,

38:38   and others, ones who were to be chained
in bonds.

38:39   This is Our gift,
so show **you** grace or hold back
without any reckoning.

38:40   Truly for him *is* a nearness with Us,
and a goodness of destination.

Sec. 4   *

38:41   Remember Our servant Job,
when he cried out to his Lord:
Truly Satan has afflicted me
with fatigue and punishment!

38:42   Stamp **your** foot;°
this is a cool place of washing,
and drink.

38:43   We bestowed on him his people,
and the like of them along with them,

as a mercy from Us
to be mindful for those who have intuition.
Take in **your** hand a bundle of rushes   38:44
and strike with it,
and fail not **your** oath,°
truly We found him one who remains steadfast.°
How excellent a servant!°
Truly he *was* penitent.
Remember Our servants Abraham,   38:45
Isaac and Jacob,
all owners of strength and insight.
Truly We made them sincere   38:46
with a special quality,
mindful of the Abode.
Truly they are to Us   38:47
among those who are favored and good.
Remember Ishmael, Elisha, and Dhu-l Kifl;°   38:48
all are among the good.
This *is* a Reminder.°   38:49
Truly for ones who are Godfearing
the Gardens of Eden *are*
a goodly destination   38:50
whereof the doors *are* ones opened for them,
ones who shall recline in them;   38:51
they shall call for
many sweet fruits and drink in it.°
With them shall be ones who are restraining (f)   38:52
in their glances, persons of the same age.
This *is* what you are promised   38:53
for the Day of Reckoning.
Truly this *is* Our provision;   38:54
for it, *there is* no coming to an end.
This is so.°   38:55
Truly for ones who are defiant,
there shall be a worse destination,
hell, where they shall roast;   38:56
a miserable cradling!
Let them experience this then: 38:57
Scalding water and filth

38:58   and other *torment* of a similar kind in pairs.

38:59   This *is an army* unit rushing with you;°
there is no welcome for them;
truly they shall roast in the fire.

38:60   They said: Rather you, *there is* no welcome for you;°
it is you who put this forward on us;°
so miserable *is* the stopping place!

38:61   They said: Our Lord!
Whoever put this forward for us,
increase him with a double punishment in the fire.

38:62   They said: What *is* the matter with us
that we see not men
whom we used to number
among the worst?

38:63   Have we taken them to ourselves as a laughing-stock
or has our sight swerved from them?

38:64   Truly this *is* true
of the disagreement of the people of the fire.

Sec. 5   *

38:65   Say: I *am* not but one who warns;°
and there *is* no god but God,
The One, The Omniscient,

38:66   the Lord of the heavens and the earth
and all that *is* between them,
The Almighty, The Forgiver.

38:67   Say: It *is* a serious tiding

38:68   when you *are* one who turns aside.

38:69   I had no knowledge of the lofty Council
when they were striving against one another;

38:70   it is revealed to me,
nothing but that I *am* a clear warner.

38:71   **Your** Lord said to the angels:
Truly I *am* One Who Creates a mortal from clay.

38:72   So when I have shaped him,
and breathed into him My Spirit,
then fall to him in prostration.

38:73   So the angels prostrated,
one and all of them together,

38:74   except Iblis;

he grew arrogant
and was among the ones who were ungrateful.
He said: O Iblis!   38:75
What prevented **you** from prostrating
to what I created with My two hands?
Have **you** grown arrogant,
or are **you** among the ones who exalt themselves?
Iblis said: I *am* better than he;°   38:76
You have created me from fire
while **You** have created him from clay.
He said: Then go forth from here   38:77
for, truly **you** are accursed.
Truly on **you** My curse   38:78
until the Day of Judgment.
Iblis said: My Lord!   38:79
Then give me respite
until the day to be raised up.
He said: Truly **you** are   38:80
of the ones who are respited
until the Day of the known time.   38:81
Iblis said: By **Your** renown,   38:82
then I shall indeed lead them one and all into error,
except **Your** devoted servants among them.   38:83
He said: Then The Truth *is* and The Truth I say *is*   38:84
that I shall fill hell with **you**   38:85
and those who heed **you**, one and all.
Say: I ask not of you any compensation for this   38:86
nor *am* I one
of the ones who takes things upon himself.
It *is* nothing other than a Reminder for the worlds,   38:87
and you shall indeed know its tidings   38:88
after a while.

CHAPTER 39
THE TROOPS (*al-Zumar*)

In the Name of God,
The Merciful, The Compassionate   Sec. 1
The sending down successively of this Book   39:1

is from God, The Almighty, The Wise.

39:2　Truly We have sent forth to **you** the Book
in Truth, so worship God
sincerely and devotedly
in the way of life for Him.

39:3　Indeed the way of life *belongs* exclusively for God.°
Those who take to themselves
protectors other than Him *say*:
We worship them not
except that they may bring us near to God.
Truly God gives judgment between them
about what they *were* at variance,°
truly God guides not
one who lies and *is* an ingrate.

39:4　Had God wanted to take to Himself a son,
He would have favored
from what He had created
what He will.°
Glory be to Him!°
He *is* God, The One, The Omniscient.

39:5　He has created
the heavens and the earth with The Truth;°
He wraps up the nighttime around the daytime
and wraps up the daytime around the nighttime;°
and He has caused to become subservient
the sun and the moon,°
each running for a determined term.°
Is He not The Almighty, The Forgiving?

39:6　He created you from one soul,
then made its mate from it;
and He has sent forth for you
eight pairs of flocks.°
He creates you in the wombs of your mothers,
creation after creation,
in threefold shadows.°
Such *is* God your Lord,
His *is* the dominion;°
there is no god but He;°
why then turn you away?

If you are ungrateful,   39:7
truly God *is* Independent of you;°
and He is not well-pleased
with ingratitude from His servants;°
and if you are thankful,
He shall be well-pleased with you,°
no soul laden shall bear the heavy load of another,°
then to your Lord *is* the return,
so He shall tell you what you were doing.°
Truly He *is* Knowing
of what *is* in the breasts.
When some distress afflicts the human being,   39:8
he calls to his Lord
as one who is repentant to Him.
Then when He grants him divine blessing
from Himself,
he forgets that for which he called to Him
before,
and he lays on rivals to God
to cause *others* to go astray from His way.°
Say: Take joy in **your** ingratitude for a while;°
truly **you** *are* of the Companions of the Fire.
Is he one who is morally obligated   39:9
during the night watch
as one who prostrates himself
or as one who is standing up,
being fearful of the world to come,
and hoping for the mercy of his Lord?°
Say: Are those who know
and those who know not on the same level?°
Those who have intuition not but recollect.

*   Sec. 2

Say: O My servants who have believed!   39:10
Be Godfearing of your Lord.°
For those who do good in the present,
there is benevolence,°
and the earth of God *is* extensive;°
ones who remain steadfast
shall have the compensation paid in full

without reckoning.

39:11 Say: Truly I am commanded to worship God
sincerely and devotedly
in the way of life for Him.

39:12 I am commanded to be
the first of ones who submit.

39:13 Say: Truly I fear if I rebel against my Lord,
the punishment of a tremendous Day.

39:14 Say: God I worship
sincerely and devotedly
in the way of life for Him.

39:15 So worship what you will besides Him,°
say: Truly the ones who are losers *are* those
who have lost themselves and their people
on the Day of Resurrection,°
truly that *is* a clear loss.

39:16 They *shall have* overshadowings above
from the fire,
and beneath them, overshadowings.°
With that, God frightens His servants.°
O my servants! Be Godfearing of Me!

39:17 Those who avoid false deities
so that they should not worship them
and are penitent to God,
for them are good tidings.°
So give good tidings to My servants,

39:18 those who listen to the saying
and follow the fairest of it.°
Those are those whom God has guided;°
and they, those who have intuition.

39:19 *Is* he upon whom the word of punishment
is to be realized?
Shall **you** save him from the fire?

39:20 But those who are Godfearing of their Lord,
for them are the highest chambers
with the highest chambers built above them,
beneath which rivers run;°
this is the solemn declaration of God;°
God never replaces His promise.

Have **you** not considered
that God has sent forth water from heaven,
and threads fountains in the earth,
then brings out crops by it
of varying hues;
then they wither,
so that **you** see them
as ones who are growing yellow,
then He makes them chaff.°
Truly in this *is* mindfulness
for those who have intuition.

*

Is he whose breast God has expanded
for submission
so that he *is* in a light from His Lord?°
So woe to those whose hearts are hardened
against the Reminder of God.°
They *are* clearly going astray.
God has sent down the fairest discourse,
a Book,
one that is consistent
in its often repeated parts of the Quran
by which shiver
the skins of those who dread their Lord,
their skins and their hearts become gentle
with the Reminder of God.°
That *is* the guidance of God;
with it He guides whom He will.°
Whomever God causes to go astray,
there is not for him anyone who guides.
What? Is he then one who fends off
the terrible punishment with his face
on the Day of Resurrection?°
It shall be said to the ones who are unjust:
Experience what you were earning.
Those before them denied,
and so the punishment approached them
from where they *were* not aware.
So God caused them to experience degradation

in this present life;°
but the punishment of the world to come is greater°
if they but knew.

Indeed We have propounded for humanity
in this Quran
every kind of parable
so that perhaps they would recollect;

39:28 an Arabic Quran without any crookedness,
so that perhaps they would be Godfearing.

39:29 God propounds a parable
of a man *owned*
by quarreling associates
and a man *owned* entirely by one man.
Are those two equal in comparison?°
The Praise *belongs* to God.°
But most of them know not.

39:30 Truly **you** are mortal
and truly they are mortal;

39:31 then truly on the Day of Resurrection before your
Lord
you shall be striving against one another.

***

Part 24

*

Sec. 4

39:32 Then who *is* one who does greater wrong
than one who lies against God,
and denies sincerity when it draws near to him?°
Is *there* not in hell a place of lodging
for the ones who are ungrateful?

39:33 He who brings about sincerity,
and he who establishes it as true,°
those are they who *are*
the ones who are Godfearing.

39:34 They *shall have* all that they will near their Lord.°
That *is* the recompense
of those who are doers of good,

39:35 so that God may absolve them
of the bad deeds of what they did
and give them recompense in compensation

535

for the fairest of what they were doing.
Has God not sufficed for His servants?°
They frighten **you** with those besides Him.°
Whom God causes to go astray,
there is not for him any one who guides.
Whomever God guides,
there is not for him anyone who leads astray,°
Is not God Almighty, The Possessor of Requital?
Truly if you ask them:
Who created the heavens and the earth?
Indeed they shall say: God.°
Say: Have you yourself considered
the things that you call to besides God?
If God wanted some distress for me, would
they *be* ones who remove His distress *from me*?
Or if He wanted mercy for me
would they *be* ones who hold back His mercy?°
Say: God *is* enough for me;°
in Him the ones who put their trust
put their trust.
Say: O my folk!
Truly act according to your ability
I too am one who acts; soon you shall know
who *it is* whom punishment approaches
that shall cover him with shame,
and on whom alights an abiding punishment.
Truly We have sent forth to **you** the Book
for humanity in Truth;°
so whoever is truly guided, it is not but for himself;°
and whoever goes astray,
goes not astray but for himself;°
you *are* not over them a trustee.
God calls the souls to Himself
at the time of their death
and those that have not died
during their slumbering;°
He holds back those for whom
He has decreed death,

and sends the others *back* for a determined term.
Truly in that *are* Signs for a folk who reflect.

39:43 Or have they taken to themselves besides God
intercessors?°
Say:
What? Even though they possessed nothing,
and are not reasonable?

39:44 Say: To God *belongs* all intercession;°
His *is* the dominion
of the heavens and the earth;°
then to Him you shall be returned.

39:45 When God alone is remembered,
the hearts shudder of those
who believe not in the world to come;°
when those besides Him are mentioned,
lo! They rejoice at the good tidings!

39:46 Say: O God!
The One Who is The Originator
of the heavens and the earth!
The One Who Has Knowledge
of the unseen and the visible!
You shall give judgment among **Your** servants
about what they *were* at variance.

39:47 If those who did wrong
had all that *is* in and on the earth,
and the like of it,
they would truly offer it as ransom
for the evil punishment
on the Day of Resurrection,°
that shall be shown to them from God
what they had not been anticipating;

39:48 that shall be shown to them
the evil deeds that they earned;
and they shall be surrounded
by what they used to ridicule.

39:49 When distress would afflict the human being,
he would call to Us;
when We have granted him divine blessing from Us
he would say:

I was not but given this because of knowledge;
rather it is only a test,
but most of them know not.
Truly those before them said that,   39:50
so what they used to earn availed them not.
The evil deeds they earned have lighted on them.°   39:51
As for those who did wrong among these,
evil deeds of what they earned shall light on them;
they shall not *be* ones who frustrate *the Will of God.*
Know they not   39:52
that God extends the provision
to whom He will,
and confines it *to whom He will.°*
Truly in this *are* Signs
for a folk who believe.
                          *   Sec. 6

Say: O My servants,   39:53
those who have exceeded all bounds
against themselves
despair not of the mercy of God.°
Truly God forgives all impieties.°
Truly He *is* The Forgiving, The Compassionate.
Be penitent to your Lord and submit to Him   39:54
before the punishment approaches you.
Then you shall not be helped.
Follow   39:55
the fairest of what *is* sent forth to you
from your Lord
before the punishment approaches you suddenly
while you are not aware,
so that a soul not say: 39:56
I regret what I neglected
of my responsibility to God
and that I was indeed
among the ones who derided.
Or it say: Had God guided me,   39:57
I should indeed have been
of the ones who are Godfearing.
Or it say at the time of seeing the punishment: 39:58

If only I might return again,
then I would be
of the ones who are doers of good.

39:59 Yea! My Signs have drawn near to **you**,
and **you** have denied them,
and have grown arrogant,
and were of the ones who were ungrateful.

39:60 On the Day of Resurrection **you** shall see
those who lied against God,
their faces clouded over.°
Is there not in hell a place of lodging
for ones who increase in pride?

39:61 God shall deliver
those who have been Godfearing,
keeping them safe;
no evil shall afflict them
nor shall they feel remorse.

39:62 God *is* The Creator of everything;°
and He *is* Trustee over everything.

39:63 To Him *belongs* the keys
of the heavens and the earth,°
and those who were ungrateful for the Signs of God;
those *are* they, ones who are the losers.

Sec. 7 *

39:64 Say: Have you commanded me to worship
other than God?
O ones who are ignorant!

39:65 Indeed it has been revealed to **you**
and to those who *were* before **you**
that if **you** ascribe a partner unto God,
indeed **your** actions shall be fruitless
and indeed **you** shall be
of the ones who are losers.

39:66 Rather **you** should worship God,
and be among the ones who are thankful!

39:67 They measure not God
with His true measure,
and the earth altogether *shall be* His handful;
on the Day of Resurrection

539

the heavens *shall be* rolled up in His right hand.°
Glory *be* to Him!
Exalted is He
above all the partners they make with Him!
The trumpet shall be blown;   **39:68**
then whoever is in the heavens shall swoon
and whoever *is* in and on the earth,
except him whom God willed;°
then it shall be blown another time,
and they *shall be* upright looking on.
The earth shall shine   **39:69**
with the Light of its Lord;
the Book shall be laid down;
the prophets and the witnesses
shall be brought;
it shall be duly decided among them;
and they shall not be done wrong.
Each soul *shall have* its account paid in full   **39:70**
for what it has done;
and He has greater knowledge
of what they accomplish.

*

         Sec. 8

Those who are ungrateful shall be driven to hell   **39:71**
in troops;°
until when they have drawn near it,
and the doors of it are flung open,
the ones who are its keepers shall say to them:
Approached you not Messengers
from yourselves
recounting to you
the Signs of your Lord,
and warning you
of the meeting of this Day?°
They would say: Yea!
Yet the word of punishment was realized
against ones who were ungrateful.
It would be said: Enter the doors of hell   **39:72**
as ones who shall dwell in it forever;°
a miserable place of lodging

for the ones who increased in pride.

39:73 Those who are Godfearing shall be driven
to their Lord in the Garden in troops;°
until when they draw near it
and its doors are let loose,
ones who are its keepers shall say:
Peace be on you!
You have fared well!
So enter it as ones who shall dwell in it forever.

39:74 They would say: The Praise *belongs* to God
Who has been sincere in His promise to us,
and has given us the earth as inheritance
that we may take our dwelling in the Garden
wherever we will!°
How excellent a compensation
for ones who work!

39:75 **You** shall see the angels,
as ones who encircle around the Throne,
glorifying with the praise of their Lord;°
it would be decided with Truth among them
and it would be said: The Praise *belongs* to God,
the Lord of the worlds.

CHAPTER 40
THE BELIEVER (*al-Mu'min*)

In the Name of God

Sec. 1 The Merciful, The Compassionate
40:1 *Ḥā Mīm;*
40:2 the sending down successively of this Book
is from God, The Almighty, The Knower,
40:3 The One Who Forgives impieties,
and One Who Accepts remorse,
The Severe in Repayment, The Possessor of Bounty;°
there is no god but He;°
to Him *is* the Homecoming.
40:4 No one disputes the Signs of God
except those who are ungrateful,
so be not disappointed

541

by one who goes to and fro through the land.
The folk of Noah denied before them   40:5
and the confederates after them;°
and every community was wont to
take its Messenger;°
they disputed with falsehood
to refute The Truth
so I took them,
and how was My repayment!
Thus was the word of **your** Lord realized   40:6
against those who were ungrateful
that they *shall be* the Companions of the Fire.
Those who carry the Throne   40:7
and all those around it
who glorify the praises of their Lord
and believe in Him and ask forgiveness
for those who have believed *saying*:
Our Lord!
You have encompassed everything
in mercy and knowledge;
so forgive those who have repented
and have followed **Your** way;
guard them from the punishment of hellfire.
Our Lord!   40:8
Cause them to enter the Gardens of Eden
which **You** have promised them
and those who were in accord with morality
among their fathers
and their wives and their offspring.°
Truly **You, You** *are* The Almighty, The Wise.
Guard them from the evil deeds.°   40:9
He whom **You** have guarded
from the evil deeds on that Day;
truly **You** *have had* mercy on him.°
That is the winning the sublime triumph!

*

Truly it shall be proclaimed   40:10
to those who are ungrateful:
Truly the repugnance of God *is* greater

than your repugnance towards one another
when you are called to believe,
but you are ungrateful.

40:11 They said: Our Lord!
You have caused us to die two times,
and **You** have given us life two times;
we acknowledge our impieties,
then is there any way of going forth?

40:12 That *is* because
when God alone was called to,
you were ungrateful;°
but when you ascribe partners to Him,
you believe.°
The determination *is* with God,
The Lofty, The Great.

40:13 It *is* He Who causes you to see His Signs,
and sends down provision for you from heaven.°
None recollect but those who are penitent.

40:14 So call you on God
sincerely and devotedly
in the way of life for Him
though the ones who are ungrateful may dislike it.

40:15 Exalter of Degrees, Possessor of the Throne;
He casts the Spirit by His command
on whom He will of His servants,
that He may warn of the Day of Encounter,

40:16 a Day when they *are* ones who depart;°
nothing about them shall be hidden from God.°
Whose *is* the dominion this Day?°
It is to God, The One, The Omniscient.

40:17 On this Day every soul shall be given recompense
for what it earned.°
Truly *there shall be* no injustice today.°
God *is* Swift in reckoning.

40:18 Warn them of the Threatened Day
when the hearts *shall be* in the throats°
choking;
there shall not *be* a loyal friend
for ones who are unjust,

nor an intercessor be obeyed.
He knows the treachery of the eyes   40:19
and whatever the breasts conceal.
God decrees with justice.°   40:20
Those whom they call to other than Him
decide not anything,°
truly God, He *is* The Hearing, The Seeing.

*   Sec. 3

What? Have they not journeyed on the earth   40:21
to look on
what was the Ultimate End
of those who were before them?°
They, they were superior to them in strength,
and in traces *they left* on the earth,
but God took them for their impieties,
and *there* was not for them
one who is a defender from God.
That *was* because   40:22
their Messengers had approached them
with clear portents,
but they were ungrateful
so God took them;
truly He *is* Strong, Severe in Repayment.
Indeed We sent Moses with Our Signs,   40:23
and a clear authority
to Pharaoh, Haman and Korah;   40:24
but they said: *He is* one who is a sorcerer, a liar.
Then when he drew near with The Truth from Us,   40:25
they said:
Kill the sons of those who believe with him
saving alive their women.°
The cunning of the ones who are ungrateful
is but going astray.
Pharaoh said: 40:26
Let me kill Moses and let him call to his Lord;°
truly I fear that he may substitute
your way of life
or that he may cause corruption to appear
in and on the earth.

40:27
Moses said:
Truly I take refuge in my Lord
and your Lord
from every one who increases in pride
and who believes not in the Day of Reckoning.

*

40:28
Said a believing man of the family of Pharaoh,
one who kept back his belief:
Would you kill a man because he says:
My Lord *is* God,
yet he has drawn near to you with clear portents
from your Lord?°
If he is a liar,
then on him shall be his lying;°
and if he is one who is sincere,
then shall alight on you
some of what he promises;°
truly God guides not
one who is excessive, one who lies.

40:29
O my folk!
Yours *is* the dominion this day,
ones who are prominent on the earth;
but who shall help us from the might of God
if it draws near to us?°
Pharaoh said: I cause you to see
not but what I see,
and I guide you
not but to the way of rectitude.

40:30
He who has believed said: O my folk!
Truly I fear for you
like the day of the confederates,

40:31
similar to the custom of a folk of Noah,
and Ad and Thamud,
and those after them.°
God wants not injustice for His servants.

40:32
O my folk! Truly I fear for you a Day
when there shall be calls to one another;

40:33
a Day when you shall turn as ones who draw back,
having no one who saves from harm

from God
and for whomever God causes to go astray;
there is not anyone who guides.
Indeed Joseph drew near to you   40:34
before with clear portents,
but you continued in uncertainty
about what he had brought you;°
until, when he perished,
you said: God shall never raise up
a Messenger after him.°
Thus God causes one who is an excessive doubter
to go astray.
Those who dispute the Signs of God   40:35
without *any* authority approaching them,°
are troublesome, repugnant to God
and to those who have believed.°
Thus God sets a seal on every heart
of one who increases in pride, haughtiness.
Pharaoh said: O Haman!   40:36
Build for me a pavilion
so that perhaps I would reach the routes,
the routes to the heavens,   40:37
and that I may peruse The God of Moses
but truly I think that he is one who lies.°
Thus it was made to appear pleasing to Pharaoh,
the evil of his actions;
and he was barred from the way.°
The cunning of Pharaoh *was* not but in defeat.

*   Sec. 5

He who had believed said: O my folk!   40:38
Follow me, I shall guide you
to the way of rectitude.
O my folk!   40:39
Truly this present life *is* nothing
but *transitory* enjoyment;
truly the world to come *is*
the stopping place, the Abode.
Whoever does an evil deed   40:40
shall not be given recompense except the like of it;°

but one who has acted in accord with morality,
whether male or female,
and is one who believes,
such shall enter the Garden
where they shall be provided in it without reckoning.

40:41 O my folk!
What *is it* to me that I call you to deliverance,
and you call me to the fire?

40:42 You call me to be ungrateful to God,
and to make partners with Him
of what I *have* no knowledge,
while I call you to
The Almighty, The Forgiver.

40:43 Without doubt, what you call me to
has no call in the present
nor in the world to come;
and our turning back shall be to God,
and truly the ones who are excessive,
they *shall be* the Companions of the Fire.

40:44 You shall remember what I say to you.°
I commit my affairs to God.°
Truly God *is* The Seeing of the servants.

40:45 So God guarded him from the evil deeds
that they planned;°
while the people of Pharaoh were surrounded
by an evil punishment:

40:46 The fire to which they were presented
the first part of the day and evening;°
and on a Day when the Hour is secure
it is said: Cause the people of Pharaoh to enter
the severest punishment.

40:47 When they dispute with one another in the fire,
the weak shall say to those who had grown arrogant:
Truly we were followers of you so shall you be
ones who avail us from a share of the fire?

40:48 Those who grow arrogant would say:
Truly we are all in it;
truly God indeed has given judgment
among *His* servants.

Those in the fire would say   40:49
to ones who are keepers of hell:
Call to your Lord
to lighten the punishment for us for a day.
They would say: 40:50
Brought not your Messengers
clear portents?°
They would say: Yea!°
They would say: Then call you yourselves,°
and the supplication of the ones who are ungrateful
not but goes astray.
*   Sec. 6

Truly We shall indeed help Our Messengers,   40:51
and those who have believed
in this present life,
and on a Day when
the ones who bear witness shall stand up,
a Day when   40:52
their excuses shall not profit the ones who are unjust;
and for them shall be the curse,
and for them *shall be* an evil abode.
Indeed We gave Moses the guidance as inheritance 40:53
for the Children of Israel
the Book,
for the mindful   40:54
and for those who have intuition.
So have patience;   40:55
truly the promise of God *is* true;
ask for forgiveness for **your** impiety
and glorify the praises of **your** Lord
in the evening and in the early morning.
Truly those who dispute about the Signs of God 40:56
without any authority having approached them,   •
there *is* nothing but having pride in their breasts;
they shall never be ones who reach *its satisfaction.*°
So seek refuge in God;°
Truly He *is* The Hearing, The Seeing.
Truly the creation   40:57
of the heavens and the earth

is greater than the creation of humanity,
yet most of humanity knows not.

40:58 Not on the same level are the *unwilling* to see
and the seeing,
nor those who have believed,
and the ones who have acted in accord with morality,
and the evil doers.°
Little do they recollect.

40:59 Truly the Hour *is* surely one that arrives,
there is no doubt about it,
yet most of humanity believes not.

40:60 Your Lord said:
Call to Me; I shall respond to you.°
Truly those who grow arrogant toward My worship,
they shall indeed enter hell
as ones who are in a state of lowliness.

Sec. 7 *

40:61 God! *It is* He Who has made for you the nighttime
so that you may rest in it,
and the daytime for you—one who perceives.°
Truly God *is* full of grace to humanity,
yet most of humanity *is* not thankful.

40:62 That *is* God, your Lord,
the Creator of all things;
there is no god but He!°
How then are you misled?

40:63 Thus are misled
those who negated the Signs of God.

40:64 God! *It is* He Who has made the earth for you
as a stopping place
and the heaven as a canopy;
and He has formed you and formed you well,
and He has provided you of what is good.°
That *is* God your Lord!°
Then blessed be God, the Lord of the worlds!

40:65 He *is* The Living!
There is no god but He!
So call to Him
sincerely and devotedly

549

in the way of life for Him,°
The Praise *belongs* to God,
the Lord of the worlds!
Say: Truly I have been prohibited from worshipping
those whom you call to other than God,
since clear portents have drawn near me
from my Lord.
I am commanded to submit
to the Lord of the worlds.
He *it is* Who created you from earthy dust,
then from seminal fluid,
then from a clot,
then He brings you out as infant children,
then you come of age and are fully grown,
then afterwards you are an old man°
and of you *is* he whom death calls to itself before;°
and that you reach a determined term
so that perhaps you would be reasonable.
He *it is* Who gives life and causes to die;°
and when He decrees an affair,
He not but says to it: Be! And it is!

                    *

Have **you** not considered
those who dispute about the Signs of God,
how they are being turned away?
Those who denied the Book
and that with which We sent Our Messengers;°
then they shall know.
When yokes *are* on their necks
and the chains,
they shall be dragged
into scalding water.
Then they shall be poured into the fire as fuel.
Then it would be said to them:
Where *are* what you used to make as partners
to God?°
They would say: They have gone astray from us;
rather we were not called to anything before.°
Thus God causes to go astray

40:66

40:67

40:68

Sec. 8
40:69

40:70

40:71

40:72

40:73

40:74

ones who are ungrateful.

40:75 That *was* because you were exultant
on the earth without right,
and that you used to be glad.

40:76 Enter the doors of hell
as ones who shall dwell in it forever;°
How miserable a place of lodging
for the ones who increase in pride!

40:77 So have **you** patience;
truly the Promise of God *is* true.°
Whether We cause **you** to see
some part of what We have promised them
or We call **you** to Ourself,
then it is to Us they all shall be returned.

40:78 Indeed We sent Messengers before **you**;
among whom We have related to **you**;
and some We have not related to **you**,°
and it was not for any Messenger
that he should bring a Sign,
except with the permission of God.°
So when the command of God would draw near,
the matter would be decided rightfully,
and *it is* then
that the ones who deal in falsehood shall lose.

Sec. 9 *

40:79 God *is* He Who has made for you flocks
that you may ride on some of them,
eat some of them;

40:80 and you *have* what is profitable from them,
that with them you may reach
the satisfaction of a need that is in your breasts,
and may be carried on them as on the boat.

40:81 He causes you to see His Signs;
so which of the Signs of God have you rejected?

40:82 Have they not journeyed through the earth
and looked on
how was the Ultimate End
of those from before them?°
They were more than them,

and *were* more vigorous in strength
and in regard to the traces *they left* on the earth.
Yet all that they earned availed them not.
Then when their Messengers drew near to them 40:83
with clear portents,
they were glad in the knowledge that they had;
and they were surrounded
by what they used to ridicule.
So when they considered Our punishment, 40:84
they said: We have believed in God alone,
and we were ungrateful in that
we used to *be* ones who were polytheists.
But their belief profited them not 40:85
when they considered Our punishment;°
this *is* the custom of God
which has been in force before among His servants,
and there, the ones who are ungrateful shall be lost.

CHAPTER 41
THEY WERE EXPLAINED DISTINCTLY
(al-Fuṣṣilat)

In the Name of God,
The Merciful, The Compassionate Sec. 1
Ḥā Mīm; 41:1
a sending down successively 41:2
from The Merciful, the Compassionate,
a Book in which its Signs are explained distinctly, 41:3
a Quran in Arabic for a folk who know,
a bearer of glad tidings and a warner, 41:4
but most of them turn aside so they may not hear.
They said: Our hearts have been sheathed 41:5
from that to which **you** call us to,
and in our ears *is* a heaviness,
and between us and between **you** is a partition.
So act;
truly we, too, *are* ones who work.
Say: I *am* nothing but a mortal like you; 41:6
it is revealed to me that your God *is* God, One;

552

so go straight to Him
and ask for forgiveness from Him;°
woe to the ones who are polytheists,

41:7 those who give not the purifying alms
and who in the world to come
are ones who are ungrateful.

41:8 Truly those who have believed,
ones who have acted in accord with morality,
for them shall be an unfailing compensation.

*

41:9 Say: What? Were you ungrateful to Him
Who created the earth in two days
and assigned you to Him rivals?
That *is* the Lord of the worlds!

41:10 He made on it mountains from above it;
He blessed it
and ordained its sustenance within it
in four days,
equally for ones who seek.

41:11 Then He turned His attention to the heaven
while it was smoke;
He said to it and to the earth:
Approach both of you
ones who are willing or unwilling;
they both said: We approach
as ones who are obedient.

41:12 Then He foreordained seven heavens in two days
and He revealed in each heaven its command.°
We made the present heaven appear pleasing,
with lamps and keeping them safe;
such *is* the decree
of the Almighty, The Knowing.

41:13 But if they turn aside,
then say: I have warned you of a thunderbolt
like the thunderbolt of Ad and Thamud.

41:14 When the Messengers drew near
before them and from behind them *saying*:
Worship none but God!
They said: Had our Lord willed,

He would indeed have sent forth angels.
So indeed in what you have been sent,
we *are* ones who disbelieve.
As for Ad, 41:15
they grew arrogant on the earth without right,
and they said:
Who is more vigorous than us in strength?°
Have they not considered that God Who created them,
was more vigorous than they in strength?°
They would negate Our Signs.
So We sent on them a raging wind 41:16
in days of misfortune
that We might cause them to experience
the punishment of degradation
in this present life;°
and truly the punishment in the world to come
shall be more degrading;°
and they shall not be helped.
As for Thamud, 41:17
We guided them, but they embraced
blindness of heart rather than guidance;
then a thunderbolt took them
with a humiliating punishment
because of what they were earning.
We delivered those who had believed 41:18
and were Godfearing.
* Sec. 3

On a Day when the enemies of God 41:19
shall be assembled to the fire,
they shall be marching in ranks
until when they draw near it, 41:20
witness shall be borne against them
by their having the ability to hear,
and by their sight and by their skins
as to what they were doing.
They shall say to their skins: 41:21
Why do you bear witness against us?
They shall say: We were given speech by God,
Who gave speech to all things.

He created you the first time,
and to Him you shall be returned.

41:22 Covered you not yourselves
so that witness not be borne against you
by your having the ability to hear,
and your sight and your skins,
but you thought that God knows not
much of what you do.

41:23 Your thought,
which you thought
about your Lord,
has dealt destruction to you,
and you have become
of the ones who are losers.°

41:24 Then if they endure patiently,
yet the fire shall be the lodging place for them.
If they ask for favor,
yet they *shall not be*
of the ones to whom favor is shown.

41:25 We have allotted for them comrades
who have been made to appear pleasing to them—
whatever was before them
and whatever was behind them.
The saying was realized against them
as against communities that have passed away
before them
of jinn and human kind;°
indeed they, they were ones who were losers.

*

Sec. 4

41:26 Those who are ungrateful said:
Hear not this Quran and talk idly about it
so that perhaps you would prevail.

41:27 But indeed We shall cause those who are ungrateful
to experience
a severe punishment,
and We shall give recompense to them
for the bad deeds of what they were doing.

41:28 That *is* the recompense of the enemies of God:
The fire;°

for them *is* the abode in it for eternity;°
as recompense
because they negated Our Signs.
Those who are ungrateful shall say: 41:29
Our Lord!
Cause us to see those who cause us to go astray
of jinn and human kind.
We shall lay them beneath our feet
so that they become of the lowest.
Truly those who say: Our Lord *is* God!   41:30
Then they go straight,
and the angels come forth to them:
Neither fear nor feel remorse,
but rejoice in the Gardens
which you have been promised.
We have been protectors in this present life   41:31
and in the world to come;°
and you *shall have* in it
that for which your souls hungered,
and you *shall have* in it what you call for,
a welcoming from   41:32
The Forgiving, The Compassionate.
*   Sec. 5

Who has a fairer saying   41:33
than he who has called to God—
one who has acted in accord with morality—
and says: I am one of the ones who submit.
Not on the same level are   41:34
benevolence and the evil deed.°
Drive back with what is fairer;
then behold, he who
between you and between him was enmity
shall be as though he were
a protector, a loyal friend.
But none shall be in receipt   41:35
except those who endure patiently,
and none shall be in receipt of it
except the possessor of a sublime allotment.
If a provocation from Satan provokes **you**,   41:36

seek refuge in God;°
truly He *is* The Hearing, The Knowing.

41:37 Of His Signs
are the nighttime and the daytime,
and the sun and the moon.°
Prostrate not to the sun nor to the moon,
but prostrate to God Who created them
if *it is* He you worship.

41:38 But if they grow arrogant,
then those who *are* with **your** Lord glorify Him
during the nighttime and daytime,
and they never grow weary.‡

41:39 Among His Signs
are that **you** see the earth as what is humbled;
but when We send forth water to it,
it quivers and swells.°
Truly He Who gives it life,
indeed He *is* the One Who Gives Life to the dead.°
Indeed He *is* Powerful over everything:

41:40 Truly those who blaspheme Our Signs
are not hidden from Us,°
is he who is cast down into the fire better off,
or he who approaches as one who is in safety
on the Day of Resurrection?°
Act as you willed;°
truly He *is* Seeing of what you do.

41:41 Truly those who were ungrateful for the Reminder
when it drew near them;°
and truly it is a mighty Book!

41:42 Falsehood approaches it not
from before it,
nor from behind it;°
it is a sending down successively
from The Wise, The Worthy of Praise.

41:43 Nothing is said to **you** except
what truly was said
to the Messengers before **you**.°
Truly **your** Lord *is*,
indeed the possessor of forgiveness,

557

and the possessor of painful repayment.
If We had made this a non-Arabic Quran,   **41:44**
they would have said:
Why *are* His Signs
not explained distinctly?°
A non-Arab *tongue*
and an Arab?°
Say: It *is* a guidance for those who believe
and a healing;°
and *as for* those who have not believed,
there is a heaviness in their ears,
and blindness in their heart.°
Those, they are given notice
from a far place.
　　　　　*   **Sec. 6**

Indeed We gave Moses the Book,   **41:45**
but *there* has been variance in it,°
and had it not been for the word
that had preceded from **your** Lord,
it would have been decided between them.°
But truly
they *are* in uncertainty,
ones whose suspicions have been aroused.°
One who has acted in accord with morality,   **41:46**
it is for himself;°
and whoever does evil, it is against *himself,*°
and **your** Lord *is* not unjust to *His* servants.
　　　　　***   **Part 25**

To Him is returned the knowledge of the Hour.°   **41:47**
No fruits go forth from their sheaths,
no female conceives or brings forth offspring
except with His knowledge.°
On a Day He shall cry out to them:
Where *are* My associates?
They would say: We proclaim to **You**
that none of us *was* a witness *to that.*
Gone astray is what they used to call to before;°   **41:48**
they shall think that *there is* for them no asylum.
The human being has not grown weary   **41:49**

of supplication for good,
but if worse afflicts him,
then he *becomes* hopeless, desperate.

41:50   Truly if We cause him to experience
mercy from Us
after some tribulation has afflicted him,
he shall surely say:
This is for me.
He thinks not
that the Hour *shall* arise,
but if I am to be returned to my Lord
truly for me with Him shall be the fair.°
Then We truly shall tell those who are ungrateful
of what they have done,
and We shall cause them to experience
a harsh punishment.

41:51   When We are gracious to the human being,
he turns aside, withdraws aside,
but when worse afflicts him,
then he is full of supplication.

41:52   Say: Have you yourselves not considered
that if it were from God,
then you are ungrateful for it,
who *is* one who goes more astray
than one who is in wide breach?

41:53   We shall cause them to see Our Signs
in the horizons and in their own selves
until it becomes clear to them that it *is* The Truth,°
Suffices it not that **your** Lord,
He is Witness over all things?

41:54   Truly they are in hesitancy
about the meeting with their Lord,°
truly He is who One Who Encloses.

Chapter 42
Consultation (*al-Shūrāʾ*)

In the Name of God,
Sec. 1   The Merciful, The Compassionate

559

Ḥā Mīm;   42:1

ᶜAyn Sīn Qāf;   42:2

thus He reveals to **you**,   42:3
and to those who are before **you**,
God *is* The Almighty, The Wise.

To Him *belongs* whatever *is* in the heavens,   42:4
and whatever *is* in the earth;°
and He *is* The Lofty, The Sublime.

The heavens were about to split asunder   42:5
from above them.°
When the angels glorify the praise of their Lord,
and ask forgiveness for those on the earth;°
truly God,
He *is* The Forgiving, The Compassionate.

As for those who take to themselves   42:6
other than Him as protectors,
God *is* Guardian over them
and **you** *are* not a Trustee over them.

Thus We have revealed to **you** an Arabic Quran   42:7
that **you** may warn
the Mother of the Towns
and whoever *is* around it,
and that you may warn of the Day of Amassing;
there is no doubt about it,°
a group of people *shall be* in the Garden,
and a group of people *shall be* in the blaze.

Had God so willed,   42:8
He could have made them one community;
but He causes to enter whom He will
into His mercy.°
The ones who are unjust,
there is for them neither protector, nor helper.

Or they take other than Him to themselves   42:9
as protectors;°
but God, He alone *is* The Protector;
He, He gives life to the dead;
He *is* Powerful over everything.

*   Sec. 2

Whatever thing about which you *are* at variance,   42:10

then its determination *belongs* with God.°
That *is* God, my Lord
in Whom I put my trust
and to Him I am penitent.

42:11 The Originator
of the heavens and the earth.°
He has made for you mates of yourselves
and of the flocks, mates;°
by which means He makes them numerous.°
There is not like Him anything;°
and He *is* The Hearing, The Seeing.

42:12 To Him *belong* the keys
of the heavens and the earth;°
He extends provision
for whomever He will
and measures it.°
Truly He *is* The Knowing of everything.

42:13 He has laid down the law of the way of life for you,
that with which He had charged Noah
and what We have revealed to **you**
and that with which We charged Abraham,
and Moses and Jesus:°
Perform the *prescribed* way of life,
and be not split up in it.°
Troublesome for the ones who are polytheists
is that to which **you** call them.°
God elects for Himself whom He will
and guides those who are penitent to Himself .

42:14 They split not up,
except after the knowledge had drawn near to them,
through insolence among themselves.°
Had it not been for a word that preceded
from **your** Lord
—a determined term—
the command would have been decided
among them.°
But truly those who were given as an inheritance
the Book after them,
are in uncertainty,

their suspicions having been aroused about it.
Then for that, call *to this;*°
and go **you** straight as **you** were commanded;°
and follow not their desires;°
and say: I have believed
in whatever Book God has sent forth;°
and I am commanded to be just among you;°
God *is* our Lord and your Lord;°
for us *are* our actions and for you, your actions;°
there is no disputation between us and between you;°
God shall gather us together,
and to Him *is* the Homecoming.
Those who argue with one another about God   42:16
after *it* has been assented to,
their disputations *are* null and void with their Lord,
and on them *is* anger;
and for them *shall be* a severe punishment.
It is God Who has sent forth the Book   42:17
with The Truth and the Balance,°
and what causes **you** to recognize it?
Perhaps the Hour *is* near.
Those who believe not in it are impatient;°   42:18
and those who believe *are* apprehensive of it,
and they know that *it is* The Truth.°
Now truly those who altercate about the Hour
are certainly gone far astray.
God *is* Subtle with His servants;   42:19
He provides to whom He will;°
and He *is* The Strong, The Almighty.
*   Sec. 3

Whoever would want to cultivate   42:20
the world to come,
We increase his cultivation for him;°
whoever would want to cultivate the present,
We give him of it,
and he has not a share in the world to come.
Or *have* they associates   42:21
who have laid down the law
of the way of life for them

for which God has not given permission?°
Had *it* not *been* for a decisive word,
it would have been decided among them,°
and truly the ones who are unjust,
for them *is* a painful punishment.

42:22 **You** shall see the ones who are unjust,
apprehensive of what they have earned,
and *it is* what falls on them,°
and those who have believed,
the ones who have acted in accord with morality,
are in the well-watered meadows of the Gardens;°
they *shall have* whatever they will
from their Lord.°
That *is* the great grace;

42:23 that *is* what God gives as good tidings
to His servants who have believed,
ones who have acted in accord with morality.°
Say: I ask you not for compensation,
except the affection for kin,°
and whoever gains benevolence,
We shall increase for him goodness in it.°
Truly God *is* Forgiving, Most Ready to Appreciate.

42:24 Or they say:
He has devised against God a lie;°
so if God will,
He would have set a seal on **your** heart,°
and God blots out falsehood,
and verifies The Truth by His words.°
Truly He *is* Knowing of what *is* in the breasts.

42:25 He *is* the One Who accepts the remorse
of His servants
and pardons their evil deeds;
and He knows what you accomplish.

42:26 He responds to those who have believed,
the ones who have acted in accord with morality,
and increases them of His grace.°
As for the ones who are ungrateful,
theirs *shall be* a severe punishment.

42:27 If God extended the provision for His servants,

they would be insolent in the earth,
but He sends down by measure
whatever He will.
Truly He *is*
The Aware, The Seeing of His servants.
He *it is* Who sends down plenteous rain water   42:28
after they have despaired,
and He unfolds His mercy.°
He *is* The Protector, The Worthy of Praise.
Among His Signs *is* the creation   42:29
of the heavens and the earth
and whatever
moving creatures He has disseminated in them.°
He *has*
the power of amassing them when He will.
*   Sec. 4
Whatever affliction lights on you   42:30
is because of what your hands have earned;
and He pardons much.
You *are* not ones who frustrate *the Will of God*   42:31
on the earth;°
and there is not for you, other than God,
any protector nor any helper.
Of His Signs *are* the ones that run in the sea   42:32
like landmarks.
If He will, He may still the wind,   42:33
then they would stay in what is motionless
on the surface.°
Truly in that *are* Signs
for every enduring and grateful one.
Or He may wreck them   42:34
because of what they have earned,
and He pardons *them* from much.
Those who dispute Our Signs know   42:35
that there *is* no asylum for them.
So whatever you have been given   42:36
were the enjoyments of this present life;°
and what *was* with God *was* better,
and what endured

for those who have believed,
who put their trust in their Lord;

42:37 those who avoid the major sins
and indecencies
and forgive when they are angry;

42:38 those who respond to their Lord,
perform their formal prayers
and their affairs are by counsel among themselves;
who spend of what We have provided them,

42:39 and those who, when insolence lights on them,
they help each other.

42:40 The recompense for an evil deed
is the like of an evil deed;°
but whoever pardons and makes things right,
his compensation *is* due from God.°
Truly He loves not the ones who are unjust.

42:41 As for those who help each other after an injustice,
so those, there *is* not any way against them.

42:42 The way *is* not but against those who
do wrong to humanity
and *are* insolent in and on the earth unrightfully;°
those, for them *is* a painful punishment.

42:43 Whoever endures patiently and forgives,
truly that is indeed of the constancy of affairs.

Sec. 5
*

42:44 Whomever God causes to go astray
has no protector apart from Him;°
you shall see the ones who are unjust
when they consider the punishment.
They shall say: *Is there* any way to avert it?

42:45 **You** shall see them presented to it
as ones who are humbled by a sense of humility,
looking on with secretive glances;°
those who have believed shall say:
Truly the ones who are losers are those
who have lost themselves and their people
on the Day of Resurrection.
Indeed truly the ones who are unjust
shall be in an abiding punishment.

That there was not for them any protector
to help them other than God,°
and he whom God causes to go astray,
there is not for him any way.

Assent to *the call of* your Lord
before a Day approaches
for which *there is* no turning back from God.°
There shall be no shelter for you on that Day,
nor *is there* for you no refusal.

But if they turn aside,
We have not put **you** forward
as a guardian over them;°
your duty *is* but to deliver the message,°
and truly when
We caused the human being to experience
mercy from Us
he was glad in it;°
but when evil deeds lights on them
because of what their hands had sent,
then truly the human being *is* ungrateful.

To God *belongs* the dominion
of the heavens and the earth.°
He creates what He will.°
He bestows females on whom He will,
and bestows males on whom He will,
or He couples them, males and females;°

and He makes barren whom He will.°
Truly He *is* Knowing, Powerful.

It was not for a mortal
that God should speak to him,
except by revelation,
or from behind a partition,
or that He send a Messenger to reveal
by His permission what He will.°
Truly He *is* Lofty, Wise.

Thus We have revealed to **you**
the Spirit of Our command.°
You were not informed what the Book *is*
nor what *is* belief,

but We have made it a light
by which We guide
whomever We will of Our servants.°
Truly **You, You** guide to a straight path—

42:53 the path of God,
to whom *belongs* whatever *is* in the heavens
and whatever *is* in and on the earth,°
truly to God all affairs come home.

CHAPTER 43
THE ORNAMENTS (*al-Zukhruf*)

In the Name of God,
Sec. 1 The Merciful, The Compassionate
43:1 *Ḥā Mīm;*
43:2 by the clear Book;
43:3 We truly have made it an Arabic Quran
so that perhaps you would be reasonable.
43:4 Truly it *is* in the essence of the Book
in Our Presence,
indeed Lofty, Wise.
43:5 Shall We turn about the Reminder from you,
turning away
because you *are* an excessive folk?
43:6 How many a prophet have We sent
among the ancient ones!
43:7 Approached them not a prophet,
but that they used to ridicule him.
43:8 Then We caused to perish
those who were more vigorous in courage than they
and the example of the ancient ones had passed.
43:9 Indeed if you ask them:
Who has created the heavens and the earth?
They shall indeed say:
The Almighty, The Knowing created them,
43:10 He Who made the earth a cradle for you
and has made in it ways for you,
so that perhaps you would be truly guided.
43:11 He Who sends down water from heaven

567

in measure;
then We revive with it a lifeless land.°
Thus you are brought out.
He Who created all the pairs,   43:12
and has assigned for you boats,
and flocks on which you ride,
so that you may sit upon their backs;   43:13
then you may remember the divine blessing
of your Lord
when you were seated on them
and you say:
Glory be to Him
Who causes this to become subservient to us;
we ourselves were not ones who are equal to it!
Truly we indeed are   43:14
ones who are turning to Our Lord.
Yet they have assigned to Him a part   43:15
of His servants.°
Truly the human being *is* indeed
clearly ungrateful.
*   Sec. 2
Or has He taken to Himself   43:16
from what He has created, daughters,
and has He selected for you sons?
If glad tidings are given to one of them   43:17
of what he cited as an example from The Merciful,
his face becomes one that is clouded over
and he chokes.
Is one who is brought up with glitter,   43:18
and in altercation unclear?
They have made the angels,   43:19
who themselves are servants to The Merciful,
females.°
Bore they witness to their creation?°
Their testimony shall be written down
and they shall be asked *about it.*
They say: If it had been the will of   43:20
The Merciful,
We would not have worshiped them.°

They *have* no knowledge of that;°
they do nothing but guess.

43:21 Or have We given them any Book before this
so they *are* ones who hold fast to it?

43:22 Rather they said: We found our fathers
in a community,
and we are indeed in their footsteps,
ones who are truly guided.

43:23 Thus We sent not
a warner to any town before **you**
without those given ease saying:
We found our fathers in a community,
we *are* indeed ones who imitate their footsteps.

43:24 He said: What? Even if I bring about
a better guidance for you
than what you found your fathers on?°
They would say:
Truly in that with which you have been sent
We *are* ones who disbelieve.

43:25 So We requited them;°
then look on how was the Ultimate End
of the ones who deny.

Sec. 3   *

43:26 When Abraham said to his father and his folk:
Truly I *am* released from obligation
to what you worship,

43:27 except Him Who originated me;
truly He shall guide me.

43:28 He made it an enduring word
among ones who came after,
so that perhaps they would return.

43:29 Rather I gave enjoyment to these
and to their fathers,
until The Truth drew near to them
and a clear Messenger.

43:30 When The Truth drew near to them, they said:
This *is* sorcery and we *are*
ones who disbelieve in it.

43:31 They said: Why was this Quran not sent down

to some eminent man of the two towns? What?
Is it they who would divide the mercy of **your** Lord°
while *it is* We have divided out among them
their livelihood in this present life.°
Exalted are some of them above others in degree,
so that some may take to themselves
others in their bondage;°
and the mercy of **your** Lord is better
than what they gather.
Were it not that all of humanity would become   43:33
one community,
We would have made
for those who disbelieve in The Merciful,
roofs of silver for their houses,
and stairways up which they scale,
and for their houses, doors, and couches   43:34
on which they would recline,
and ornaments.°   43:35
Yet all this would have been nothing but
the enjoyment of this present life.°
The world to come with your Lord
is for the ones who are Godfearing.

*

Sec. 4

Whoever renders himself weak-sighted   43:36
to the Remembrance of The Merciful,
We allot for him a satan,
so he is a comrade for him.
Truly they bar them from the way,   43:37
but they assume that they are
ones who are truly guided;
until when he draws near to us, he says: 43:38
Would that *there* were
a distance between me and between **you**
of two sunrises!
Then miserable is the comrade.
It shall never profit you this Day;   43:39
as you did wrong,
you shall be ones who are partners in the punishment.
So shall **you** cause someone *unwilling* to hear, to hear,   43:40

or shall **you** guide the *unwilling* to see
or someone who has clearly gone astray?

43:41 Even if We take **you** away,
We shall indeed be
ones who requite them,

43:42 or We shall cause them to see
what We promised them.
Then truly
We *are* Ones Who are Omnipotent over them.

43:43 So hold **you** fast
to what is revealed to **you**;°
truly **you** *are* on a straight path.

43:44 Truly this is indeed a reminder for **you**
and **your** folk;°
and you shall be asked.

43:45 Ask
those of Our Messengers whom We sent before **you**:
Made We ever gods other than The Merciful
to be worshiped?

*

43:46 Indeed We sent Moses with Our Signs
to Pharaoh and his Council.
So he said: Truly I *am* a Messenger
of the Lord of the worlds.

43:47 But when he drew near them with Our Signs,
lo! They laughed at them.

43:48 We caused them not to see any Sign
except it was greater than its sister *Sign*;°
and We took them with the punishment,
so that perhaps they would return.

43:49 They said: O one who is a sorcerer!
Call for us **your** Lord
by the compact He has made with **you**;
truly We *shall be* ones who are truly guided.

43:50 But when We remove the punishment from them,
lo! They break their oath!

43:51 Pharaoh proclaimed amongst his folk
he said: O my folk!
Is not the dominion of Egypt for me

and these rivers running beneath me?°
Perceive you not?
Or I am better than this one who *is* despicable,   43:52
who almost makes things not clear.
Why *are* bracelets of gold not cast down on him   43:53
or the angels draw near to him
as ones who are connected with another?
Thus he irritated his folk,   43:54
and they obeyed him.°
Truly they were a disobedient folk.
So when they provoked against Us,   43:55
We requited them
and drowned them one and all,
and We made them a thing of the past   43:56
and a parable for later *ages*.

*

When the son of Mary is cited as an example,   43:57
lo! The folk cry aloud
and say: *Are* our gods better or *is* he?°   43:58
They cite him to **you**
not but to be argumentative.°
Rather they *are* a contentious folk.
He was but a servant to whom We were gracious,   43:59
and We made him an example
to the Children of Israel.
If We will,   43:60
We would have assigned angels
among you on the earth to be your successors.
It *is* knowledge for the Hour,   43:61
so contest not about it and follow Me.°
This *is* a straight path.
Let not Satan bar you;°   43:62
truly he *is* a clear enemy to you.
When Jesus drew near with clear portents,   43:63
he said: Truly I have drawn near to you
with wisdom
and in order to make manifest to you
some of that about which you were at variance;°
so be Godfearing of God and obey me.

43:64 Truly God He is my Lord and your Lord
so worship Him.°
This *is* the straight path.

43:65 The confederates were at variance among themselves;°
so woe to those who did wrong
from the punishment of a painful Day.

43:66 Have they looked on but for the Hour
that shall approach them suddenly,
while they are not aware.

43:67 Friends on that Day,
shall be enemies to one another,
except ones who are Godfearing.

Sec. 7
*

43:68 O My servants!
This Day *there is* no fear in you,
nor shall you feel remorse.

43:69 Those who have believed in Our Signs
and were ones who submit:

43:70 Enter the Garden, you and your wives,
walking with joy!

43:71 There shall be passed around among them
platters of gold and goblets;°
and in it shall be whatever souls hunger for,
and all that in which the eyes delight;°
and you *shall be* ones who dwell in it forever.

43:72 This *is* the Garden
which you have been given as inheritance
because of what you were doing.

43:73 For you *there shall be* much sweet fruit,
which you shall eat.

43:74 Truly ones who sin
shall be in the punishment of hell,
ones who shall dwell in it forever.

43:75 It shall not be decreased for them,
and they *shall be* ones seized with despair in it.

43:76 We did not wrong them,
but they were the ones who were unjust.

43:77 They would cry out: O Malik!
Let **your** Lord finish us!°

He would say: Truly you *shall be* one who abides.
Indeed We have brought about The Truth to you,   43:78
but most of you *are* ones who dislike The Truth.
Or *have* they fixed on some affair?   43:79
Then We, too, *are* Ones Who Fix.
Assume they that We hear not   43:80
their secret *thoughts* and their conspiring secretly?°
Yea!
Our messengers are near them writing down.
Say: If The Merciful had a son,   43:81
then I *would be* the first
of ones who are worshippers.
Glory be to the Lord   43:82
of the heavens and the earth,
the Lord of the Throne,
from all that they allege!
So let them engage in idle talk and to play   43:83
until they encounter their Day
which they were promised.
It is He Who *is* God in the heaven   43:84
and God on the earth.°
He *is* The Wise, The Knowing.
Blessed is He   43:85
to whom *belongs* the dominion
of the heavens and the earth,
and whatever *is* between them,
with Whom is the knowledge of the Hour,
to Whom shall you be returned.
Those whom they call to possess no power   43:86
for intercession
other than Him,
except those who bear witness to The Truth,
and they know.
If **you** ask them: 43:87
Who created them?
They shall indeed say: God!°
How then are they misled?
His saying: O my Lord!   43:88
Truly these *are* a folk who believe not;

so overlook them and say: Peace.°
Soon they shall know.

CHAPTER 44
THE SMOKE (*al-Dukhān*)

In the Name of God,

The Merciful, The Compassionate

44:1   *Ḥā Mīm;*

44:2   by the clear Book;

44:3   truly We sent it forth
on a blessed night.°
Truly We were ones who warn.

44:4   Every wise command is made clear in it,

44:5   a command from Us.°
Truly We were ones who sent it

44:6   as a mercy from **your** Lord.°
Truly He *is* The Hearing, The Knowing,

44:7   the Lord of the heavens and the earth
and whatever *is* between them;°
if you *were* ones who are certain.

44:8   *There is* no god but He;
it is He Who gives life and causes to die;°
your Lord and the Lord of your ancient fathers.

44:9   Rather they play in uncertainty.

44:10   Then be **you** on the watch for a Day
when the heavens shall bring a clear smoke,

44:11   overcoming humanity;°
this *is* a painful punishment.

44:12   Our Lord! Remove from us the punishment!
Indeed we *are* ones who believe.

44:13   How mindful are they
when a clear Messenger has already drawn near them.

44:14   Then they turned away from him,
and they said: One who is taught,
one who is possessed.

44:15   Truly We *are* ones who remove the punishment
for a little.°
Truly you *are* ones who revert.

On the Day when We shall seize by force   44:16
with the greatest attack,
truly We *shall be* ones who requite.
Indeed We tried   44:17
a folk of Pharaoh before them,
when there drew near to them
a generous Messenger.
Give the servants of God back to me;   44:18
truly I am a trustworthy Messenger to you.
Rise not up against God;°   44:19
truly I am one who arrives with a clear authority.
Truly I take refuge in my Lord and your Lord   44:20
so that you should not stone me.
But if you believe not in me,   44:21
then withdraw.
So he called on his Lord: 44:22
Indeed these *are* a sinning folk.
He said: Set **you** forth with My servants by night;   44:23
indeed you *shall be* ones who are followed;
and leave the sea calmly as it is;°   44:24
truly they indeed shall be a drowned army.
How many they left behind   44:25
of gardens and springs,
crops and generous stations,   44:26
ones with continual prosperity,   44:27
ones who are joyful in it!
Thus°   44:28
We gave them as inheritance to another folk.
Neither the heavens wept for them,   44:29
nor the earth,
nor were they ones who were given respite.
*   Sec. 2
Indeed We delivered the Children of Israel   44:30
from the despised punishment
of Pharaoh.°   44:31
Truly He was one who exalted himself
and was of the ones who are excessive.
Truly We chose them with knowledge   44:32
above the worlds,

44:33	and gave them the Signs in which there was a clear trial.
44:34	Truly these say:
44:35	There *is* nothing but our first singled out death, and we *shall* not *be* ones who are revived.
44:36	Then bring our fathers back, if you *would be* ones who are sincere.
44:37	Are they better or a folk of Tubba and those before them?° We caused them to perish;° they indeed were ones who sinned.
44:38	We created not the heavens and the earth, and all that *is* between them as ones who play!
44:39	We created them not but with The Truth; but most of them know not.
44:40	Truly the Day of Decision is the time appointed for all of them,
44:41	a Day when one who protects shall not avail *another* one who protects at all, nor shall they be helped,
44:42	except him on whom God has mercy.° Truly He *is* The Almighty, The Compassionate.
Sec. 3	*
44:43	Truly the tree of Zaqqum
44:44	*shall be* the food of the sinful.
44:45	Like molten copper it shall bubble in the bellies,
44:46	like boiling, scalding water.
44:47	*It shall be said*: Take him and drag him violently into the depths of hellfire;
44:48	then unloose over his head the punishment of scalding water!
44:49	Experience *this*! Truly **you, you** *were* the mighty, the generous!
44:50	Truly this *is* what you used to contest.
44:51	Truly the ones who are Godfearing shall be in the station of trustworthiness,
44:52	among Gardens and springs,

wearing fine silk and brocade,   **44:53**
as ones who face one another.
Thus   **44:54**
We shall give in marriage lovely-eyed houris.
They shall call on them for every kind of sweet fruit   **44:55**
as ones that are safe;
they shall not experience death in them   **44:56**
except a first singled out death;°
and He shall protect them
from the punishment of hellfire,
a grace from **your** Lord.°   **44:57**
That *shall be* the winning the sublime triumph!
Truly We have made this easy in **your** language   **44:58**
so that perhaps they would recollect.
So be on the watch!   **44:59**
Truly they *are* ones who are on the watch.

CHAPTER 45
THE ONES WHO KNEEL (*al-Jāthiyah*)

In the Name of God,
The Merciful, The Compassionate   **Sec. 1**
Ḥā Mīm;   **45:1**
the sending down the Book successively   **45:2**
is from God, The Almighty, The Wise.
Truly in the heavens and the earth   **45:3**
are Signs for the ones who believe:
In your creation,   **45:4**
and what He disseminated of moving creatures
are Signs for a folk who are certain.
The alternation of the nighttime and the daytime,   **45:5**
and what God has sent forth
from the heaven of provision,
He gives life with it to the earth after its death,
and the diversifying of the winds—
all are the Signs for a folk who are reasonable.
These *are* the Signs of God   **45:6**
which We recount to **you** with The Truth;°
then in which discourse,

after God and His Signs, shall they believe?

45:7 Woe to every false, sinful one!

45:8 He hears the Signs of God
being recounted to him,
yet he persists *as* one who grows in arrogance
as if he heard them not;°
so give him good tidings
of a painful punishment!

45:9 Should he know anything about Our Signs,
he takes them in mockery.°
Those, there *is* for them a despised punishment.

45:10 Behind them *there is* hell;°
what they have earned
shall not avail them at all,
nor what they have taken
other than God as protectors;°
and for them *shall be* a tremendous punishment.

45:11 This is a guidance;°
those who were ungrateful for the Signs of their Lord
for them there is a punishment
of a painful wrath.

Sec. 2
＊

45:12 God *is* He
Who has caused the sea to become subservient to you
that the boats may run through it by His command
and so that you may look for His grace,
and perhaps you shall be thankful.

45:13 He has caused for you to become subservient
whatever *is* in the heavens
and whatever *is* in and on the earth;
all *is* from Him.°
Truly in that *are* Signs
for a folk who reflect.

45:14 Say to those who have believed:
Forgive those who hope not for the days of God
that He may give recompense to a folk
according to what they were earning.

45:15 One who acts in accord with morality,
it is for his own self;°

and whoever does evil, he *is* against *his own self*;°
then to your Lord you shall be returned.
Indeed We gave the Children of Israel

the Book, the critical judgment and the prophethood,
and We provided them from what is good,
and We gave them advantage above all the worlds;
and We gave them clear portents of the command;°

and they were not at variance
until after the knowledge drew near to them
through insolence among themselves.°
Truly **your** Lord shall decree between them
on the Day of Resurrection
about what they were at variance.
Then We have assigned **you**

an open way of the command
so follow it
and follow not the desires of those who know not.
Truly they shall never avail **you**

against God at all.°
Truly the ones who are unjust,
some of them *are* protectors of others;°
but God *is* Protector
of the ones who are Godfearing.
This *is* a clear evidence for humanity

and a guidance and a mercy
for a folk who are certain.
Have those who seek to do evil deeds assumed

that We shall make them *equal*
with those who have believed,
the ones who have acted in accord with morality?
Are their living and dying equal?°
Evil *is* the judgment they give!
*

God created the heavens and the earth

with The Truth,
so that every soul would be given recompense
for what it has earned,
and they *shall* not *be* done wrong.
Have **you** considered him who has taken to himself

his own desire as his god,
and whom God causes to go astray knowingly,
and has set a seal on his hearing and his heart
and laid a covering on his sight?
Who then shall guide him after God?°
Shall you not then recollect?

45:24 They said:
There is nothing but this present life of ours;
we die and we live
and nothing causes us to perish,
but a long course of time.°
There is for them not any knowledge;°
truly they are but surmising.

45:25 When are recounted to them
Our Signs, clear portents,
then disputation was not but that they said:
Bring our fathers,
if you were ones who were sincere.

45:26 Say: God gives you life,
then causes you to die;
then He shall gather you
on the Day of Resurrection
in which *there is* no doubt,
but most of humanity knows not.

*

Sec. 4

45:27 To God *belongs* the dominion
of the heavens and the earth.°
On a Day that the Hour shall be secure,
the ones who deal in falsehood shall lose.

45:28 **You** shall see each community
as one that kneels.°
Each community shall be called to its Book:
This Day you shall be given recompense
for what you were doing.

45:29 This *is* Our Book that speaks for itself
against you with The Truth.°
Truly We have registered what you were doing.

45:30 Then as for those who have believed,
the ones who have acted in accord with morality,

their Lord shall cause them to enter in His mercy.°
That *shall be* the winning the clear triumph.
But as for those who are ungrateful: 45:31
Were not My Signs recounted to you,
but you grew arrogant
and you were a sinning folk?
When it was said: 45:32
Truly the promise of God *is* The Truth
and the Hour, *there is* no doubt about it.
You said: We are not informed about the Hour;
truly We think it but as an opinion,
and we ascertain not.
The evil deeds they have done 45:33
shall show themselves to them;
they shall be surrounded
by what they used to ridicule.
It would be said: This Day We shall forget you 45:34
as you forgot the meeting of this Day of yours.
Your place of shelter *shall be* the fire,
and *there is* not for you any one who helps.
This *is* because you took the Signs of God to yourself 45:35
in mockery
and this present life has deluded you.°
So this Day they shall not be brought out from there,
nor shall they ask to be favored.
So The Praise *belongs* to God, 45:36
the Lord of the heavens and the Lord of the earth,
and the Lord of the worlds.
His *is* the dominion 45:37
of the heavens and the earth;°
and He *is* The Almighty, The Wise.
*** Part 26

CHAPTER 46
THE CURVING SANDHILLS (al-Aḥqāf)

In the Name of God,
The Merciful, The Compassionate Sec. 1
Ḥā Mīm; 46:1
the sending down successively of the Book 46:2

46:3   We have not created the heavens and the earth
and whatever is between the two
except with The Truth
and for a determined term,
but those who are ungrateful
are ones who turn aside
from what they are warned about.

46:4   Say: Have you considered
what you associate with God?
Cause me to see
what of the earth they have created
or of the heavens.
Bring me a Book from before this,
or a vestige of knowledge
if you would be ones who are sincere.

46:5   Who *is* one who has gone more astray
than one who calls
to other than God,
one who would not respond to him
until the Day of Resurrection?
They *are* of their supplication to them,
ones who are heedless.

46:6   When humanity is assembled,
they would become their enemies
and would be ones who disavow
their worship.

46:7   When Our Signs are recounted,
clear portents,
those who are ungrateful for The Truth,
when it draws near them,
say: This *is* clear sorcery!

46:8   Or say they: He has devised it?°
Say: If I have devised it,
you still possess nothing for me against God;°
He has greater knowledge
of what you press on about;°
He suffices as a Witness
between me and between you;°
and He *is* The Forgiving, The Compassionate.

Say: I *am* not an innovation
among the Messengers;
nor am I informed what shall be wreaked on me,
nor with you;°
I follow not but what is revealed to me
and I *am* not but a clear warner.
Say: Have you considered that
if this is from God and you were ungrateful for it,
and a witness bore witness
from among the Children of Israel
to its like
and has believed *in it* yet you grew arrogant?°
Truly God guides not the unjust folk.
*

Those who were ungrateful
say to those who have believed:
Had it been good,
they would not have preceded us toward it.°
When they are not truly guided by it,
they say: This is a ripe, aged calumny.
Yet before it *was* the Book of Moses
as a leader and a mercy.°
This *is* a Book establishing as true
in the Arabic language
to warn those who did wrong
and as good tidings
to the ones who are doers of good.
Truly those who say: Our Lord *is* God;
and then go straight,
there is neither fear in them,
nor shall they feel remorse.
Those are the Companions of the Garden,
ones who shall dwell in it forever,
as a recompense for what they were doing.
We have charged the human being
with kindness to ones who are his parents;°
his mother carried him painfully
and she painfully brought him forth;°
and the bearing of him and the weaning of him

46:9

46:10

Sec. 2
46:11

46:12

46:13

46:14

46:15

584

are thirty months.°
When he be fully grown, having come of age
and reached forty years,
he says: My Lord!
Arouse me that I may be thankful
for **Your** divine blessing,
that with which **You** have been gracious to me
and to ones who were my parents,
so that I would do
as one who acts in accord with morality,
that **You** be well-pleased with it;
and make things right for me and my offspring;°
truly I have repented to **You**
and truly I am of the ones who submit.

46:16   Those are they from whom We shall receive
the fairest of what they have done
and we shall pass over their evil deeds;
they are among the Companions of the Garden;°
this is a promise of sincerity
which they have been promised.

46:17   But he who says to ones who are his parents:
Fie on you both!
Are you promising me that I shall be brought out,
when generations before me have passed away?
While they both cry to God for help:
Woe unto **you**!
Believe! Truly the promise of God *is* True.
But he says:
This *is* nothing but fables of the ancient ones.

46:18   Those are they against whom the saying was realized
about the communities
that have passed away before
of the jinn and human kind;°
truly they were ones who were losers.

46:19   For each there *shall be* degrees
according to what he did,
that He may pay them their account in full
for their actions;
and they shall not be done wrong.

On a Day when those who were ungrateful   46:20
shall be presented to the fire:
You caused what are good to dissipate
in your present life
and you enjoyed them.
Now on this Day you shall be given recompense
with a punishment of humiliation
because you grew arrogant on the earth
without right,
and because you were disobedient.
*   Sec. 3
Remember the brother of Ad   46:21
when he warned his folk in the curving sandhills;
warners have passed away
before and after him *saying*:
Worship nothing but God;
truly I fear for you the punishment
of a tremendous Day.
They said: 46:22
What! Have **you** drawn near to us
to mislead us away from our gods?
Then bring us that with which **you** have promised us,
if **you** are one of the ones who are sincere.
He said: 46:23
The knowledge is not but with God
and I state to you what I have been sent,
but I see that you *are* a folk who are ignorant.
Then when they saw it as a dense cloud   46:24
proceeding towards their valleys,
they said: This is a dense cloud
that shall give us rain.°
Rather *it is* what you were impatient for;°
a wind in which there is a painful punishment,
destroying everything by the command of its Lord,   46:25
so it came to be in the morning
that nothing was to be seen
except their dwellings.°
Thus have We given recompense to the sinning folk.
Indeed We had established them firmly   46:26

in what We have not established you,
and We have made for them
the ability to hear and sight and minds,
yet having the ability to hear availed them not,
nor their sight, nor their minds in any way
since they used to negate the Signs of God,
and they are surrounded
by what they used to ridicule.

*

46:27   Indeed We have caused to perish
towns around you
and We have diversified the Signs
so that perhaps they would return.

46:28   Then why helped them not
those whom they had taken to themselves as gods,
other than God,
as a mediator?
Rather they have gone astray from them.°
That *was* their calumny,
and what they had been devising.

46:29   When We turned away toward **you**
groups of jinn
who listened to the Quran,
when they found themselves in its presence,
they said: Pay heed!°
When it was finished,
they turned away to their folk
as ones who warn.

46:30   They said: O our folk!
Truly We have heard a Book
sent forth after Moses,
establishing as true what *was* in advance of it.
It guides to The Truth
and to a straight road.

46:31   O our folk! God answers to one who calls,
so believe in Him;
He shall forgive you your impieties,
and shall grant protection to you
from a painful punishment.

Whoever answers not   46:32
to one who calls to God,
he is not one who frustrates *the Will of God*
in and on the earth,
and there shall not be for him
other than God as protectors.°
Those *are* clearly gone astray.
What! Have they not considered that   46:33
God Who created the heavens and the earth,
and was not wearied by their creation,
is One Who Has Power to give life to the dead.°
Yea! He truly *is* Powerful over all things.
On a Day when those who are ungrateful   46:34
shall be presented to the fire:
Is not this The Truth?
They would say: Yea! By our Lord!
He shall say: Then experience the punishment
because you were ungrateful!
So have patience   46:35
as endured patiently those with constancy
of the Messengers;
and let them not be impatient for it.°
As truly on a Day they shall see
what they are promised;
as though they had not lingered in expectation
except for an hour of daytime.°
This is delivering the message!°
Shall any be caused to perish
except the disobedient folk?

CHAPTER 47
MUHAMMAD (*Muḥammad*)

In the Name of God,
The Merciful, The Compassionate   Sec. 1
Those who were ungrateful,   47:1
and who barred from the Way of God—
He has caused their actions to go astray.
Those who have believed,   47:2

the ones who have acted in accord with morality,
and have believed in what was sent down
to Muhammad,

.   for it *is* The Truth from their Lord,
He shall absolve them of their evil deeds
and make right their state of mind.

47:3   That *is* because those who were ungrateful
followed falsehood,
while those who believed followed The Truth
from their Lord.°
Thus God propounds their parables
for humanity.

47:4   So when you have met those who were ungrateful,
then strike their thick necks
until you have given them a sound thrashing;
then tie them fast with bonds,
and afterwards either *have* good will *toward them*
or take ransom for them
until the war lays down its heavy load.°
Thus! So!
But had God willed,
He Himself would have indeed avenged you,
but *it is* to try some of you with others,°
as for those who are slain in the way of God,
He shall never cause their actions to go astray.

47:5   He shall guide them,
and He shall make right their state of mind.

47:6   He caused them to enter the Garden
with which He had acquainted them.

47:7   O those who have believed!
If you help God, He shall help you,
and make firm your feet.

47:8   As for those who are ungrateful,
let *them* fall into ruin!
He has caused their actions to go astray.

47:9   That *is* because they disliked
what God has sent forth,
so He has caused their actions to fail.

47:10   What! Have they not journeyed through the earth

and looked on
how was the Ultimate End of those before them?°
God destroyed them;°
and for ones who are ungrateful *is* its likeness.
That *is* because God *is* the One Who Protects 47:11
those who have believed;
as for the ones who are ungrateful,
there is no one who protects them.

*

Truly God shall cause to enter 47:12
those who have believed,
the ones who have acted in accord with morality,
gardens beneath which rivers run;°
while those who were ungrateful,
were taking joy in eating as flocks eat,
the fire *shall be* their place of lodging.
How many a town *has there been* 47:13
which *was* stronger in strength than **your** town
which has driven **you** out,
We have caused to perish,
and *there was* no one who helped them!
What! Is he who was on a clear portent 47:14
from his Lord like him
to whom his terrible actions
were made to appear pleasing
while they have followed their own desires?
This is the parable of the Garden 47:15
which has been promised ones who are Godfearing;°
in it are rivers of unpolluted water
and rivers of milk,
the taste of which *is* not modified,
and rivers of intoxicants
delightful to ones who drink,
and rivers of clarified honey;°
and in it for them every kind of fruit,
and forgiveness from their Lord;°
Are they like those who *are*
ones who shall dwell forever in the fire
and would be given scalding water to drink

so that it cuts off their bowels?

47:16 Among them are some
who listen to **you**,
but when they go forth from **you**,
they say to those
who have been given knowledge:
What was that he said just now?°
Those are they upon whose hearts
God has set a seal,
and they have followed their own desires.

47:17 As for those who are truly guided,
He has increased them in guidance,
and He has given to them their Godfearingness.

47:18 Look they then on anything except that the Hour
should approach them suddenly?°
But indeed some of its tokens have drawn near.°
But how shall they be mindful
when it draws near?

47:19 So know that *there is* no god but God;
ask forgiveness for **your** impieties
and for the ones who are male believers
and the ones who are female believers;°
God knows your going to and fro
and your place of lodging.

Sec. 3   *

47:20 Those who have believed say:
Why has a chapter of the Quran not been sent down?°
But when has been sent forth
a definitive chapter of the Quran,
and fighting is remembered in it,
• **you** see those in whose hearts is a sickness
looking on **you**
with the look of one who is fainting at death;°
but better for them would be

47:21 obedience and a moral saying!°
When the affair has been resolved,
then if they had been sincere to God,
it would have been better for them.

47:22 Shall it be that if you turned away,

591

CHAPTER 47 MUHAMMAD (*Muḥammad*) STAGE 6 PART 26 SECTION 3 47:16–47:22

you would make corruption in the earth
and cut off blood relations?
Those are they whom God has cursed,   47:23
so He has made them unhearing,
and their sight, *unwilling* to see.
What? Meditate they not then on the Quran   47:24
or are there locks on *their* hearts?
Truly those who go back, turning back   47:25
after the guidance has become clear to them,   •
it was Satan who had enticed them,
and He granted them indulgence.
That is because they said   47:26
to those who disliked what God had sent down:
We shall obey **You** in some of the affair;°
and God knows what they keep secret.
Then how *shall it be for them*   47:27
when the angels shall call them to themselves,
striking their faces and their backs?
That *is* because they have followed   47:28
what displeased God
and they have disliked His contentment,
so He has caused their actions to fail.
                              *   Sec. 4

Or assumed those in whose hearts *is* a sickness   47:29
that God shall never bring out their rancor?
If We willed, We would have caused **you** to see them,   47:30
and **you** would have recognized them
by their marks.°
But indeed **you** shall recognize them
by the twisting of speech.°
God knows all your actions.
Indeed We shall try you   47:31
until We know the ones who struggle among you,
and the ones who remain steadfast,
and We shall try your news.
Truly those who were ungrateful,   47:32
and barred from the way of God,
and made a breach with the Messenger
after guidance had become clear to them,

they never injure God in the least,
but He shall cause their actions to fail.

47:33 O those who have believed!
Obey God and obey the Messenger
and prove not our actions untrue.

47:34 Truly those who were ungrateful,
and barred from the way of God—
while they *were* the ones who were ungrateful—
God shall never forgive them.

47:35 So be not faint and call for peace
while you *have* the upper *hand*;
God *is* with you,
and shall never cheat you out of your actions.

47:36 This present life *is* but a pastime and a diversion.°
But if you believe and are Godfearing,
He shall give you your compensation,
and shall not ask of you for your property.

47:37 If He were to ask it of you, and be importunate,
you would be miserly,
and He would bring out your rancor.

47:38 Behold! You *are* those
being called to spend in the way of God,
yet among you *are* some who *are* miserly;°
and whoever *is* miserly,
then he is miserly not but to himself.°
God *is* Sufficient and you *are* poor.°
If you turn away,
He *shall have* a folk other than you in exchange;
then they shall not be the like of you.

CHAPTER 48
THE VICTORY (*al-Fatḥ*)

In the Name of God,
Sec. 1 · The Merciful, The Compassionate
48:1 Truly We have given victory to **you**,
a clear victory,
48:2 that God may forgive **you**
what was former of **your** impiety

and what shall come later,
that He may fulfill His divine blessing on **you**
and guide **you** on a straight path,
and that God may help **you** with a mighty help. 48:3
It is He Who sent forth the tranquility 48:4
into the hearts of the ones who believe
that they may add belief to their belief,°
and to God *belongs* the armies
of the heavens and the earth.°
God *is* Knowing, Wise;
that He causes to enter 48:5
the ones who are male believers
and the ones who are female believers,
Gardens beneath which rivers run,
ones who shall dwell in them forever,
and that he may absolve them
of their their evil deeds;°
that was to God
winning of a sublime triumph;
and that He may punish 48:6
the ones who are male hypocrites,
and the ones who are female hypocrites,
and also the ones who are male polytheists,
and the ones who are female polytheists,
and the ones who think
morally evil thoughts about God;
for them is a morally evil turn of fortune;°
God *was* angry with them,
He has cursed them,
and prepared hell for them;°
how evil indeed a Homecoming!
To God *belongs* the armies 48:7
of the heavens and the earth.°
God is Almighty, Wise.
Truly We have sent **you** as one who bears witness, 48:8
and one who gives good tidings and as a warner,
so that you may believe in God 48:9
and His Messenger,
and that you may support him,

and revere Him and glorify Him
in the early morning at dawn and eventide.

48:10 Truly those who take the pledge of allegiance to **you**
take the pledge of alliance not but to God;
the hand of God is over their hands.°
Then whoever has broken his oath,
has broken his oath not but to *the harm* of himself;°
and whoever has lived up
to what he has made as a contract with God,
He shall give him a sublime compensation.

Sec. 2
*

48:11 Nomads, ones who were left behind, shall say to **you**:
Our property and our people occupied us,
so ask forgiveness for us.°
They say with their tongues
what is not in their hearts.°
Say: Who then has any sway for you against God
if He has wanted to distress you
or has wanted to bring you profit?°
Rather God has been Aware of what you do.

48:12 Rather you thought
that the Messenger and the ones who believe
would never turn about to their people;
that was made to appear pleasing
in your hearts;
but you thought morally evil thoughts,
and you became a lost folk.

48:13 Whoever believes not in God
and His Messenger,
truly We have made ready
a blaze for the ones who are ungrateful.

48:14 To God *belongs* the dominion
of the heavens and the earth.°
He forgives whom He will
and punishes whom He will.°
God *is* Forgiving, Compassionate.

48:15 The ones who were left behind shall say
when you set out to take the gains:
Let us follow you;°

they want to substitute for the assertion of God.°
Say: You shall not follow us;
thus God has said beforehand;°
then they shall say: Rather you are jealous of us.°
Rather they understand not but a little.
Say to the ones who have been left behind

among the nomads:
You shall be called against a folk
of severe might.
You shall fight them or they shall submit;°
then if you obey,
God shall give you a fair compensation;°
but if you turn away
as you turned away before,
He shall punish you *with* a painful punishment.
There is no fault on the blind,

no fault on the lame,
no fault on the sick,°
and whoever obeys God
and His Messenger,
He shall cause him to enter Gardens
beneath which rivers run;°
and whoever turns away,
He shall punish him with a painful punishment.
*

Indeed God was well-pleased

with the ones who believe
when they took the pledge of allegiance to **you**
beneath the tree,
for He knew what *was* in their hearts;
He sent forth the tranquility on them;
He repaid them with a victory near at hand.
They shall take much gain,°

and God *is* Almighty, Wise.
God has promised you much gain

that you shall take;
He has quickened this for you;
He has limited the hands of humanity from you,
so that perhaps it would be a Sign

to the ones who believe
that He may guide you to a straight path,

48:21 and other *gains,*
which *are* not yet within your power;
indeed God comprehends them.°
God *is* Powerful over all things.

48:22 If those who were ungrateful fought you,
they would have turned their backs;
then they would have found
neither protector nor helper.

48:23 That *has been* the custom of God
which had been in force before;°
you shall never find in the custom of God
any substitution.

48:24 He *it is who* limited their hands from you
and your hands from them
in the hollow of Makkah;
after He had made you victors over them.°
God *is* Seeing of what you do.

48:25 They are ones who were ungrateful;
they barred you from the Masjid al-Haram
and detained the sacrificial gift
from reaching its place of sacrifice.°
Had it not been
for the ones who are male believers,
and for the ones who are female believers
whom you know not
so that you should not tread on them
and guilt should light on you
without *your* knowledge°
that God may cause to enter into His mercy
whomever He will,°
if they should have been severed,
We would have punished
those who were ungrateful
among them
with a painful punishment.

48:26 When those who were ungrateful
laid bigotry into their hearts,

like the bigotry of the Age of Ignorance,
then God sent forth His tranquility
on His Messenger,
and to the ones who believe,
and fastened on them the word
of Godfearingness,
and they had better right to it
and were more worthy of it.°
God is Knowing of everything.
*

Indeed God has been sincere
to His Messenger's dream
with The Truth:°
You shall indeed enter the Masjid al-Haram,
had God willed,
as ones who are in safety,
as ones who have shaved your heads
or as ones whose *hair* is cut short;
you fear not;°
He knew what you knew not,
and He assigned besides that
a victory near at hand.
He *it is* Who has sent His Messenger
with guidance
and the way of life of The Truth
that He may uplift it over all of the ways of life.°
God suffices as a witness.
Muhammad *is* the Messenger of God;°
and those who *are* with him
are severe against the ones who are ungrateful,
but compassionate among themselves;°
you see them as ones who bow,
as ones who prostrate themselves;
they are looking for grace from God
and contentment;°
on their faces are their marks
from the effects of prostration.°
This *is* their parable in the Torah,°
and their parable in the Gospel *is*:

Like sown seed
that brings out its shoot, then is invigorated;
it then becomes stout,
and rises straight on its plant stalk,
impressing the ones who are sowers
so that He may enrage
the ones who are ungrateful by them,°
God has promised
those who have believed,
the ones who have acted in accord with morality,
for them
forgiveness and a sublime compensation.

CHAPTER 49
THE INNER APARTMENTS (al-Ḥujurāt)

In the Name of God,

Sec. 1 The Merciful, The Compassionate

49:1 O those who have believed!
Put not *yourselves* forward
in advance of God and His Messenger;°
be Godfearing of God.°
Truly God *is* Hearing, Knowing.

49:2 O those who have believed!
Exalt not your voices
above the voice of the Prophet
nor openly publish a saying to him
as you would openly publish something to others,
so that your actions not be fruitless
while you *are* not aware.

49:3 Truly those who lower their voices
near the Messenger of God,
those *are* the ones God has put to test
their hearts for Godfearingness.°
For them *is* forgiveness
and a sublime compensation.

49:4 Truly those who cry out to **you**
from behind the inner apartments,
most of them are not reasonable.

If they had endured patiently   49:5
until **you** would go forth to them,
it would have been better for them.°
God *is* Forgiving, Compassionate.
O those who have believed!   49:6
If one who disobeys draws near to you
with a tiding, be you clear
so that you not light on a folk out of ignorance;
then you would become ones who are remorseful
for what you have accomplished.
Know you that the Messenger of God *is* of you.°   49:7
If he were to obey you in many of the affairs,
you would indeed fall into misfortune;
but God has endeared belief to you
and made it appear pleasing
to your hearts,
and He has caused to be detestable to you
ingratitude and disobedience and rebellion.°
They, those *are* the ones who are right minded,
as a grace from God and His divine blessing.°   49:8
God *is* Knowing, Wise.
If two sections   49:9
among the ones who believe
fight against each other,
then make things right between them both;°
but if one of them is insolent against the other,
then fight the one who is insolent
until it changes its mind about the command of God.°
Then if it changes its mind,
make things right between them
justly and equitably;°
truly God loves the ones who are equitable.
The ones who believe are not but brothers,   49:10
so make things right between your brothers.°
Be Godfearing of God
so that perhaps you would find mercy.
*
                                                             Sec. 2
O those who have believed!   49:11
Let not a folk deride another folk;

600

it may be that the latter *are* better than they,
nor women *deride other* women;°
it may be that they are better than they;
nor find fault with one another,
nor insult one another with nicknames;°
misery is the name of disobedience after belief!°
Whoever repents not,
then they, those *are* the ones who are unjust.

49:12 O those who have believed!
Avoid suspicion much;
truly some suspicion is a sin;°
and spy not nor backbite one another.°
Would one of you love
to eat the flesh of his lifeless brother?
You would dislike it.°
Be Godfearing of God.°
Truly God *is*
One Who Accepts Repentance, Compassionate.

49:13 O humanity!
Truly We have created you
from a male and a female,
and made you into peoples and types
that you may recognize one another.°
Truly the most generous of you with God
is the most devout.°
Truly God *is* Knowing, Aware.

49:14 The nomads have said: We have believed!
Say to them: You believe not,
instead say: We have submitted,
for belief has not *yet* entered into your hearts;°
but if you obey God and His Messenger,
He shall not withhold any of your actions.°
Truly God *is* Forgiving, Compassionate.

49:15 The ones who believe *are* not but those
who have believed in God and His Messenger;
then they were not in doubt,
but they struggled with their wealth,
and themselves in the way of God.°
They, those *are* the ones who are sincere.

Say: Would you teach God about your way of life   **49:16**
when God knows all that *is* in the heavens
and all that *is* in and on the earth?°
God *is* Knowing of everything.
They show grace to **you**   **49:17**
in that they have submitted!°
Say: Your submission shows not grace to me;°
rather God shows grace to you
in that He has guided you to belief,
if you indeed be ones who are sincere.
Truly God knows the unseen   **49:18**
of the heavens and the earth.°
God *is* Seeing of what you do.

CHAPTER 50
QAF (*Qāf*)

In the Name of God,   Stage 7
The Merciful, The Compassionate   Sec. 1
Qāf;° by the glorious Quran!   **50:1**
Rather they marveled   **50:2**
that *there* has drawn near to them
one who warns
from among themselves;
so the ones who were ungrateful said:
This *is* a strange thing;
What? When we have died   **50:3**
and have become earthy dust;°
that *is* a far-fetched returning!
Indeed we know what the earth reduces   **50:4**
from them;°
and with Us *is* a guardian Book.
Rather they have denied The Truth   **50:5**
when it drew near to them,
so they *are* in a confused state of affairs. What?
Have they not looked on the heaven above them,   **50:6**
how We have built it and made it appear pleasing?
There *are* not any gaps in it.
The earth, We have stretched it out,   **50:7**

and cast on it firm mountains,
and have caused to develop in it
of every diverse pair,

50:8 for contemplation and mindfulness
to every repentant servant.

50:9 We sent down blessed water from heaven,
then We caused gardens to develop from it
and reaped wheat;

50:10 and high-reaching date palm trees,
with ranged spathes

50:11 as provision for My servants;°
We gave life by them to a lifeless land.°
Thus shall *be* the going forth.

50:12 The folk of Noah denied *what came* before them,
and the Companions of Rass and Thamud,

50:13 Ad and Pharaoh and the brothers of Lot,

50:14 the Companions of the Wood
and the folk of Tubba.°
All denied the Messengers,
so My threat was realized.

50:15 Were We then wearied by the first creation?°
Rather they *are* in perplexity about a new creation.

Sec. 2

*

50:16 Indeed We have created the human being;
We know what evil his soul whispers to him;°
We are nearer to him
than the jugular vein.

50:17 When the two receivers receive,
seated on the right hand and on the left hand

50:18 he utters not a saying
but that *there is* a watcher ready near him.

50:19 When in truth the agony of death draws near:°
That is what **you** were to shun.

50:20 The trumpet shall be blown:
That *is* the threatened Day.

50:21 Then every person shall draw near,
along with one who drives and a witness.

50:22 Indeed **you** were heedless of this,
so We have removed **your** screen from **you**

so that **your** sight this Day is sharp.

His comrade would say: 50:23

This *is* what *is* ready near me.

Both of you cast into hell 50:24

every stubborn ingrate,

one who delays the good, 50:25

one who is an aggressor, one who arouses suspicion,

he who made another god besides God! 50:26

Then cast him into the severe punishment!

His comrade would say: Our Lord! 50:27

I made him not overbold,

but he was going far astray

He would say: Strive not against one another 50:28

near Me,

for indeed I put forward to you the threat.

The saying from Me is not to be substituted, 50:29

and I *am* not unjust to the servants.

*

On a Day when We shall say to hell: 50:30

Are **you** full?

It shall say: Are there any more?

The Garden shall be brought close 50:31

to the ones who are Godfearing,

not far off.

This *is* what you were promised 50:32

for every penitent and guardian

who dreaded The Merciful in the unseen 50:33

and drew near with a repentant heart.

Enter you there in peace;° 50:34

that *is* the Day of Eternity!

They *shall have* what they will in it; 50:35

with Us *there is* yet an addition.

How many have We caused to perish 50:36

before them of generations

who *were* stronger than they in courage

so that they searched about on the land.

Was there any asylum?

Truly in that *is* mindfulness 50:37

for one who has a heart

or give listen;
he *is* one who has an attentive mind.

50:38 Indeed We created
the heavens and the earth
and whatever *is* between
in six days,
and no exhaustion afflicted Us.

50:39 So have patience with whatever they say,
and glorify with the praise of **your** Lord
before the coming up of the sun
and before sunset;

50:40 glorify Him in the end part of the night
and after the prostrations.

50:41 Listen on a Day
when one who calls out shall call
from a near place.

50:42 On a Day when they shall hear the Cry
with The Truth.°
That shall be the Day of going forth.

50:43 Truly it is We who give life and cause to die,
and to Us *is* the Homecoming.

50:44 On a Day when the earth shall be split open
swiftly,°
that shall be an easy assembly for Us.

50:45 We have greater knowledge of what they say;°
you *are* not haughty over them;°
so remind by the Quran him who fears My threat.

CHAPTER 51
THE WINNOWING WINDS (*al-Dhāriyāt*)

In the Name of God,
Sec. 1 The Merciful, The Compassionate

51:1 By the winnowing winds of ones that winnows;

51:2 by the burden-bearers who carry a heavy burden,

51:3 the ones that run with ease,

51:4 the ones that distribute the command,

51:5 truly what you are promised *is* sincere,

51:6 and truly the judgment *is* what surely falls.

By the heaven full of tracks, 51:7

you *are* ones who are at variance in *your*sayings. 51:8

He is mislead there by him who would be misled. 51:9

Accursed be *those who* guess, 51:10

those who *are* inattentive because of obstinacy. 51:11

They ask: When *shall* the Day of Judgment *be*? 51:12

A Day when they are tried over the fire: 51:13

Experience your test; 51:14

this *is* that for which you were impatient.

Indeed the Godfearing *shall be* in the Garden 51:15
and springs,

ones who take what their Lord has given them.° 51:16

Truly they have before been
ones who are doers of good.

They used to slumber little during the night; 51:17

and at the breaking of the day, 51:18
they ask for forgiveness.

There was a consideration in their wealth 51:19
for the ones who ask,
and the ones who are outcasts.

In the earth *are* Signs for the ones who are certain, 51:20

and in yourselves.° 51:21

Perceive you not?

In the heaven *is* your provision, 51:22
as you are promised

by the Lord of the heaven and the earth; 51:23
it *is* indeed The Truth
just as you yourself speak.

*   Sec. 2

Truly has the discourse about 51:24
the honored guests of Abraham approached **you**?

When they entered to him 51:25
they said: Peace;°
he said: Peace.
An unknown folk.

Then he turned upon his people 51:26
and produced a fattened calf;

so he brought it near to them *and* he said: 51:27
Shall you not eat?

51:28	Then he sensed a fear of them;°
	they said: Be not in awe;°
	they gave him good tidings of a knowing boy.
51:29	Then his wife came forward with a loud cry;
	she smote her face
	and said: *I am* an old barren woman!
51:30	They said: Thus has **your** Lord spoken;°
	truly He *is* The Wise, The Knowing.

***

Part 27

51:31	*Abraham* said:
	O ones who were sent, what is your business?
51:32	They said: We have been sent to a sinning folk,
51:33	to send on them rocks of clay
51:34	marked by **your** Lord
	for the ones who are excessive.
51:35	So We brought out those who were in it
	of the ones who believe.
51:36	But We found
	nothing in it but a house of ones who submit.
51:37	We left a Sign in it
	for those who fear the painful punishment,
51:38	and in Moses,
	when We sent him to Pharaoh
	with a clear authority.
51:39	But *Pharaoh* turned away to his court and
	said: One who is a sorcerer or one who is possessed!
51:40	So We took him and his armies,
	and cast them forth into the water of the sea;
	he *was* one who was answerable.
51:41	And in Ad, when We sent against them
	the withering wind;
51:42	it forsake not anything it approached,
	but made it decay.
51:43	And in Thamud, when it was said to them:
	Take joy for awhile.
51:44	But they defied the command of their Lord,
	so the thunderbolt took them
	while they were looking on.
51:45	They were neither able to stand up

nor were they ones who would aid themselves.

The folk of Noah from before;°
truly they were a disobedient folk.

*

We built the heaven with potency 51:47
and truly We are ones who extend wide.
The earth, We have spread it forth; 51:48
how excellent *are* the ones who spread!
Of everything We have created mates 51:49
so that perhaps you would recollect.
So run away towards God;° 51:50
truly I *am to you* a clear warner from Him.
Make not with God any other god;° 51:51
truly I *am* to you a clear warner from Him.
There approached not 51:52
those who were before them
any Messenger,
but that they said: One who is a sorcerer
or one who is possessed.
Are they recommending this to one another? 51:53
Rather they *are* a defiant folk!
So turn away from them 51:54
that **you** *are* not one who is to be reproached.
Remind, 51:55
for truly being mindful profits
the ones who believe.
I created not but jinn and human kind 51:56
so that they should worship Me.
I want no provision from them, 51:57
nor want I that they should feed Me.
Truly God, He *is* The Provider, 51:58
The Possessor of Strength, The Sure.
Truly the portion of those who do wrong 51:59
is like the portion of their companions;
so let them not be impatient.
Then woe to those who were ungrateful 51:60
for that Day of theirs that they were promised.

CHAPTER 52
THE MOUNTAIN (al-Ṭūr)

In the Name of God,

Sec. 1 The Merciful, The Compassionate

52:1 By the mountain

52:2 and by a Book inscribed,

52:3 on an unrolled scroll of parchment,

52:4 by the frequented House,

52:5 by the exalted roof,

52:6 by the pouring over sea,

52:7 truly the punishment of **Your** Lord
is what fails not;

52:8 *there is* none that *shall* avert *it*.

52:9 On a Day when the heaven shall spin
a spinning,

52:10 and the mountains shall journey a journey;

52:11 then woe on a Day to the ones who denied,

52:12 they, those who *are* engaging in play;

52:13 on a Day they shall be driven away with force
to the fire of hell with a driving away:

52:14 This *is* the fire which you were denying!

52:15 *Is* this then sorcery, or *is it that* you perceive not?

52:16 Roast you *in it!*
Whether you have patience,
or you patiently endure not,
it is all the same to you;°
you shall be given recompense
not but for what you were doing.

52:17 Truly for the ones who are Godfearing
shall be Gardens and bliss,

52:18 ones that are joyful
for what their Lord has given them,
and their Lord has protected them
from the punishment of hellfire.

52:19 Eat and drink with a wholesome appetite
because of what you were doing.

52:20 They shall be ones who are reclining
on couches arrayed;°

609

We shall give in marriage to them
lovely-eyed houris.
Those who have believed,   52:21
and their offspring who followed them in belief,
We cause them to join their offspring,
and we shall not deprive them
of anything of their actions.°
Every man *shall be* pledged for what he has earned.
We have furnished relief to them   52:22
with sweet fruit and meat
such as that for which they *have* a good appetite.
They shall contend with one another for a cup   52:23
around which *there is* no idle talk,
nor accusation of sinfulness.
Boys of theirs shall go around them   52:24
as if they were well-guarded pearls.
Some of them shall come forward to others   52:25
inquiring of one another;
they say: Truly we were before   52:26
ones who were apprehensive among our people,
but God has shown grace to us,   52:27
and has protected us
from the punishment of the burning wind.
Truly we used to call to Him before;°   52:28
truly He, He *is* The Source of Goodness,
The Compassionate.

*   Sec. 2

So remind   52:29
by the divine blessing of **your** Lord;
you *are* not a soothsayer
nor one who is possessed.
Or they say: A poet,   52:30
we await for the misfortunes of time for him.
Say: Await, for I *am*   52:31
among the ones who are waiting.
Are they commanded by   52:32
their faculties of understanding to this?°
Are they a defiant folk?
Or they say: He has fabricated it.°   52:33

Rather they believe not.

52:34　Then let them bring a discourse like it,
if they are ones who are sincere.

52:35　Or were they created from nothing,
or *were* they *of themselves* the ones who create?

52:36　Or created they the heavens and the earth?°
Rather they *have* not certainty.

52:37　Or *are* the treasures of **your** Lord with them,
or are they registrars?

52:38　Or *have* they a ladder
by means of which they listen?°
Then let ones who are listening bring
a clear authority.

52:39　Has He daughters and they *have* sons?

52:40　Or ask **you** from them for a compensation
so that they are weighed down
from something owed?

52:41　Or *is* the unseen with them,
and they write it down?

52:42　Or want they cunning?°
But *it is* those who were ungrateful
who are the ones who are outwitted.

52:43　Or *have* they a god other than God?°
Glory be to God
from all that they make partners *with Him*!

52:44　If they were to consider
a piece of the heavens falling,
they would say: Heaped up clouds!

52:45　So forsake them until they encounter their day
in which they shall be swooning,

52:46　a day when their cunning shall avail them
nothing at all, nor shall they be helped.

52:47　Truly for those who do wrong
there is a punishment besides that,
but most of them know not.

52:48　So have patience for the determination of **your** Lord,
for truly **you** *are* under Our eyes;°
and glorify the praises of **your** Lord
when you have stood up at the time of *dawn*;

CHAPTER 53
THE STAR (*al-Najm*)

In the Name of God,
The Merciful, The Compassionate   Sec. 1
By the star when it is hurled to ruin,   53:1
neither has your companion gone astray,   53:2
nor has he erred
nor speaks he out of desire.   53:3
This is but a revelation that is revealed,   53:4
taught him by One stronger in strength,   53:5
Possessor of Forcefulness, then he stood poised   53:6
while he was on the loftiest horizon.   53:7
Then he came to pass near and hung suspended   53:8
until he was *at a distance of* two bow lengths or nearer.   53:9
Then He revealed to His servant   53:10
what He revealed.
The mind lied not against what it saw.   53:11
Shall you altercate with him   53:12
about what he saw?
Indeed he saw it another time,   53:13
near the Lote Tree of the Final End,   53:14
near which is the Garden of the Place of Shelter.   53:15
When overcame the Lote Tree what overcame it,   53:16
the sight swerved not nor was it defiant.   53:17
Indeed he saw   53:18
some of the greatest Signs of his Lord.
Have you then seen al-Lat and al-Uzza,   53:19
and Manat, the third, the other?   53:20
Have you males and has He, females?   53:21
That then *is* an unfair division.   53:22
They are but names that you have named,   53:23
you and your fathers,
for which God has not sent forth any authority.°
They follow nothing but opinion
and that for which their souls yearn;°

indeed the guidance has drawn near to them
from their Lord.

53:24 Or *shall* mankind *have* what he covets

53:25 yet to God *belongs* the Last and the First?

Sec. 2

*

53:26 How many an angel in the heavens *is there*
whose intercession shall avail nothing at all
except that God gives permission
to whom He will and He is well-pleased.

53:27 Truly those who believe not in the world to come
name the angels with female names,

53:28 while they *have* no knowledge of it;°
they follow nothing but opinion;°
and truly opinion avails them
nothing at all against The Truth.

53:29 So turn aside from him who turns away
from Our Reminder
and he wants nothing but this present life.

53:30 That *is* their attainment of knowledge.°
Truly **your** Lord,
He *is* the One Who has Greater Knowledge
of those who go astray from His way;
and He has greater knowledge
of those who are truly guided.

53:31 To God *belongs*
whatever *is* in the heavens
and whatever *is* in and on the earth
that He may give recompense
to those who did evil
for what they have done,
and give recompense
to those who did good with fairness.

53:32 Those who avoid the major sins,
and the indecencies
except the lesser offenses,°
truly **your** Lord *is* One Who is Extensive
in forgiveness.°
He has greater knowledge of you
when He caused you to grow from the earth

and when you *were* an unborn child
in the wombs of your mothers;°
so ascribe not purity to yourselves;°
He has greater knowledge of him
who is Godfearing.

*

Have **you** considered him who turned away
and gave a little, giving grudgingly?
Is the knowledge of the unseen with him
so that he sees *it*?
Has he been told what *is* in the scrolls of Moses?
Or of Abraham who paid his account in full,
so that the soul laden
not bear the heavy load of another?
There is nothing that *belongs* to mankind
except that for which he endeavors,
and that his endeavor shall be seen.
He shall be given recompense for it
with a more true recompense:
That towards **your** Lord is the Utmost Boundary;
that *it is* He, He Who causes laughing
and causes weeping;
that *it is* He, He Who causes to die and gives life;
that *it is* He, He creates the pairs,
male and female,
from seminal fluid when it is emitted;
and with Him *is* another growth;
that *it is* He, He Who has Enriched
or has made rich;
that it is He, He Who *is* the Lord of Sirius;
that it is He Who caused to perish
the former Ad,
and Thamud,
causing none to remain,
and the folk of Noah before;°
truly they, they were
ones who did greater wrong,
ones who were defiant.
He has overthrown cities

53:33	
53:34	
53:35	
53:36	
53:37	
53:38	
53:39	
53:40	
53:41	
53:42	
53:43	
53:44	
53:45	
53:46	
53:47	
53:48	
53:49	
53:50	
53:51	
53:52	
53:53	

	that He caused to tumble,
53:54	so enwrapped them with what enwraps.
53:55	Then which of the benefits of **your** Lord
	shall **you** quarrel with?
53:56	This *is* a warning
	like the previous warners.
53:57	The Day of Threat is threatening.
53:58	None other than God *is* One Who Uncovers it.
53:59	Then marvel you at this discourse?
53:60	Shall you laugh and not weep
53:61	while you *are* ones who pass life in enjoyment?
53:62	So prostrate *yourselves* to God and worship *Him*.‡

CHAPTER 54
THE MOON (*al-Qamar*)

	In the Name of God,
Sec. 1	The Merciful, The Compassionate
54:1	The Hour is near
	and the moon has been split.
54:2	If they see a Sign, they turn aside and say:
	Incessant sorcery.
54:3	They deny and follow their own desires.°
	Every affair is continuous.
54:4	Indeed draws near to them the tidings
	that are a deterrent,
54:5	a far-reaching wisdom;°
	yet warnings avail not.
54:6	So turn away from them.•
	On a Day when The One Who Calls shall call
	to a horrible thing,
54:7	their sight shall be humbled
	and they shall go forth from the tombs
	as if they were diffused locusts,
54:8	ones who run forward with their eyes fixed in horror
	towards The One Who Calls;°
	the ones who are ungrateful shall say:
	This *is* a difficult Day!
54:9	*The* folk of Noah denied before them,

they denied Our servant and said:
One who is possessed; and he was deterred.
So he called to his Lord *saying*: 54:10
I *am* one who is vanquished, so help me.
So We opened the doors of heaven 54:11
with torrential water.
We caused the earth to gush forth with springs, 54:12
so the waters met each other
according to a measured command.
We carried him 54:13
on a vessel made of planks and caulked
running under Our eyes, 54:14
a recompense for him who has been ungrateful.
Indeed We have left this as a Sign; 54:15
then *is there* one who recalls?
So how were My punishment and My warnings? 54:16
Indeed We have made the Quran easy 54:17
as a Reminder
then *is there* one who recalls?
Ad denied. 54:18
So how were My punishment and My warnings?
Truly We sent a raging wind against them 54:19
on a day of continuous misfortune
tearing out humanity, 54:20
as if they were uprooted palm-trees, uprooted.
So how were My punishment and My warnings? 54:21
Indeed We have made the Quran easy 54:22
as a Reminder;
then *is there* one who recalls?

* Sec. 2

The Thamud denied the warnings 54:23
for they said: 54:24
Are we to follow a lone mortal from among us?
Truly we *would be* then
going astray and insane.
Is the Reminder cast down to him 54:25
from among us?
Rather he *is* a rash liar!
They shall know tomorrow who the rash liar *is*! 54:26

54:27 Truly We are ones who send the she-camel
as a test for them;
so be on the watch for them
and maintain patience.
54:28 Tell them
that the division of the water *is* between them;°
every drink *is* one that is divided, for each in turn.
54:29 But they cried out to their comrade,
and he took her in hand and crippled her.
54:30 So how were My punishment and My warnings?
54:31 Truly We sent against them one Cry,
and they became like the straw
of the one who is a pen-builder.
54:32 Indeed We have made the Quran easy
as a Reminder.
Then *is there* one who recalls?
54:33 The folk of Lot denied the warnings.
54:34 Truly We sent against them a storm of pebbles,
except the people of Lot
when we delivered them at the breaking of day,
54:35 as a divine blessing from Us.°
Thus We give recompense to him who is thankful.
54:36 Indeed he had warned them of Our attack,
but they quarreled over the warnings.
54:37 Indeed they sought to solicit his guests,
so We obliterated their eyes:
So experience My punishment and My warnings.
54:38 Truly it came to be in the morning,
early morning at dawn,
a settled punishment.
54:39 So experience My punishment and My warnings.
54:40 Indeed We have made the Quran easy
as a Reminder;
then *is there* one who recalls?

*

Sec. 3
54:41 Indeed to the People of Pharaoh
drew near the warnings.
54:42 They denied Our Signs, all of them.°
So We took them with a taking

of an Almighty, One Who is Omnipotent.

Are ones who are ungrateful better than those,   54:43
or *have* you an immunity in the scrolls?

Or say they: 54:44
We *are* a great aided multitude.

Their multitude shall be put to flight   54:45
and they shall turn their backs.

Rather the Hour   54:46
is what has been promised them
and the Hour *shall be*
more calamitous and more distasteful.

Truly ones who sin *are* going astray and insane.   54:47

On a Day they shall be dragged into the fire   54:48
on their faces:

Experience the touch of Saqar!

Truly We have created all things   54:49
in measure,

and Our command *is* not   54:50
but one, as the twinkling of the eye.

Indeed We have caused   54:51
their partisans to perish;
then *is there* one who recalls?

Each and everything   54:52
they have accomplished *is* in the scroll.

Every small and great thing   54:53
is what is inscribed.

Truly the ones who are Godfearing   54:54
shall be in Gardens and rivers,

in a position of sincerity,   54:55
near an Omnipotent King.

CHAPTER 55
THE MERCIFUL (*al-Raḥmān*)

In the Name of God,
The Merciful, The Compassionate   Sec. 1

The Merciful.   55:1

He taught the Quran;   55:2

He created mankind   55:3

55:4	and He taught him the clear explanation.
55:5	The sun and the moon *are* to keep count.
55:6	The stars and the trees both prostrate.
55:7	The heaven He has exalted,
	and He has set in place the Balance:
55:8	Be not defiant in the Balance.
55:9	Set up the weight with justice,
	and skimp not in the Balance.
55:10	He has set the earth in place for the human race.
55:11	On and in it *are* many kinds of sweet fruit,
	and date palm-trees with the sheaths of a fruit tree,
55:12	and grain with husks and fragrant herbs.
55:13	So which of the benefits of your Lord
	shall you both deny?
55:14	He created mankind
	from dry clay like potter's clay.
55:15	He created the spirits
	from a smokeless flame of fire.
55:16	So which of the benefits of your Lord
	shall you both deny?
55:17	The Lord of the Two Easts,
	and the Lord of the Two Wests!
55:18	So which of the benefits of your Lord
	shall you both deny?
55:19	He has let forth the two seas to meet each other.
55:20	Between them *is* a barrier
	which they wrong not.
55:21	So which of the benefits of your Lord
	shall you both deny?
55:22	From both of them go forth pearls and coral.
55:23	So which of the benefits of your Lord
	shall you both deny?
55:24	His *are* ones that run displayed in the sea
	like landmarks.
55:25	So which of the benefits of your Lord
	shall you both deny?
	*
Sec. 2	
55:26	All that is in or on it
	is that which is being annihilated,

yet the Face of **your** Lord shall remain forever,   55:27
Possessor of Majesty and Splendor.
So which of the benefits of your Lord   55:28
shall you both deny?
Of Him asks whoever *is*   55:29
in the heavens and in and on the earth.°
Everyday He *is* on an affair.
So which of the benefits of your Lord   55:30
shall you both deny?
We shall attend to you at leisure   55:31
O you two dependents.
So which of the benefits of your Lord   55:32
shall you both deny?
O you both, assembly of jinn and human kind!   55:33
If you are able to pass through
the quarters of the heavens and the earth
then pass through *them*!°
But you shall not pass through
except with an authority.
So which of the benefits of your Lord   55:34
shall you both deny?
There shall be sent against you both   55:35
a flame of fire and heated brass,
and you shall not help yourselves.
So which of the benefits of your Lord   55:36
shall you both deny?
Then when the heaven is split   55:37
and it becomes crimson like red leather.
So which of the benefits of your Lord   55:38
shall you both deny?
On that Day   55:39
no one shall be asked about his impiety
neither human kind nor spirits.
So which of the benefits of your Lord   55:40
shall you both deny?
Ones who sin shall be known by their mark,   55:41
and they shall be taken
by their forelocks and their feet.
So which of the benefits of your Lord   55:42

shall you both deny?

55:43   This *is* hell which the ones who sin denied!

55:44   They shall go around between it
and scalding boiling water!

55:45   So which of the benefits of your Lord
shall you both deny?

*

55:46   For him who feared the station before his Lord
are two Gardens.

55:47   So which of the benefits of your Lord
shall you both deny?

55:48   With wide shade.

55:49   So which of the benefits of your Lord
shall you both deny?

55:50   Two springs shall be running.

55:51   So which of the benefits of your Lord
shall you both deny?

55:52   In them both every kind
of sweet fruit of diverse kinds.

55:53   So which of the benefits of your Lord
shall you both deny?

55:54   Ones who are reclining on places of restfulness
the inner linings of which *are* of brocade,°
and the fruit plucked from trees while fresh
drawn near from the two Gardens.

55:55   So which of the benefits of your Lord
shall you both deny?

55:56   In them both
are ones who restrain their glances,
whom no human kind has touched a female sexually
before nor ones who are spirits.

55:57   So which of the benefits of your Lord
shall you both deny?

55:58   *They are* as if they *were* like rubies and coral.

55:59   So which of the benefits of your Lord
shall you both deny?

55:60   *Is* the recompense for kindness
other than kindness?

55:61   So which of the benefits of your Lord

shall you both deny?

Besides these *are* two other Gardens. 55:62

So which of the benefits of your Lord 55:63
shall you both deny?

Dark green 55:64

So which of the benefits of your Lord 55:65
shall you both deny?

In them both *are* two springs gushing. 55:66

So which of the benefits of your Lord 55:67
shall you both deny?

In them both *are* sweet fruits 55:68
and date palm trees and pomegranates.

So which of the benefits of your Lord 55:69
shall you both deny?

In them both *are* the good works, fair. 55:70

So which of the benefits of your Lord 55:71
shall you both deny?

Restrained black-eyed ones in pavilions. 55:72

So which of the benefits of your Lord 55:73
shall you both deny?

Whom no human kind has touched a female sexually 55:74
before them and no spirits.

So which of the benefits of your Lord 55:75
shall you both deny?

Ones who are reclining on green pillows 55:76
and fair carpets.

So which of the benefits of your Lord 55:77
shall you both deny?

Blessed be the Name of **your** Lord 55:78
The Possessor of The Majesty, Splendor.

CHAPTER 56
THE INEVITABLE (*al-Wāqiʿah*)

In the Name of God,
The Merciful, The Compassionate Sec. 1

When The Inevitable comes to pass, 56:1
its descent is not a lie. 56:2

It shall be abasing, exalting, 56:3

56:4	when the earth has been rocked with a rocking,
56:5	and the mountains have crumbled to dust,
	in a great crumbling
56:6	and they have become dust scattered abroad;
56:7	you have been of three diverse pairs:
56:8	The Companions of the Right Hand,
	who *are* the Companions of the Right Hand?
56:9	The Companions of the Left Hand,
	who *are* Companions of the Left Hand?
56:10	The Ones Who Outstrip
	are the Ones Who Outstrip.
56:11	Those *are* the ones who are brought near
56:12	in the Gardens of Bliss.
56:13	A throng of the ancient ones,
56:14	and a few of the later *ones*,
56:15	*are* on lined couches,
56:16	ones who are reclining on them,
	ones who are facing one another.
56:17	Immortal children circle around them,
56:18	with cups and ewers
	and goblets from springs of water.
56:19	Neither shall they suffer headaches
	nor shall they be exhausted.
56:20	*There shall be* sweet fruit of what they may specify,
56:21	and the flesh of birds
	for which they have an appetite
56:22	and lovely-eyed ones, black-eyed,
56:23	like the parable of the well-guarded pearls.
56:24	A recompense for what they used to do.
56:25	They shall not hear any idle talk in it,
	nor any accusation of sinfulness,
56:26	but the saying of: Peace! Peace!
56:27	The Companions of the Right Hand,
	who *are* the Companions of the Right Hand?
56:28	Among thornless lote-trees,
56:29	acacias one on another,
56:30	spread out shade,
56:31	by outpoured water,
56:32	and many sweet fruit,

there is neither what is cut off, 56:33
nor what is inaccessible;
it is an exalted place of restfulness. 56:34
Truly We have caused them to grow, *a good* forming, 56:35
and made them virgins, 56:36
full of love, of the same age, 56:37
for the Companions of the Right Hand. 56:38
* Sec. 2

A throng of the ancient ones, 56:39
and a few of the later *ones,* 56:40
and the Companions of the Left Hand. 56:41
Who *are* the Companions of the Left Hand?
Those in burning wind, boiling water, 56:42
and shade of black smoke, 56:43
neither cool nor generous. 56:44
Truly they were before that given ease, 56:45
and they persisted in tremendous wickedness. 56:46
They used to say: 56:47
What? When we have died,
and have become as earth dust and bones,
shall we then be ones who are raised up?
Our ancient fathers as well? 56:48
Say: Truly the ancient ones 56:49
and the later *ones,*
shall be ones who are gathered to a time appointed 56:50
on a known Day,
then truly you, O ones who go astray, 56:51
are the ones who denied.
Indeed you *shall be* ones who eat of a tree of Zaqqum. 56:52
Then you *shall be* ones who fill your bellies from it; 56:53
ones who drink boiling water after it, 56:54
so you *shall be* ones who drink 56:55
like the drinking of thirsty camels.
This *shall be* their welcome 56:56
on the Day of Judgment!
We, We created you; 56:57
why establish it not as true?
Have you considered what you spill? 56:58
Is it you who create it, or *are* We the ones who create? 56:59

56:60	We have ordained death among you
	and We *are not* ones who are to be outstripped
56:61	from substituting you with your likes
	and causing you to grow in what you know not.
56:62	Indeed you have known the first growth;
	shall you not recollect?
56:63	Have you considered the soil that you till?
56:64	*Is it* you who sows it or are We the ones who sow?
56:65	If We will, We would indeed make it into chaff,
	and you would continue to joke:
56:66	We *are* ones who are debt-loaded!
56:67	Rather we are ones who were deprived.
56:68	Have you considered the water that you drink?
56:69	*Is it* you who sends it forth from the cloud vapor,
	or *are* We the ones who send forth?
56:70	If We will, We would make it bitter.
	Why then are you not thankful?
56:71	Have you considered the fire which you kindle?
56:72	*Is it* you who causes the tree to grow
	or *are* We the ones who cause it to grow?
56:73	We have made it an admonition,
	and sustenance for ones who are desert people.
56:74	Glorify with the name of **your** Lord, The Sublime.
Sec. 3	*
56:75	No! I swear by the orbits of the stars.
56:76	Truly *that is* an oath to be sworn
	if you know, sublime.
56:77	Truly it *is* indeed a generous Recitation,
56:78	in a well-guarded Book;
56:79	none touches it but the ones who are purified,
56:80	a sending down successively
	from the Lord of the worlds.
56:81	Then *is* it this discourse
	that you *are* ones who scorn?
56:82	You make *it* your provision
	that you, you deny.
56:83	Then why not when it reaches the wind-pipe,
56:84	and you at that moment are looking on,
56:85	We *are* nearer to him than you,

but you perceive not.
Then why not if you *are* exempt   56:86
from being ones who are judged?
Return it if you are ones who are sincere.   56:87
Then if he were of those brought near *to God,*   56:88
there is solace and fragrant herbs   56:89
and a Garden of Bliss.
If he were   56:90
of the Companions of the Right Hand,
then: Peace to **you**   56:91
for the Companions of the Right Hand.   56:92
Yet if he were of the straying ones who deny,   56:92
then a welcome of boiling water   56:93
and broiling in hellfire.   56:94
Truly this *is* The Truth of certainty.   56:95
So glorify the Name of **your** Lord,   56:96
The Almighty.

CHAPTER 57
IRON (*al-Ḥadīd*)

In the Name of God,
The Merciful, The Compassionate   Sec. 1
Whatever *is* in the heavens glorifies God   57:1
and *whatever is* in and on the earth;°
He *is* The Almighty, The Wise.
To Him *belongs* the dominion   57:2
of the heavens and the earth;°
He gives life and causes to die;°
and He *is* Powerful over all things.
He *is* The First and The Last,   57:3
and the One Who is Outward,
and The One Who is Inward,
and He *is* Knowing of everything.
It is He Who created the heavens and the earth   57:4
in six days,
then He turned His attention to the Throne.°
He knows what penetrates into the earth
and what goes forth from it;

what comes down from the heaven
and what goes up to it;°
He *is* with you wherever you may be.°
God *is* Seeing of what you do.

57:5 To Him *belongs* the dominion
of the heavens and the earth.°
All commands return to God.

57:6 He causes the nighttime to be inserted
into the daytime,
and causes the daytime to be inserted
into the nighttime.°
He *is* Knowing
of whatever *is* in the breasts.

57:7 Believe in God and His Messenger
and spend out of that which
He has made you ones who are the successors;°
for those of you who have believed
and have spent,
for them *is* a great compensation.

57:8 What *is* the matter with you
• that you believe not in God
while the Messenger calls to you
to believe in your Lord
and He has taken your solemn promise,
if you are ones who believe?

57:9 *It is* He Who sends down
to His servant clear portents, Signs,
that He may bring you
out from the shadows into the light.°
Truly God
is to you Gentle, Compassionate.

57:10 What *is* the matter with you
that you not spend in the way of God?
To God *belongs* the heritage
of the heavens and the earth?°
Not on the same level are those among you
who spent and fought before the victory.°
Those *are* more sublime in degree
than those who spent afterwards and fought.°

God has promised fairness to all.°
God *is* Aware of what you do.

*

Who *is* he that shall lend to God a fair loan
that He may multiply it for him?
He *shall* he *have* a generous compensation.
On a Day **you** shall see
the ones who are male believers
and the ones who are female believers
their light coming eagerly in advance of them,
and on their right:
Good tidings for you this Day;
Gardens beneath which rivers run,
are ones who shall dwell in them forever.°
That *is* the winning the sublime triumph!
On a Day shall say
the ones who are male hypocrites
and the ones who are female hypocrites
to those who have believed:
Wait for us
that we may borrow a light from your light;
it shall be said: Return behind
and search out for a light;
there shall be set up a fence between them,
for which *there is* a door;
inside it there *is* mercy,
and outside it, towards the punishment.
The hypocrites shall cry out to *the believers*:
Were we not with you?°
They shall say: Yea!
But you let yourselves be tempted,
and you awaited and you were in doubt,
and you were deluded following *your* desires
until the command of God drew near,
and the deluder deluded you in regard to God.
So this Day ransom shall not be taken from you,
nor from those who were ungrateful.°
Your place of shelter *is* the fire;°
that *is* what protects you;°

and how miserable *is* the Homecoming!

Was it not the time for those who had believed
so that their hearts are humbled
by the Reminder of God,
and to The Truth that has come down to them,
and that they not become like
those who were given the Book
. before
and the space of time was long for them,
and so their hearts became hardened;°
. and many of them *were* ones who disobey?

57:17 Know that God gives life to the earth
after its death.°
Indeed We have made manifest the Signs to you
so that perhaps you would be reasonable.

57:18 Truly the ones who are males who give in charity
and the ones who are females who give in charity,
they who shall lend to God a fair loan
that He may multiply it for him
they *shall* he *have* a generous compensation.

57:19 Those who have believed in God
and His Messengers,
they, those are the just persons;°
and the witnesses to their Lord;
for them *is* their compensation
and their light;°
but those who were ungrateful
and denied Our Sign,
those *are* the Companions of Hellfire.

*

Sec. 3

57:20 Know that this present life
is not but a pastime, a diversion, an adornment,
a mutual boasting among you,
and a rivalry in respect to wealth and children;°
like drops of rain water,
the vegetation impresses ones who are ungrateful;
then it withers becoming yellow,
and you see it as growing yellow;
then it becomes chaff;°

while in the world to come
there is severe punishment,
and forgiveness from God and contentment.°
This present life *is*
nothing but a delusion of enjoyment.
Race towards forgiveness from your Lord,   57:21
and *towards* the Garden
whose depth is as the breadth
of the heavens and earth;
it is prepared for those who have believed in God
and His Messengers.°
That *is* the grace of God;
He gives it to whom He will.°
God *is* Possessor of the Sublime Grace.
No affliction lights on the earth   57:22
nor on yourselves
but *it is* in a Book that We fashioned before.°
Truly that *is* easy for God,
so that you not grieve over   57:23
what has passed away from you,
nor be glad because of what has been given to you;°
God loves not any proud, boastful *one*.
Those who are misers   57:24
and who command humanity to miserliness,°
and whoever turns away;
then truly God,
He *is* The Sufficient, The Worthy of Praise.
Indeed We have sent Our Messengers   57:25
with clear portents;
We sent forth with them the Book,
and the Balance
so that humanity may uphold equity;
We sent forth iron
in which *is* vigorous might
and uses for mankind;
so that perhaps God would know
those who help him
and His Messengers in the unseen.°
Truly God *is* Strong, Almighty.

*

Indeed We sent Noah and Abraham.
We assigned to their offspring
prophethood and the Book;°
and of them *are* ones who are truly guided;°
while many of them *are* ones who disobey.

57:27 Then We sent in their footsteps Our Messengers;
We followed *them with* Jesus son of Mary;
We gave him the Gospel;
We assigned in the hearts
of those who followed him
tenderness and mercy.
But as for monasticism, they made it up *themselves.*
We prescribed it not for them
except looking for the contentment of God;
but they gave it not the right attention,
its due attention,
so We gave those who believed among them
their compensation;°
but many of them *are* ones who disobey.

57:28 O those who have believed!
Be Godfearing of God
and believe in His Messenger;
He shall give you a double component of His mercy;
He has assigned you a light to walk by;
He shall forgive you;
and God is Forgiving, Compassionate.

57:29 So that the People of the Book may know
that they *have* no power over anything
• of the grace of God,
and that the grace of God *is* in the hand of God;
He gives it to whomever He will.°
God *is* Possessor of the Sublime Grace.

***

Part 28

CHAPTER 58
SHE WHO DISPUTES (*al-Mujādilah*)

In the Name of God,
Sec. 1 The Merciful, The Compassionate

Indeed God has heard the saying 58:1
of she who disputes with **you** about her husband;
she complains to God
and God hears the conversing between you both.°
Truly God *is* Hearing, Seeing.
Those of you who 58:2
divorce their wives *saying: Be as my mother's back,*
they (f) *are* not your mothers;°
their mothers are only those who gave them birth.°
Truly they say
a saying of one who is immoral
and an untruth.°
Truly God *is* Pardoning, Forgiving.
Those of you who 58:3
divorce their wives *saying: Be as my mother's back,*
and then retract what they have said,
then let go of a bondsperson
before they both touch one other,°
that *is* of what you are admonished.°
God *is* Aware of what you do.
He who finds not such means, then formal fasting 58:4
for two successive months
before they both touch each other;
but for him who *is* unable to do so,
the feeding of sixty needy *persons;*
that *is* in order that you may believe in God
and His Messenger.°
Those *are* the ordinances of God,°
and for the ones who were ungrateful,
a painful punishment.
Truly those who oppose God 58:5
and His Messenger,
they shall be thwarted
as those before them were thwarted.°
Indeed We have sent forth
clear portents, Signs;
and for the ones who are ungrateful
a despised punishment,
on a Day when God shall raise them up 58:6

altogether
and tell them what they did.°
God has counted it while they have forgotten it.°
God *is a* Witness over all things.

*

58:7 Have **you** not considered that
God knows whatever *is* in the heavens
and whatever *is* in and on the earth?°
There is no secret conspiring of three,
but He *is* their fourth,
nor of five, but He *is* the sixth,
nor of fewer than that nor of more,
but He *is* with them wherever they might be;°
then He shall inform them of what they did
on the Day of Resurrection.°
Truly God *is* Knowing of everything.

58:8 Have **you** not considered those who were
prohibited from conspiring secretly,
then those who after that reverted
to that from which they had been prohibited,
and held secret counsel
in sin and deep-seated dislike
and in opposition to the Messenger?
When they drew near to **you**
they gave **you** greetings with that
with which God gave not *as a* greeting to **you**.
They say to themselves:
Why should God not punish us for what we say?°
Hell shall be enough for them;
they shall roast in it;°
how miserable indeed *is* that Homecoming!

58:9 O those who have believed!
When you hold secret counsel,
hold not secret counsel
in sin and deep-seated dislike
in opposition to the Messenger;
but hold secret counsel for virtuous conduct
and Godfearingness;°
be Godfearing of God

before Whom you shall be assembled.

Indeed conspiring secretly *is* not but from Satan 58:10
that he may cause grief
to those who have believed,
but he is not one who distresses anything,
except with the permission of God.°
In God let the ones who believe put their trust.

O those who have believed! 58:11
When it is said to you:
Make ample space in the assemblies,
then make room;
God shall make room for you.
When *it is* said: Move up,
then move up;
God shall exalt those among you who have believed,
and those who have been given knowledge
in degrees.°
God *is* Aware of what you do.

O those who have believed! 58:12
When you converse privately
with the Messenger,
put charity forward
in advance of your conversing privately.°
That *is* better for you and purer.°
But if you find not *the means,*
then truly God *is* Forgiving, Compassionate.

Are you apprehensive 58:13
about putting forward charity in advance
before your conversing privately?°
If then you accomplish *it* not,
God has turned in forgiveness to you.
Perform the formal prayer and give the purifying alms
and obey God and His Messenger.°
God *is* Aware of what you do.°

* Sec. 3

Have **you** considered 58:14
those who turn as a friend to a folk
against whom God is angry?
They *are* not of you, nor *are you* of them,

and they swear to a lie
while they know.

58:15 God has prepared a severe punishment for them;°
indeed they, how evil is what they used to do!

58:16 They have taken their oaths as a pretext,
and they have barred from the way of God;
so for them *is* a despised punishment.

58:17 Their wealth and their children shall not avail them
against God at all.°
They *shall be* the Companions of the Fire;°
they, ones who shall dwell in it forever.

58:18 On a Day when God shall raise them up altogether,
then they shall swear to Him
as they swear to you,°
assuming that they are something.°
Lo! They, they *are* ones who lie.

58:19 Satan has gained mastery over them,
so he has caused them to forget
the Reminder of God.°
Those *are* of the Party of Satan.°
Surely the Party of Satan,
they *shall be* the ones who are losers.

58:20 Truly those who oppose God
and His Messenger,
those *are* among the humiliated in spirit.

58:21 God has prescribed: Truly I shall prevail,
I and My Messengers
truly God *is* Powerful, Almighty.

58:22 **You** shall not find any folk who believe in God
and the Last Day
who make friends with
those who have opposed God and His Messenger
even though they were their fathers
or their sons
or their brothers or their kinspeople.°
Those, He has prescribed belief in their hearts,
and confirmed them with a Spirit from Himself;°
and He shall cause them to enter Gardens
beneath which rivers run,

as ones who shall dwell in them forever;
God has been well-pleased with them,
and they have been well-pleased with Him.°
Those *are* the Party of God.°
Surely the Party of God,
they *are* the ones who prosper.

CHAPTER 59
THE BANISHMENT (*al-Ḥashr*)

In the Name of God,
The Merciful, The Compassionate   Sec. 1
Whatever *is* in the heavens glorifies God,   59:1
and whatever *is* in and on the earth;°
and He *is* The Almighty, The Wise.
It is He Who drove out those who were ungrateful,   59:2
the People of the Book
from their houses
at the first assembly.°
You thought not that they would go out
while they thought that they *are*
ones who are secure in their fortresses
from God;
but God approached them
from where they anticipated not;°
and He hurled alarm into their hearts.°
They devastated their own abodes
with their own hands
and the hands of the ones who believe;
then learn a lesson, O you with sight!
If God had not prescribed banishment for them,   59:3
He would have indeed punished them
in the present;°
and for them in the world to come
would be the punishment of the fire.
That *is* because they made a breach with God   59:4
and His Messenger;°
whoever has made a breach with God,
then truly God *is* Severe in repayment.

59:5
Whatever palm-trees you severed
or left them as ones that arise from their roots,
it was with the permission of God,
and so that He might cover
the ones who disobey with shame.

59:6
What God gave as spoils of war
to His Messenger from them
for which you spurred not an animal
neither any horse nor riding camel,
but God gives authority to His Messenger
over whomever He will.°
God *is* Powerful over all things.

59:7
What God gave His Messenger as spoils of war
from the people of the towns
is for God and His Messenger,
the kin and the orphans,
the needy and the traveler of the way
so that it may not *just* change hands
among the rich of you.°
Whatever the Messenger gives you, take it,
and whatever he prohibits you from,
refrain yourselves *from it.*°
Be Godfearing of God;
truly God *is* Severe in repayment.

59:8
For the poor of the ones who were emigrants,
those who were driven out from their abodes
and their property, look for grace from God
and contentment, and they are helping God
and His Messenger.°
They, those *are the* ones who are sincere.

59:9
Those who took dwellings for their abodes
and *had* belief before them,
love them who migrated to them;
they find not in their breasts a need
for what they have been given;
and they hold them in greater favor over themselves
even though destitution was on them.°
Whoever *is* protected from his own stinginess,
then those *are* the ones who prosper.

637

Those who drew near after them,
they say: Our Lord!
Forgive us and our brothers
who have preceded us in belief;
make not in our hearts any grudge
against those who have believed.
Our Lord! Truly **You** are
Gentle, Compassionate.

*

Have **you** not considered
those who were hypocrites?
They say to their brothers,
those who were ungrateful
among the People of the Book:
If you are driven out,
we indeed shall go forth with you;
we shall not obey anyone about you ever.
If you were fought against,
we shall indeed help you.
God bears witness
that they truly *are* ones who lie.

Indeed if they are driven out,
they shall never go forth with them;
if they are fought against
they shall not help them;
if they were to help them,
they would turn their backs;
so they shall not be helped.

Truly you are a more severe fright
in their breasts than God.°
That is because they are a folk who understand not.

They fight not against you altogether,
but in fortified towns,
or from behind walls.°
Their might among themselves *is* very vigorous.°
You would assume them united,
but their hearts are toward diverse ends.°
That *is* because they *are* a folk
who are not reasonable.

59:15 Like those who *were* shortly before them,°
they experienced the immediate mischief
of their affair
and for them *is* a painful punishment.

59:16 Like Satan
when he says to a human being: Be ungrateful!
then when he is ungrateful,
Satan says: I *am* free of **you**;
I fear God the Lord of the worlds.

59:17 So the Ultimate End of both of them
was that they *be* in the fire,
ones who shall dwell in it forever.°
That *is* the recompense
of the ones who are unjust.

Sec. 3
*

59:18 O those who have believed!
Be Godfearing of God,
and let every person look on
what it has put forward for tomorrow;°
be Godfearing of God.°
Truly God *is* Aware of what you do.

59:19 Be not like those who forgot God,
and He caused them to forget themselves.°
They, those *are* the ones who disobey.

59:20 The Companions of the Fire are not equal
to the Companions of the Garden.°
The Companions of the Gardens,
they *are* the ones who are victorious.

59:21 If We had sent forth this Quran on a mountain,
you would have seen it as one that is humbled,
one that is split open from the dread of God.°
Those parables, We propound them
for humanity,
so that perhaps they would reflect.

59:22 He *is* God; *there is* no god but He;°
The One Who Has Knowledge
of the unseen and the visible;°
He *is* The Merciful, The Compassionate.

59:23 He *is* God; *there is* no god but He,

The King, The Holy,
The Peaceable, The Bestower, The Preserver
The Almighty, The Compeller
The One Who is Supreme.°
Glory be to God,
above whatever partners they make *with Him.*
He *is* God, The Creator,   **59:24**
The One Who Fashions,
The One Who is The Giver of Form;°
to Him *belong* the Fairest Names.°
Whatever *is* in the heavens glorifies Him
and *whatever is* in and on the earth;°
He *is* The Almighty, The Wise.

CHAPTER 60
SHE WHO IS PUT TO A TEST (*al-Mumtaḥinah*)

In the Name of God,
The Merciful, The Compassionate   **Sec. 1**
O those who have believed!   **60:1**
Take not My enemy to yourselves
and your enemy as protectors,
showing affection towards them
while they have been ungrateful
for what has drawn near to you of The Truth.
They have driven out
the Messenger and yourselves
because you believe in God your Lord.
If you have gone forth to struggle in My way,
looking for My good pleasure,°
you keep secret affection for them
while I *am* Aware of what you have concealed
and what you have spoken openly.°
Whoever accomplishes that among you,
then indeed he has gone astray
from the right path.
If they come for you,   **60:2**
they shall be enemies against you,
extending their hands against you

and their tongues with evil.
They wished that you would be ungrateful.

60:3 Your blood relations shall never profit you
nor your children—°
^on the Day of Resurrection^
He shall distinguish among you.°
God *is* Seeing of what you do.

60:4 Indeed there was a good example for you
in Abraham
and those with him
when they said to their folk:
Truly we are released from obligation to you,
and whatever you worship other than God.
We disbelieve in you.
Between us and between you has shown itself
in enmity and hatred eternally
unless you believe in God alone—
except for Abraham saying to his father:
Truly I shall ask for forgiveness for **you**,
and I possess not anything for **you** before God;
Our Lord! In **You** we have put our trust
and to **You** we are penitent
and to **You** *is* the Homecoming!

60:5 Our Lord!
Make us not be a cause of their pleasure,
those who were ungrateful,
and forgive us;
our Lord!°
Truly **You, You** *are* The Almighty, The Wise.

60:6 Indeed there has been
a good example in them for you
for those who would hope for God
and the Last Day.°
Whoever turns away,
then truly God,
He *is* Sufficient, Worthy of Praise.

*

Sec. 2

60:7 Perhaps God shall assign
between you and between those

with whom you are at enmity,
affection among them.°
God *is* Powerful.°
God *is* Forgiving, Compassionate.
God prohibits you not from those   60:8
who fought not against you
on account of *your* way of life,
nor have driven you out of your abodes
that you be good and equitable toward them.°
Truly God loves the ones who are equitable.
God prohibits you not but with regard to those   60:9
who fought against you on account of *your* way of life
and have driven you out of your abodes,
and were behind those who expelled you,
that you turn to them in friendship.°
Whoever turns to them in friendship,
then they, those are the ones who are unjust.
O those who have believed!   60:10
When ones who are female believers draw near to you,
ones who are emigrants,
put them (f) to a test;°
God *has* greater knowledge as to their (f) belief;°
then if you have known them (f)
to be ones who are female believers,
return them (f) not to the ones who are ungrateful;°
they (f) are not allowed to them (m);°
nor are they (m) lawful for them (f);
and give them (m) what they (m) have spent.°
There is no blame on you that you (m) marry them (f)
when you have given them (f) their compensation.
Hold back *conjugal* ties
with the ones who are ungrateful.
Ask for what you (m) have spent,
and let them ask for what they (m) have spent.
That is the determination of God;
He gives judgment among you;
God *is* Knowing, Wise.
If any of your wives   60:11
slip away from you

to the ones who are ungrateful,
then you retaliate
and give the like to those whose wives have gone
of what they have spent.°
Be Godfearing of God
in Whom you *are* ones who believe.

60:12 O Prophet!
When draw near to **you**
the ones who are female believers
to take the pledge of allegiance to **you**
that they shall not make partners with God,
nor shall they steal nor shall they commit adultery,
nor shall they kill their children,
nor shall they approach
making false charges to harm another's reputation
that they devise
between their (f) hands and their (f) feet,
and that they rebel not against **you**
in anything that is moral,
then take their (f) pledge of allegiance
and ask forgiveness from God for them (f);°
truly God *is* Forgiving, Compassionate.

60:13 O those who have believed!
Turn not in friendship to a folk
against whom God is angry;
surely they have given up hope
in the world to come,
just as the ones who are ungrateful
have given up hope
as the occupants of the graves.

CHAPTER 61
THE RANKS (*al-Ṣaff*)

In the Name of God,
Sec. 1 The Merciful, The Compassionate
61:1 Whatever *is* in the heavens glorifies God
and whatever *is* in and on the earth;°
He *is* The Almighty, The Wise.

O those who have believed!   61:2
Why say you what you accomplish not?
It is most repugnant to God   61:3
that you say what you accomplish not.
Truly God loves those   61:4
who fight in His Way in ranks,
as if they were a well-compacted structure.
When Moses said to his folk: 61:5
O my folk! Why inflict torment on me
while surely you know
that I *am* the Messenger of God to you?°
So when they swerved,
God caused their hearts to swerve.°
God guides not the disobedient folk.
When Jesus son of Mary said: 61:6
O Children of Israel!
I *am* the Messenger of God to you,
one who establishes as true
what was in advance of me in the Torah,
and one who gives good tidings of a Messenger to
approach after me;
his name *shall be* Ahmad;°
but when he brought about clear portents to them,
they said: This is clear sorcery!
Who has done more wrong than   61:7
the one who devised against God a lie
while he is being called to submission?°
God guides not the unjust folk.
They want to extinguish the light of God   61:8
with their mouths and God *is* The Fulfiller of His light
even though the ones who are ungrateful dislike it.
He *it is* Who has sent His Messenger   61:9
with guidance and the way of life of The Truth
to uplift it over all other ways of life
even though the ones who are polytheists dislike it.
                          *
                                                        Sec. 2
O those who have believed!   61:10
Shall I point you to a transaction
that shall rescue you from a painful punishment?

61:11   That you believe in God and His Messenger
and struggle in the way of God
with your wealth and your lives.°
That is better for you if you would know.

61:12   He shall forgive you your impieties
and cause you to enter into Gardens
beneath which rivers run,
and into good dwellings
in the Gardens of Eden.°
That is the winning the sublime triumph.

61:13   Another *thing* you love:
Help from God and victory in the near future,
so give good tidings to the ones who believe.

61:14   O those who have believed!
Be helpers of God
as Jesus son of Mary said
to the disciples:
Who *are* my helpers for God?
The disciples said:
We are the helpers for God;°
then a section of the Children of Israel believed,
and a section disbelieved;°
so We confirmed those who believed
against their enemies;
and they became ones who were uppermost.

CHAPTER 62
THE CONGREGATION (*al-Jumuᶜah*)

In the Name of God,

Sec. 1   The Merciful, The Compassionate

62:1   Whatever *is* in the heavens glorifies God
and whatever *is* in and on the earth,
The King, The Holy, The Almighty, The Wise.

62:2   He *it is* Who raises up among the unlettered
a Messenger from them
recounting His Signs to them,
and making them pure,
and teaching them the Book and wisdom,

even though before they had
gone clearly astray,
and also others among them   62:3
who have not yet joined them.°
He *is* The Almighty, The Wise.
That *is* the grace of God;   62:4
He gives it to whom He will.°
God *is* Possessor of the Sublime Grace.
The parable   62:5
of those who were entrusted with the Torah,
but then carried it not
is as the parable of a donkey
who carries writings.°
How miserable is the parable of a folk
who deny the Signs of God!°
God guides not the unjust folk.
Say: O those who became Jews!   62:6
If you claimed that you are the protectors of God
to the exclusion of humanity,
then covet death
if you are ones who are sincere.
But they shall not covet it ever   62:7
because of what their hands have put forward.°
God knows well the ones who are unjust.
Say: Truly the death from which you run away   62:8
then *shall be* indeed one you will encounter;
then you shall be returned
to the One Who has Knowledge
of the unseen and the visible;
He shall tell you what you used to do.
*

Sec. 2

O those who have believed!   62:9
When the formal prayer is proclaimed
on the day of Friday
then hasten to the Reminder of God,
and forsake trading.°
That *is* better for you
if you were to know.
Then when the formal prayer has ended,   62:10

be you diffused through the earth,
looking for the grace of God.
Remember God much
so that perhaps you would prosper.

62:11 When they consider a transaction or a diversion,
they break away toward it,
and leave **you** as one who has been stood up.°
Say: What *is* with God
is better than any diversion
or any transaction.°
God *is* The Best of the ones who provide.

CHAPTER 63
THE HYPOCRITES (*al-Munāfiqūn*)

In the Name of God,
Sec. 1 The Merciful, The Compassionate
63:1 When the ones who are hypocrites draw near to **you**,
they say: We bear witness
that you are indeed the Messenger of God,°
and God knows that **you** *are* indeed
His Messenger;
God bears witness that
the ones who are hypocrites *are* surely ones who lie.
63:2 They have taken their oaths to themselves
as a pretext;
then they barred from the way of God.°
Truly they, how evil *is* what they have been doing!
63:3 That *is* because they believed and then disbelieved,
so a seal was set on their hearts
so they understand not.
63:4 When **you** see them
their bodies impress **you**;°
when they speak, **you** hear their saying;°
it is as if they were propped up timber;°
they assume that every cry *is* against them;°
they are the enemies so beware of them.°
May God take the offensive!°
How they are misled!

647

When it is said to them: Approach now,   63:5
the Messenger of God asks forgiveness for you;
they twist their heads;
you would see them dissuading
while they *are* ones who grow in arrogance.
It is the same to them   63:6
whether **you** ask for forgiveness for them
or ask not for forgiveness for them;
God shall never forgive them.°
Truly God guides not the disobedient folk.
They *are* the ones who say: Spend not   63:7
on those who are with the Messenger of God
until they break away,°
yet to God *belongs* the treasures
of the heavens and the earth.
But the ones who are hypocrites understand not.
They say: If we returned to the city,   63:8
indeed the more mighty would drive out
the humiliated in spirit from it.°
Yet to God *belongs* the renown,
and to His Messenger,
and to the ones who believe;
but the ones who are hypocrites know not.
                    *   Sec. 2
O those who have believed!   63:9
Let not your wealth divert you
nor your children
from the Reminder of God.°
Whoever accomplishes that,
then those *are* the ones who are losers.
Spend what We have provided you   63:10
before death approaches one of you
and he shall say: My Lord!
If only **You** would postpone *it* for a little term,
then I would be charitable and be among
the ones who work righteousness.
But God shall never postpone *it* for a soul   63:11
when its term draws near.°
God *is* Aware of what you do.

CHAPTER 64
THE MUTUAL LOSS AND GAIN (al-Taghābun)

In the Name of God,
The Merciful, The Compassionate

64:1 Whatever *is* in the heavens glorifies God
and whatever *is* in and on the earth;°
His *is* the dominion;
to Him *belongs* all the praise;°
He *is* Powerful over everything.

64:2 He *it is* Who has created you:
So of you *is* one who is ungrateful
and of you *is* one who believes.
God *is* Seeing of what you do.

64:3 He has created the heavens and the earth
with The Truth;
He has formed you and formed your forms well;°
to Him is the Homecoming!

64:4 He knows what *is* in the heavens and the earth
and He knows what you keep secret
and what you speak openly;
God *is* The Knowing
of what is in the breasts.

64:5 Has there not approached you the tiding
of those who were ungrateful before?
They experienced the mischief of their affair
and *there is* a painful punishment for them.

64:6 That *is* because their Messengers approached them
with clear portents,
but they said:
Shall mortals guide us?
So they were ungrateful and turned away.°
God was Sufficient.°
God *is* Rich, Worthy of Praise.

64:7 Those who were ungrateful claimed:
They shall never be raised up.°
Say: Yea! By my Lord,
you shall indeed be raised up,
then you shall be told of what you did.°

That *is* easy for God.
So believe in God and His Messenger,   **64:8**
and in the Light which We have sent forth.°
God *is* Aware of what you do.
On a Day when He shall amass you   **64:9**
for the Day of Gathering;°
that *shall be* the day of the mutual loss and gain;°
whoever believes in God,
one who has acted in accord with morality,
He shall absolve him of his evil deeds;
He shall cause him to enter Gardens
beneath which rivers run,
as ones who shall dwell in them forever.°
That *shall be* the winning the sublime triumph.
But for those who are ungrateful and deny Our Signs,   **64:10**
those *are* the Companions of the Fire,
ones who shall dwell in it forever;°
how miserable is that Homecoming!
No affliction would light   **64:11**
except with the permission of God;°
whoever believes in God, He guides his heart.°
God *is* Knowing of everything.
*   **Sec. 2**

Obey God and obey the Messenger.°   **64:12**
But if you turn away,
then *it is* not but for Our Messenger
to deliver the clear message.
God, *there is* no god except He.°   **64:13**
In God
let the ones who believe put their trust.
O those who have believed!   **64:14**
Truly *there are* among your wives
and your children
enemies for you,
so beware of them.°
If you would pardon, overlook and forgive,
then truly God *is* Forgiving, Compassionate.
Your wealth and your children *are* not but a test.°   **64:15**
God, with Him *is* a sublime compensation.

So be Godfearing of God as much as you are able
and hear and obey
and spend;
that is good for yourselves;°
whoever is protected from his own stinginess,
then they, those *are the* ones who prosper.

If you lend to God a fair loan,
He shall multiply it for you and will forgive you.°
God *is*
Ready to Appreciate, Forbearing,

One Who has Knowledge
of the unseen and the visible
The Almighty, The Wise.

CHAPTER 65
DIVORCE (*al-Ṭalāq*)

In the Name of God,
Sec. 1 The Merciful, The Compassionate
65:1 O Prophet!
When you divorce your wives,
then divorce them (f) after their (f) waiting periods
and count their (f) waiting periods,°
and be Godfearing of God, your Lord;°
drive them (f) not out from their (f) houses
nor *let* them (f) go forth
unless they approach a glaring indecency.°
Those *are* the ordinances of God.°
Whoever violates the ordinances of God,
then indeed he has done wrong to himself.°
You are not informed,
so that perhaps God would cause to be evoked
something after that affair.
65:2 Then when they (f) have reached their (f) term,
either hold them (f) back *as* one who is honorable,
or part with them (f) as one who is honorable,
and call to witness two just persons
from you
and perform testimony for God.°

That is admonished
for whomever believes in God
and the Last Day.°
He who is Godfearing of God,
He shall make a way out for him.
He shall provide him   **65:3**
from where he not anticipate.°
Whoever puts his trust in God,
then He shall be enough for him.°
God *is* One Who Carries Through His command.°
Indeed God has assigned a measure to everything.
As for those who give up hope   **65:4**
of menstruation among your women,
if you are in doubt,
their (f) waiting period is three months,
and for those who have not yet menstruated.°
As for those who are pregnant women,
their (f) waiting period is until they bring forth a baby.°
Whoever is Godfearing of God,
He shall make his affair easy for him.
That *is* the command of God   **65:5**
which He has sent forth to you.°
Whoever is Godfearing of God,
He shall absolve him of his evil deeds
and shall enhance for him a compensation.
Cause them (f) to dwell where you inhabit   **65:6**
according to what you are able to afford,
and press them (f) not as to put them (f) in straits;
if they are pregnant women,
then spend on them (f)
until they bring forth their (f) baby;
then if they (f) suckle for you,
give them (f) their compensation
each of you take counsel between you
as ones who are honorable,
but if you make difficulties for each other
then another may suckle for him.
The rich man shall spend according to his plenty;   **65:7**
he whose provisions are measured,

he shall spend out of what God has given him.
God places not a burden on any person
but what He has given him.°
God shall make ease after hardship.

*

65:8 How many a town has defied
the command of its Lord and His Messengers,
so we made a reckoning, a severe reckoning;
We punished it *with* a horrible punishment.

65:9 So it experienced the mischief of its affair
and the Ultimate End of its affair was loss.

65:10 God prepared for them a severe punishment;°
so be Godfearing of God,
O those who have intuition, those who have believed!
Indeed God has sent forth to you a Reminder,

65:11 a Messenger,
who recounts to you
the Signs of God made manifest,
that he may bring out those who have believed,
the ones who have acted in accord with morality,
from the shadows to the light.°
Whoever believes in God,
one who has acted in accord with morality,
He shall cause him to enter into Gardens
beneath which rivers run,
ones who shall dwell in them forever, eternally;°
indeed God *has made* a good provision for him.

65:12 *It is* God Who created the seven heavens
and of the earth, like them;
the command comes forth between them
so that perhaps you would know
that God *is* Powerful over all things,
and that God indeed *is* One Who Comprehends
all things in *His* Knowledge.

CHAPTER 66
FORBIDDING (*al-Taḥrīm*)

In the Name of God,

The Mercize, The Compassionate

O Prophet! Why have **you** forbidden
what God has permitted to **you**;°
were **you** looking for the good pleasure of **your** wives?
God *is* Forgiving, Compassionate.

God has imposed on you
the dissolution of *such of* your oaths.°
God *is* One Who Protects;°
He *is* The Knowing, The Wise.

When the Prophet confided
to one of his wives
a discourse,
she communicated it and disclosed it;
God acquainted him of it;°
then when he told *her* some of it,
she said: Who told **you** this?°
He said:
The Knowing, The Aware has told me.

If you two repent to God—
the hearts of you both has bent towards *it;*°
if you help one another against him,
then truly God, He *is* One Who Protects,
and Gabriel, and
ones acts in accord with morality among the believers,
and the angels after that *are his* sustainers.

It may be if he divorce you (f),
his Lord shall give him in exchange
wives better than you (f):
Ones who are females who submit to God,
ones who are female believers,
ones who are morally obligated females,
ones who are females who repent,
ones who are females who worship,
ones who are females inclined to fasting,
ones who are previously married and virgins.

O those who have believed!
Protect yourselves and your people from a fire
whose fuel *is* humanity and rocks
over which *are* angels, harsh,

severe and terrible,
who do not disobey
whatever God commands them;
they accomplish what they are commanded.

O those who were ungrateful!
Make not excuses this Day;°
you are not but given recompense
for what you were doing.

*

O those who have believed!
Turn to God for forgiveness remorsefully, faithfully;
perhaps your Lord
shall absolve you of your evil deeds
and cause you to enter into Gardens
beneath which rivers run.
On the Day
God shall not cover the Prophet with shame
and those who have believed with him;°
their light shall hasten about before them
and on their right;
they shall say: Our Lord!
Fulfill for us our light and forgive us.
Truly **You** *are* Powerful over all things.

O Prophet!
Struggle hard against the ones who are ungrateful,
and the ones who are hypocrites;
be harsh against them.°
Their place of shelter shall be hell;°
and how miserable *is* the Homecoming!

God has propounded an example
for those who were ungrateful *like* the wife of Noah
and the wife of Lot;°
they were
under two servants of Our servants,
ones who are in accord with morality,
but they both (f) betrayed them
so they availed them nothing against God at all;
and it was said:
Enter the fire along with ones who enter.

God has propounded an example
for those who have believed:
The wife of Pharaoh when she said:
My Lord, build for me near **You** a house
in the Garden
and deliver me from Pharaoh and his action;
deliver me from the unjust folk.
Mary, the daughter of Imran,
she guarded the virginity of her private parts,
so We breathed into it of Our Spirit,
and she established as true the words of her Lord
and His Books,
and she was among
the ones who are morally obligated.

***

66:11

66:12

Part 29

CHAPTER 67
THE DOMINION (*al-Mulk*)

In the Name of God,
The Merciful, The Compassionate
Blessed be He in whose hands *is* the dominion
for He *is* Powerful over everything!
He Who has created death and this life
that He might try you *as to*
which of you *is* fairest in action.°
He *is* The Almighty, The Forgiving
Who created the seven heavens
one on another;°
you see not
any imperfection in the creation of The Merciful;°
then return your sight! See **you** any flaw?
Return your sight twice again,
and your sight shall turn about to **you**
one that is dazzled, while it *is* weary;
indeed We have made to appear pleasing
the lower heaven with lamps,
and have assigned them things to stone satans;°
We have made ready for them
the punishment of the blaze.

Sec. 1

67:1

67:2

67:3

67:4

67:5

67:6	For those who were ungrateful to their Lord
	is the punishment of hell;°
	how miserable is the Homecoming!
67:7	When they have been cast down into *it*,
	they would hear it sighing while it is boiling,
67:8	and about to burst forth with rage;°
	as often as a unit *of them* had been cast down into it,
	the ones who are keepers there asked them:
	Has not a warner approached you?
67:9	They shall say: Yea! A warner had drawn near to us,
	but we denied him, and we said:
	God has not sent down anything;
	you *are* not but in a great going astray.
67:10	They would say:
	If we had heard or been reasonable,
	we would not have been among
	the Companions of the Blaze.
67:11	They would acknowledge their impiety;
	then curse the Companions of the Blaze!
67:12	Truly those who dread their Lord in the unseen,
	for them *is* forgiveness and a great compensation.
67:13	Keep your saying secret or publish it,°
	truly He *is* Knowing of what is in *your* breasts.
67:14	Would He who has created not know?
	He *is* The Subtle, The Aware.
Sec. 2	*
67:15	*It is* He who has made the earth submissive to you,
	so walk in the tracts
	and eat of his provision;°
	to Him *is* the rising.
67:16	Are you so safe that He Who *is* in the heaven
	shall not cause the earth to swallow you up
	when it spins?
67:17	Are you so safe that He Who *is* in the heaven
	shall not send against you a storm of pebbles?°
	Soon shall you know how My warning has been!
67:18	Certainly those who were before them had denied,
	but how horrible it was!
67:19	Have they not considered the birds above them

spreading and closing their wings?°
Nothing holds them back but The Merciful.°
Truly He *is* Seeing of everything.
Or who *is* it that *is* your army   67:20
who may help you other than The Merciful?°
Truly those who are ungrateful
are not but in delusion.
Or who *is* this that shall provide for you   67:21
if He holds back His provision?°
Rather they were resolute,
turning in disdain *and* aversion.
Is then he who walks as one who is prone   67:22
on his face
better guided or he who walks without fault
on a straight path?
Say: *It is* He who has caused you to grow   67:23
and assigned you
the ability to hear, sight, and minds;°
yet how little you thank!
Say: *It is* He who   67:24
has made you numerous on the earth
and to Him you shall be assembled.
They say: When shall this promise be   67:25
if you would be ones who are sincere?
Say: The knowing of this is not but with God,   67:26
and I *am* not but a clear warner.
But when they have seen it nigh,   67:27
the faces of those who were ungrateful
shall be troubled;
and it shall be said to them:
This *is* that for which you were calling.
Say: Have you yourselves considered   67:28
whether God would cause me to perish,
and those who *are* with me,
or have mercy on us;
who shall grant protection
to the ones who are ungrateful
from a painful punishment?
Say: He *is* The Merciful;   67:29

we have believed in Him,
and in Him we have put our trust;°
you shall know
who *is* he who *is* clearly going astray.

67:30 Say: Have you yourselves considered?
If it came to be in the morning
that your water *be* sunk into the ground,
who shall then come to you with water springs?

Chapter 68
The Pen (*al-Qalam*)

In the Name of God,
Sec. 1 The Merciful, The Compassionate
68:1 *Nūn;*°
68:2 by the pen and what they inscribe:
You are not, through the blessing of **your** Lord,
one who is possessed.
68:3 Truly *there is* for **you**
surely an unfailing compensation.
68:4 Truly **you** are of sublime morals,
68:5 soon **you** shall perceive and they shall perceive
68:6 which of you *is* the one who is demented.
68:7 Truly **your** Lord, He has greater knowledge
of those who have gone astray from His Way,
and He has greater knowledge
of those who are truly guided.
68:8 Then obey not ones who deny;
68:9 they wished that **you** would compromise,
and they shall compromise with **you**.
68:10 Obey **you** not anyone who is a worthless swearer,
68:11 defamer,
one who goes about with slander, slandering,
68:12 one who delays good, a sinful aggressor,
68:13 cruel and after that, ignoble,
68:14 because he is the master of wealth and children.
68:15 When Our Signs would be recounted to him,
he said: Fables of the ancient ones!
68:16 We shall mark him on the snout!

659

Truly We have tried them   68:17
as We tried the Companions of the Garden
when they swore an oath
that they would pluck the fruit,
ones doing it, happening in the morning.
They make no exception *for God.*   68:18
Then a visitation from **your** Lord visited it   68:19
while they *were* ones who were sleeping.
It came to be in the morning   68:20
that it was like a plucked Garden!
They called to one another   68:21
happening in the morning:
Set forth early to your cultivation   68:22
if you would be ones who pluck fruit.
So they set out and they *were* whispering *saying*:   68:23
No needy man this day shall enter it against you. 68:24
They set forth with the design   68:25
of ones who have the power.
When they saw it, they said: 68:26
Truly we *are* ones who have gone astray!
Rather we *are* ones who are deprived.   68:27
The most moderate of them said: 68:28
Said I not to you:
Why glorify you not?
They said: Praise *belongs* to God, our Lord!   68:29
Truly we have been ones who are unjust.
They came forward to blame one another.   68:30
They said: Woe be to us!   68:31
Truly we have been ones who are defiant.
Perhaps our Lord shall exchange *for* us   68:32
a better one in its place;
truly we are ones who are avid about our Lord.
Thus *is* the punishment;°   68:33
but the punishment of the world to come
is greater°
if they but knew!
                    *   Sec. 2

Truly for those who are Godfearing   68:34
are Gardens of Bliss with their Lord.

68:35	Shall we make ones who have submitted
	as ones who are sinners?
68:36	What *is* the matter with you?
	How you give judgment!
68:37	Or have you a Book in which you study?
68:38	Truly you *shall have* in it
	whatever you specify!
68:39	Or *are there* oaths from Us,
	ones that are carried through
•	to the Day of Resurrection *saying*:
	You shall have whatever you give as judgment?
68:40	Ask them then which of them
	shall be a guarantor for that.
68:41	Or *have* they ones they associate *with God*?
	Then *let them* approach
	with the ones they associate *with God,*
	if they were ones who are sincere.
68:42	On a Day the great calamity shall be uncovered,
	and they shall be called to prostrate themselves,
	but they shall not be able *to do so.*
68:43	Their sight *is* as one who is humbled;
	abasement shall come over them;°
	they have been called to prostrate themselves
	while they *are* ones who are healthy.
68:44	So forsake Me
	with him who denies this discourse;°
	We shall draw them on gradually
	from where they know not,
68:45	and I shall grant them indulgence.°
	Truly My cunning *is* sure
68:46	Or ask **you** of them for a compensation,
	so that they are weighed down
	with something owed?
68:47	Or have they knowledge of the unseen with them
	so they are writing *it* down?
68:48	So be patient until the determination of **your** Lord,
	and be not like the Companion of the Fish
	when he cried out one who was suppressed by grief.
68:49	Had a blessing not followed him from his Lord,

he would have been cast forth into the wilderness
while he was one who was condemned.
But his Lord elected him and made him   **68:50**
of the ones who are in accord with morality.
It was almost like those who were ungrateful   **68:51**
looked at you sternly with their sight
when they heard the Reminder;
they said: He *is* one who is possessed.
It *is* nothing but a Reminder to the worlds.   **68:52**

CHAPTER 69
THE REALITY (*al-Ḥāqqah*)

In the Name of God,
The Merciful, The Compassionate   **Sec. 1**
The Reality!   **69:1**
What *is* The Reality?   **69:2**
What would cause you to recognize   **69:3**
what The Reality *is*?
Thamud and Ad denied   **69:4**
the Day of Disaster.
Then as for Thamud,   **69:5**
they were caused to perish
by a storm of thunder and lightning.
As for Ad,   **69:6**
they were caused to perish
by a fierce and roaring, raging wind.
He compelled against them   **69:7**
for seven uninterrupted nights and eight days
so **you** would have seen the people laid prostrate
as if they were the uprooted fallen down palm trees.
Then see **you** any ones who endure among them?   **69:8**
Pharaoh and those who came before him,   **69:9**
and the cities overthrown,
were ones of inequity;
they rebelled against the Messenger   **69:10**
of their Lord,
so He took them with a mounting taking.
When the waters became turbulent,   **69:11**

	we carried you in the floating Ark,
69:12	that We might make it a Reminder for you,
	and attentive ears would hold onto it.
69:13	When the trumpet
	has been blown with one gust,
69:14	and the earth and the mountains are mounted
	then ground to powder in one grinding,
69:15	on that Day The Reality
	shall have suddenly come to pass.
69:16	The heaven shall have split,
	for on that day they shall be very frail,
69:17	and the angels shall be at its borders.°
	The Throne of your Lord above them shall be carried
	by eight on that Day.
69:18	That Day you shall be presented;
	your private matters shall not be hidden.
69:19	As for him who is given his book
	in his right hand
	he shall say: Take! Recite my book!
69:20	Truly I thought that
	I would be one who encounters my reckoning.
69:21	He *is* in a well-pleasing, pleasant life,
69:22	in a magnificent Garden,
69:23	its clusters *are* drawn near.
69:24	Eat and drink with wholesome appetite
	for what you have done in the past,
	in the days gone by.
69:25	But as for him who is given his book
	in his left hand
	he shall say: O would that
	I had not been given my book,
69:26	and that I had not been informed of
	what this my reckoning *was*!
69:27	O would that it had been the end of me!
69:28	My wealth has not availed me;
69:29	my authority has perished from me:
69:30	Take him and restrict him.
69:31	Then broil him in hellfire.
69:32	Then in a chain of the length

of seventy cubits,
insert him *in it*.
Truly he did not believe in God, The Sublime.   69:33
Nor did he urge to give food to the needy.   69:34
This day he *shall have* no loyal friend here   69:35
and no food but the foul pus   69:36
which none eat   69:37
except ones who are inequitable.

*   Sec. 2

So I swear an oath by what you perceive,   69:38
and what you perceive not,   69:39
that this is the saying of a generous Messenger,   69:40
and not the saying of a poet.°   69:41
Little do you believe!
Nor *is it* the saying of a soothsayer.°   69:42
Little do you recollect!
It is a sending down from the Lord of the worlds.   69:43
Had he fabricated against Us any sayings,   69:44
truly We would have taken him   69:45
by the right hand
and then We would have severed his life-vein.   69:46
None of you would *be*   69:47
ones who hindered Us from him.
Truly it is an admonition   69:48
for ones who are Godfearing.
We well know that   69:49
there are some of you who are ones who deny.
Truly it shall be a regret   69:50
for those who are ungrateful.
Truly it is The Truth of certainty.   69:51
So glorify the Name of **your** Lord, The Sublime.   69:52

CHAPTER 70
THE STAIRWAYS OF ASCENT (al-Maʿārij)

In the Name of God,
The Merciful, The Compassionate   Sec. 1
A supplicant asked   70:1
for a punishment *that shall be* falling

70:2	for the ones who are ungrateful,
	for which there shall be none to avert.
70:3	*It is* from God,
	the Possessor of the Stairways of Ascent.
70:4	The angels and the Spirit go up to Him
	in a day whose measure is
	fifty thousand years.
70:5	So be patient *with* a sweet patience.
70:6	Truly they see it as distant,
70:7	but We see it as near at hand.
70:8	On a Day the heaven
	shall become as molten copper,
70:9	and the mountains as wool clusters,
70:10	and no loyal friend shall ask a loyal friend,
70:11	*although* they are given sight of them.°
	One who sins would wish that
	he might ransom himself
	from the punishment of that day
	at the price of his children,
70:12	his companion wife and his brother,
70:13	his relatives who gave him refuge,
70:14	and all who are on the earth
	so that it might rescue him.
70:15	Nay!° Truly *it is* the furnace,
70:16	removing them by their scalps.
70:17	It calls him who has drawn back,
	turned away,
70:18	and amassed and gathered.
70:19	Truly mankind was created fretful;
70:20	when the worst afflicts him,
	he is impatient.
70:21	When good afflicts him, begrudging,
70:22	except those who *are* at their formal prayer,
70:23	as ones who continue,
70:24	and those in whose wealth
	there is a known obligation
70:25	for the one who begs and the outcast,
70:26	and those who sincerely
	validate the Day of Judgment,

and those who *are* apprehensive
about the punishment of their Lord. 70:27
Truly the punishment of their Lord, 70:28
there is no security *from it*.
Those who *are* ones who guard their private parts, 70:29
except with their wives 70:30
or what their right hands possess,
truly they are not ones who shall be reproached.
But whoever be looking beyond that, 70:31
they, those *are* ones who are turning away.
They, those *are* 70:32
ones who preserve their trust and their covenant;
they, those *are* ones who uphold 70:33
their testimony;
they, those *are* 70:34
watchful of their formal prayers;
those *shall be* in Gardens, 70:35
ones who are honored.

*

Sec. 2

What *is* with those who were ungrateful, 70:36
ones who run forward with their eyes fixed in horror
toward you from the left and the right, tied in knots. 70:37
Hopes not every man of them to be caused to enter 70:38
into a Garden of Bliss?
Nay!° Truly We have created them 70:39
of what they know.
So I swear an oath by the Lord 70:40
of the rising places
and the setting places
that We *are* ones who have the power
to substitute better for them. 70:41
We are not ones to be outrun.
So let them engage and play 70:42
until they encounter the day of theirs,
that they were promised,
the day when they shall go forth 70:43
swiftly from their tombs
as though they were hurrying
to their goal

70:44 　　　　　　with their humbled sight,
　　　　　abasement shall come over them.°
That *is* the Day which they were promised.

Chapter 71
Noah (*Nūḥ*)

In the Name of God,

Sec. 1 　　The Merciful, The Compassionate

71:1 　Truly We sent Noah to his folk *saying*:
Warn **your** folk before a painful punishment
　　　　　approaches them.

71:2 　　　　He said: O my folk!
Truly I *am* a clear warner to you:

71:3 Worship God and be Godfearing of Him and obey me,

71:4 　that He may forgive you some of your impieties
and shall postpone you until a determined term.°
Truly the term of God, when it draws near,
shall not be postponed, should you know.

71:5 　　　　He said: My Lord!
Truly I have called my folk nighttime and daytime,

71:6 but my supplication increases not except their flight.

71:7 　Truly whenever I have called them
that **You** would forgive them,
they laid their finger tips over their ears,
and covered themselves with their garments;
they maintained their arrogance
as they grew arrogant.

71:8 　Then I called them with openness;

71:9 　　I spoke openly to them
and kept their secrets secret.

71:10 　I said: Ask for forgiveness of your Lord;
truly He has always been a Forgiver.

71:11 　He shall cause the heavens
to send abundant rain on you.

71:12 He shall furnish you relief with wealth and children;
He shall assign for you Gardens
and assign for you rivers.

71:13 　What *is* it with you *that* you hope not

for dignity from God
since He has created you by stages?   **71:14**
Have you not considered how God has created   **71:15**
the seven heavens, one stage on another?
He has made the moon in them as a light   **71:16**
and has made the sun as a burning lamp.
God has caused you to develop   **71:17**
and brought forth from the earth.
Then He shall cause you to return again into it,   **71:18**
and bring you out as an expulsion.
God has made the earth as a carpet for you   **71:19**
that you may thread ways, ravines.   **71:20**
*
Sec. 2

Noah said: My Lord!   **71:21**
Truly they have rebelled against me;
they followed him whose wealth and children
do not increase him except in loss.
They planned a magnificent plan   **71:22**
and have said: **71:23**
Forsake not your gods,
nor forsake Wadd, nor Suwa
nor Yaghuth, and Yauq, and Nasr.
They have caused many to go astray.   **71:24**
Increase **You** not the ones who are unjust
except in causing them to go astray
and because of their transgressions,   **71:25**
they were drowned
and caused to enter into a fire;
they found not for themselves
any helpers other than God.
Noah said: My Lord!   **71:26**
Allow not even one on the earth
from among ones who are ungrateful.
Truly **You**, if **You** were to allow them,   **71:27**
they would cause **Your** servants to go astray;
they would not but procreate
wicked ingrates.
My Lord! Forgive me and ones who are my parents,   **71:28**
and everyone who has entered my house

as ones who believe,
the ones who are male believers
and the ones who are female believers;
increase not the ones who are unjust but in ruin.

CHAPTER 72
THE JINN (*al-Jinn*)

In the Name of God,

Sec. 1 The Merciful, The Compassionate

72:1 Say: It has been revealed to me
that a group of jinn overheard *me*
and said: Truly we have listened
to a wonderful Recitation.

72:2 It guides to the right judgment
so we have believed in it;°
we shall never make anyone partners
with our Lord.

72:3 Truly He, exalted is the Grandeur of our Lord,
has taken no companion (f) to Himself
nor son.

72:4 Yet he, our foolish one, has said
an outrageous lie about God!

72:5 But we truly thought
that neither the human being nor the jinn
would ever lie about God.

72:6 That truly there were individuals of human kind
who would take refuge with individuals of the jinn,
but they increased them in vileness.

72:7 Truly they thought, as you thought,
that God would never raise up anyone.

72:8 We stretched towards the heavens
and we found it
filled with stern guards and meteor showers.

72:9 We would sit in its positions for listening,
but whoever has the ability to hear now
finds a band of meteor showers for himself.

72:10 We are not informed
whether the worst is intended

669

for those who are on earth,
or whether their Lord intends
right mindedness for them.
There are some among us,   72:11
who ones who are in accord with morality,
and there are some among us who are contrary;°
we have been of differing ways from one another.
We truly thought   72:12
that we should never be able to weaken God
on the earth
and never could we weaken Him by flight.
So truly when we heard the guidance,   72:13
we believed in it;°
whoever believes in his Lord,
he shall fear neither meagerness nor vileness.
Truly we *are* the ones who have submitted;   72:14
among us *there are*
the ones who swerve from justice;°
whoever has submitted,
then those seek right mindedness.
As for the ones who have swerved from justice,   72:15
they have become as firewood for hell.
Would they but go straight on the way,   72:16
We truly would give them to satiate *themselves*
of copious water,
so that We try them in it.°   72:17
But whoever turns aside
from the reminder of his Lord,
He shall dispatch him
to a rigorous punishment.
Truly the places of prostration *belong* to God,   72:18
so call not to any other with God.
Truly when the servant of God stood up,   72:19
calling on Him,
they almost became a swarm.

*

Sec. 2

Say: Truly I call to not but my Lord;   72:20
I make no partners with Him.
Say: Truly I possess not the power   72:21

to hurt nor *to bring* right mindedness for you.

72:22 Say: Truly none would ever
grant me protection from God,
nor shall I ever find any haven other than Him.

72:23 *To me is* not but the delivering from God
of His messages.°
Whoever disobeys God
and His Messenger,
then for him *is* the fire of hell,
ones who shall dwell in it forever, eternally.

72:24 Until when they have seen what they are promised,
then they shall know who *is* weaker in helpers
and fewer in number.

72:25 Say: I am not informed
if what you are promised *is* near,
or if my Lord shall assign for it a space of time.

72:26 The Knower of the unseen,
He discloses not the unseen to anyone,

72:27 except a Messenger with whom He is content;
then truly He dispatches in advance of him
and behind him
a succession of a band of watchers,

72:28 that he shall know
that they have expressed the messages
of their Lord;
He comprehended whatever *is* with them;
He has counted everything with numbers.

CHAPTER 73
THE ONE WHO IS WRAPPED (*al-Muzzammil*)

In the Name of God,
Sec. 1 The Merciful, The Compassionate
73:1 O **you**, the one who is wrapped,
73:2 stand up during the night, except for a little part,
73:3 for half of it,
or reduce it a little.
73:4 Or increase it and chant the Quran,
a good chanting

for We shall cast on **you** a weighty saying.   73:5
Truly the beginning of the nighttime   73:6
is when impression *is* more vigorous
and speech more upright.
Truly for **you** in the daytime   73:7
is a lengthy occupation.
Remember the Name of **your** Lord;   73:8
devote yourself to Him with total devotion.
The Lord of the East and of the West,   73:9
there is no god but He.
So take Him to **yourself** as **your** Trustee;
have patience with regard to what they say;   73:10
abandon them with a sweet abandonment.
Forsake to Me the ones who deny,   73:11
those with prosperity; **you** respite them for a little.
Truly with Us *are* shackles and hellfire,   73:12
and food which sticks in the throat and chokes   73:13
and a painful punishment.
On a Day when the earth shall tremble   73:14
and the mountains,
would become a slipping heap of sand poured forth.
Truly We have sent you a Messenger,   73:15
as one who bears witness to you,
as We had sent a Messenger to Pharaoh.
But Pharaoh rebelled against the Messenger   73:16
so We took him a remorseless taking.
If you are ungrateful, how shall you avoid   73:17
a day that shall make the children grey haired
and the heaven *shall be* split apart by it;   73:18
His promise would be accomplished.
Truly this is an admonition;°   73:19
so let whoever has willed
take himself on the way to his Lord.

*   Sec. 2

Truly **your** Lord knows   73:20
that **you** stand up
for nearly two thirds of the night
or a half of it or a third of it,
along with a section

of those who *are* with **you**.°
God ordains the nighttime and the daytime.°
He knows that you would never count it,
so He has turned towards you in forgiveness;°
then recite of the Quran as much as is easy.°
He knows that some of you *are* sick,
and others journey on the earth
looking for the grace of God,
and others fight in the way of God;°
so recite of it as much as is easy.°
Perform the formal prayer,
give the purifying alms and lend to God a fair loan.°
For whatever of good you put forward for your souls,
you shall find the same with God.
That *is* better
and a sublime reward.°
Ask God for forgiveness;°
for God *is* Forgiving, Compassionate

CHAPTER 74
THE ONE WHO IS WRAPPED IN A CLOAK
(*al-Muddaththir*)

In the Name of God,
Sec. 1 The Merciful, The Compassionate
74:1 O **you**,
the one who is wrapped in **thy** cloak!
74:2 Stand up and warn!
74:3 **Your** Lord, magnify
74:4 **Your** garments, purify
74:5 and defilement, abandon!
74:6 Show grace not to acquire more.
74:7 For **your** Lord, persevere, then have patience.
74:8 Then when the horn has been sounded,
74:9 truly that Day *shall be* a difficult day,
74:10 not easy for the ones who are ungrateful.
74:11 Leave Me with him whom I created alone.
74:12 I have assigned to him
the spreading out of abundant wealth,

and children as ones who witness;   **74:13**

I have made affairs smooth for him,   **74:14**

a *good* making smooth.

Then he is desirous that I increase *it*.   **74:15**

Nay!° Truly he was stubborn about Our Signs.   **74:16**

I shall constrain him with a hard ascent.   **74:17**

Truly he deliberated and ordained.   **74:18**

May he be accursed! How he ordained!   **74:19**

Then again, may he be accursed! How he ordained!   **74:20**

Then he looked on;   **74:21**

then he frowned and scowled;   **74:22**

then he drew back and grew arrogant.   **74:23**

He said: This *is* nothing but fabricated   **74:24**

from old sorcery.

These *are* nothing but the saying of a mortal.   **74:25**

Soon I shall scorch him in Saqar.   **74:26**

How shall you recognize what Saqar is?   **74:27**

It forsakes not, nor causes anything to remain,   **74:28**

scorching the mortal,   **74:29**

over it *there are* nineteen.   **74:30**

We have made   **74:31**

not but angels as Companions of the Fire;   •

We have made the number of them

not but as a test for those who were ungrateful

so that those who were given

the Book may be reassured

and to add to the belief of those who have believed;

and that those who were given the Book;

that the ones who have believe may not be in doubt;

that those in whose hearts

there *is* a sickness,

the ones who are ungrateful, *may say*:

What wanted God by this example?

Thus God causes to go astray

whom He will,

He guides whom He will.°

None knows the army of **your** Lord

but He.°

It *is* not other than for the mortals to be mindful.

674

*

74:32	Nay! By the moon
74:33	and the night when it draws back,
74:34	and the morning when it is polished.
74:35	Truly it *is* one of the greatest *of all things*,
74:36	as a warner to mortals,
74:37	to whomever has willed among you,
	that he go forward or remain behind.
74:38	Every soul *is* a pledge for what it has earned,
74:39	except the Companions of the Right.
74:40	*They shall be* in Gardens
	and shall inquire
74:41	of the ones who are sinners:
74:42	What thrust you into Saqar?
74:43	They would answer:
	We were not
	among ones who formally prayed;
74:44	we were not used to feeding the needy;
74:45	we engaged in idle talk
	along with the ones who engage in idle talk;
74:46	we used to deny the Day of Judgment,
74:47	until certainty approached us.
74:48	Then the intercession shall not profit them
	from ones who are intercessors.
74:49	Then what *is* the matter with them
	that they *are* ones who turn aside
	from the admonition
74:50	as though they *were* frightened donkeys
74:51	that had run away from a lion?
74:52	Rather every man among them wants
	to be given unrolled scrolls.
74:53	Nay! They fear not the world to come.
74:54	Nay! Truly it *is* an admonition.
74:55	So let whoever has willed remember.
74:56	But they shall not remember unless God will.
	He *is* Worthy of the Godfearingness
	and He *is* Worthy of the forgiveness.

CHAPTER 75
THE RESURRECTION (*al-Qiyāmah*)

In the Name of God,
The Merciful, The Compassionate   Sec. 1
No! I swear an oath by the Day of Resurrection;   75:1
no! I swear an oath by the reproachful soul.   75:2
Assumes mankind   75:3
that We shall never gather his bones?
Yea, indeed! We are ones who have the power   75:4
to shape his fingers again.
Rather the human being wants   75:5
to act immorally.
He asks: What *is* this Day of Resurrection?   75:6
But when their sight is astonished,   75:7
and the moon shall cause the earth to be swallowed,   75:8
and the sun and the moon shall be gathered,   75:9
mankind shall say on that Day: 75:10
Where *is* a place to run away?
Nay! *There is* no recourse!   75:11
With **your** Lord on that Day   75:12
shall be the stable place.
Mankind shall be told on that Day   75:13
what he has put forward
and what he has postponed.
Rather the human being   75:14
is clear evidence against himself.
Although he would cast his excuses,   75:15
impel not **your** tongue to hasten it.   75:16
Truly on Us   75:17
is his amassing and his Recitation.
But when We recite it,   75:18
follow its Recitation.
Then from Us *is* its clear explanation.   75:19
Nay! You love the transitory   75:20
and forsake the world to come.   75:21
Some faces on that Day *shall be* radiant,   75:22
ones who beam towards their Lord;
looking at their Lord;   75:23

75:24	and faces on that day *shall be* scowling,
75:25	**you** shall think that a crushing calamity
	has been wreaked against them.
75:26	Nay! When it reaches the collar bone,
75:27	and it is said: Who *is* one who enchants,
75:28	he thought it to be his parting;
75:29	one leg is intertwined with the other leg,
75:30	that Day he shall be driven toward **your** Lord.
Sec. 30	*
75:31	For he established not the true,
	nor offered the formal prayer;
75:32	he denied and turned away.
75:33	Then he went to his people, going arrogantly.
75:34	Closer to **you** and closer!
75:35	Then closer to **you** and closer!
75:36	Assumes mankind that he shall be left aimless?
75:37	Was he not a sperm-drop
	that was spilled from seminal fluids?
75:38	Then he was a clot
	and He created *him* and shaped *him.*
75:39	Then He made of him a pair,
	the male and the female.
75:40	Is not that One who has the power
	to give life to the dead?

CHAPTER 76
THE HUMAN BEING (*al-Insān*)

	In the Name of God,
Sec. 1	The Merciful, The Compassionate
76:1	Has there approached the human being
	a long course of time
	when he was nothing remembered?
76:2	Truly We have made the human being
	of a mingling of seminal fluids,
	that We may test him,
	so We have made him hearing, seeing.
76:3	Truly We have guided him on the way,
	whether *he be* one who is thankful or unthankful.

Truly We have made chains and yokes ready 76:4
for ones who are ungrateful
and a burning blaze.
Truly the pious shall drink from a cup 76:5
that *is* mixed with camphor,
a spring where the servants of God drink; 76:6
they shall cause it to gush forth, a great gushing.
They live up to their vows, 76:7
and they fear a day
where the worst would fly far and wide.
They contribute food, because they cherish Him, 76:8
to one who is needy and *the* orphan
and *the* prisoner of war:
We contribute not but for the countenance of God; 76:9
we want no recompense from you,
nor any thankfulness.
Truly we fear our Lord 76:10
on a frowning, inauspicious day.
So God would protect them 76:11
from the worst on that day
and would make them find radiancy and joyfulness;
He would give them recompense 76:12
for their enduring patiently
with a Garden and silk,
and ones who are reclining in it on benches;° 76:13
in it they shall see neither sun
nor excessive cold;
what draws near them *is* its shade, 76:14
and clusters *of grapes* brought low, a bringing low;
receptacles of silver 76:15
and goblets that are of crystal
would be passed among them of crystal like silver 76:16
which they measure *with an exact* measuring.
They shall be given to drink in it 76:17
a cup of a ginger mixture;
there is a spring in it named Salsabil, 76:18
and immortal youths shall circle around them; 76:19
whom, when **you** have seen them,
you shall assume them to be scattered pearls;

76:20	when **you** have seen *them,*
	then **you** shall have seen bliss and a great dominion.
76:21	On them *are* garments of fine green silk
	and brocade;°
	they would be adorned with bracelets of silver;
	and their Lord shall draw undefiled water for them.
76:22	Truly this was your recompense;
	what is thanked was your endeavoring.
76:23	Truly We have sent down to **you**
	the Recitation, a sending down successively.
Sec. 2	*
76:24	So have patience
	for the determination of **your** Lord,
	and obey not any one of them,
	the ones who are perverted or the ungrateful.
76:25	Remember the Name of **your** Lord
	in the early morning and in the eventide;
76:26	during the night, prostrate **yourself** to Him;
	glorify Him a lengthy part of the night.
76:27	Truly they, those love the transitory,
	and they forsake a weighty day behind them.
76:28	We have created them;
	We strengthened their frame;°
	and when We have willed,
	We have substituted their likes with a substitution.
76:29	Truly this *is* an admonition;°
	so whoever has willed
	take a way to his Lord.
76:30	But you will *it* not,
	unless God will *it,*°
	for God is Knowing, Wise.
76:31	He causes to enter whom He will
	into His mercy.°
	But for the ones who are unjust
	He has made ready for them a painful punishment.

In the Name of God,
The Merciful, The Compassionate · Sec. 1
By ones who are sent successively; · 77:1
by the storm and raging winds; · 77:2
by the ones who are the unfolders; · 77:3
by what causes vegetation to revive;
by the ones who separate, a separation; · 77:4
by ones who cast a reminder, · 77:5
excusing or warning, · 77:6
truly what you are promised shall surely fall. · 77:7
Then when the stars are · 77:8
the ones who are obliterated,
when the heaven has been cleaved, · 77:9
when the mountains have been scattered, · 77:10
when the time has been set · 77:11
for the Messengers *to bear witness*
—for which Day has been appointed; · 77:12
for the Day of Decision! · 77:13
What would cause **you** to recognize · 77:14
what this Day of Decision *is*?
Woe on that Day to the ones who deny! · 77:15
Caused We not the ancient ones to perish? · 77:16
Then We shall also cause the later generations to perish · 77:17
who pursued after them.
Thus We accomplish with the ones who sin. · 77:18
Woe on that Day to the ones who deny! · 77:19
Have We not created you of despicable water, · 77:20
then We made in a secure stopping place · 77:21
for a known measuring? · 77:22
We measured. · 77:23
How bountiful *are* the ones who measure!
Woe on that day to the ones who deny! · 77:24
Have We not made the earth · 77:25
a place of drawing together
the living and the lifeless? · 77:26
We made on it soaring, firm mountains; · 77:27

We satiated you with the sweetest kind of water.

77:28 Woe on that Day to the ones who deny!

77:29 Set out to what you denied.

77:30 Set out to the three-massing shade,

77:31 that is neither shading,

nor shall it avail you against the flame!

77:32 Truly it shall throw up sparks of fire

high like palaces

77:33 as though they *were* saffron-colored male camels.

77:34 Woe on that Day to the ones who deny!

77:35 This Day they shall not speak,

77:36 nor shall they be given permission

so that they may excuse themselves.

77:37 Woe on that Day to the ones who deny!

77:38 This *is* the Day of Decision;°

We have gathered altogether you and the ancient ones.

77:39 So if there *is* cunning for you, then try to outwit Me.

77:40 Woe on that Day to the ones who deny!

Sec. 2 *

77:41 Truly the ones who are Godfearing

shall be amidst shade and springs,

77:42 and sweet fruit for which they *have* an appetite:

77:43 Eat and drink with wholesome appetite

for what you were doing;

77:44 truly We thus give recompense

to the ones who do good.

77:45 Woe on that Day to the ones who deny!

77:46 Eat, take joy for a little; you *are* ones who sin.

77:47 Woe on that Day to the ones who deny!

77:48 When it is said: Bow down, they bow not down.

77:49 Woe on that Day to the ones who deny!

77:50 Then in what discourse after this shall they believe?

Part 30 ***

CHAPTER 78
THE TIDING (*al-Nabā'*)

In the Name of God,

Sec. 1 The Merciful, The Compassionate

78:1 About what inquire you of one another?

Of the sublime tiding   78:2

about which they *are* ones who are at variance?   78:3

Nay! Truly they shall know.   78:4

Then again nay truly they shall know.   78:5

Have We not made the earth as a cradle,   78:6

and the mountains as stakes?   78:7

Have We not created you in pairs?   78:8

We made your sleep as a rest,   78:9

and We made the nighttime as a garment;   78:10

We made the daytime for *you* to earn a living;   78:11

We have built over you seven superior ones,   78:12

and We made a bright, light-giving lamp.   78:13

We have sent forth   78:14

clouds bringing rain, water cascading,

with which We bring forth grain and plants,   78:15

and luxuriant Gardens.   78:16

Truly the Day of Decision   78:17

is a time appointed,

a Day the trumpet shall be blown;   78:18

then you shall approach in units,

and the heaven shall be opened   78:19

and would be as doors;

the mountains would be set in motion   78:20

and become as vapor.

Truly hell has become a watching place,   78:21

a destination for the ones who are defiant,   78:22

who shall linger in expectation in it for many years. 78:23

They shall not experience in it   78:24

any coolness or any drink,

except scalding water and filth,   78:25

a suitable recompense!   78:26

Truly they had hoped   78:27

that they would not be brought to a reckoning,

and they denied Our Signs, a denying.   78:28

But everything have We counted in a Book.   78:29

Experience *it*! We shall not increase you   78:30

except in punishment.

*   Sec. 2

Truly for the Godfearing, a place of security,   78:31

682

78:32	plantations and grapevines,
78:33	swelling breasted maidens of the same age,
78:34	and an overflowing cup.
78:35	They shall hear no idle talk in it,
	nor any denial.
78:36	A recompense from **your** Lord,
	a gift, a reckoning.
78:37	The Lord of the heavens and the earth,
	and of whatever *is* between them,
	The Merciful°
	with Whom they possess no argument.
78:38	On a Day
	the Spirit and the angels shall stand up
	in ranks;°
	they shall not assert themselves
	except him whom the Merciful has permitted,
	and who says what is pious.
78:39	This is the true Day;°
	so whoever has willed, has taken his Lord to himself
	as the destination.
78:40	We have warned you of a near punishment
	on a Day when the man shall look on
	at what his hands have put forward;
	the ones who are ungrateful shall say:
	O would that I were earthy dust!

CHAPTER 79
THE ONES WHO TEAR OUT (al-Nāziʿāt)

	In the Name of God,
Sec. 1	The Merciful, The Compassionate
79:1	By the ones who tear out vehemently;
79:2	by the ones who draw out a drawing out;
79:3	by the ones who swim, swimming;
79:4	the preceding Ones Who Outstrip;
79:5	by the ones who manage a command.
79:6	On a day when the first bang trembles,
79:7	succeeded by the one that comes behind it,
79:8	hearts on that day *shall be* beating painfully;

their sight *is* of one who is humbled. 79:9

They shall say: Are we ones who are being restored 79:10
to our original state?

What? After we have become crumbled bones? 79:11

They say: This then *shall be* a losing return again. 79:12

Truly it *shall be* but one scare. 79:13

Lo! They *are* the ones awakening. 79:14

Has the discourse of Moses approached **you**? 79:15

When his Lord cried out to him 79:16
in the sanctified valley Tuwa:

Go **you** to Pharaoh; truly he has been defiant, 79:17

say: Would **you** purify **yourself**? 79:18

I shall guide **you** to **your** Lord, 79:19
then **you** shall dread *Him*.

He caused him to see the great Sign, 79:20

but he denied and rebelled. 79:21

Then he drew back, hastening about; 79:22

he assembled them, then proclaimed, 79:23

so he said: I am your lofty lord. 79:24

So God took him with an exemplary punishment 79:25
for the Last and for the First.

Truly in that *is* a lesson for him who dreads. 79:26

* Sec. 2

Is your constitution more difficult *to create* 79:27
or the heaven which God has built?

He exalted its vault, and shaped it, 79:28

and He has made it dark, 79:29
and has brought out its forenoon.

He spread out the earth after this; 79:30

He brought out from it 79:31
its water and its pasture;

the mountains He set firm, 79:32

an enjoyment for you and for your flocks. 79:33

When the Great Catastrophe shall draw near, 79:34

on that Day the human being shall recollect 79:35
for *what* he endeavored;

hellfire shall be advanced for whoever sees. 79:36

As for whoever was defiant, 79:37

and held this present life in greater favor, 79:38

79:39 then truly hellfire shall be the place of shelter!

79:40 As for him who has feared
the Station of his Lord,
and has prohibited desire from his soul,

79:41 truly the Garden shall be the place of shelter!

79:42 They ask **you** concerning the Hour,
when shall it berth?

79:43 A*re* **you** being mindful?

79:44 To **your** Lord *is* its Utmost Boundary of it.

79:45 **You** are not but a warner
to him who dreads it.

79:46 It shall seem to them on a Day they see it
that they had not lingered in expectation
except an evening or a forenoon.

CHAPTER 80
HE FROWNED (ʿ*Abasa*)

In the Name of God,

Sec. 1 The Merciful, The Compassionate

80:1 He frowned and turned away

80:2 because the blind man drew near him;

80:3 and what shall cause **you** to recognize
so that perhaps he would purify himself,

80:4 or yet recollect and being mindful *would* profit him?

80:5 But as for one who was self-complacent,

80:6 then attend to him.

80:7 What *is it* to **you**
if he purifies not himself?

80:8 But as for him who draws near to **you**,
coming eagerly,

80:9 he dreads *God*;

80:10 thus **you** pay no heed to him!

80:11 Nay! Truly this *is* an admonition;

80:12 so whoever has willed shall remember it

80:13 in scrolls held in esteem,

80:14 ones that are exalted and ones that are purified

80:15 by the hands of generous writers

80:16 and ones who are kind.

May the human being be accursed!   80:17
How ungrateful he is!
From what thing has He created him?   80:18
He created him from a seminal fluids   80:19
and determined he *be*;
He made the way easy for him;   80:20
then He caused him to die and buried him.   80:21
When He has willed, He revives him.   80:22
Nay! He has not yet fully decided   80:23
what He had commanded him.
Yet the human being expects his food.   80:24
Truly how We unloosed rain in a pouring out;   80:25
then We split the earth, a splitting;   80:26
We put forth in it grain,   80:27
grapevines and reeds,   80:28
olives and date palm trees;   80:29
dense orchards,   80:30
and sweet fruits and whatever grows on the earth,   80:31
an enjoyment for you and your flocks.   80:32
Then when the blare draws near,   80:33
on that Day a man shall run away   80:34
from his brother, his mother, his father,   80:35
his companion wife and his children.   80:36
For every man of them on that Day,   80:37
shall be a matter that shall preoccupy him.
Some faces on that Day *will be* as   80:38
ones that are polished,
ones who are laughing,   80:39
and ones who are rejoicing at the good tidings;
and some faces on that Day *shall be* dust-stained.   80:40
Gloom shall come over them;   80:41
they, those *are* the ones who were ungrateful,   80:42
ones who acted immorally.

CHAPTER 81
THE DARKENING (*al-Takwīr*)

In the Name of God,

Sec. 1 The Merciful, The Compassionate

81:1 When the sun is darkening,

81:2 when the stars plunge down,

81:3 when the mountains have been set in motion,

81:4 when the pregnant camels have been ignored,

81:5 when the savage beasts
have been assembled together,

81:6 when the seas have been caused to overflow,

81:7 when the souls have been mated,

81:8 when the buried infant girl has been asked

81:9 for what impiety she was slain,

81:10 when the scrolls have been unfolded,

81:11 when the heaven has been stripped off,

81:12 when hellfire has been caused to burn fiercely,

81:13 when the Garden has been brought close,

81:14 every soul shall know to what it is prone.

81:15 So no! I swear an oath by the stars that recede,

81:16 by the ones that run, the setting stars

81:17 by the night, when it swarms,

81:18 by the morning, when it sighs,

81:19 truly that is the saying of a generous Messenger,

81:20 possessed of strength,
secure with the Possessor of the Throne,

81:21 one who is obeyed and trustworthy.

81:22 Your companion *is* not one who is possessed.

81:23 Certainly he saw him on the clear horizon.

81:24 He *is* not greedy for the unseen,

81:25 nor *is* it the saying
of the accursed Satan.

81:26 So with what are you going off!

81:27 Truly it *is* no other than a Reminder
to the worlds

81:28 for whoever among you has willed to go straight.

81:29 But you will not
unless God will, the Lord of the worlds.

687

Chapter 82
The Splitting Apart (*al-Infiṭār*)

In the Name of God,
The Merciful, The Compassionate   Sec. 1
When the heaven has been split apart,   82:1
when the stars have been scattered,   82:2
when the seas gush forth   82:3
when the graves   82:4
are scattered about,
every soul shall have known what it has put forward,   82:5
and what it has postponed.
O human being!   82:6
What has deluded **you**
as to **your** generous Lord,
He Who created **you**,   82:7
then shaped **you** in proportion,   82:8
He composed **you** in whatever form He will.
Nay! But you deny *this* way of life.   82:9
Truly there are ones who guard you,   82:10
a generous scribe;   82:11
they know whatever you accomplish.   82:12
Truly the pious *shall be* in bliss,   82:13
but truly the ones who act immorally   82:14
shall be in hellfire.
They shall roast on the Day of Judgment,   82:15
and they *shall* not *be* among ones who are unseen.   82:16
What shall cause **you** to recognize   82:17
what the Day of Judgment is?
Again what shall cause **you** to recognize   82:18
what the Day of Judgment is?
It is a Day whereon one soul shall not possess   82:19
anything to avail another soul;°
and the command on that Day *shall belong* to God.

688

CHAPTER 83
THE ONES WHO GIVE SHORT MEASURE
(al-Muṭaffifīn)

In the Name of God,

Sec. 1 The Merciful, The Compassionate

83:1 Woe be to the ones who give short measure;

83:2 those, who, when they measure against humanity take full measure;

83:3 but when they measure for them, or weigh for them, they skimp.

83:4 Think they not that they shall be raised up

83:5 on the sublime Day,

83:6 a Day *when* humanity shall stand up for the Lord of the worlds?

83:7 Nay! Truly the Book of the ones who act immorally is in Sijjīn;

83:8 and what shall cause **you** to recognize what Sijjīn is?

83:9 It is a written book.

83:10 Woe on that Day to the ones who deny!

83:11 The ones who deny the Day of Judgment!

83:12 None denies it but every sinful aggressor,

83:13 who, when **you** recount Our Signs to him, he said: Fables of the ancient ones!

83:14 Nay! Rather their hearts were overcome with rust from what they had earned.

83:15 Nay! Truly they *shall be* partitioned on that Day;

83:16 and they shall roast in hellfire.

83:17 Then it shall be said to them: This is what you used to deny.

83:18 Nay! Truly the book of the good is in Illiyyūn.

83:19 What shall cause you to recognize what Illiyyūn is?

83:20 *It is* a written book,

83:21 the ones who are brought near to God bear witness to it.

83:22 Truly the pious *shall be* in bliss,

83:23 on raised benches, looking on;

you shall recognize bliss in their faces. 83:24

They shall be given to drink sealed, exquisite wine; 83:25

its seal *shall have* the lingering smell of musk.° 83:26

So for that, then the ones who strive, strive.

The mixture shall be of Tasnim, 83:27

a spring from which the ones shall drink 83:28

who are brought near.

Truly those who sin were laughing 83:29

at those who had believed.

When they passed by them, 83:30

they wink at one another.

When they turn about to their people, 83:31

they turned about,

acting as ones who are unconcerned;

when they saw them, 83:32

they would say:

Truly those are ones who have gone astray.

But they were not sent as ones who guard. 83:33

Then on this Day those who have believed 83:34

shall laugh at the ones who were ungrateful.

They are seated on raised benches, looking on. 83:35

Have those who were ungrateful not been 83:36

rewarded for what they were accomplishing?

CHAPTER 84
THE SPLITTING OPEN (al-Inshiqāq)

In the Name of God,

The Merciful, The Compassionate Sec. 1

When the heaven has been split open, 84:1

gives ear to its Lord, 84:2

and it has been justly disposed;

when the earth has been stretched out, 84:3

has cast what is in it, and voids itself, 84:4

and gives ear to its Lord, 84:5

it has been justly disposed.

O human being! 84:6

Truly **you** *are* one who is laboring

toward **your** Lord laboriously

and **you** *shall be* one who encounters Him.

84:7　　　　　　As for him who is given
　　　　　　　his book in his right hand,

84:8　　then he shall be reckoned an easy reckoning,

84:9　　　　and shall turn about to his people
　　　　　　　　as one who is glad.

84:10　　But as for him who is given his book
　　　　　　　　behind his back,

84:11　　　　　he shall call damnation;

84:12　　　　　he shall roast in a blaze.

84:13　He once lived among his people, one who was glad.

84:14　　　　　　Truly he thought
　　　　　　he would never retreat.

84:15　　Yea! Truly but his Lord sees him.

84:16　　Then I swear an oath by the twilight;

84:17　　by the night and all that it envelopes;

84:18　　　by the moon when it is full;

84:19　that you shall truly ride plane after plane.

84:20　Then what *is it* for those who believe not

84:21　that when the Recitation is recited to them,
　　　　　　　they prostrate not?‡

84:22　　Rather those who are ungrateful deny;

84:23　　　but God *has* greater knowledge
　　　　　　　　of what they amass.

84:24　　　So give them good tidings
　　　　　　of a painful punishment;

84:25　　but those who have believed,
　the ones who have acted in accord with morality,
　for them *is* an unfailing compensation.

CHAPTER 85
THE CONSTELLATIONS (*al-Burūj*)

　　　　　In the Name of God,
Sec. 1　　The Merciful, The Compassionate

85:1　By the heaven possessing the constellations;

85:2　　　　by the promised Day;

85:3　　by ones who witness and are witnessed;

85:4　may the Companions of the Ditch be accursed!

The fire possessing the fuel,   85:5
when they *were* ones who sat by it;   85:6
they were ones who witnessed   85:7
what they had accomplished
against the ones who believe.
They took revenge on them only   85:8
because they were ones who believed in God,
The Almighty, The Worthy of Praise,
to whom *belongs* the dominion   85:9
of the heavens and the earth.°
God *is* a Witness over everything.
Truly those who persecute   85:10
the ones who are male believers
and the ones who are female believers,
and then have not repented,
for them *is* prepared the punishment of hell;
for them is the punishment of the burning.
Truly those who have believed,   85:11
the ones who have acted in accord with morality,
for them *shall be* Gardens
beneath which rivers run.°
That *will be* the great triumph.
Surely the seizing by force of your Lord *is* severe.   85:12
He causes to begin and He causes to bring back.   85:13
He *is* the The Forgiving, The Loving,   85:14
the Possessor of the Glorious Throne   85:15
Who achieves what He wants.   85:16
Has there approached you   85:17
the discourse of the armies
of Pharaoh and of Thamud?   85:18
Rather those who are ungrateful deny;   85:19
and God *is* One Who Encloses them   85:20
from behind.
Rather it *is* a glorious Recitation   85:21
on the Guarded Tablet.   85:22

CHAPTER 86
THE NIGHT VISITOR (al-Ṭāriq)

In the Name of God,

Sec. 1   The Merciful, The Compassionate

86:1   By the heaven and the night visitor,

86:2   what shall cause **you** to recognize
what the night visitor *is*?

86:3   *It is* the piercing star.

86:4   Every soul has one who guards it.

86:5   *Let* the human being look
of what he was created.

86:6   He was created of water that gushes forth,

86:7   going forth from
between the loins and the breast bone.

86:8   Truly He *is* One Who has the Power
of returning him.

86:9   On a Day
all secrets shall be tried.

86:10   Then there *shall* not *be* for him
any strength nor ones who help.

86:11   By the heaven possessing the return;

86:12   by the earth splitting with verdure,

86:13   truly this *is* a saying possessing decisiveness,

86:14   and not with merriment;

86:15   truly they are devising a strategy;

86:16   but I, too, am devising a strategy.

86:17   So respite the ones who are ungrateful!
Grant **you** them a delay for awhile.

CHAPTER 87
THE LOFTY (al-Aᶜlā)

In the Name of God,

Sec. 1   The Merciful, The Compassionate

87:1   Glorify the Name of **your** Lord, The Lofty,

87:2   Who has created and shaped;

87:3   Who has ordained and then guided;

87:4   Who brought out the pasture,

693

then made it dark colored refuse.	87:5
We shall make **you** recite,	87:6
and **you** shall not forget,	
but what God has willed.°	87:7
He knows what is openly published,	
and what is hidden.	
We will make easy for you, an easing.	87:8
So remind, because being mindful has profited them.	87:9
Whoever dreads God shall recollect,	87:10
but the unhappy shall scorn it,	87:11
even he who shall roast in the great fire.	87:12
Then he shall not die in it, nor shall he live.	87:13
He has certainly prospered,	87:14
he who has purified himself,	
and remembered the Name of his Lord	87:15
and invoked blessings.	
Rather you hold this present life in greater favor,	87:16
yet the world to come *is* better,	87:17
and what endures.	
Truly this *is* in the previous scrolls,	87:18
the scrolls of Abraham and Moses.	87:19

CHAPTER 88
THE OVERWHELMING EVENT (al-Ghāshiyah)

In the Name of God,	
The Merciful, The Compassionate	Sec. 1
Has the discourse approached **you**	88:1
of the overwhelming event?	
Faces on that Day *shall be*	88:2
as ones who are humbled,	
ones that work and those that are fatigued;	88:3
they shall be in a hot fire.	88:4
They shall be given to drink of a scalding spring.	88:5
Is it not that there is no food for them	88:6
but a thorn fruit;	
it shall not fatten,	88:7
neither shall it avail hunger.	
Faces on that Day shall be ones that are pleasant,	88:8

694

88:9	ones who are well-pleased by their endeavor.
88:10	*They shall be* in a magnificent Garden;
88:11	you shall not hear in it babble.
88:12	In it *is* a running spring;
88:13	in it *are* exalted couches,
88:14	and goblets set down,
88:15	and cushions arrayed,
88:16	and rugs dispersed.
88:17	Look they not then on the camel, how it has been created?
88:18	Of the heaven, how it is lifted up?
88:19	The mountains, how they are hoisted up?
88:20	The earth, how it is stretched out?
88:21	Remind then for **you** are not but one who reminds.
88:22	**You** are over them a registrar.
88:23	But whoever turned away, and was ungrateful,
88:24	God shall punish him with the greatest punishment.
88:25	Truly to Us *is* their reversion,
88:26	then truly on Us *is* their reckoning.

CHAPTER 89
THE DAWN (*al-Fajr*)

	In the Name of God,
Sec. 1	The Merciful, The Compassionate
89:1	By the dawn
89:2	and the ten nights;
89:3	by the even number and the odd number
89:4	and at night when it sets forth.
89:5	*Is there* not in that an oath for a possessor of intelligence?
89:6	Have **you** not considered how **your** Lord accomplished with Ad
89:7	or Iram of the pillars,
89:8	the likes of which have never been created in the land;
89:9	and with Thamud, those who hollowed out the rocks

and with Pharaoh, 89:10
the possessor of the stakes,
those who were defiant in the land 89:11
and made much corruption in it? 89:12
So **your** Lord unloosed on them 89:13
a scourge of punishment.
Truly **your** Lord *is* surely on the watch. 89:14
Then as for the human being, 89:15
whenever his Lord has tested him,
and honored him and lauded him,
he says: My Lord has honored me.
But whenever he tests him, 89:16
and constricts his provision for him,
he says: My Lord has despised me.
Nay!° Rather you do not honor the orphan; 89:17
and you encourage not one another 89:18
about food for the needy;
you consume the inheritance, a greedy eating; 89:19
you cherish wealth with an ardent love. 89:20
Nay! When the earth has been ground to powder, 89:21
a thorough grinding to powder,
your Lord draws near, 89:22
and the angels, rank by rank;
on that Day hell shall be brought.° 89:23
On that Day shall the human being recollect;
how shall the mindfulness *avail* him?
He shall say: Would that I had put forward 89:24
for my present life!
Then on that Day no one shall punish 89:25
the like of His punishment;
nor shall any bind His bonds. 89:26
O soul, one that is at peace! 89:27
Return to **your** Lord, 89:28
as one who is well-pleasing, well-pleased:
Enter **you** among My servants; 89:29
and enter **you** My Garden! 89:30

CHAPTER 90
THE LAND (*al-Balad*)

	In the Name of God,
Sec. 1	The Merciful, The Compassionate
90:1	No! I swear by this land;
90:2	**you** are a lodger in this land;
90:3	by one who was your parent,
	and what was procreated.
90:4	Truly We created the human being in trouble.
90:5	What? Assumes he that no one has power over him?
90:6	He says: I have caused abundant wealth to perish.
90:7	What? Assumes he that no one has seen him?
90:8	Have We not made two eyes for him,
90:9	a tongue and two lips
90:10	and guided him to the two open highways?
90:11	Yet he has not rushed onto the steep ascent.
90:12	What shall cause **you** to recognize
90:13	what the steep ascent *is*?
	It is the liberating of a bondsperson,
90:14	or feeding an orphan among near of kin
90:15	on a day of famine,
90:16	*or* a needy in misery
90:17	while being among those who have believed;
	counselled one another to patience,
	and counselled one another to clemency.
90:18	Those *shall be* the Companions of the Right Hand.
90:19	But they who were ungrateful for Our Signs,
	they *shall be* the Companions of the Left Hand
90:20	and over them fire *shall be* a cover.

CHAPTER 91
THE SUN (*al-Shams*)

	In the Name of God,
Sec. 1	The Merciful, The Compassionate
91:1	By the sun and its forenoon;
91:2	by the moon when it relates to it;
91:3	by the daytime when it displays it;

by the nighttime when it overcomes it; 91:4
by the heaven and what built it; 91:5
by the earth and what widened it; 91:6
by the soul and what shaped it, 91:7
and then inspired it to act immorally 91:8
or with Godfearingness.
He who makes it pure has prospered; 91:9
but he who is seduced by it has been frustrated. 91:10
Thamud denied because of their overboldness, 91:11
when the disappointed among them were aroused, 91:12
and the Messenger of God said to them: 91:13
Water the she-camel of God.
But they denied him, then they crippled her, 91:14
so their Lord doomed them for their sin,
then He leveled them.
He fears not its Ultimate End. 91:15

CHAPTER 92
THE NIGHT (*al-Layl*)

In the Name of God,
The Merciful, The Compassionate Sec. 1
By the nighttime when it overcomes; 92:1
by the daytime when it self-discloses; 92:2
by He who has created 92:3
the male and the female.
Truly your endeavors *are* to diverse ends. 92:4
As for him who gave and *is* Godfearing, 92:5
and established the fair as true, 92:6
We shall make easy for him the easing. 92:7
But as for him who was a miser 92:8
and was self-sufficient,
and denied the fair, 92:9
We shall make *falling into* difficulty easy for him; 92:10
his wealth shall not avail him 92:11
when he has passed.
Truly guidance *is* from Us; 92:12
indeed the last and the first *belong* to Us. 92:13
I have warned you of a fire that blazes fiercely, 92:14

92:15	it roasts none but the wretched
92:16	who have denied and turned away.
92:17	But the most devout shall be turned aside from it;
92:18	he who gives of his wealth to purify himself
92:19	expects no divine blessing to be given as recompense
92:20	but only looks for the countenance
	of his Lord, The Lofty.
92:21	He shall be well-pleased.

CHAPTER 93
THE FORENOON (*al-Ḍuḥā*)

In the Name of God,
Sec. 1	The Merciful, The Compassionate
93:1	By the forenoon;
93:2	by the brooding night,
93:3	**your** Lord has not deserted **you**,
	nor hates **you**.
93:4	Truly the Last *shall be* better for **you**
	than the First;
93:5	**soon your** Lord shall give **you**
	that with which **you** will be well-pleased.
93:6	Found He **you** not an orphan
	and He gave **you** refuge?
93:7	Found He **you** not one who goes astray,
	then has He not guided **you**?
93:8	Found He **you** not one who wants,
	then He enriched **you**?
93:9	As for the orphan, oppress him not.
93:10	As for one who begs, scold him not.
93:11	As for **your** Lord's blessing, divulge it!

CHAPTER 94
THE EXPANSION (*al-Inshirāḥ*)

In the Name of God,
Sec. 1	The Merciful, The Compassionate
94:1	Have we not expanded **your** breast for you;
94:2	and lifted from **you**

699

the heavy loaded burden
which weighed heavily on **your** back?   94:3
Exalted We not **your** Reminding?   94:4
So truly with hardship, ease,   94:5
truly with hardship, ease.   94:6
So when **you** have been emptied, work on,   94:7
and have **your** Lord as **your** quest.   94:8

Chapter 95
The Fig (*al-Tīn*)

In the Name of God,
The Merciful, The Compassionate   Sec. 1
By the fig and the olive;   95:1
by the mountain of Sinai,   95:2
by this trustworthy land;   95:3
truly We have created the human being   95:4
of the fairest symmetry,
then We returned him to the lowest of the low,   95:5
except those who have believed,   95:6
the ones who have acted in accord with morality;
for them *is* an unfailing compensation.
What shall cause **you** to deny   95:7
the Judgment?
Is not God the most just of ones who judge?   95:8

Chapter 96
The Blood Clot (*al-ᶜAlaq*)

In the Name of God,
The Merciful, The Compassionate   Sec. 1
Recite in the name of **your** Lord   96:1
Who has created;
He has created the human being   96:2
from a clot.
Recite: **Your** Lord *is* the Most Generous   96:3
Who taught by the pen,   96:4
Who taught the human being   96:5
what he knew not.

96:6	Nay! Truly the human being is defiant
96:7	when He considers himself
	to be one who is self-sufficient.
96:8	Truly to **your** Lord *is* the returning.
96:9	Have **you yourself** considered one who prohibits
96:10	a servant when he invokes blessings?
96:11	Have **you yourself** considered if he was on guidance
96:12	or commanded Godfearingness?
96:13	Have **you yourself** considered if he denies
	and turns away?
96:14	Knows he not that God sees?
96:15	Nay! Truly if he refrains himself not,
	We shall surely lay hold of him by the forelock,
96:16	a lying, inequitable forelock.
96:17	Have him call to his conclave;
96:18	We shall call the guards of hell.
96:19	Nay! Truly obey **you** him not
	but continue to prostrate **yourself** *to God*
	and be near *to Him*.‡

CHAPTER 97
THE NIGHT OF POWER (*al-Qadr*)

	In the Name of God,
Sec. 1	The Merciful, The Compassionate
97:1	Truly We sent it forth on the night of power.
97:2	What shall cause **you** to recognize
	what *is* the night of power?
97:3	The night of power
	is better than a thousand months.
97:4	The angels come forth,
	and the Spirit during it
	with their Lord's permission,
	with every command.
97:5	Peace! *It is* until the time of the rising dawn.

701

CHAPTER 98
THE CLEAR PORTENT (*al-Bayyinah*)

In the Name of God,
The Merciful, The Compassionate

Those who were ungrateful
among the People of the Book,
and the ones who were polytheists,
were not ones who were set aside
until the clear portent approached them—
a Messenger from God
who recounted to them purified scrolls
wherein are truth-loving Books.
They split not up among themselves
until the Book was given
after the clear portent had drawn near to them.
They were commanded nothing but to worship God
sincerely and devotedly
in the way of life for Him
as innate monotheists;
to perform the formal prayer,
to give the purifying alms.
That is the truth-loving way of life.
Truly those who were ungrateful
of the People of the Book,
and the ones who are polytheists
shall be in the fire of hell,
ones who shall dwell in it forever.°
Those *are* the most evil of existents.
But those who have believed,
the ones who have acted in accord with morality,
those *are* the best of existents.
Their recompense *is* with their Lord—
Gardens of Eden,
beneath which rivers run,
ones who shall dwell in them forever, eternally;°
God is well-pleased with them;
they are well-pleased with Him.°
That *is* for him who has dreaded his Lord.

Sec. 1
98:1

98:2

98:3
98:4

98:5

98:6

98:7

98:8

CHAPTER 99
THE CONVULSION (*al-Zalzalah*)

In the Name of God,

Sec. 1   The Merciful, The Compassionate

99:1   When the earth has been convulsed
with a convulsion,

99:2   and the earth has brought out its ladings

99:3   and the human being has said: What *is* with it?

99:4   On that Day it shall divulge its news,

99:5   for that Day your Lord revealed it.

99:6   On that Day humanity shall issue, radiating out,
that they may be caused to see their actions.

99:7   Whoever does
an atom's weight of good shall see it.

99:8   Whoever does
an atom's weight of the worst shall see it.

CHAPTER 100
THE CHARGERS (*al-ʿĀdiyāt*)

In the Name of God,

Sec. 1   The Merciful, The Compassionate

100:1   By the chargers, panting;

100:2   by the kindlers of fire, striking fire;

100:3   by the raiders in the morning,

100:4   then they plowed it *to* dust,

100:5   and they penetrated the center with it
altogether;

100:6   truly the human being
is unthankful to his Lord.

100:7   Truly he *is* a witness to that.

100:8   He *is* more severe in the cherishing of the best.

100:9   Knows he not that when all that
is in the graves is scattered,

100:10   what *is* hidden in the breasts
is shown forth,

100:11   truly on that day their Lord *shall be* Aware
of them.

703

CHAPTER 101
THE DISASTER (*al-Qāriᶜah*)

In the Name of God,	
The Merciful, The Compassionate	Sec. 1
The Disaster!	101:1
What *is* the Disaster?	101:2
What shall cause **you** to recognize	101:3
what the Disaster *is*?	
On a Day human beings	101:4
shall be like dispersed moths,	
the mountains shall become	101:5
like plucked wool clusters.	
Then as for him	101:6
whose balance is heavy,	
he has a pleasant life, one that is well-pleasing.	101:7
But he whose balance *is* light,	101:8
his abode of rest *shall be* the pit.	101:9
What shall cause **you** to recognize what it *is*?	101:10
It is a hot fire.	101:11

CHAPTER 102
THE RIVALRY (*al-Takāthur*)

In the Name of God,	
The Merciful, The Compassionate	Sec. 1
Rivalry diverted you	102:1
until you stopped by the cemetery.	102:2
Nay! Soon you shall surely know!	102:3
Again, nay! You shall surely know!	102:4
Nay! Soon you shall know	102:5
with the knowledge of certainty,	102:6
Nay! You would indeed see hellfire,	102:7
again you would indeed see it	
with the eye of certainty.	102:8
Then you shall surely be asked	
on that day about the bliss.	

CHAPTER 103
BY TIME (*al-ᶜAṣr*)

In the Name of God,
Sec. 1   The Merciful, The Compassionate
103:1   By time;
103:2   truly the human being *is* at a loss,
103:3   except those who have believed,
the ones who have acted in accord with morality,
and have counselled one another to The Truth,
have counselled each other to endure patiently.

CHAPTER 104
THE SLANDERER (*al-Humazah*)

In the Name of God,
Sec. 1   The Merciful, The Compassionate
104:1   Woe to every slandering backbiter,
104:2   who has gathered wealth
and counts it over and over!
104:3   He assumes that his wealth
has made him immortal.
104:4   Nay! He shall be cast forth
into the Crusher.
104:5   What shall cause you to recognize
what the Crusher is?
104:6   The starting of *the* fire of God
104:7   that will peruse the minds of humanity
104:8   closing in on them
104:9   with outstretched pillars.

CHAPTER 105
THE ELEPHANT (*al-Fīl*)

In the Name of God,
Sec. 1   The Merciful, The Compassionate
105:1   Have **you** not considered
what **your** Lord accomplished
with the Companions of the Elephant?

705

Had He not led their cunning to nothing?	105:2
He sent upon them flocks of birds,	105:3
throwing at them rocks of baked clay.	105:4
Then made He them like	105:5
consumed stalks of husked grain?	

Chapter 106
The Quraysh (*al-Quraysh*)

In the Name of God,	
The Merciful, The Compassionate	Sec. 1
For the solidarity of the Quraysh;	106:1
their solidarity *is*	106:2
the winter and the summer travel.	
Let them worship the Lord of this House,	106:3
Who has fed them against hunger,	106:4
and secured them against fear.	

Chapter 107
Small Kindnesses (*al-Māʿūn*)

In the Name of God,	
The Merciful, The Compassionate	Sec. 1
Have **you** considered one who denies *this* way of life?	107:1
That *is* he who drives away the orphan	107:2
with force	
and urges not to give food to the needy.	107:3
So woe to ones who formally pray,	107:4
who *are* inattentive to the formal prayer,	107:5
those who show off,	107:6
and repulse small kindnesses.	107:7

Chapter 108
The Abundance (*al-Kawthar*)

In the Name of God,	
The Merciful, The Compassionate	Sec. 1
Truly We have given **you** the abundance.	108:1
So invoke blessings for **your** Lord	108:2

and make sacrifice.

108:3 Truly the one who detests **you** *is* one who is cut off.

CHAPTER 109
THE UNGRATEFUL (*al-Kāfirūn*)

In the Name of God,

Sec. 1   The Merciful, The Compassionate

109:1   Say: O you who are ungrateful!

109:2   I worship not what you worship

109:3   nor are you ones who worship what I worship

109:4   nor shall I worship
what you have worshipped;

109:5   nor shall you worship what I worship.

109:6   For you *is* your way of life,
and for me *is* my way of life.

CHAPTER 110
THE HELP (*al-Naṣr*)

In the Name of God,

Sec. 1   The Merciful, The Compassionate

110:1   When the help of God draws near
and the victory,

110:2   and **you** have seen humanity
entering into God's way of life in units;

110:3   then praise the glory of **your** Lord
and ask for His forgiveness.°
Truly He has been ever The Accepter of Repentance.

CHAPTER 111
THE FLAME (*al-Lahāb*)

In the Name of God,

Sec. 1   The Merciful, The Compassionate

111:1   Perdition be the hands of Abu Lahab,
and he is in perdition.

111:2   His wealth availed him not,
nor whatever he had earned.

and his wife, the carrier of firewood, 111:4

around her long neck *is* a rope of palm fibers. 111:5

CHAPTER 112
SINCERE EXPRESSION (*al-Ikhlāṣ*)

In the Name of God,

The Merciful, The Compassionate Sec. 1

Say: He *is* God, One; 112:1

God, the Everlasting; 112:2

He has neither procreated 112:3

nor was He procreated;

and there is nothing comparable to Him. 112:4

CHAPTER 113
DAYBREAK (*al-Falaq*)

In the Name of God,

The Merciful, The Compassionate Sec. 1

Say: I take refuge with the Lord of Daybreak, 113:1

from the worst of those things 113:2

which He has created;

from the worst 113:3

of the darkening of the night when it intensifies;

from the worst 113:4

of the women who blow on the knots;

from the worst 113:5

of one who *is* jealous when he is jealous.

CHAPTER 114
HUMANITY (*al-Nās*)

In the Name of God,

The Merciful, The Compassionate Sec. 1

Say: I take refuge with the Lord 114:1

of humanity,

The King of humanity, 114:2

The God of humanity, 114:3

114:4	from the worst of the sneaking whisperer
114:5	who whispers evil
	in the breasts of the humanity,
114:6	from among the jinn and the humanity.

• Bibliography •

Ali, Syed Anwar. *The Quran: The Fundamental Law*. Karachi, Pakistan: Hamdard Foundation, 1982.

Anṣārī, Khawjeh ᶜAbdullah. *Kashf al-asrār*. Tehran: Kitab Khaneh Ibn Sina,   1334.

Badran, Margot. "Feminism and the Quran," ed. Jane McAuliffe, *Encylopedia of the Quran*, vol. 2 (Leiden: Brill, 2002); "Gender in the Quran," ed. Jane McAuliffe, *Encyclopedia of the Quran*, vol. 2 (Leiden: Brill, 2002); "Gender Journeys into Arabic," Langues and Linguistique: Revue Internationale de Linguistique, special issue on Langauge and Gender in the Arab World," eds., Margot Badran, Fatima Sadiqi, and Linda Stump al-Rashidi, 9 (2002: Fex, Morocco). "Sisters," ed. Jane McCaulifee, *Encyclopedia of the Quran*, vol. 5 (Leiden: Brill, 2006).

Bukhari, Imam. *Ṣaḥiḥ al-Bukhārī*. Chicago: Kazi Publications, 1976.

El-Ḥarere, *Commentary on the Mukāmat*. Paris, 2nd Edition.

Hughes, Thomas Patrick. *Dictionary of Islam*. Chicago: Kazi Publications, 1994.

Kassis, Hanna. *The Concordance of the Quran*. California: University of California Press, 1986.

Lane, Edward. *Arabic-English Lexicon*. Lahore, Pakistan: Sh. Muhammad Ashraf, 1984.

McAuliffe, Jane Dammen, General Editor. *The Encyclopedia of the Quran*. Boston: E. J. Brill, 2003.

Mutahhari, Murtaza. *Hijab: Islamic Modest Dress*. Chicago: Kazi Publications, 1988.

Shariati, Ali. *Shariati on Shariati and the Muslim Woman*. Chicago: ABC International Group, 1996.

Qutb, Seyyed. *In the Shade of the Quran*. Leicester, UK: The Islamic Foundation, 2001.

Wadud, Amina. *Quran and Woman*. Oxford: Oxford University Press, 1999.